The Critical Shusterman

SUNY series in American Philosophy and Cultural Thought

Randall E. Auxier and John R. Shook, editors

The Critical Shusterman

Richard Shusterman

Edited and with an Introduction by
Crispin Sartwell

SUNY
PRESS

Published by State University of New York Press, Albany

EU GPSR Authorised Representative:
Logos Europe, 9 rue Nicolas Poussin, 17000, La Rochelle, France
contact@logoseurope.eu

For information, contact State University of New York Press, Albany, NY
www.sunypress.edu

Library of Congress Cataloging-in-Publication Data

Names: Shusterman, Richard, author. | Sartwell, Crispin, 1958–
Title: The critical Shusterman / Richard Shusterman ; [Crispin Sartwell,
    editor].
Description: Albany : State University of New York Press, [2025] | Series:
    SUNY series in American philosophy and cultural thought | Includes
    bibliographical references and index.
Identifiers: LCCN 2024044569 | ISBN 9798855802504 (hardcover : alk. paper) |
    ISBN 9798855802511 (ebook)
Subjects: LCSH: Philosophy, American—20th century. | Philosophy, American—
    21st century.
Classification: LCC B945.S6471 S27 2025 | DDC 191—dc23/eng/20250106
LC record available at https://lccn.loc.gov/2024044569

For my teachers, in grateful memory

Contents

III. Aesthetics

IV. Somaesthetics

Preface

When the editors of this series invited me to do a book titled *The Critical Shusterman*, I was flattered but puzzled. I had recently encountered the first of their critical readers, which was devoted to Joseph Margolis, who, for many years, was my senior colleague at Temple University. He had just died at the age of ninety-seven, the year *The Critical Margolis* (2021) was published. I did not feel ready to follow him in producing a defining final statement of what was critical in my work, because I hoped still to have some important new milestones to reach in my philosophical journey. In fact, I felt in the midst of fresh turns in that journey, having just published a long book introducing a new dimension of my somaesthetic theory, *Ars Erotica: Sex and Somaesthetics in the Classical Arts of Love* (Cambridge, 2021), that also involved a different style in my philosophical writing, combining thick cultural history with philosophical argument. At the same time, I was preparing a new book, *Philosophy and the Art of Writing* (Routledge, 2022), to explore the role of writing in the practice of philosophy when philosophy is conceived as an embodied art of living rather than a mere textual genre. Perhaps such recent and forthcoming texts will prove ultimately more important than what is now regarded as critical in my work.

Justifiably described as a nomadic philosopher, because of my wandering among different philosophical traditions (analytic, continental, pragmatist, and Asian), I am uneasy about decisively defining the critical center of my work, because a new turn in my thinking may alter that apparent central core. For example, in 2010 I published a short essay, "What Pragmatism Means to Me: Ten Principles," that summarized what I advocated as essential to pragmatist philosophy. But I soon realized, through deeper immersion in Peirce and James, that I had neglected to highlight the role of affect, which I now regard as crucial, as I explain in "Thought in the Strenuous Mood: Pragmatism as a Philosophy of Feeling" (2012) and "Affective Cognition"

(2013), and in a 2018 Chinese book on affect and action in pragmatism.[1] Nevertheless, *The Critical Shusterman* certainly collects some of my most significant work inspired mainly by the American pragmatist tradition. Whether or not these texts are truly critical, the task of selecting *them* rather than others and of putting them in a coherent, convincing order is a work of interpretive and evaluative criticism. So, this book deserves the title "critical" in at least the sense in which any thoughtful anthology is a work of criticism.

What was the thinking that governed its selection? The sixteen articles, divided into four equal parts, do not all belong to my favorite essays, nor to my most cited texts, although several of them fit those categories. Instead, the texts were chosen to represent a definitive, influential timespan of my pragmatist-inspired work and to indicate the range of my views on the more general topics of philosophy. I therefore excluded not only texts that focus on particular thinkers (Wittgenstein, Dewey, James, Peirce, Rorty, Foucault, de Beauvoir, Merleau-Ponty, Bourdieu, Danto, Burke, T. S. Eliot, etc.) but also texts focusing on particular artistic genres (poetry, rap, dance, photography, architecture, film, fashion, etc.). I also omit my more biographical philosophical essays as well as the numerous texts connected with my performance work with the Man in Gold, including the graphic novel *The Adventures of the Man in Gold*.[2] Many of these texts on particular topics and thinkers are central to my public profile as a philosopher and to my own sense of what I've done and who I've been. But they seemed either too narrow in scope or too personal in tone to serve the function of this anthology, as I understood it: namely, to provide materials that outline the general principles and essential elements of my philosophical vision and my key views on traditional topics in philosophy, including new approaches to such topics that emerge through my work in somaesthetics.

That I've never formulated a detailed philosophical system does not preclude there being a structural coherence or unity of outlook in my work. If such a unity exists, its basic elements and general lineaments can be found in these sixteen texts. One can also find these core features and unifying thrust (expressed with more graceful concision) in Crispin Sartwell's superbly insightful introduction, which not only explains how these texts respond in a distinctive way to crises in contemporary philosophy but also creatively suggests how their arguments and vision should be further developed in future philosophical inquiry. The sixteen texts selected here serve, then, as the general skeleton of my body of work in philosophy, the underlying bare bones rather than the juicier flesh of my more concrete essays on diverse genres of art and styles of life that some readers find more attractive. Sartwell is right to see aesthetic desire as an essential *fil conducteur* in my texts, as it is in my life. But in this collection my more conventional philosophical libido is on display.

The articles span twenty-five years, from 1990 to 2014, a period that begins with my initial steps in the writing of *Pragmatist Aesthetics* (1992) and extends into the development of my pragmatist thinking on topics of ethics, politics, ontology, epistemology, philosophy of mind, and, of course, somaesthetics. That field, I should stress, is not a departure from but an expansion of my work in pragmatism. This twenty-five-year period covers my books *Practicing Philosophy* (1997), *Performing Live* (2000), *Surface and Depth* (2002), *Body Consciousness* (2008), and *Thinking through the Body* (2012). I have slightly revised some of the texts to update references or develop certain points.

Regrettably, there was no room here for any of my early work in analytic philosophy, on topics concerning the logics of interpretation and evaluation (*Philosophical Quarterly* 1978, 1980) and the role of convention in philosophy of language and action (*Philosophical Investigations*, 1986). That work, inspired by Wittgenstein and Austin (key foci of my studies at Jerusalem and Oxford), prepared my path to pragmatism through their themes of pluralism, empirical observation of usage, and the crucial roles of action and context in questions of meaning and understanding. My transition to pragmatist philosophy was much easier because of what I learned from those pragmatic analytic masters and from the analytic philosophers who taught me at the Hebrew University (Yehoshua Bar-Hillel, Eddy Zemach, and Joseph Raz) and at Oxford (J. O. Urmson and Peter Hacker). In taking a different philosophical path, I am no less grateful to the teachers who first shaped me in philosophy. I gratefully remember them here, along with three more recent mentors whose exemplary writings and personal kindness enriched my subsequent philosophical career in America and Europe: Richard Rorty, Arthur Danto, and Pierre Bourdieu. Their work has been critical to whatever is critical in mine. Crispin Sartwell has my special thanks for his invaluable work as editor of this volume, and I also thank T. J. Bonnet and Megan Spring for help with the proofreading and index. I close by expressing my deep and enduring gratitude to the Schmidt Family Foundation, which generously endowed the Humanities chair I hold at Florida Atlantic University and whose support I have enjoyed since 2005.

Acknowledgments

This book's chapters are printed with permission (and with updating revisions) from the following original publications. I have slightly altered a few of the original titles for greater clarity and simplicity.

1. "Beneath Interpretation, Against Hermeneutic Holism," *Monist* 73 (1990): 181–204.

2. "Dewey on Experience: Foundation or Reconstruction?" *Philosophical Forum* 26 (1994): 127–48.

3. "Organic Unity: Deconstruction and Analysis," *Redrawing the Boundaries: Analytic Philosophy, Deconstruction, and Literary Theory*, ed. R. W. Dasenbrock (Minneapolis: University of Minnesota Press, 1989), 92–115.

4. "Affective Cognition: From Pragmatism to Somaesthetics," *Intellectica* 60, no. 2 (2013): 49–68.

5. "Postmodern Ethics and the Art of Living," chapter 9 of *Pragmatist Aesthetics* (Oxford: Blackwell, 1992).

6. "Self-Knowledge and Its Discontents," *Philosophy and Education Yearbook* (the Kneller Lecture) (2007): 25–37.

7. "Putnam and Cavell on the Ethics of Democracy," *Political Theory* 25 (1997): 193–214.

8. "Multiculturalism and the Art of Living," chapter 9 of *Performing Live* (New York: Cornell University Press, 2000).

9. "The End of Aesthetic Experience," *Journal of Aesthetics and Art Criticism* 55 (1997): 29–41.

10. "Art as Dramatization," *Journal of Aesthetics and Art Criticism* 59 (2001): 363–72.

11. "Entertainment: A Question for Aesthetics," *British Journal of Aesthetics* 43, no. 3 (2003): 289–307.

12. "Art and Religion," *Journal of Aesthetic Education* 42, no. 3 (2008): 1–18.

13. "Somaesthetics and the Body/Media Issue," chapter 7 of *Performing Live* (New York: Cornell University Press, 2000).

14. "Thinking through the Body, Educating for the Humanities: A Plea for Somaesthetics," *Journal of Aesthetic Education* 40, no. 1 (2006): 1–21.

15. "Muscle Memory and the Somaesthetic Pathologies of Everyday Life," *Human Movement* 12, no. 1 (2012): 4–15.

16. "Somaesthetics and Politics: Incorporating Pragmatist Aesthetics for Social Action," *Beauty, Responsibility, and Power,* ed. Leszek Koczanowicz and Katarzyna Liszka (Amsterdam: Rodopi, 2014), 5–18.

Introduction

Dance of Ideas: Richard Shusterman's Embodied Philosophy

Crispin Sartwell

I. Situating Shusterman in Intellectual History

At a certain point in late twentieth century intellectual life, the question of whether anything could happen after postmodernism—and, if so, what—became urgent. What creative or rehabilitative possibilities remained, after Michel Foucault, Richard Rorty, Jacques Derrida, Charles Taylor, Gayatri Spivak, even after late Ludwig Wittgenstein? After narrative theory and the linguistic construction of reality, after neopragmatism, deconstructionism? After the end? The postmodern thinkers raised devastating suspicions about many philosophical and cultural myths, but also about many things to which intellectuals, or people in general, aspired: things like authenticity, identity, freedom, truth. Sometimes (call those times the 1980s) it seemed that no idea, no thing, could escape being deconstructed or narrativized.

By late in their lives, several of these figures had made moves to take concepts like justice or truth seriously, even as deconstructed or reconstrued pragmatically, and also to recapture the physical world studied by science, for example, and to recentralize the human body as making an ethical claim or a claim to justice, the body as constituting a plea or demand to end suffering, if also as a "field of power" and a "zone of inscription." But the next generation, including the postmodernists' own students and younger colleagues in the '70s and '80s, needed to emerge and get on to some next

1

set of issues and positive projects. It was hard, at a certain moment, to see how we could. These were very formidable figures, after all. Say you were proposing to attack Derrida; well, he was already there ahead of you, deconstructing himself. Refuting Donald Davidson or Roland Barthes: first you'd have to figure out what they meant; specialists will not concede that you've got it right. Then you'd have to develop some sort of systematic criticism. Good luck with that, as the saying goes.

One reason it seemed hard to get beyond this era and those figures, even for themselves, is that postmodernism, as the name indicates, already had an "after" quality: after modernism, after Heidegger, after liberalism, after truth, even. So here we are asking what came, or what could possibly come after after, postpost. Initially, it sounds kind of pitiful, like a further petering out. It could have taken the form of a playful or despairing rummaging around in the remaining scraps and fragments of a culture and a tradition. Or it could have amounted to a straightforward reaction, demanding a naive return to "truth" and "reality." Such responses occurred.

The postmodern generation of philosophers, that is, left younger thinkers with a practical and disciplinary problem: how and why to keep going. Indeed, my teacher and Shusterman's friend and mentor Richard Rorty was one of many twentieth-century philosophers who argued that philosophy was over or should never have existed at all, that it was entirely misguided or in error. With bold perversity, they argued for the end of their own discipline. But then again, they were already ensconced in endowed chairs. Their students and younger colleagues, however, had to figure out what could come after the alleged end. This was more than a sheer question about who would have a job (though it definitely had that aspect); finding and practicing or defending some form of philosophy became urgent at that time for people who had come to study this subject because they loved the activity of addressing "the big questions." Even if, once we got into graduate study, we heard from its own professors that the discipline in which we applied was illegitimate or over, we had gone there because we thought philosophy was important and absorbing. Perhaps we thought it was a route to truth, as well, or we would never have started. So, now, when your teachers tell you this is naive, or just start snickering, what do you do?

∾

But I hope historians of the post-postmodern, or the "pre-" of something still to be defined, will centralize the systematic, constructive response and creative project of Richard Shusterman: a decent and (dare I say) a true philosophy that emerges partly in sophisticated response to the postmodern crisis of truth and reality. Shusterman takes the postmodern critique of culture, art, ideology, and truth fully seriously, and has known many of its most eminent practitioners, such as Rorty and Pierre Bourdieu. However, he has responded, for forty years now, not simply by going further down the same road, or by refuting Derrida book by book, or by pretending the whole thing never happened, but rather by facing the critique in its most fearsome versions and carefully forging a viable alternative that rests on insights that should fuel decades more of development. Calmly, with good sense and an impulse to see what's right even in his opponents, accompanied with a resolution to say what he believes and endorse what he experiences, Shusterman lays a groundwork for new disciplines and new extensions of old ones.

One opening toward the Shustermanian future was provided by the major postmodern figures themselves. Starting by the '70s, people such as Rorty, Taylor, and Richard Bernstein were, almost uniquely, interested and competent in all three of the major strands of Western philosophy in the twentieth century: analytic philosophy (represented by figures such as Bertrand Russell and W. V. O. Quine), continental philosophy (Martin Heidegger and Hans-Georg Gadamer, for example), and American pragmatism (Peirce-James-Dewey, in the classic triumvirate). For Shusterman, this crossing of borders was completely natural by the early '90s, though it was still the exception across the field. And he has gone on, adding yet more elements, including—profoundly—from Asian and ancient Greek thought.

American pragmatism has, from the beginning, formed a great deal of the basis of Shusterman's philosophy. In aesthetics, this takes him back to Dewey's thought. But with regard to basic "metaphysical" questions, such as what sorts of things there are and how human beings experience them, his approach leans as heavily on the thought of C. S. Peirce and William James. One lesson Shusterman draws from the pragmatist tradition is that in trying to figure out what sorts of things we are, we had better start by acknowledging that we are physical organisms in a physical environment. Now, that may appear obvious or trivial on almost anyone's philosophy. But the neopragmatists such as Rorty took the pragmatist tradition in a different direction, emphasizing the constructed nature of experience, or holding, with Gadamer for example, that we experience the world always as already interpreted, as though it were a text to be decoded.

The physical reality of the body could not, for these thinkers, be exempted from cultural critique; they held that centralizing the body in this way was a version of "the myth of the given" or "the metaphysics of presence," a slightly covert but indefensible foundationalism that had, they said, long ago been superseded. That is, returning to the body as the center of our experience would be a reactionary gesture, wildly implausible given the political and philosophical critiques that concepts like "physical reality" had been subjected to in the previous half century and more. Or, "physical reality" and "the body" were supposed themselves to be ideological constructions rather than bottom-line facts. And it's true, "the body" and "physical reality" are words, even if the body and physical reality are not. We can designate things like the latter only by using things like the former, and it seems that all we're directly experiencing is the designators.

⁓

The outline of Shusterman's profound response were formulated early in his authorship and is represented here in the second chapter, which addresses the concept of experience in Dewey and Rorty. "Though appreciative of the linguistic turn," he writes,

> I am also wary of its totalizing tendencies and am reluctant to abandon pragmatism's traditional concern with the somatic and nondiscursive. . . . Before burying the body or simply textualizing it, we need to assess more critically philosophy's resistance to nondiscursive experience. Such resistance is based not only on arguments but on deeply entrenched biases that work beneath the level of conscious thought. . . . There is no allocation for [the body] in traditional Western philosophical space, no "subdiscipline of the body" to complement philosophy of mind (as hatha yoga serves the more spiritual raja yoga in Indian thought). The result is that nondiscursive somatic experience is either ignored—relegated to other fields like psychology or neuroscience—or instead subsumed under clearly discursive projects, such as epistemological justification or genealogical accounts or "reading the body" as a social text on which a society's practices of formative power are inscribed. (see chapter 2, "Experience," section 5)

Notice here the provisional identification of the "somatic" and the "nondiscursive," which signals one of the main uses or functions of the body in Shusterman's thought: as a critique of the linguistically oriented philosophy of the era in which it was composed. But, of course, this passage also indicates some of the many other reasons we might want or need to return to embodiment in philosophy or cultural critique. Shusterman has richly developed a somatic aesthetics, and has made substantive beginnings on somatic ethics, epistemology, and even political philosophy. Perhaps, as he says, there was no allocation for this fundamental topic when he started writing it into existence, no subdiscipline of Western philosophy concerned primarily with the body, embodied experience, or the nondiscursive. Now there is.

Shusterman, that is, spends some time carefully arguing against some aspects of postmodernism, particularly in Rorty's version. But his response to the postmodern moment or generation, as well as to many other features of his and our intellectual environment, has been more than a critique; he has attempted carefully to construct an alternative, or to try to push us into a next constructive phase. So much of the postmodern intellectual formation was critical, and so little of it seemed constructive, that developing a positive vision would itself constitute the deepest critique. At this point, certainly, not only has the outline of Shusterman's alternative been sketched and many basic questions broached. The subdiscipline that we might call *somaphilosophy* has been established. The time is right, in other words, for a point of access that can help us see the basic construction on which people are already building. Or, the time is right for *The Critical Shusterman*.

However, though this volume gives you the very center of Richard Shusterman, philosopher, the man himself does many other things too, all of which seem to form a single practice. Indeed, one of his books is titled *Practicing Philosophy*; for Shusterman, philosophy (unlike this book) consists of much more than words. (This emphasis is captured here particularly in chapter 8, "Ethics of Democracy.") He's written a philosophy of the body, but he is also a practitioner and teacher of the body movement discipline known as the Feldenkrais Method, as well as other disciplines for bodily cultivation and transformation. He's written widely on hip-hop music, which he was early in treating as an important art form, and on other forms of popular music. He's contemplated the history of philosophy critically, but he's also engaged in Zen training quite seriously. He has written one of the most cohesive and compelling philosophies of art, and he is also an artist, the courageous and funny performer known as "the Man in Gold." To understand Shusterman's body philosophy, it helps to understand his body art and other practices. He has done some of most elaborate and sophisticated work in the history of philosophy on sexuality and the erotic, which is indicated in this volume rather than presented in its full development (for that, consult his *Ars Erotica* [2021]).

∽

The Critical Shusterman, then, does not distill all of his philosophy, much less all of his intellectual and aesthetic activity. What it does instead is to gather and represent Shusterman's most philosophical philosophy, focusing on his fundamental positions on fundamental philosophical questions and also his position in the unfolding intellectual developments of his period. The idea here is to present Shusterman's central ideas in a relatively compact form. These ideas, throughout Shusterman's career, have begun with a commitment to understanding the power of the arts and the nature of aesthetic experience. But they bear on many other matters in ethics, epistemology, metaphysics, and cultural studies: For Shusterman, aesthetic questions about the nature of sensory experience and interpretation, representation, cultivation, and even liberation ramify outward from philosophy of art to an account of what human life is, and what it's like to have one, and what it's for, or what could give it meaning. Questions emerging from the arts broadly construed and aesthetic experience at the widest scope amount in the writings collected here to an attempt to a return to and realization of the ancient ambition of the most accomplished philosophers.

Notoriously, one central feature of the postmodern era was a de-emphasis on the material and the physical, which one might have initially insisted on as a conspicuous and essential and recalcitrant aspect of our lives and cultures, and even a key (as in Marxist materialism) to political liberation. Now, it's rather hard to see why Western thought, or any thought really, could turn away from or de-emphasize the body, how anyone could try to account for what it's like to be a person while ignoring what it's like (as Richard puts it) both to have and to be a particular body living among other human bodies in a real physical environment. But that's just what postmodernism—and not only postmodernism—did. Much Western philosophy seems to put the value and even the reality of the body under question or threat, from Plato's treatment of physical reality as a reflection or representation of a realm of abstractions, to Descartes' treatment of the body as a hydraulic machine connected to a nonmaterial mind, to Kant's idea that space and time are forms of human perception rather than real dimensions inhabited by material bodies. So Shusterman's approach implies or entails various critiques of postmodernism but also of many other aspects of Western intellectual history, which has a weird problem or an unaccountable blind spot just here. The dualisms and the idealisms of so much philosophy tend to devalue the body on principle, if they do not deny its reality. But dualists and idealists are mammals too, if rather sophisticated ones, and could possibly also use a philosophy appropriate to creatures such as they are. Shusterman's philosophy, in short, is not exactly the opposite of deconstruction. It takes account of deconstruction, uses and criticizes it. But we might say that Shusterman's philosophy is exactly the opposite of destruction. All this time, he has been building.

II. From Pragmatist Aesthetics to Somaesthetics

Perhaps the very first thing to notice about the arc of Shusterman's thought, again, is that it centralizes aesthetics. Of course, the basic questions of aesthetics—about the nature of art and beauty, the nature of aesthetic judgment, pictorial representation and the role and value of art in human experience—are, traditionally, central philosophical questions, and Shusterman has addressed them systematically for decades. For him, indeed, aesthetic questions are key to all philosophical issues and all human questions too. He argues with John Dewey that aesthetic experience can "be achieved in any domain of action, since all experience, to be coherent and meaningful, requires the germ of aesthetic unity and development" (see chapter 9, "The End of Aesthetic Experience," section 3). He hints that art, beauty, and aesthetic experience form the telos of human life, are what gives us meaning. "The concept [of aesthetic experience] is directional," he says, "reminding us of what is worth seeking in art and elsewhere in life" (chapter 9, section 3). This sounds questionable when flatly asserted; perhaps it sounds like the "aestheticism" of Wilde and Pater, for example. And Shusterman is not denying that there are many things that people want or that could give human lives meaning. But he is asserting that none of these goals could be fully realized in isolation from aesthetics, once we conceive aesthetics richly enough, as including a sense of what is fitting and coherent, "balanced" and "poised," for example.

That's probably not a thesis best directly argued for (though many passages in this book could be taken as arguments for it), rather, it ought to be "demonstrated"—we should take the aesthetic categories out into the field, out into ethics and politics, sports and arts, food and fashion, and see what can be done with them: a pragmatic test of truth. Shusterman reverts to aesthetic concepts to understand the form or the value, or at least a central dimension of the form and value, of almost anything that exists, and the character of it in his own or in our experiences. What it's like to be what and who you are or to experience the things you experience, or how to characterize the whole world in which you are experiencing whatever you are experiencing: such matters immediately and inevitably invoke the aesthetic, on Shusterman's view, or according to his temperament. It's everywhere, all the time.

Now this itself is a revival and a pushing forward. By the time Shusterman started writing in the 1980s, aesthetics had been rather marginalized in mainline analytic philosophy (if less so in continental), and certainly it had been relegated to a marginal subdiscipline; aesthetic concepts were not bandied about in analytic ethics, metaphysics, or political philosophy. Shusterman was trained in this analytic material and edited an anthology summarizing its history (*Analytic Aesthetics*, 1989). Analytic aesthetics remains a touchstone, if nothing more than a cautionary tale about how the essential thing can be lost. Although some of it, such as the work of Nelson Goodman and Arthur Danto, was rich and important (and highly appreciated by Shusterman), Shusterman began to realize that this vein of philosophy would not be the most useful for his work, a realization already implicit in the analytic aesthetics anthology he edited.

If there is a fundamental single source for Shusterman's philosophy, it is Dewey's aesthetics. To a great extent we could see Shusterman's authorship as an elaboration and correction of the fundamental insights of *Art as Experience* (1934) connecting art to everyday life, treating it as a central way of understanding many or even all of the things we experience. For Dewey, all experiences are either "esthetic" or "anesthetic," either drawing us toward some sort of coherent "consummation"—the sort of satisfying "click" we get when the plot is satisfactorily resolved or insight gleaned or high point attained—or a lapsing or scattering away from such resolution. For Dewey, art is a crystallization of the sheer fact that we can have a series or group of experiences that all in turn cohere into a single experience: a meal, a journey, a love affair, or for that matter crafting a useful object or painting a masterpiece. And the needs and abilities that lead to art are of the most practical kind in their origin: organizing things into objects or graspable and satisfying sequences or narratives. Without the aesthetic element, experience would disintegrate into an unconnected series or a chaotic conflagration, and we could not respond effectively to our environments or (and this is central) make a mutually comprehensible culture.

The relentless emphasis on the unity of "consummatory" experiences with which Dewey associated all art and aesthetics comes in for suspicion in Shusterman (see chapter 3, "Organic Unity"). He points out rightly that fragmentation, incompletion, internal tension that may not be resolved, confrontation, and even confusion can be important elements in the arts. After all, Shusterman emerged in the postmodern era; Dewey's obsession with "unified" experiences seemed almost quaint by 1990, and indeed was probably not fully adequate to understanding the modernist works that Dewey did admire; it seems more appropriate to a classical aesthetic of proportion, harmony, and unity in variety. But emblematically for Shusterman's thought, both unity and disintegration had to be acknowledged, as possible threats and as possible values. But even while questioning and refining some elements of Dewey's aesthetics, Shusterman draws perhaps his most basic inspiration from Dewey's reintegration of art and life, and of the human organism and natural environment. These integrations remain a touchstone throughout Shusterman's philosophical oeuvre, as well as in his art and body practices.

The commitment to integrating insights from different traditions that seem to be in tension arises from deep conceptual and biographical sources. Indeed, as the reader will see even in this volume, which in general represents the less personal side of Shusterman's authorship, he has not been reticent about avowing the sources of his interests and also the character of his solutions in biographical facts about himself. In this and in other ways, his authorship anticipates some current developments, as authors such as Agnes Callard and the pragmatist John Kaag combine philosophical reflection with confessional self-revelation. An American who moved to Israel as a teen, to Oxford in his late twenties (where he studied with the likes of Stuart Hampshire and J. O. Urmson), then back to Philadelphia, and eventually to Paris and Boca Raton, Shusterman describes one source of his reflections as "a tendency toward doubleness, which pervades so much of my life: a binational, a double-major in college, twice married with two sets of children, I do research in both analytic and continental philosophy, and for most of my career I have simultaneously held academic appointments at two institutions. When my life is not double," he remarks, "it seems even more multiple."[1]

But there's no doubt that from these multiple or even opposed sources he has forged a single philosophy, though he has also tried to make it playful, commodious, and open-ended enough to engage pluralities, his own included:

Despite all that doubleness and plurality—and probably because of it—my philosophical work has been very much devoted to overcoming presumed dualisms that polarize our thought and impoverish our lives by excluding possibilities of interaction and synthesis that could enrich experience. So along with my insistence on pluralism, there is a compensating recognition that pluralities can very often be held together within a reasonably unified and stable field of focus. I see the meaning of an event, of an artwork, of one's life as examples of reconstructed unities that embrace plurality and change.

Pragmatist Aesthetics: Living Beauty, Rethinking Art (1992) was Shusterman's third book, after *The Object of Literary Criticism* (1984) and *T. S. Eliot and the Philosophy of Criticism* (1988). Eliot has remained a touchstone (see chapter 7, "Dialectics of Multiculturalism," for example), and some of the fruits of his work on literary interpretation are evident in this volume's first essay. But it is the third book that sets the pragmatist direction of the whole subsequent authorship. What Shusterman finds in Dewey, centrally, is just what Rorty devalued or ignored: an acknowledgment of nondiscursive modes of experience and a relatively straightforward understanding of aesthetic experience as centered in the physical human organism in interchange with its environment. He describes Dewey's aesthetics as "rooting aesthetics in natural needs, constitution, and activities of the human organism." Dewey "aims at recovering the continuity of aesthetic experience with normal processes of living" and connects the roots of art and beauty to "basic vital functions": the biological realities that humans share with "bird and beast." Shusterman writes that, "for Dewey, all art is the product of interaction between the living organism and its environment, an undergoing and a doing which involves a reorganization of energies, actions, and materials. Though the fine arts have become increasingly more spiritualized, 'the organic substratum remains as the quickening and deep foundation,' the sustaining source of the emotional energies of art which make it so enhancive of life."[2] These Deweyan observations could stand as a foundational manifesto for somaesthetics, though perhaps those of us who first read them in the early '90s couldn't foresee the directions in which, or the richness with which, these thoughts could develop over the long run under Shusterman's auspices, and how far they could emerge from their Deweyan sources.

One immediate result of bringing aesthetics back to earth this way was that it suggested that various hierarchies and "dualisms," such as the distinction between fine and popular art, could be dismantled. For example, though there are many differences between a Mahler symphony and a rap by "the Brooklyn crew Stetsasonic," each is an aesthetic object deeply rooted in human cognitive needs and biological capacities. Both engage the body, if somewhat differently. Above all, they emerge from the need to organize and reorganize social worlds in sound. The point might not be to exalt one and devalue the other or to think about which one is better but to see each as crystallization of its context and a way of understanding it.

The egalitarian impulse in aesthetics that allowed Shusterman to become one of the first philosophers to take hip-hop and some other popular arts fully seriously, and his own multicultural background, allowed him to recentralize and redescribe pleasure in a way that corresponded much more closely to the experiences that people of our generation were actually having:

> The strongest and most urgent reason for defending popular art is that it provides us (even us intellectuals) with too much aesthetic satisfaction to accept its wholesale denunciation as debased, dehumanizing, and aesthetically illegitimate. To condemn it as only fit for the barbaric taste and dull wit of the unenlightened, manipulated masses is to divide us not only against the rest of our community but against ourselves. We are made to disdain the things that give us pleasure and feel ashamed of the pleasure they give. (*Pragmatist Aesthetics*, 170)

At an intense moment of political critique of the arts, from feminists and Marxists, Pierre Bourdieu and Frederic Jameson, critical theorists and reactionary traditionalists, political figures such as Tipper Gore and Bill Clinton, Shusterman's plea for attention to the popular arts was notably refreshing. Even merely in frankly avowing his own actual pleasures, Shusterman brought a certain directness back to philosophy, and a kind of openness, effervescence, or tendency to dance. Indeed, I think of *Pragmatist Aesthetics* as one of the first books to really take popular arts seriously (though not uncritically) in the realm of philosophical aesthetics, and to give an account that encompassed them naturally.

One way to understand the development from pragmatist to body aesthetics is in terms of the fascinating theory of art that Shusterman developed around 2000, which focuses on the concept of drama and the process of dramatization, in several senses (represented in chapter 10, "Art as Dramatization"). The Deweyan idea of a sequence of events that is unified by a single tone or mood, or organized into a coherent aesthetic whole, lurks in the background here, but Shusterman characterizes dramatization simultaneously in terms of "experiential intensity" (as when we speak of a "dramatic event") and "social frame." A play on a stage is set apart from ordinary life by a set of codified social practices, provisionally or for practical purposes, and thus marked as art. And as his aesthetics developed, Shusterman has continued to highlight the importance of the social frame. But somaesthetics tends to focus on the dimension of experiential intensity, at least initially. Or, it arises in focusing on questions of experiential intensity and integrity or coherence and of their loss as well. All such experiences presuppose and center on the body, he asserts. This appears obvious, I suppose. But it profoundly challenges the Western aesthetic tradition, from Kant to what Shusterman calls Nelson Goodman's "semantic anesthetics" (see chapter 8, section 3), which again melted all image and performance into symbols and their logics of syntax and semantics.

Shusterman used the term "somaesthetics," his own coinage, as early as 1997,[3] and boldly declared the dawn of a new discipline in 1999, in "Somaesthetics: A Disciplinary Proposal" in the *Journal of Aesthetics and Art Criticism*. The "somatic" in Shusterman highlights the "nondiscursive": not necessarily what is immediately given but what precedes or exceeds the possibilities of being fully captured by verbal description. And hence somaesthetics provides a way of redressing what he terms here "philosophy's dominant ideology of textualism" (see chapter 2, section 5) represented by figures such as Rorty, Gadamer, and Derrida.

"Soma," of course, is the Greek term for "body," though Shusterman uses it in a particular but also etymologically defensible way, as referring to the human being not merely as a physical object but also something more. Soma is the living, experiencing, perceiving body, or it is the body as both had by and lived as a particular person. "The body," he observes, "captures the ambiguous human condition of subject and object, power and vulnerability, dignity and indignity, freedom and constraint, commonality and difference, knowledge and ignorance. . . . Even at rest, however, the soma is not a motionless thing but a complex field of multiple movement, a surge of life, a projection of energy that Bergson describes as *élan vital*" (chapter 2, section 2). The return of vitalism might be just one of many surprises waiting down the Shusterman Road.

He's characterized the discipline of somaesthetics in a number of ways, all closely related, but we might take the following formulation as paradigmatic: "Somaesthetics is devoted to the critical, ameliorative study of one's experience and use of one's body as a locus of sensory-aesthetic appreciation (*aistheisis*) and creative self-fashioning. It is therefore devoted to the knowledge, discourses, practices, and bodily disciplines that structure such somatic care or can improve it" (see chapter 13, "Soma and Media," section 2). The continuity with the pragmatist orientation should already be evident, particularly in the emphasis on "ameliorative" physical practices. But the data of somaesthetics, once one gets the concept on board, is vast, and complexly related to the traditional discipline of philosophical aesthetics. To begin with, the human body is perhaps the most frequently depicted thing in the arts. And there's no question of experiencing art, or making it, without the body, even in virtual reality. We see with our eyes. We move through and around works of art and built or otherwise constructed environments. But there is more: the nature of art, as Shusterman shows, always engages the body, and also has the potential to transform bodily experience in ways from the mundane (now I see green; that is, light at certain wavelengths runs through my eyes and into my head) to the profound (occupying one's own body, one's own life, with greater awareness or understanding). Dance is a model artform in these respects; in it, body is medium and instrument, artist and art, subject and object, at once. Dance is always central to Shusterman, I think. I speculate that it was reflections on dance and dancers that led him toward a philosophy of the body. Recall that *Pragmatist Aesthetics* was dedicated to "Three Dancing Graces."

Body crafts, disciplines, and arts—practical therapeutic ameliorative transformations and aesthetic reenvisionings—are keys to understanding Shusterman's philosophy, and also hoped-for results of it. For the idea that the practice of philosophy can be separated from the life of the body is no more plausible than the idea that the practice of art can be. Shusterman repeatedly centralizes body disciplines and transformative practices such as yoga, *taijiquan*, the Feldenkrais Method, and the Alexander Technique, and points to their aesthetic aspects and some of their relations to the arts, and to ways of life and thought at the broadest scope.

Shusterman demands an art and a philosophy of and for living (see especially chapter 8, "The Ethics of Democracy"); and he suggests that dancing or yoga, for example, might actually be ways of doing philosophy, as some cultures have conceived martial arts and other bodily disciplines as central expressions of their belief systems. He writes:

> The soma also plays a crucial role in aesthetics; we can neither create art nor appreciate it without bodily means. We use our

> hands to paint and sculpt, our vocal cords to sing, our limbs to dance, and our eyes and ears to appreciate an opera. Moreover, since all affect is grounded in the body, the soma is essential for appreciating the qualitative feelings expressed in art and for enjoying the emotions of aesthetic experience, whether aroused by art or nature. Improving our somatic aptitudes and sensibilities can help us improve our aesthetic capacities. (chapter 13, section 2)

Getting theoretically clearer is intellectually important, but transforming one's experience practically is urgent, as it can be necessary to living a decent life; and at any rate the theoretical clarity may tend to follow rather than precede the physiological transformations.

This fundamental change of emphasis suddenly opens new aesthetic vistas, or reopens old ones from a new angle. Shusterman has begun enumerating subdisciplines for the new discipline (which has a journal and a center and conferences already), including "representational" and "practical" somaesthetics, examining how bodies are depicted and interpreted and how their condition can be improved, among other matters (see chapter 13, section 3). The aesthetics of sex, for example, surely the site of many of our most intense experiences of pleasure and experiences of beauty, as well as of many difficulties and fraught issues personal and political, can be considered aright for the first time from this point of view, as Shusterman shows in *Ars Erotica*. The aesthetics of sport, a still underexplored area, can be discussed much more naturally from within somaesthetics than from most other standpoints. Somaesthetics provides new ways to take seriously and begin to understand the aesthetics of food. It's obviously in play in the aesthetics of fashion. And once we get rid of the idea that the physical is low and that the high arts should concern themselves only with the spiritual or the intellectual, we can recover many of the experiences of popular arts, crafts, and expressive forms of movement and gesture as revealing central aspects of the aesthetic and the human. Hence somaesthetics is, among other things, a cure for and an alternative to Kantian formalism: the idea that when we look at a painting, for example, qua work of art, we are registering its formal properties intellectually and getting pleasure from that, looking at the arrangement of lines and colors, as though at an abstract form. Art, for Shusterman, engages every aspect of our real physical lives.

The newly defined discipline is at its greatest sweep when it opens up ways of talking about beauty, and ways of experiencing it too:

Beauty of color, shape, movement, and song are part of the dance of life, of the wider natural world that humans belong to and through which they are constituted. The energies and material that constitute aesthetic experience for the human subject belong to a wider environing world; aesthetic experience, properly speaking, is never located only in the head of the human subject but always exists in a wider context that frames the subject's interaction with the object of art or natural beauty. And . . . the human subject itself is but a shifting, temporary construction from the materials and energies of the larger world of nature and history. (chapter 11, "Entertainment," section 4)

I would like in particular to draw attention to the passage reprinted in this volume in the chapter on art and religion (chapter 12, "Art and Religion," section 4), describing a transformational experience in Zen training. Shusterman's teacher, he tells us, allowed him to meditate on a bench overlooking "Japan's beautiful inland sea": a picturesque view, except that it was interrupted by two rusting metal barrels in his immediate line of sight, "the kind I had often seen used as makeshift open-air stoves by homeless people." The natural scene was "spoiled," by the commonplace and merely ugly human artifacts. As Shusterman continues to meditate for some time, however, the point of view suddenly reverses (I won't quote the whole description, but you should definitely read it). He suddenly finds the barrels beautiful ("savoring the subtle sumptuousness" of their colors, irregular textures, "flaking and peeling crusts embellishing the hard iron shell"), perhaps more beautiful than the sea itself. "Thus I too felt transfigured," he writes, "without feeling that either barrels or I had changed ontological categories and levitated into transcendent reality. Conversely, I realized that it was more the idea of the sea that I had been regarding as beautiful, not the sea itself, which I saw through a veil of romantic thoughts" (chapter 12, section 4).

This passage is exemplary of Shusterman's thought in a number of dimensions. The aesthetic transformation, or the detection of the reality that is already there and hence its beauty, depends on a physical transformation of the soma. The sense of human experience as continuous, from physical sensation to philosophical understanding to spiritual transformation, and from real environment to conscious interaction, is profound. These sorts of continuities, which I was calling "integrations" earlier, perhaps constitute Shusterman's most basic insight.

In reconnecting the human and the natural worlds through the human body, Shusterman heals some of the lacerations of postmodernism and creates an aesthetics for a time in which we are almost forced, or in which we really need, to consider ourselves as fundamentally physical things inhabiting a physical world to which we are connected at all times. The postmodern analysis of experience exclusively into words and languages and images seems, for example, ill-suited to address environmental aesthetics, or for that matter to provide a vocabulary for engaging real environmental threats. That we are real bodies in a real world is at this point a bottom-line presupposition for our ethics and our politics as well as for our arts, and perhaps directly for our survival.

III. A Fully-Embodied Philosophy

Though it begins in aesthetics and returns to it continuously, Shusterman's work explicitly provides resources for reconstruing all the subdisciplines of philosophy. (Well, with the possible exception of logic, though one never can tell.) Shusterman wields or deploys the body in critique of various elements of the Western tradition, especially the sequence that runs from "modern" philosophy (Descartes, Locke, and Kant, for example) to the postmoderns, a history of figures who explicitly devalue or question the existence of the body and think that philosophical questions can be answered without centralizing or understanding it. But in bringing the body to bear, using its traction or leverage, Shusterman, in texts collected here and elsewhere, has also identified and adumbrated useful historical elements, reinterpreting ancient Greek and Asian treatments of the body, including their erotic reflections, as well as more modern figures such as Nietzsche, the pragmatists, and late Foucault. In other words, the history of human thought reconfigures around Shusterman's structure, just the sort of thing you would expect from a significant new systematic philosophical development. And this leads us toward some relatively well-defined and underexplored projects that still beckon.

SOMATIC METAPHYSICS

"What does it mean for philosophy to recognize [the] somatic dimension?" Shusterman asks below (chapter 2, section 5). "Simply to say that it exists, even as a necessary feature of human existence, seems an empty gesture. The importance of nondiscursive experience does not mean that it is *philosophically* important. And how could it be, since philosophy as traditionally practiced can apparently do nothing with it except misuse it discursively for foundationalist fantasies?" This registers the objections to centralizing the body brought to bear by Rorty, for example, or Gadamer. Such figures put the question: Why do you *want* to believe in an apparently brute, explicitly "nondiscursive" reality allegedly underlying all knowledge and indeed all phenomena that knowledge could be knowledge of? Perhaps you are looking for unquestionable foundations in the very nature of things for the sorts of beliefs you already have, or are engaged in a "quest for certainty" of the sort that Dewey criticized: a sheer fantasy, everyone now seems to agree.

But Shusterman's treatment of the body in philosophy is supple, flexible, dancing. He does not regard physical reality as an absolute bottom line justifying all other claims or naturalizing some ideology. The body for Shusterman is itself is a site for "creative self-fashioning" and "sensory appreciation," and though these are more than discursive, they are also fully cultural, which is also true of the dance. Much or even most of Shusterman's work shows that the body does not, for us, remain a mere object, that our living bodies are much more than twitchy corpses, that they are moving cultural as well as physical things. Chapter 13 ("Soma and Media") contains a typical expression of this view, where Shusterman both deploys and compromises the distinction between direct and mediated experience, and hence between bodies and other sorts of things, showing both their difference and their continuity. Here the "doubleness" that is so often near the center of Shusterman's reflection (and which he typically accommodates on principle, as productive complementarity or complexity rather than a danger to unitary thinking) takes on the status of a direct description of fact. We ought not to contrast too sharply an unmediated experience of the physical with a mediated experience online, say. "Since the soma is more basic, familiar, and organic than the newer electronic media, the soma comes to seem so immediate. . . . Nevertheless the somatic constructor of reality is itself also continuously constructed through other varieties of media and mediations (including reconstructive surgery)" (chapter 13, section 4). The body is cultural as well as natural, and, for example, is adorned and interpreted according to rich sets of cultural norms that give it meaning in different contexts. Here, Shusterman's somaphilosophy is compatible with Judith Butler's insight that gender resolves largely to culturally articulated bodily performance, while also insisting on the physical reality of the body.

That we are not dealing ultimately or only with mere inert physical stuff is signaled by the use of the term "soma," which, again, indicates the living and perceiving and moving body, the body inhabiting a physical and social environment and moving in relation to it. Hence soma is engaged both in relatively direct experience and the processing or interpretation of that experience. Here, Shusterman's thought takes in the postmodern critique of foundationalism and responds to it with a return to the body, now playing a less naive role than it has had in previous philosophy, a role both more real and more open; not a sheer swarm of atoms or committee of organs but a "live creature" negotiating an environment from which it is not fully distinct, an intelligent creature negotiating this environment creatively, delimited by the body's physical capacities and the culture's representational resources but also reaching toward unexpectable new resolutions.

This, we might say, is Shustermanian metaphysics, and one thing we might hope still to get from this very living philosopher is more development in this regard, though that may not reflect his current interests, which are liable to be more practical, or more arts-oriented. At any rate, Shusterman's ontology does not appear to be a form of sheer materialism, though unlike so much Western philosophy, it straightforwardly acknowledges the existence of a fully material environment and fully material bodies. The hints, already mentioned, of Bergsonian vitalism, which also had an influence on Shusterman's hero William James; the account of what makes the soma distinct from a sheer pile of stuff; the idea that we or the whole world are driven forward together by a fully embodied life energy, dynamic and perhaps erotic, remain to be more fully developed, I think.[4]

If the implications for ontology still seem largely nascent, Shusterman—in developing somaesthetics—has also given much more than hints about somatic ethics, somatic epistemology, and even somatic political philosophy. We might, in other words, see the thought captured in this volume as a system of philosophy, albeit one still in process, and perhaps one that should or can never be completely finished, because it remains embodied and alive.

SOMATIC EPISTEMOLOGY

Just as profound as the potential ontological developments in somaesthetics are the implications for epistemology, or questions about the nature of the knower and of the known. In a remarkable passage (in chapter 14, "Thinking through the Body"), Shusterman draws out some of the implications: "As both an indispensable source of perception and an insurmountable limit to it, the soma epitomizes the human condition of knowledge and ignorance.

Because, as a body, I am a thing among things in the world in which I am present, that world of things is also present and comprehensible to me. Because the body is thoroughly affected by the world's objects and energies, it incorporates their regularities and thus can grasp them in a direct, practical way." This is a fundamental insight: the reason we can know what the world is like, and the way we can know it, is not that we can mirror facts accurately or run through a series of premises in our heads. We can know the world is because we are chunks or portions of it, events within it; we are the same sort of thing that we find in our world, and continuous with such things.

The laws of nature actually run through the body of each of us; we are physical phenomena, whatever else we may be. Each of us is fully embedded as a body in the world's body, which we can know, as it were, from inside. The Western epistemological tradition, from this point of view, is far too intellectual and stands in need of correction from the physical. Even the basic idea of a "standpoint" (a concept that has been central to feminist epistemology, for example) or "point of view" essentially makes use of or depends on embodiment for their sense: "To see the world, we must see it from some point of view: a position that determines our horizon and directional planes of observation, that sets the meaning of left and right, up and down, forward and backward, inside and outside, and eventually shapes the metaphorical extensions of these notions in our conceptual thought. The soma supplies that primordial point of view through its location both in the spatiotemporal field and in the field of social interaction."

No philosopher in her right mind, of course, denies the centrality of perception to knowledge, but many of the accounts of perception in the Western tradition seem bizarrely disembodied, portraying the process as like sitting passively in a theater watching a screen on which visual images appear, or our sensory organs and capacities as devices for processing sensory data into texts, assertions, theories, accounts, and justifications. Rather, perception is an active process of an organism moving in and through an environment, absorbing some bits of it and extruding bits of itself back into it: a process by which organism and environment become de-distinguished. And here too, Shusterman makes a characteristic reversal: questions about the body and knowledge are not only theoretical; they are practical. Making use of Xenophon's Socrates, who seems better for this purpose than Plato's, and of the great Confucian ethicist Mencius, Shusterman observes that "rather than rejecting the body because of its sensory deceptions, we should try to correct the functional performance of the senses by cultivating improved somatic awareness and self-use, which can also improve our virtue by giving us greater perceptual sensitivity and powers of action" (chapter 14, section 2).

SOMATIC ETHICS

The idea of trying to do ethics without bodies is quite ridiculous, of course. And if, for example, utilitarian ethics turns on questions of pleasure and pain, then it is essentially about the body. Shusterman starts to draw the implications in such texts as "Entertainment,":

> I begin with pleasure, as my aesthetics has been criticized for hedonism, even though I never claim that pleasure is the only or the highest value in art and life. I do, however, think that post-Kantian aesthetics wrongly tends to dismiss the importance of pleasure by failing to realize the complexity of its logic and the diversity of its forms and uses. This diversity is even suggested in the vast vocabulary of pleasure that far exceeds the single term. Besides the traditional contrast between sensual voluptuousness (*voluptas*) and the sacred heights of religious joy (*gaudium*), there is delight, pleasantness, gratification, gladness, elation, titillation, fun, exhilaration, enjoyment, exultation, bliss, rapture, ecstasy, and more. While fun and pleasantness convey a sense of lightness that could suggest triviality, the notions of rapture, bliss, and ecstasy clearly evoke just how profound and potently meaningful pleasures can be. Such pleasures, as much as truth, help constitute our sense of the sacred and can establish or enforce our deepest values. (chapter 11, section 4)

Passages such as this make one realize how superficial or blank are the usual concepts of pleasure and pain, happiness and unhappiness, well-being and its opposite, especially in recent Western ethics, and how an ethics that centralizes pleasure and pays real attention to what it's like to have different sorts of pleasures on different occasions, could be a very rich ethics fully engaged in and articulated by particular representational, aesthetic, and cultural practices.

Even more urgently for ethics and political philosophy, the same is true of pain; and here the outlines of a somaethics start to emerge. In "Thinking through the Body," Shusterman quotes a "strangely brutal" passage in Wittgenstein's notebooks in which the latter points out that concepts such as "self-respect" and "dignity" (and, we could add, "integrity") that are central to the post-Kantian Western ethical tradition all depend on "the habitual, normal state of our bodies." These concepts could not mean what they mean if individuals lived in conditions where bodily integrity could never be maintained. By the same token, although we may "dehumanize" people by ridiculing them or describing them in certain ways incompatible with full personhood, dehumanization is clearest and most profound through something physical done to their bodies:

> In a world where bodies were always mutilated, starved, and abused, our familiar concepts of duty, virtue, charity, and respect for others could get no purchase and make no sense. Moreover, bodily abilities set the limits of what we can expect from ourselves and others, thus determining the range of our ethical obligations and aspirations. If paralyzed, we have no duty to leap to the rescue of a drowning child. Virtue cannot require constant labor with no rest or nourishment because these needs are physical necessities. (chapter 14, section 2)

An ethics that does not centralize the body is just not a possible ethics for creatures such as ourselves, as I suspect antitorture activists and Amnesty International would agree. This seems entirely obvious, but figures such as Foucault have really only made a start on questions like these, taken from this point of view. In this, Shusterman may participate in a much wider intellectual and practical rethinking of many ethical questions, emblematized by such books as Elaine Scarry's *The Body in Pain* (1985) and focused on the real treatment of bodies in physical space.

SOMATIC POLITICAL PHILOSOPHY

With some persistence—and, I hope, in texts that will still emerge—Shusterman develops some of the ethical implications of somaesthetics in the direction of political philosophy. Even just broaching the topic from this somatic angle accomplishes something; we'd all better realize that a politics that ignores or transcends bodies is fantastical or evil. But it might also yield some directly practical insights, moment by moment. In this light, Shusterman has been particularly concerned to describe how our cultural somatic trainings lead us into prejudices that we experience as direct and visceral, because pre- or more-than-discursive. His treatment of this matter raises an important point about his account of the body and nondiscursive experience. These have phenomenological immediacy in many instances, and hence are particularly compelling. But they are not exempt from or entirely independent of cultural vocabularies, as we have seen, though they may also exceed or challenge familiar categories.

Structural oppressions such as racism and sexism are encoded in the body; they are "incorporated." Shusterman suggests that the current fashion for anti-racist training in corporations and colleges, for example, is inadequate to the extent that it does not address the bodily comportments and visceral/cultural reactions in which racism is largely contained. "Feelings of discomfort from 'foreign' bodies are almost entirely the results of learning or habit rather than innate instinct," he observes, and "as such they are malleable to efforts of reformation." Somatic philosophy, he says, can help initiate change, "suggesting how sensitizing, consciousness-raising somatic training can deal with issues of racism, sexism, homophobia, and violence" (chapter 16, "Somaesthetics and Politics," section 2).

Oppression is encoded in bodies in a thousand ways. One could read the social structure of oppression from the bodily comportment of oppressors and oppressed people, for example, which are embedded inextricably in both biologic and in semiotic systems, in systems of cultural meanings playing across and within bodies:

> Entire ideologies of domination can thus be covertly materialized and preserved by encoding them in somatic norms that, as bodily habits, get typically taken for granted and so escape critical consciousness: for example, the norm that women of a given culture should speak softly, eat dainty foods, sit with their knees close together, keep the head and the eyes down while walking, and assume the passive or lower position in copulation. However, just as repressive power relations are encoded in our bodies, so they can be challenged by alternative somatic practices. (chapter 13, section 2)

To address or remediate oppression, we might need to accomplish a revolution or to lobby for new laws. But as feminists and critical race theorists, everyone from Frederick Douglass to Iris Marion Young, have emphasized, we will have to become aware, too, of how oppression is reflected in the bodies of both oppressed and oppressors, or is expressed and made real in our physical comportment, and indeed depends on it. Young's insight, for example, that "throwing like a girl" is not a natural biological condition but a cultural discipline imposed on bodies, or Douglass's that, in manifesting an upright and proud bearing he was negating his own treatment as chattel, shows some of the ways that social systems, resistance to them, and the bodies embedded in them are mutually articulated. Shusterman argues in chapter 8 that his treatment of aesthetics, as Dewey conceived his own, has democratic implications, that it indicates ways that our mutual space can be collectively shaped so that differently embodied individuals can more fruitfully connect, merge, and diverge. It suggests, Shusterman argues, ways to conceive the relation of the individual and the collective.

"Somaesthetics echoes Marx in rejecting the presumed dichotomy between individual and social existence," Shusterman writes (chapter 16, "Somaesthetics and Politics," section 4), which Marx says can only be resolved practically, as a "real problem of life." But how political liberation could change our bodies or how our bodies can be changed to contribute to it: these profound matters also await more elaborate treatment. In some ways, somaesthetics could be interpreted as a rethinking of materialism, both as a metaphysics and as a liberatory program.

IV. Somaphilosophy Now

I write this less than a year after the broad release of artificial intelligence apps such as ChatGPT that challenge our traditional sense of the distinctness of human intelligence. People sometimes claim that the body is becoming less significant in every dimension with the rapid developments of social media, artificial intelligence, robotics, and virtual reality. Many people seem to experience themselves, or at least others, primarily as avatars inhabiting a virtual space. And this space seems to be functioning as our museum and our art studio. It is also "where" many of our deepest ethical and political dilemmas are being sorted through or exacerbated. Indeed, our apparently thoroughly mediated lives now might seem to be the practical realization of postmodernism's constructed realities, as though in the end Rorty and Goodman beat Shusterman not with arguments they are no longer around to make but through cultural/technological developments.

In closing, or in opening to the texts that follow, I would like to urge just the opposite. Questions about real bodies in real space are more urgent than ever, and if we lost the sense of ourselves as bodies, there would no longer be any artificial environment to enter, and there would be no way to get there anyway. There are many reasons to move in the direction that Shusterman suggests. The idea that there is nothing outside the text, or nothing real that is being represented in our representations, again, leaves us without a way to respond even to environmental destruction that physically threatens our bodies, the bodies of other animals, and the body of the earth. As many people began to work virtually or "distantly" from one another (initially because of what the COVID virus does to particular human bodies when it leaps from one to another), this somatic isolation led to a spike in mental illness. Psychology has given up on trying to understand its subject matter apart from neurology; identity of bodily and emotional and cognitive conditions is in some sense taken for granted. In spite of the proliferation of the virtual, which also depends on the physical, or because of the proliferation of the virtual, we seem to be in a condition now of yearning for deeply embodied experiences of interaction and physical presence with one another. The moment when the real world seems to be threatened by virtual realities is the moment that somatic philosophy becomes entirely indispensable.

And, despite all our physical limitations and despite all the threats to our bodies and hence to our spirits, Shusterman's somaphilosophy is an attempt to bring us back into our bodies and hence back to the earth we coinhabit. Richard Shusterman's philosophy is devoted above all to cultivating awareness of the body, or learning to love being the bodies that we are, despite our obvious imperfections and mortality. It is a philosophy that opens up possibilities of joy, which I don't think one could say of most philosophies: "There is every reason to regard our somatic selves with grateful wonder and enthusiastic curiosity for the vulnerable yet astoundingly complex and well-functioning organization of biological, social, psychological, and cultural materials that we indeed are" (chapter 6, "Self-Knowledge and Its Discontents," section 6).

I

Cognition, Interpretation, and Ontology

Chapter One

Beneath Interpretation

I

Kohelet, that ancient postmodern who already remarked that all is vanity and there is nothing new under the sun, also insisted that there is a time for everything: a time to be born and a time to die, a time to break down and a time to build up, a time to embrace and a time to refrain from embracing. There is no mention of a time for interpretation, but surely there is one; and just as surely that time is now. Our age is even more hermeneutic than it is postmodern, and the only meaningful question to be raised at this stage is whether there is ever a time when we refrain from interpreting. A host of holist hermeneuts answer this firmly in the negative, maintaining that simply to perceive, read, understand, or behave intelligently at all is already, and must always be, to interpret. They hold that whenever we experience anything with meaning, such meaningful experience always must be a case and product of interpretation.

This position of hermeneutic universalism[1] dominates contemporary theory. Loss of faith in foundationalist and realist objectivity has made it the current dogma. Having abandoned the ideal of reaching a naked, rock-bottom, unmediated God's-eye view of reality, we seem impelled to embrace the opposite position—that we see everything through an interpretive veil or angle. Indeed, one might further argue that since the terms "veil" and "angle" inappropriately suggest that we can even make sense of the idea of a naked, perspectiveless reality, we do not merely *see* everything through interpretation, but everything *is* in fact constituted by interpretation. In other words, there is nothing real (and certainly nothing real for us) that

27

is not interpreted. This theory can, of course, be traced back to Nietzsche's famous remark, "Facts are precisely what there is not, only interpretations";[2] and it is not surprising that today's hermeneutic universalists have resurrected Nietzsche as a major philosopher and as a precursor of the postmodern. Alexander Nehamas's fine book on Nietzsche is a contemporary defense of Nietzschean perspectivism and universal hermeneutics.[3] Nehamas in fact identifies the two positions by defining Nietzsche's perspectivism as "the thesis that every view is an interpretation," and he goes on to assert that not only all views but "all practices are interpretive," since "all our activity is partial and perspectival" (*N* 66, 70, 72).

Pragmatists, like Nietzscheans, insist on rejecting the very idea of any foundational, mind-independent, and permanently fixed reality that could be grasped or even sensibly thought of without the mediation of human structuring. Such structuring or shaping of perception is today typically considered to be interpretation, and so we find contemporary pragmatists like Stanley Fish repeatedly insisting that interpretation comprises all of our meaningful and intelligent human activity, that "interpretation is the only game in town."[4] All perception and understanding must be interpretation, since "information only comes in an interpreted form." Thus, even in our most primitive and initial seeing of an object, "interpretation has already done its work."[5] Moreover, quite apart from such radical Nietzschean and pragmatist perspectives, we find hermeneutic universalism firmly endorsed by a traditionalist like Gadamer who baldly asserts that "all understanding is interpretation."[6]

In short, the various camps of the ever-growing antifoundationalist front seem united by the belief that interpretation subsumes all meaningful experience and reality, that there is nothing beneath interpretation that serves as the object of interpretation, since anything alleged to be such is itself an interpretive product. Though I share their rejection of foundationalism and their commitment to interpretation's pervasive and irreplaceable role, I think its role is better understood by more modest pretentions than hermeneutic universalism. Interpretation is better served by letting it leave room for something else (beneath or before it), by slimming it down from an overly bloated state that courts coronary arrest, by saving it from an ultimately self-destructive imperialist expansion.

In this chapter I challenge hermeneutic universalism by critically examining what appear to be its best arguments. Having shown that those arguments need not compel belief in hermeneutical universalism, I then suggest why such a belief is more dangerous and unprofitable than the contrary idea that our intelligent and meaningful intercourse with the world includes noninterpretational experience, activity, and understanding, so that we should not think interpretation is the only game in town. Finally, I shall try to determine what distinguishes interpretation from those uninterpreted understandings and experiences that hermeneutic universalists insist on fully subsuming under the concept of interpretation. In drawing this distinction, I am not claiming it is a rigid ontological one, where interpretation and understanding are different natural kinds that can never share the same objects. But I hope to show that some functional distinction between them is pragmatically helpful and illuminating, and can itself be helpfully illuminated.

II

Before undertaking these tasks, however, I need to distance my challenge of interpretation from an earlier and influential critique advanced by Susan Sontag in "Against Interpretation."[7] Sontag's attack is directed not at interpretation per se but at the global claims of interpretation over *art*. Indeed, she explicitly endorses hermeneutic universalism's notion of "interpretation in the broadest sense, the sense in which Nietzsche (rightly) says, 'There are no facts, only interpretations'" (AI 5). But what *are* the claims of interpretation's dominion over art? Arthur Danto and others have argued that a work of art is ontologically constituted by interpretation. Since physically identical things can be different works if they have different interpretations, "interpretations are what constitute works, there are no works without them"; without them, works would be the "mere things" of their material substance.[8] This view that the art object is not a physical or foundational fact but must itself be constituted by an interpretive perspective is essentially an application of the Nietzschean view of objects that Danto here confines to the domain of art, elsewhere remaining a realist. Such *constitutive* interpretation of art, as Danto notes, should not be the target of Sontag's attack, though its alleged necessity—that art cannot be meaningfully experienced without being interpreted—will be a target of mine.

The interpretation Sontag instead impugns is the deliberate act of explaining, disclosing, or decoding the content or meaning of the object (interpretively) constituted. Such interpretation of content is indicted as a corruptive act "of translation. . . . The interpreter, without actually erasing or rewriting the text, *is* altering it," making it "into something else," distracting us from "experiencing the luminousness of the thing in itself" by putting us on a false quest for its meaning (AI 5, 6, 8, 13). Rather than opening us up to the powerful sensuous experience of art's surface form, which is the essence of art's liberational challenge to the primacy of the cognitive and discursive, interpretation "poisons our sensibilities" and represents "the revenge of the intellect upon art" at the expense of our "sensual capability" (AI 7). Sontag therefore urges, "In place of a hermeneutics we need an erotics of art," and she conceives this erotics in terms of a criticism that gives "more attention to form in art," "that dissolves consideration of content into those of form," and that "would supply a really sharp, loving description of the appearance of a work of art," "to *show how it is what is*" (AI 12–14).

Though I support Sontag's protest against hermeneutics' imperialist conquest of all artistic understanding and share her insistence on greater recognition of sensuous immediacy in aesthetic experience, I cannot accept her critique of interpretation. This is not because its repudiation of content for pure form and eros seems to reflect and legitimate what is arguably the worst of American culture—meaningless sex, empty formalism, and contempt of intellect. Such ideological complaints we can leave for other occasions and our moments of alienated discontent. What I instead aim to show is that whatever our verdict on its ideological stance, Sontag's critique is severely crippled by deep confusions and unwarranted assumptions.

First, in claiming that all interpretation "sustains the fancy that there really is such a thing as the content of a work of art" and in subsequently demanding that criticism instead confine itself to form, which is contrastingly real, Sontag relies on a naively rigid content/form distinction that suggests that form itself has no content and that she herself wishes to deny (AI 5, 11–12). Secondly, Sontag betrays a naive realism about the work of art's identity and form. This is not only unconvincing but totally at odds with the Nietzschean interpretive position she claims to endorse. Her attack on interpretation for necessarily "altering" or "translating" the work "into something else" rather than describing the work as "just what it is," "the thing in itself," presumes first that there is some foundational identity of the work "just as it is" apart from our constitutive and perspectival grasping of it, and secondly that we can transparently grasp that identity (AI 6, 8, 11, 13). "Transparence," which Sontag claims as the highest value in art and criticism, "means experiencing the luminousness of the thing in itself" (AI 13). But the Nietzschean notion of interpretation as constituting identity not only rejects such nonperspectival transparency; it repudiates the very idea of the uninterpreted "thing in itself" as a dogmatic notion.[9]

Sontag's third confusion is her presumption that while interpretive content represents "the revenge of the intellect on art" by taming art's sensuous liberational power into something "manageable, conformable" (AI 8), form, on the other hand, is neither intellectual nor constraining but simply liberationally erotic. This is obviously false, as the very morphology of the word "conformable" makes clear. Indeed, since the time of Plato and Aristotle, who essentially formed our notion of form, we regard form as something paradigmatically intellectual and constraining. Moreover, as has been emphasized since Kant, the formalistic appreciation of aesthetic objects demands much more intellectual power and repressive austerity than appreciation based on content, which can simply rely on our ordinary feelings associated with and immediately evoked by the content. Formalists such as Kant and Clive Bell condemn the more natural, less intellectualized appreciation of content as philistine barbarism.[10] Sontag similarly condemns interpretation of content as philistinism, while privileging the appreciation of form. But she mistakenly confuses formal analysis with unintellectual "sensuous immediacy" (AI 9), when it instead requires no less (and usually much more) intellectual mediation than the interpretation of content.

This leads to the fourth crucial error in Sontag's position—her failure to recognize that she is not really sustaining a global rejection of interpretation; for the formalistic analysis she advocates is itself a recognized form of interpretation. It is simply a mistake to think that all interpretation is governed by the depth metaphor of uncovering hidden layers or kernels of meaning. Interpretation is also practiced and theorized in terms of formal structures with the aim not so much of exposing hidden meanings but of connecting unconcealed features and surfaces so as to see and present the work as a well-related whole. Recognition of this formalist interpretive mode that aims "to grasp the whole design" of the work is what swayed an earlier and more strident rejector of interpretation, T. S. Eliot, from his view that "the work of art cannot be interpreted" to an acceptance of interpretation's ineliminable role and value.[11]

Sontag should similarly recognize that her apparent critique of all interpretation is but a privileging legitimation of one interpretive form above and against all others. She provides no argument that we ever should or could do without interpretation altogether or that in fact we ever do without it in at least its Nietzschean constitutive sense. She does not even consider hermeneutic universalism's arguments for holding that interpretation is necessarily present in any meaningful experience of art, or of anything else. In short, Sontag's critique is simply normative, that we should not interpret for content. What I instead contest is the view that, logically and necessarily, we are always interpreting whenever we meaningfully experience or understand anything, the view expressed in Gadamer's dictum that "all understanding is interpretation." I must therefore address the powerful arguments for this view.

III

Since our current hermeneutic turn derives in large part from the rejection of foundationalism, it is not surprising that the central arguments for hermeneutic universalism turn on rejecting foundationalist ideas of transparent fact, absolute and univocal truth, and mind-independent objectivity. For such ideas underwrite the possibility of attaining some perfect God's-eye grasp of things as they really are, independent of how we differently perceive them, a seeing or understanding that is free from the corrigibility and perspectival pluralities and prejudices that we willingly recognize as intrinsic to all interpretation.

I think the universalists are right to reject such foundational understanding but wrong to conclude from this that all understanding is interpretation. Their mistake, a grave but simple one, is to equate the nonfoundational with the interpretive. In other words, what the universalists are successfully arguing is that all understanding is nonfoundational; that it is always corrigible, perspectival, and somehow prejudiced or prestructured; that no meaningful experience is passively neutral and disinterestedly nonselective. But since, in the traditional foundationalist framework, interpretation is contrasted and designated as *the* form of nonfoundational understanding, the inferior foster home of all corrigible, perspectival perception, it is easy to confuse the view that no understanding is foundational with the view that all understanding is interpretive. Yet this confusion of hermeneutic universalism betrays an unseemly residual bond to the foundationalist framework in the assumption that what is not foundational must be interpretive. It thus prevents the universalists from adopting a more liberating pragmatist perspective, which (I shall argue) can profitably distinguish between understanding and interpretation without thereby endorsing foundationalism. Such pragmatism more radically recognizes uninterpreted realities, experiences, and understandings as already perspectival, prejudiced, and corrigible; in short, as nonfoundationally given.

So much for a general overview of the universalist arguments. I now want to itemize and consider six of them in detail. Though there is some overlap, we can roughly divide them into three groups, respectively based on three ineliminable features of all understanding: (a) corrigibility, (b) perspectival plurality and prejudice, and (c) mental activity and process.

(1) What we understand, what we grasp as truth or fact, frequently turns out to be wrong, to require correction, revision, and replacement by a different understanding. Moreover, this new understanding is typically achieved by reinterpreting the former understanding, and can itself be replaced and shown to be not fact but "mere interpretation" by a subsequent understanding reached through interpretive thought. Since any putative fact or true understanding can be revised or replaced by interpretation, it cannot enjoy an epistemological status higher than interpretation; and interpretation is paradigmatically corrigible and inexhaustive. This is sometimes what is meant by the claim that there are no facts or truths but only interpretations.

The inference, then, is that since understanding is epistemologically no better than interpretation, it is altogether no different from interpretation (as if all meaningful differences had to be differences of apodicticness!). The conclusion is reinforced by the further inference that since all interpretation is corrigible, and all understanding is corrigible, then all understanding is interpretation. Once formulated, the inferences are obviously, indeed pathetically, fallacious. But we tend to accept their conclusion, since we assimilate all corrigible and partial understanding to interpretation, as if genuine understanding itself could never be revised or enlarged, as if understanding had to be interpretive to be corrigible. But why make this rigidly demanding assumption? Traditionally, the reason was that understanding (like its cognates truth and fact) was itself defined in contrast to "mere interpretation" as that which *is* incorrigible. But if we abandon foundationalism by denying that any understanding is incorrigible, the idea of corrigible understanding becomes possible and indeed necessary; and once we recognize this idea, there is no need to infer that all understanding must be interpretation simply because it is corrigible. When hermeneutic universalists make this inference, they show an unintended and unbecoming reliance on the foundationalist linkage of uninterpreted understanding with incorrigible, foundational truth.

(2) The second argument for hermeneutic universalism derives from understanding's ineliminable perspectival character and the inevitable plurality of perspectives. We already noted how Nehamas builds his argument that all understanding is interpretive on the premise that all understanding, indeed, "all our activity is partial and perspectival." I think the premise is

perfectly acceptable, and can be established by an argument that Nehamas does not supply. All understanding must be perspectival or aspectual, since all thought and perception exhibit intentionality (in the phenomenological sense of being about something), and all intentionality is aspectival, that is, grasping its object in a certain way. But the very idea of perspective or aspect implies that there are other possible perspectives or aspects, which lie (in Gadamer's words) outside "the horizon" of a particular perspectival standpoint and thus outside its "range of vision" (*TM* 269). There can be no univocal and exclusive understanding of anything, but rather many partial and perspectival ways of seeing it, none of which provides total and exclusive truth.

So much for the premise, but how does it follow that all understanding is interpretive? Again, in the traditional foundationalist framework, interpretation marks the realm of partial, perspectival, and plural ways of human understanding in essential contrast to some ideal understanding that grasps things as they really are univocally, exhaustively, and absolutely. Rejecting the very possibility and intelligibility of such univocal and complete understanding (as Nehamas and Gadamer rightly do), the universalists infer that all understanding is thereby reduced to interpretation—the foundationalist category for understanding that is not necessarily false and illegitimate (not a *mis*understanding) but that cannot represent true understanding since it is perspectivally plural and not necessarily and wholly true. However, again we should realize that once we are free of foundationalism's doctrines; there is no need to accept its categorizations. There is thus no need to deny that true understanding can itself be perspectivally partial and plural, and consequently no reason to conclude that since all understanding must be perspectival, it must also be interpretation.[12]

(3) In speaking of understanding as perspectival and hence partial, we have so far meant it cannot exclude different perspectives and can in principle always be supplemented. But partiality also has the central sense of bias and prejudice. The third argument why understanding must always be interpretation is that it is always prejudiced and never neutrally transparent. This is a key point in the Nietzschean, Gadamerian, and even pragmatist attacks on foundationalist understanding. Any understanding involves the human element that prestructures understanding in terms (and in service) of our interests, drives, and needs, which significantly overlap but also frequently diverge among different societies and individuals. Moreover, for Nietzsche, Gadamer, and the pragmatists the fact that understanding is always motivated and prejudiced by our needs and values is a very good

thing; it is what allows us to thrive and survive so that we can understand anything at all.

From the premise that "all understanding necessarily involves some prejudice" (*TM* 239), "that every view depends on and manifests specific values" and "antecedent commitments" (*N* 67–68), it is but a short step to the view that all understanding and perception is interpretation. But it is a step that the more canny pragmatist refuses to take, and where she parts company from grand continental hermeneuts such as Nietzsche and Gadamer. In rejecting the foundationalist idea and ideal of transparent mirroring perception, she recognizes that understanding is always motivated and prejudiced, just like interpretation. But she wonders why this makes understanding always interpretive. It just does not follow, unless we presume that *only* interpretation could be prejudiced, while (preinterpretive) understanding or experience simply could not be. But to her, this inference is as strange and offensive as a sexist argument that all humans are really women because they all are influenced by emotions, while presumably real men are not.

(4) The fourth argument for hermeneutic universalism inhabits the overlap between the ineliminability of perspectival partiality and its active process. The argument is basically that since all understanding is selective—focused on some things but not others, grasping certain but not all features—all understanding must therefore be interpretive. The fact that understanding is perspectivally partial (in both senses of incompleteness and purposive bias) implies that it is always selective. It always grasps some things rather than others, and what it grasps depends in part on its antecedent purposes.

This selectivity seems uncontestable. What I challenge is the inference that since understanding (or indeed any intelligent activity) is always selective, it is therefore always interpretive. Such a conclusion needs the further premise that all purposive selection must be the product of interpretive thinking and decision. But this premise is false, an instance of the philosophical fallacy Dewey dubbed "intellectualism."[13] For most of the selection involved in our ordinary acts of perception and understanding is done automatically and unconsciously (yet still intelligently and not mechanically) on the basis of intelligent habits, without any reflection or deliberation at all.[14] Interpretation, in its standard ordinary usage, certainly implies conscious thought and deliberate reflection; but not all intelligent and purposive selection is conscious or deliberate. Walking down the stairs requires selecting how and where to place one's feet and body; but such selection involves interpreting only in cases of abnormal conditions when descent of the staircase presents a problem (as with an unusually dark or narrow winding staircase, a sprained ankle, or a fit of vertigo).

Just as it is wrong to confuse all purposive intelligent choice with interpretive decisions requiring ratiocination, so we need not confuse perceptions and understandings that are immediately given to us (albeit only corrigibly, and mediated by prior experience) from understandings reached only by interpretive deliberation on the meaning of what is immediately given. When I awake on the beach at Santa Cruz with my eyes pierced by sunlight, I immediately perceive or understand it is daytime; only when I instead awake to a darkish gloom do I need to interpret that it is no longer night but only another dreary morning in Philadelphia.

In short, I am arguing that though all understanding is selective, not all selective understanding is interpretive. If understanding's selection is neither conscious nor deliberate but prereflective and immediate, we have no reason to regard that selection or the resultant understanding as interpretation, since interpretation standardly implies some deliberate or at least conscious thinking, while understanding does not.[15] We can understand something without thinking about it at all; but to interpret something we need to think about it. This may recall a conclusion from Wittgenstein's famous discussion of seeing-as, where he distinguishes seeing from interpreting: "To interpret is to think, to do something; seeing is a state."[16]

(5) Though insightful, Wittgenstein's remark is also quite problematic. For it suspiciously suggests that we could see or understand without doing anything; and this suspicion suggests the fifth argument for hermeneutic universalism. Understanding or perceiving, as Nietzscheans, pragmatists, and even Gadamerians insist, is active. It is not a passive mirroring but an active structuring of what it encounters. To hear or see anything, before we even attempt to interpret it, involves the activity of our bodies, certain motor responses and tensions in the muscles and nerves of our organs of sensation. To characterize seeing or understanding in sharp contrast to interpretation as an achieved "state" rather than as "doing something" suggests that understanding is static rather than active; and if passively static, then it should be neutral rather than selective and structuring. The fifth argument for hermeneutic universalism therefore rejects this distinction between understanding as passively neutral and interpretation as actively structuring, and infers that since all understanding is active, all understanding must be interpretive.

My response to this argument should already be clear. As a pragmatist, I fully assent to the premise that all perception and understanding involve doing something; but I deny this entails that they always involve interpretation. The inference relies on an implicit premise that all "doings" that are cognitively valuable or significant for thought are themselves already cases of thinking. Hence any active selection and structuring of perception must already be a thoughtful, deliberate selection, one involving an interpretive decision. This is the premise I contest, the assimilating conflation of all active, selective, and structuring intelligence with the active, selective, and structuring of the interpreting intellect. Understanding can actively structure and select without engaging in interpretation, just as action can be intelligent without engaging thought or the intellect. When, on my way to the beach, I am told that the surf is up, I immediately understand what is said, prereflectively selecting and structuring the sounds and meanings I respond to. I do not need to interpret what is said or meant. It is only if I were unfamiliar with idiomatic English, or unable to hear the words, or in a situation where the utterance would seem out of place, that I would have to interpret it. Only if there were some problem in understanding, some puzzle or doubt or incongruity, would I have to thematize the utterance as something that needed interpretation, something to think about and clarify or resolve.

(6) But this assertion is precisely what is challenged by the sixth argument for hermeneutic universalism, an argument that highlights the intimate link between the hermeneutic turn and the linguistic turn in both continental and Anglo-American philosophy. Briefly and roughly, the argument goes as follows. All understanding is linguistic, because all understanding (as indeed all experience) involves concepts that require language. But linguistic understanding is essentially a matter of decoding or interpreting signs that are arbitrary rather than natural and whose translation into meaningful propositions thus requires interpretation. To understand the meaning of a sentence, we need, on the Quinean-Davidsonian model, to supply a translation or interpretation of it in terms already familiar to us (whether those terms be in the interpreted language itself or in another more familiar "home" language). So Davidson baldly asserts, "All understanding of the speech of another involves radical interpretation," and he firmly equates "the power of thought" with "speaking a language."[17] And from the continental tradition, Gadamer concurs by basing the universal scope of hermeneutics on "the essential linguisticality of all human experience of the world" and on a view of language as "itself the game of interpretation that we are all engaged in every day."[18] Hence, not only all understanding but all experience is interpretive, since both are ineliminably linguistic—a conclusion endorsed by Rorty, Derrida, and a legion of hermeneutical universalists.

Though the consensus for this position is powerful and pervasive, the argument strikes me as less than persuasive. It warrants challenging on two points at least. First, we can question the idea that linguistic understanding is always the decoding, translation, or interpretation of arbitrary signs in terms of specific rules of meaning and syntax. This is, I think, an overly formalistic and intellectualized picture of linguistic understanding. Certainly, it is not apparent that we always (or ever) interpret, decode, or translate the uncoded and unproblematic utterances we hear in our native tongue simply in order to understand them. That is precisely why ordinary language distinguishes such direct and simple understandings from decodings, translations, and interpretations.

The hermeneutic universalists will object that we must be interpreting here, even if we don't realize it, since no other model can account for our understanding. But an alternative model *is* available in Wittgenstein, where linguistic understanding is a matter of being able to make the right responses or moves in the relevant language game, and where such ability or language acquisition is first gained by brute training or drill.[19] Language mastery is (at least in part) the mastery of intelligent habits of gesture and response for engaging effectively in a form of life, rather than the mastery of a system of semiotic rules for interpreting signs.

So I think a case can be made for some distinction between understanding and interpreting language, between an unreflective but intelligent trained habit of response and a thoughtful decision about how to understand or respond. I have to interpret or translate most utterances I hear in Italian in order to understand them. I understand most sentences I hear in English without interpreting them; I interpret only those that seem unclear or insufficiently understood. To defend the conflation of understanding and interpretation by arguing that in simply understanding those alleged uninterpreted utterances, I am in fact already interpreting sounds as words—or, perhaps further, that my nervous system is busy interpreting vibrations into sounds—is not only to stretch the meaning of "interpretation" for no productive purpose; it also misrepresents our actual experience. Certainly we can make a distinction between the words and the sounds, and between the sounds and the vibrations that cause them. But this does not mean they are really distinct or distinguishable in experience and that I therefore must interpret the sounds in order to understand them as words. On the contrary, when I hear a language that I understand, I typically don't hear the sounds at all but only the understood words or message. If any interpretive effort is needed, it is to hear the words as sounds or vibrations, not vice versa.

Secondly, even if we grant that linguistic understanding is always and necessarily interpretive, it would still not follow that all understanding is interpretive. For that requires the further premise that all understanding and meaningful experience is indeed linguistic. And such a premise, though it be the deepest dogma of the linguistic turn in both analytic philosophy and continental hermeneutics, is neither self-evident nor immune to challenge. Certainly, there seem to be forms of bodily awareness or understanding that are not linguistic in nature and in fact defy adequate linguistic characterization, though they can be somehow referred to through language. As dancers, we understand the sense and rightness of a movement or posture proprioceptively, by feeling it in our spine and muscles, without translating it into conceptual linguistic terms. We can neither learn nor properly understand the movement simply by being talked through it.

Moreover, apart from the nonlinguistic understandings and experiences of which we are aware, there are more basic experiences or understandings of which we are not even conscious but whose successful transaction provides the necessary background selection and organization of our experiential field that enable consciousness to have a focus and emerge as a foreground. We typically experience our verticality and direction of gaze without being aware of them, but without our experiencing them, we could not be conscious of or focused on what we are in fact aware of, and our perceptual field would be very different. As Dewey insisted, there is a difference between not knowing an experience and not having it. "Consciousness . . . is only a very small and shifting part of experience," and relies on "a context which is non-cognitive," a "universe of non-reflectional experience."[20]

To all such talk of nonlinguistic experience or understanding, the hermeneutical universalists have a ready and seemingly irresistible response. How can I claim any experience is nonlinguistic, when in that very claim I have had to talk about it, refer to it, by language? Any attempt to characterize something as nonlinguistic or describe it as linguistically inexpressible self-refutingly renders it linguistic and linguistically expressed. Therefore whatever can be said to exist, or even is explicitly thought to exist (since explicit thinking can be seen as conceptual and language-dependent), is and must be linguistic. Hence Gadamer, for example, concludes, "Being that can be understood is language" (*TM* 432), and the likes of Derrida and Rorty similarly deny any "*hors-texte*."

This argument has some suasive power, and it once swayed me. But now I see it more like a sophistic paradox about talking without language than a deep truth about human experience and the world. Surely, once we have to talk about something, even merely to affirm or deny its existence, we must bring it into the game of language, give it a linguistic visa or some conceptual-textual identity; even if the visa be one of alien or inferior linguistic status, like "inexpressible tingle" or "nondiscursive image." But this only means that we can never talk (or explicitly think) about things existing without their being somehow linguistically mediated; it does not mean that we can never experience them nonlinguistically or that they cannot exist for us meaningfully but not in language.

We philosophers fail to see this because, disembodied talking heads that we are, the only form of experience we recognize and legitimate is linguistic: thinking, talking, writing. But neither we nor the language that admittedly helps shape us could survive without the unarticulated background of prereflective, nonlinguistic experience and understanding.[21] Hermeneutic universalism thus fails in its argument that interpretation is the only game in town because language is the only game in town. For there is both uninterpreted linguistic understanding and meaningful experience that is nonlinguistic. They reside in those unmanageably illiterate and darkly somatic neighborhoods of town that we philosophers and literary theorists are occupationally accustomed to avoid and ignore but on which we rely for our nonprofessional sustenance and satisfactions.[22] After the conference papers are over, we go slumming in their bars.

IV

Thus far I have resisted the universalists' arguments that understanding and interpretation cannot possibly be distinguished since all understanding is and must be interpretation. What remains, for the final sections of this essay, is to show why the distinction is worth making and how it should be made and understood. There are three reasons why I think it important to preserve some distinction between understanding and interpretation.

First and most simply, it provides interpretation with a "contrast-class" to help delimit and thus shape its meaning. Without an activity to contrast to interpretation, what can interpretation really mean? The possibility of alternatives is a necessary condition of meaningfulness. This principle of choice, endorsed not only in structuralist semantics but also in analytic information theory, recognizes that the meaning of a term or proposition is a function of those terms or propositions that it opposes or excludes.[23] Notions of unlimited extension, like tautologies that are universally true, tend to evaporate into semantic emptiness. If everything we do or experience is always and must always be interpretation, the notion of interpretation comes to signify nothing definite at all. It becomes synonymous with all human life and activity, and thus loses any real meaning or specific role of its own. Uninterpreted understandings and experiences provide a relevant contrast-class for interpretations, enabling interpretation to be distinguishable as having some definite meaning of its own, since its meaning is in some way defined and limited by what falls outside it and is contrasted to it.

Secondly, understanding provides interpretation not only with a meaning-giving contrast but also with a meaning-giving ground. It supplies something on which to base and guide our interpretations, and thus distinguish between different levels or sequential acts of comprehension. How does understanding ground and guide interpretation? We can find the makings of an answer in Heidegger and Wittgenstein, two revered progenitors of hermeneutic universalism who I think wisely resisted that doctrine. The complexly reciprocal and leveled relationship between understanding and interpretation is suggested in the second dimension of the hermeneutic circle, which Heidegger calls to our attention in his famous remark that "any interpretation which is to contribute understanding must already have understood what is to be interpreted."[24]

Elucidating this idea with respect to a literary text, we can say that before and while we try to interpret its meaning, we must be struck and directed by some sense of what it is we are trying to interpret. At the very least, we need some primitive understanding of what we are individuating as the textual object of interpretation, simply to identify it as such. Moreover, it is our initial understanding or experience of the text as something meaningful and perhaps worth understanding more fully that generates our desire to interpret it. We do not interpret every text we encounter. But our attempt to interpret the given text is not only motivated but also guided by this prior understanding, though it be inchoate, vague, and corrigible. For we form our interpretive hypotheses about the text (and accept or reject alternative interpretations) on the basis of what we already understand as properly belonging to the text rather than falsely foisted onto it.

But how do we determine whether our initial guiding understanding is valid and not a misunderstanding? We cannot appeal to the apodicticness or incorrigibility of understanding, because we have rejected all foundationalist accounts of understanding. Nor can we simply test the validity of our initial understanding by measuring it against the meaning of the text. For, since the text's meaning is not self-evidently given but is precisely what is in question, we would first have to determine more clearly what this meaning is. Yet to do this we must interpret, and thus we can only test our prior understanding by subsequent interpretation. In other words, though interpretation of the text must be based on some prior understanding of it, this understanding itself requires interpretation of the text for its own clarification and justification, if indeed we wish to pursue this. But that clarificatory and justificatory interpretation depends again on the very understanding it has to sharpen or validate. And so the hermeneutic circle revolves in a cycle of understanding and interpretation.

Considerations of this sort have led Gadamer and other hermeneutical universalists to the radical claim that "all understanding is interpretation" (*TM* 350). But this claim, I have argued, is not only uncompelling but misleading in suggesting that we can never understand anything without interpreting it. For in many cases we are simply satisfied with our initial understanding and don't go on to interpret; there are always other—and usually better—things to do.

Moreover, if we could never understand anything without interpreting it, how could we ever understand the interpretation itself? It too would have to be interpreted, and so would its interpretation, and so on ad infinitum. As Wittgenstein notes, "Any interpretation still hangs in the air along with what it interprets." Interpretation must ultimately depend on some prior understanding, some "way of grasping . . . which is *not* an interpretation."[25] This is just a point of philosophical grammar about how these notions are related: understanding grounds and guides interpretation, while interpretation enlarges, validates, or corrects understanding. We must remember that the distinction is functional or relational, not ontological.[26] The prior and grounding understanding "which is not an interpretation" may have been the product of prior interpretations, though now it is immediately grasped. Moreover, it need not be an explicitly formulated or conscious understanding, and the ground it provides is not an *incorrigible* ground.[27]

Though the universalists are wrong to deny that any valid and helpful distinction can be drawn between simply understanding something and interpreting that which was understood, their attempts to deny it have not been unhelpful. For they showed that there is no rigid or absolute dichotomy but rather an essential continuity and degree of interdependence between understanding and interpretation. What is now immediately understood may once have been the product of a labored interpretation and may form the basis for further interpretation. Words of a French song I once labored to interpret are now immediately understood, and this understanding affords me the ground for an interpretation of their deeper poetic meaning. Though frequently what we encounter neither demands nor receives interpretation, many things are felt to be insufficiently understood until they are interpreted by us or for us. We seek an interpretation because we are not satisfied with the understanding we already have—feeling it partial, obscure, shallow, fragmented, or simply dull—and we want to make it fuller or more adequate. Yet the superior interpretation sought must be guided by that prior inadequate understanding. We no longer feel the need to interpret further when the new, fuller understanding that interpretation has supplied is felt to be satisfactory. Criteria of what is satisfactory obviously will vary with context and will depend on the sort of understanding sought. Wittgenstein effectively puts this pragmatic point: "What happens is not that this symbol cannot be further interpreted, but: I do no interpreting. I do not interpret, because I feel at home in the present picture."[28]

The third reason I think it worth distinguishing between understanding and interpretation is to defend the ordinary: not only ordinary usage, which itself draws and endorses the distinction, but ordinary experiences of understanding, whose legitimacy and value tend to get discredited by hermeneutic universalism's assimilation of all experience into interpretation. In commonplace discourse, not all understanding is interpretation. There are countless contexts where one might justifiably reply to a query of how one interpreted something by denying that one actually interpreted it at all: "I didn't bother interpreting what he said; I just took it at face value." "I didn't pause to interpret her command (question); I immediately complied with it (ignored it)."

Even if these direct or immediate understandings are always based on habits and capacities resulting from prior interpretation, there is still a difference between such effortless, unthinking acts of understanding and acts of interpretation, which call for deliberate, focused thought. In marking a difference between interpretation and the more direct experiences or understandings on which it is based, ordinary language respects the role of the unformulable, prereflective, and nondiscursive background from which the foreground of conscious thinking emerges and without which it could never arise. In rejecting this distinction by asserting that all experience is interpretation, hermeneutic universalists deny this very ordinary but very crucial *unthinking* dimension of our lives and indeed of our thinking.

We can see a variation of this discrediting denial of the ordinary and unreflective in Stanley Fish's account of reading. As hermeneutic universalist, he asserts that all our activity is essentially interpretive. We cannot simply read or even recognize a text without interpreting it, since the text can be constituted as such only by an act of interpretation. Now since interpretation implies active thinking and discourse, it cannot be a merely mirroring representation of the text, but must in some way supplement, shape, or reconstruct the text. Hence all our apparent practices of reading are really "not for reading but for writing texts." And having conflated reading with interpretation, Fish further conflates interpretation with the institutionalized interpretation of professional academic criticism, where an interpretation must not only be discursively formulated but must provide "something different" or significantly new in order to be legitimate and "be given a hearing." Hence any proper reading of a text involves "changing it" in some professionally meaningful way.[29] The result is that ordinary, unreflective, nonprofessional modes of reading are discredited and dismissed as foundationalist myth. Yet precisely these unreflective unoriginal readings, which anticipate the attempt to interpret, are what in fact provides the basis for professional transformative interpretations by supplying some shared background of meaning that enables us to identify what we agree to call "the same text" so that we can then proceed to interpret it differently.

Here, as elsewhere, universal hermeneutics' dismissal of the preinterpretive reflects an intellectualist blindness to the unreflective, nondiscursive dimension of ordinary experience, a bias at once haughtily elitist and parochially uncritical. To defend this ordinary, unassuming, and typically silent dimension, we need to preserve something distinct from interpretive activity, even if it cannot and perhaps should not be immune from interpretation and may indeed rest on what was once interpretation.

V

I have argued that we can eschew foundationalism without maintaining that all experience and understanding must be interpretation. We can do so by insisting that understanding should itself be understood nonfoundationally, that is, as corrigible, perspectival, pluralistic, prejudiced, and engaged in active process. I further offered a few good reasons for admitting some meaningful human activity or experience other than interpretation, and thus for allowing, or indeed drawing, some distinction between interpretation and understanding. What remains is to suggest how this distinction might best be drawn or understood, largely by recollecting and recasting some of the central points already made here.

First, the distinction between understanding and interpretation is not a rigid ontological one, where the two notions cannot share the same objects. Secondly, they cannot be distinguished by epistemological reliability, where understanding implies univocal truth while interpretation connotes pluralistic error. Nonetheless, understanding and interpretation are epistemologically different in terms of their functional relations: understanding initially grounds and guides interpretation, while the latter explores, validates, or modifies that initial ground of meaning.

Other differences to be drawn between understanding and interpretation are probably more debatable. While understanding—even highly intelligent understanding—is often unreflective, unthinking, indeed unconscious (even if always purposive), interpretation proper involves conscious, deliberate thought: the clarification of something obscure or ambiguous, the deciphering of a symbol, the unraveling of a paradox, the articulation of previously unstated formal or semantic relations between elements. While understanding is frequently a matter of smoothly coordinated, unproblematic handling of what we encounter,[30] interpretation characteristically involves a problem situation. We only stop to interpret in order to resolve a problem—some obscurity, ambiguity, contradiction, or, more recently, the professional academic problem of *generating* an interpretive problem. The intrinsic problem-solving character of interpretation (which includes amusing puzzles) explains why it involves conscious, deliberate inquiry. Solving a problem demands thinking; seeing the obvious does not.

On this question of consciousness, ordinary linguistic usage (to which I earlier appealed) does not give unchallengeable support. Although it sounds strange to speak of someone unconsciously interpreting some remark or event, it is not a blatant contradiction or solecism. But that is simply because language aims more at loose flexibility than at precision, and because hermeneutic universalism has accustomed us to think loosely of interpretation as subsuming all construals, understandings, or meaningful experiences, some of which are obviously unconscious. If our ordinary speech does not always draw a distinction between interpreting and understanding, it makes it more often than not and never implies that it is not worth making. The conscious and problem-solving character of interpretation suggests yet another feature that might help distinguish it from understanding. Though both are inevitably perspectival, interpretive activity seems intrinsically aware that alternative interpretations may be given (or have been given) to resolve the problem, while understanding can be unreflectively blind to the existence or possibility of alternative understandings, since it can be unaware of any problem of understanding that might present alternative solutions.

I conclude with one last suggestion for distinguishing interpretation from more primitive or basic understandings and experiences, one that reaffirms the link I established between hermeneutic universalism and the linguistic turn. Interpretation is characteristically aimed at linguistic formulation, at translating one meaningful expression into another one. A criterion for having an interpretation of some utterance or event would be an ability to express in some explicit, articulated form what that interpretation is. To interpret a text is thus to produce a text.[31] Understanding, on the other hand, does not require linguistic articulation; a proper reaction, a shudder or a tingle, may be enough to indicate one has understood. Some of the things we experience and understand are never captured by language, not only because their particular feel defies adequate linguistic expression but also because we are not even aware of them as "things" to describe. They are the felt background we presuppose when we start to articulate or to interpret.

"There are, indeed, things that cannot be put into words. They *show* themselves. They are the mystical."[32] So said the greatest twentieth-century philosopher of language in his first philosophical masterpiece. What Wittgenstein fails to emphasize here is that the ineffable but manifest is as ordinary as mystical, and it is only mystifying to those disembodied philosophical minds who recognize no understanding other than interpretation, and no form of meaning and experience beyond or beneath the web of language.

Chapter Two

Experience

Foundation or Reconstruction?

I

Pragmatism, as I conceive it, is antifoundationalist, breaking with philosophy's traditional quest to guarantee our knowledge by basing it on fixed, unquestionable grounds. These were long sought in self-evident first principles, primal essences, necessary categories, and privileged primary certainties: in notions like the cogito, the Kantian categories, sense data, and the a priori laws of thought. Such indubitable, incorrigible foundations, John Dewey argued, are neither available nor required for human knowledge and social practices. In freeing philosophy from its search for foundations, Dewey hoped to enlist it for practical reform, directing its critical acumen and imaginative energy to the resolution of concrete social and cultural problems. Since these could be deeply entrenched through the ideology of past philosophies, new philosophical thinking may be needed to resolve them: by making room for new solutions that do not fit with established ways of thinking. Philosophy should be transformational instead of foundational. Rather than a metascience for grounding our current cognitive and cultural activities, it should be cultural criticism that aims to reconstruct our practices and institutions so as to improve the experienced quality of our lives. Improved experience, not originary truth, is the ultimate philosophical goal and criterion.

Experience is surely at the heart of Dewey's philosophy. But, paradoxically, it is also where his disciple Richard Rorty thinks Dewey's philosophy is most vulnerable and dangerous, since foundationally retrograde. With characteristic bluntness (and noting Dewey's own doubts), he argues that "Dewey should have dropped the term 'experience'" rather than making it the center of his philosophy.[1] Pragmatism, in taking a needed linguistic turn, must replace this central notion with that of language and insist on a radical discontinuity between linguistic and sublinguistic behavior, which the term "experience" can only blur. Since the value of "experience" represents the major divide between classical Deweyan (and Jamesian) pragmatism and the neopragmatism advocated by Rorty and others, the question of Dewey's use and abuse of this concept is crucial.[2]

This chapter probes the extent of Dewey's experiential foundationalism in order to see whether, *pace* Rorty, the idea of experience still has a vital role to play in pragmatism. I think it does; and much of its value lies even in that notion of experience—immediate, nondiscursive experience—that seems most vulnerable to charges of foundationalism. Since the most salient locus of nondiscursive immediacy is bodily feeling, somatic experience will become the focus. My claim is that in emphasizing nondiscursive experience and its cognitive role, Dewey was on to something valuable that he unfortunately confused and devalued by treating it as the necessary guarantor of all thought. Repudiating this nondiscursive dimension, Rorty seeks to discredit it by identifying it with an already discredited foundationalism, with which it is, in fact, most typically linked. My goal is to separate the nondiscursive from the foundational better than Dewey did, so as to avoid Rorty's charges of foundationalism as well as other charges that are more convincing. We should start, then, by sketching Dewey's use of nondiscursive experience and its Rortian critique.

II

One of Dewey's major goals in deploying his concept of experience was to advance a "naturalistic humanism" that could overcome the traditional dualisms of metaphysics and epistemology, dualisms that ultimately stemmed from the primal dualism of mind and matter. Given this dualism and secular culture's acceptance of the scientific materialist world-picture, the metaphysical question was how to find room in objective reality for the mental phenomena of consciousness, knowledge, and value without trying to justify them as "superimposed" from a superior, extranatural world and without trying to reduce them to purely mechanistic networks of neurophysiology.

There was also the epistemological question, at least as old as Descartes, of how material reality could be known by a mind defined as its radical other.

Dewey's naturalistic thesis of continuity and emergence answered both these questions. Inspired by Darwin, it argued that the higher human expressions of life emerge naturally from more simple organic forms through increasingly greater organization and more discriminating behavior. Mind was not an outside observer of the natural world but an emergent part of it; knowledge and value were not transcendental imports but emerging products (and tools) of natural interactions. Experience, Dewey thought, was the best general notion to bridge these different but continuous dimensions of nature. Since "experience" could cover both *what* was experienced and the specific *how* of experiencing, it could span the object/subject split that spurs epistemology; and since it could also be attributed to lower animals, it could bridge the gap between discursive mental life and cruder forms of existence. To affirm such continuity is surely one (but not, in my view, the best) reason why Dewey insists that experience be conceived more widely than its standard philosophical construal as conscious, intellectual experience:

> When intellectual experience and its material are taken to be primary, the cord that binds experience and nature is cut. That the physiological organism with its structures, whether in man or in the lower animals, is concerned with making adaptations and uses of material in the interest of maintenance of the life process, cannot be denied. The brain and nervous system are primarily organs of action-undergoing; biologically, it can be asserted without contravention that primary experience is of a corresponding type. Hence, unless there is breach of historic and natural continuity, cognitive experience must originate within that of a non-cognitive sort. And unless we start from knowing as a factor in action and undergoing we are inevitably committed to the intrusion of an extra-natural, if not supernatural, agency and principle. (*EN* 29–30)

Rorty cites this passage in repudiating its notion of experience. Though sympathetic to Dewey's naturalism and critique of dualisms, he argues that experience is not only unnecessary for realizing Dewey's aims but also renders them suspect by contamination with foundationalist confusions and myths: confusions of justifying knowledge through appeal to original causes, and myths of an immediate given. Experience is unnecessary because its target of dualism can be overcome through other means:

> Dewey . . . confuses two ways of revolting against philosoph-
> ical dualisms. The first way is to point out that the dualism
> is imposed by a tradition for specific cultural reasons, but has
> now outlived its usefulness. This is the Hegelian way—the way
> Dewey adopts in "An Empirical Study of Empiricisms." The
> second is to describe the phenomenon in a nondualistic way
> which emphasizes "continuity between lower and higher pro-
> cesses." This is the Lockean way—the way which led Locke to
> assimilate all mental acts to raw feels, thus paving the way for
> Humean skepticism. (DM 82)

Dewey's notion of experience, Rorty argues, serves the Lockean way of foundationalist epistemology by blurring the line between cognitive and noncognitive existence so that the latter can ground the former. Rather than eliminating "epistemological problems by eliminating the assumption that justification must repose on something other than social practices and human needs," Dewey tries "to solve" them by finding " 'continuities' between nervous systems and people, or between 'experience and nature.' " But "one does not need to justify our claim to know that, say, a given action was the best we could take by noting that the brain is an 'organ of action-undergoing' " (DM 82).

We should surely not try to justify specific knowledge claims by mere appeal to the causal conditions of knowing. But Rorty never shows that Dewey commits this confusion in asserting the continuity of cognitive and noncognitive experience. To make his case Rorty cites Dewey's view that language gives meaning to more primitive qualities of organic experience, thus objectifying them in conscious, definite feelings. "This 'objectification' is not a miraculous ejection from the organism or soul into external things, nor an illusory attribution of psychical entities to physical things. The qual-ities never were 'in' the organism; they always were qualities of interactions in which both extraorganic things and organisms partake" (*EN* 211–12). Rorty then critiques this notion of experience's "qualities of interaction" for simply dodging the standard questions of dualistic epistemology, for example, "Is my *interaction* with this table brown, rather than, as I had previously thought, the *table* being brown?" (DM 83).

But this ambiguous use of experience and its failure to resolve the debate between idealism and realism surely do not amount to using non-cognitive experience as justificational evidence for our conscious cognitive claims. In asserting the general continuity of cognitive and noncognitive experience, Dewey is *not* claiming that the latter functions cognitively as a criterion for the truth of the former. In fact, on the very page Rorty cites, Dewey denies this by asserting that primitive noncognitive experience is simply *had* but not *known*, and that its qualities cannot be known until "with language they are discriminated and . . . 'objectified'" (*EN* 98).[3] Since not even known as "had," immediate experience is unavailable for use as evidence to support specific knowledge claims. Indeed, in insisting that only language constitutes qualities as objects of knowledge, Dewey has already taken the linguistic turn, which requires that the realm of cognitive justification be entirely linguistic. This suggests that Dewey's claims for nonlinguistic experience are ultimately motivated by something other than the quest for epistemological foundations, a suggestion I later develop in terms of aesthetic values.

The closest Dewey comes to foundationalism in *Experience and Nature* is to suggest that although any particular knowledge claim may be questioned, we can't take global skepticism seriously because we are linked to the world in a primal way before the question of knowledge claims can even arise. For even the formulation of skeptical doubts presupposes a behavioral background and use of world materials, organs, and language. There can be no total, unbridgeable gulf between subject and object (or mind and world) since both are only constituted as distinct terms through experiential interaction. Rorty himself often employs the same kind of antiskeptical strategy through his preferred notion of language. Rather than a continuum of experience (extending from the precognitive hence preskeptical), we have a continuum of linguistic behavior ranging from merely practical, noncognitive use to the making and justification of knowledge claims. Since we can have no sense of the world apart from how it is used, determined, and known through language, there is no wedge for a radical skepticism that language is completely out of touch with the world. Here the subject/object dualism is dissolved not in the common solvent of experience but in the network of language as a social practice through which particular minds and particular objects are constituted as individuals.

Rorty is right that language works much better than experience for such epistemological purposes; not only because language is a much clearer notion but also because epistemology is a distinctively linguistic enterprise. But this does not mean that noncognitive experience is intrinsically a foundational notion, while language is intrinsically immune to such uses. Protocol sentences have been used foundationally, and even the Wittgensteinian linguistic approach I share with Rorty is open to such misconstrual. Consider Wittgenstein's claim that justifications must come to an end and the way he typically ends them by invoking the fact that "*this language game is played*," that this is how we were taught to use words and to live our "forms of life."[4] While Wittgenstein was seeking therapy from philosophy's quest for ultimate foundations, his remarks could be read instead as substituting empiricism's myth of the given with an allegedly nonmythical *linguistic* given. The huge project of analytic metaphysics through philosophy of language constitutes such a foundational reading. Even if the notion of immediate, nonlinguistic experience does not *entail* epistemological foundationalism, philosophy has most often used it for precisely this purpose. Dewey himself does not always completely resist such temptations. Let us see precisely where he succumbs and whether immediate experience can be stripped also of Dewey's apparent foundationalist use and still be philosophically important. If not, Rorty has good grounds for urging pragmatism to renounce it.

III

Dewey's most thorough accounts of how immediate experience relates to knowledge occur in his essay "Qualitative Thought" (1930) and in his culminating treatise *Logic: The Theory of Inquiry* (1938).[5] Here, as elsewhere, he firmly eschews epistemology's standard foundationalist strategy of using the qualities of immediate experience as indubitable, incorrigible evidence for particular claims of knowledge. They could not possibly have such a role because they are simply *had* rather than *known*, and they would have to be linguistically reconstructed and formulated in order to serve as a foundational justification or ground of truth. But Dewey courts a different, more subtle variety of foundationalism when he argues that the experience of immediate, nondiscursive quality not only underlies but must guide all discursive thought. Here immediate experience is invoked not to justify particular truth claims but to ground the coherence of *any* thinking from which such claims emerge. Dewey claims that even if such experience is unknowable and ineffable, its functioning can be recognized and inferred as necessary in all our thinking. For it performs (as I count them) five logical functions needed for thought which, Dewey maintains, are otherwise not available. His argument for experiential foundations opposes the atomistic foundationalism of traditional empiricism and instead rests on the good holist premise that "we never experience nor form judgements about objects and events in isolation, but only in connection with a contextual whole. This latter is called a 'situation'" (L 72).

1. But if all thinking is contextual, what determines the relevant context or situation? What makes it the single context it is, and gives it the unity, structure, and limits necessary for providing thought with an effective framework? Dewey's answer is immediately experienced quality: "a situation is a whole in virtue of its *immediately pervasive quality*" (L 73). It is "held together, in spite of its internal complexity, by the fact that it is dominated by a single quality," "constituted by a pervasive and internally integrative quality" (Q 97). "The pervasively qualitative is not only that which binds all constituents into a whole but it is also unique; it constitutes in each situation an *individual* situation, indivisible and unduplicable" (L 74).

2. In constituting the situation, this immediate quality also controls the distinction of objects or terms that thinking later identifies and employs as parts of the situation (e.g., whether we notice a sound sequence as one message or two, or instead disregard it as background noise). Hence, for Dewey, "A universe of experience is a precondition of a universe of discourse. Without its controlling presence, there is no way to determine the relevancy, weight, or coherence of any designated distinction or relation" (L 74).[6] Yet this controlling immediate quality lies below the level of thematized consciousness and language. It "surrounds and regulates the universe of discourse but never appears as such within the latter" (L 74); and when we bring it into speech and awareness, we are transforming it into an object of a new situation defined by its own immediate and ineffable unifying quality.

3. Immediate quality also provides a sense of what is adequate in judgement, what level of detail, complexity, or precision is sufficient to render the contextual judgement valid. Is the earth really round? Is running good for your health? Does water boil at 100 degrees centigrade? We can always make our judgements more detailed and precise. "But enough," as Dewey says, "is always enough, and the underlying quality is itself the test of the 'enough' for any particular case" (Q 108).

4. A fourth function of immediate quality is to determine the basic sense or direction of the situation and to sustain it over time, despite the confusing general flood of experience. Although the quality is nondiscursively "dumb," it has "a movement or transition in some direction" that provides

the needed sense of unity and continuity in ongoing inquiry (Q 107). "This quality enables us to keep thinking about one problem without our having constantly to stop to ask ourselves what is it after all that we are thinking about." This "unique quality" is "the thread" or "directive clue" that "not only evokes the particular inquiry engaged in but that exercises control over its special procedures. Otherwise, one procedure in inquiry would be as likely to occur and to be as effective as any other" (Q 99; L 109).[7]

5. Finally, Dewey argues that immediate experience's integrative quality is the only adequate way to explain the association of ideas. The standard explanations of physical contiguity and similarity are insufficient to make the link, because "there is an indefinite number of particulars contiguous to one another in space and time" and because everything in some respect is similar to everything else. Mere spatiotemporal proximity and similarity cannot explain, for example, why I associate an empty nest with a bird I never saw rather than with "the multitudinous leaves and twigs which are more frequently and more obviously juxtaposed" to the nest (Q 111). And why should mere similarity and contiguity lead my thought from this hammer to a nail rather than to another nearly identical hammer in the store? Something else is needed to make the connections of associative thinking. For Dewey this can only be the ineffable quality of immediate experience which binds through its sense of relevance: "What alternative remains save that the quality of a situation as a whole operates to produce a functional connection?" Association must be "an intellectual connection" produced through "an underlying quality which operates to control the connection of objects thought of"; "there must be relevancy of both ideas to a situation defined by unity of quality" (Q 111).

Had Dewey simply claimed that immediate quality often grounds or directs our thinking, his position would be more convincing. Unfortunately, however, such quality is claimed as "the background, the point of departure, and the regulative principle in all thinking," determining, *in every particular situation*, the coherence of thought, the structure of discourse, and the measure of adequacy in judgement (Q 116; L 74). Moreover, it does all this without being a distinct object of awareness or term of discourse. We can never really analyze it, because doing so transforms it into something else. Yet, Dewey argues, we know it must exist and function as described, for if it did not, coherent thought would be impossible. Here Dewey's radical empiricism forsakes him for a foundational metaphysics of presence justified by transcendental argument. Why accept this ineffable experiential foundationalism, if Dewey himself provides the means to avoid it? Thought and action, he elsewhere argues, are governed by the habits, purposes, and needs of the organism, and by the specific saliencies of the situation (as shaped by the organism's habits, purposes, and needs and the surrounding environment). Such factors, which typically function unreflectively, can perform all the five necessary tasks for which immediate qualitative experience was invoked as thought's indispensable foundational guide.

Unity of situation is provided by the practical unity of purpose and the continuity and direction of habit.[8] Purpose binds together the situational elements enlisted in its pursuit, and habit already implies an internal organization of activity that projects itself on further organization. Habit and purpose not only shape our distinctions of objects and relations within the situation but also guide our judgements of their relevance and importance.[9] Habit and purpose can moreover give the situation its sustained direction. Since "all habit has *continuity*" and is "projective" by its very nature, our thinking habits naturally continue their directional course and tend to resist interruption or distraction (*HNC* 31, 168). Purpose also "gives unity and continuity" of action, its "end-in-view" calling forth a series of coordinated means to reach it.[10] These factors, rather than a mysterious qualitative presence, are what bind and control the successive steps of inquiry. Purpose better explains what is adequate in judgement; hence Dewey, even while claiming immediate quality as the criterion of adequacy, reverts to purpose: "Any proposition that serves the purpose for which it is made is logically adequate" (Q 108). Finally, habit and purpose can explain our association of ideas without invoking a mysterious ineffable quality to link them. "When I think of a hammer," Dewey asks, "why is the idea of nail so likely to follow?" (Q 111). The obvious answer is not the qualitative glue of immediate experience but the entrenched habit of their functional association for practical purposes of building. Dewey's argument for the necessity of immediate experience as the guiding ground for all thinking is both unconvincing and inimical to his antifoundationalist agenda.

IV

Why then does Dewey affirm nondiscursive experience as an epistemological foundation? His deep motive, I believe, was not to provide such foundations but to celebrate the importance of nondiscursive immediacy. Its importance was firstly *aesthetic*, being central to the realm of experienced value. He always insisted that our most intense pleasures and vivid values are those of on-the-pulse experienced quality and affect, not the abstractions of discursive truth. For Dewey, aesthetic satisfaction takes privilege over science, which is simply "a handmaiden" providing the conditions for achieving such satisfaction more frequently, stably, and fully (*EN* 269). He further saw that nondiscursive somatic experience also played an important role in cognition and action. Proprioceptive discriminations beneath the level of thematized consciousness structure our perceptual field, just as unformulated feelings ("expansions, elations, and dejections") influence our behavior and orient our thinking (*EN* 227).

Wanting to celebrate the importance of this nondiscursive experience Dewey did so in the way philosophers have habitually emphasized factors they thought primary and essential—by erecting it as a theoretical foundation. This was a bad confusion of what was (or should have been) his true aim—to establish and improve the quality of immediate experience as a practical end and useful tool. Dewey wanted philosophers to see that nondiscursive experience could be used to enrich knowledge, not just the "felt" quality of living. That such experience had no value for philosophy's favorite cognitive goal of epistemological justification did not mean that it has no other cognitive value. A better measured sense of breathing could promote a calmer, better measured process of thought; an ineffable flush of energetic excitation could spur one to think beyond habitual limits. Though traditionally focused on discursive reason, philosophy's presumed task of giving a full account of human reality required recognition of the role of nondiscursive experience.[11] Moreover, if pragmatism sought not simply to explain but to improve reality, the value of nondiscursive experience became still more important as a project to be realized; and its crucial but much neglected locus was the body.[12]

A major inspiration here was F. Matthias Alexander, the renowned body therapist and founder of the "Alexander Technique," whose influence on Dewey's thought has not been adequately recognized.[13] Long a devoted student of Alexander (not simply of his texts but of his somatic exercises as well), Dewey wrote encomiastic introductions to three of his books, defending Alexander's work against skeptical reviewers and praising it as having "demonstrated a new scientific principle with respect to the control of human behavior, as important as any principle which has ever been discovered in the domain of external nature."[14] Alexander argued that many of the physical and mental ills that we suffer in modern life result from disharmony between our more advanced intellectual behavior and our more basic bodily functions. While the efforts of millennia were devoted to developing the intellect, bodily functioning—long scorned as belonging to the base realm of flesh and unchangeable instinct—has been left to entrenched habits and instincts inherited from ancient times when the body worked in different conditions. Contemporary civilized conditions are unsuited to our inherited forms of somatic comportment while subjecting us, often unconsciously, to troubling new customs and regimes of body control (like Foucauldian disciplines of biopower). The result "is the larger number of physical disorders which inflict themselves exclusively upon civilized man [e.g., lower-back syndrome], and the large number of neuroses which express themselves in intellectual and moral maladies."[15] Yet no serious inquiry had been devoted to develop somatic functioning so as to make it not only better coordinated and more suited to the contemporary world, but to render it an effective stimulus for improving that world to answer human needs of psychosomatic fulfilment.

Alexander therefore urged a reeducation of our somatic functioning, which required a reeducation for somatic awareness, a new attention to bodily experiences that have so far gone unattended and thus unimproved. More importantly, he offered a concrete method of such reeducation. Its key was to extend "conscious control" over bodily actions formerly abandoned to unconscious habit by focusing conscious awareness on previously unnoticed and unattended somatic experience. *Conscious* somatic control is increasingly necessary in today's rapidly changing technological world, where old and slowly, unconsciously formed physical habits become ever more quickly outmoded and unfit. This insistence on *thinking* through the body so as to achieve more conscious control and more acute perception of its condition, clearly distinguishes Alexander's approach from standard forms of calisthenics and body building. In fact, he vehemently attacked such exercise styles for dealing only with externals by means of brute drill rather than bringing greater sensitivity and quality to inner experience by means of heightened consciousness (*MSI* 13–28).

Dewey's emphasis on immediate nondiscursive experience and its continuity with higher intellectual activity is perhaps best understood in this Alexandrian context: not as foundational epistemology but as a reconstruction-aimed panegyric to the somatic in the face of centuries of denigrating philosophical scorn. In his 1918 introduction to Alexander's *Man's Supreme Inheritance*, seven years before advancing his theory of experiential and mind-body continuity in *Experience and Nature* (in which Alexander's work is twice invoked and his terminology appropriated), Dewey writes:

Men are afraid, without even being aware of their fear, to recognize the most wonderful of all the structures of the vast universe—the human body. They have been led to think that a serious notice and regard would somehow involve disloyalty to man's higher life. The discussions of Mr. Alexander breathe reverence for this wonderful instrument of our life, life mental and moral as well as that life which somewhat meaninglessly we call bodily. When such a religious attitude toward the body becomes more general, we shall have an atmosphere favorable to securing the conscious control which is urged. (IMSI 351)

Recognizing that body functioning influences the mind, Alexander likewise grasped the mind's potential for the body. His project was to improve somatic (and consequently mental) functioning by using the mind, employing a method of "constructive conscious control" directed by the individual on her body.[16] Our bad bodily habits (e.g., bad posture or poorly coordinated movement) are usually performed without thinking and are taken for granted. Moreover, when we *do* focus on them, they seem right because they are familiar as our habits. When asked to stand or move differently we may be unable to, not because we are anatomically impaired but simply because we cannot yet feel ourselves into an alternative way. To improve our bodily habits and psychosomatic integration we need to bring our somatic functioning and its attendant feelings into greater consciousness, so we can learn both to detect subtly different modalities of posture and movement and to assess the quality of their coordination and their attendant affectivity. Without detecting these modalities we could never learn how to perform different somatic actions that could be developed into better habits; without qualitative appreciation we would not learn which somatic behavior should be rendered habitual so as to provide a better background of unconscious psychosomatic functioning. For example, we need to become conscious both of how to hold the head in different positions and of which position gives us the best "felt" quality and ease of breathing in order to select this position over others for a new habituation. But having been reconstructed through this concentrated attention, the now improved habit can well be returned to its unreflective character in order to allow consciousness to concentrate on other tasks.

Such an improved habit, even if it functions unconsciously, can also enhance our conscious thought, since better breathing can mean better awareness and more steady concentration. We must recall, however, that *conscious* attention was required to improve this unconscious functioning; and so, by the way, is language—as the means for designating body parts, movements, and feelings on which we are instructed to concentrate. The interdependent continuity of mind and body can be seen as reflected in the similar continuity of conscious thinking and the nondiscursive background that orients thought, an often unconscious somatic background that can however be brought into consciousness.[17]

We can now understand what Dewey's experiential foundationalism was concerned with, and how it erred. He was wrong to think that an unconscious, nondiscursive immediate quality was the necessary grounding guide or regulatory criterion for all our thinking, though he was right to insist that nondiscursive background experience influences our conscious thought. Rather than such unnoticed quality being the necessary unifying guide of all conscious thought, it is the noticing of such quality that can help give thinking greater unity and better affect, by improving the coordination of thought's nondiscursive experiential background and better integrating the psychosomatic and the intellectual. Dewey's mistake is not in emphasizing the unifying quality of experience, but only in positing it as an antecedent foundational fact rather than regarding it as an *end* and *means* of reconstruction.

Through the Alexander perspective we can see the limits of Rorty's critique. *Pace* Rorty, the dominant pragmatic aim of Dewey's philosophy of experience is not the metaphysical goal "of obtaining continuity between us and the brutes" by our "sharing something called 'experience'—something not the same as consciousness or thought but something of which consciousness or thought are more developed forms." Nor is it the epistemological goal of ensuring that our perceptions are not " 'out of touch' with nature," since both belong to the unity of experience (DHD 58–59).[18] Instead, Dewey's prime purpose was (or surely should have been) the aesthetic and practical aim of improving experience by making it the focus of our inquiry: to enrich and harmonize our experience, for example, by affirming and enhancing the continuity between soma and psyche, between nondiscursive experience and conscious thought. The aim, as he presents it in advocating the Alexander Technique, is "to integrate into harmonious coordination our animal inheritance and our distinctively human capacities of intelligence" (RR 355).

So even if Rorty is right that experience cannot solve the theoretical problems of metaphysical and epistemological continuity, this does not nullify the point of Dewey's philosophy of experience. For this philosophy (in its most useful construal) is not so much aimed at proving theoretical continuity but instead at enhancing continuity *in practice*, at healing the painfully (though often unconsciously) experienced fragmentation of human life. This, he believed, could be achieved only by recognizing the immediate dimension of somatic experience, a recognition that he occasionally misconstrued in foundational terms.

V

But what does it mean for philosophy to recognize this somatic dimension? Simply to say that it exists, even as a necessary feature of human existence, seems an empty gesture. The importance of nondiscursive experience in actual living does not entail that it is *philosophically* important. And how could it be, since philosophy as traditionally practiced can apparently do nothing with it except misuse it discursively for foundationalist fantasies? Somatic and nondiscursive experience, so central to the pragmatist thought of Dewey and James, are therefore abandoned by today's leading pragmatists as philosophically useless and troublesome notions. Indeed, as Rorty puts it, we should drop the whole notion of experience and instead insist that language exhausts the realm of philosophy, following Peirce's cue that "my language is the sum total of myself" (DHD 55).[19]

Though appreciative of the linguistic turn, I am also wary of its totalizing tendencies and am reluctant to abandon pragmatism's traditional concern with the somatic and nondiscursive (which even Peirce recognized in his notion of Firstness). Before burying the body or simply textualizing it, we need to assess more critically philosophy's resistance to nondiscursive experience. Such resistance is based not only on arguments but also on deeply entrenched biases that work, most effectively, beneath the level of conscious thought. The reason Rorty most frequently gives for banishing nondiscursive experience from the domain of philosophy is that it involves us in the foundationalist "myth of the given." In our search to base knowledge on something immune to error, we retreat to a brute experiential immediacy whose nondiscursivity makes it immune even to linguistic error. But this appeal to a nondiscursive given is mythical, because such experience can function as justificatory evidence only if it is rendered discursive.

This critique of the so-called myth of the given seems impeccable. But it does not follow that philosophy should never concern itself with the nondiscursive. Drawing this conclusion means assuming that philosophy's only possible use for nondiscursive experience is in justificational epistemology, and that assumption is neither self-evident nor argued for. Finding more fruitful ways for philosophy to treat the nondiscursive remains a vital task for pragmatism. Prefigured in Dewey's advocacy of immediate experience, it is today more urgently demanded by our culture's increasing devotion to techniques of somatic transformation yet continuing failure to give them adequate philosophical study.[20]

This somatic option is implicitly denied by Rorty's second argument for banishing the nonlinguistic: that introducing somatic experience into philosophical practice undermines philosophy's distinctive role and logical space by confusing between causes and reasons. This argument again concerns the myth of the given. For in this myth, nondiscursive physical sensation—which may be the antecedent *cause* of knowing something (e.g., a burning sensation resulting in awareness that the plate is hot)—is falsely taken for a *reason* that justifies such knowledge, a reason that seems irrefutable by its brute immediacy. But nondiscursive experience cannot, as such, play a role in the language game of epistemological justification, whose regimentation has always been philosophy's distinctive task. Such experience may be "a causal condition for knowledge but not a ground for knowledge."[21] Since philosophy is concerned with the rational justification of our beliefs, not their psychological or physiological causes, it should therefore resist trafficking with things like somatic experience that belong to the nondiscursive domain of causes; it should remain within "the logical space of reasons." For "nothing is to be gained . . . by running together the vocabularies in which we describe the causal antecedents of knowledge with those in which we offer justifications of our claims to knowledge" (*PMN* 182; DM 81).

Nothing gained, that is, for epistemology, from whose standpoint Rorty attacks the nondiscursive. But why should philosophy be confined to its standard role of justifying by reasons rather than modifying through causes, of merely legitimating beliefs and practices rather than creating or transforming them? Such justificational restriction seems particularly foreign to pragmatism, and Rorty himself boldly rejects it when he comes to his own central philosophical topic—language. Here Rorty advocates a philosophy of causation rather than legitimation. The aim is to create new vocabularies and transform our ways of speaking, not to ground those already in place.[22] He even insists on blurring the very cause/reason distinction he elsewhere strictly defended: "Once we raise the question of how we get from one vocabulary to another, from one dominant metaphoric to another, the distinction between reasons and causes begins to lose utility," for here there is insufficient common ground to provide decisive *reasons* for change (*CIS* 48).

Building on Rorty's own example, we can argue: if philosophy takes for its pragmatist goal not the grounding of knowledge but the production of better lived experience, then it need not be confined to the realm of discursive truth and the language games of their justification. Philosophy can aim more directly at the practical end of improving experience by advocating and embodying practices that achieve this. And if the practice of linguistic invention provides one such tool, why can't the practice of somatic disciplines focusing on the nondiscursive provide a complementary other? This option is never admitted, however, because philosophy's dominant ideology of textualism represses the nonlinguistic. This ideology, common to analytic and continental philosophy, insists that language exhausts the scope of experience, since whatever lies outside of language cannot be thought or given content. Hence Sellars claims that "*all* awareness . . . is a linguistic affair"; Gadamer stresses "the essential linguisticality of all human experience of the world"; Rorty asserts that we humans are "nothing more than sentential attitudes"; and Derrida declares that there cannot be a "*hors-texte*," "a reality . . . whose content could take place, could have taken place outside of language."[23]

Textualist ideology has been extremely helpful in dissuading philosophy from misguided quests for absolute foundations outside our contingent linguistic and social practices. But in making this therapeutic point by stressing what Rorty terms the "the ubiquity of language,"[24] textualism also encourages an unhealthy idealism that identifies human being-in-the-world with linguistic activity and so tends to neglect, minimize, or overly textualize nondiscursive somatic experience. Celebrated by Rorty as "the contemporary counterpart of [nineteenth-century] idealism," textualism displays idealism's disdain for nondiscursive materiality, hence for the corporeal. Seeking to secure a realm of spirituality after natural science had displaced religion's authority and despiritualized the world, idealism focused on mental consciousness and inherited, by and large, the dominant Christian impulse to depreciate the body.[25] After Freud's disenchantment of consciousness, language has become the new representative of soul in contrast to corporeal nondiscursivity. The whole project of policing the borders between "the logical space of reasons" and the realm of "physical causes" so as to confine philosophy to the former can be seen as just one more assertion of the old dualism of separating the concerns of the superior soul from the corruption of the material body; study of the latter is thus consigned not to the human but the natural sciences.

Textualism's resistance to the nondiscursive soma goes well beyond its modern idealist heritage. Such resistance is built into the old Platonic project of philosophy as a saliently linguistic discipline devoted to the *logos*. The *alogon* was at once the nonlinguistic and the irrational. Two factors thus tend to repress philosophy's treatment of the nondiscursive. The first is simply structural censorship by the philosophical field through disciplinary inertia. Despite a fine heritage of materialist thinkers, philosophy's long dominance by idealist logocentrism and its entrenched practice as a linguistic form have structured the discipline in a way that excludes serious focus on the nondiscursive.[26] There is no allocation for it in traditional Western philosophical space, no subdiscipline of "philosophy of body" to complement philosophy of mind (as hatha yoga serves the more spiritual raja yoga in Indian thought). The result is that nondiscursive somatic experience is either ignored—relegated to other fields like psychology or neuroscience—or instead subsumed under clearly discursive projects, such as epistemological justification or genealogical accounts of "reading the body" as a social text on which a society's practices of formative power are inscribed.

The second implicit ground for ignoring the nondiscursive involves what might be called the *disciplinary fallacy*: the idea that whatever a discipline ignores (or does not treat seriously) cannot be important for that discipline. Such reasoning precludes disciplinary growth and would have denied chemistry's importance for botany or the central role of the unconscious for psychology. This fallacy is especially dangerous in philosophy, which sees itself both as a specialized profession (concerning technical, strictly regimented questions) and also as a basic, time-honored human enterprise of universal significance and scope. Through the former self-conception, philosophy materially reproduces itself as a professional institution, while the latter, broader conception affords it a charismatic aura of deep relevance and wisdom (often lacking in its actual institutional expression) that helps legitimate its institutional reproduction. By the dominant professional conception (especially as understood through textualism), nondiscursive somatic experience has no place in philosophy. And if we take this conclusion as including philosophy's broader conception, then somatic experience cannot be important for better understanding human life; hence no new place should be made for it in philosophy. The upshot of this equivocation is that philosophy is right to shirk the nondiscursive as unimportant, because its very doing so proves this unimportance.

The disciplinary fallacy seems persuasive because it expresses a good pragmatic point. An individual discipline can't do everything, so it should therefore concentrate on doing what it does best and avoid doing what it can't do. Since philosophy is strongly centered on language and seems ill-equipped to handle the somatic and nondiscursive, it should not try to treat them. For what, after all can philosophy do with these notions, except embroil itself, as even Dewey did, in foundationalist regressions?[27] This question presents a major task for somatic philosophy that I cannot discharge here. Let me at least briefly suggest three ways that philosophy can productively engage nondiscursive somatic experience.

First and most simply, philosophy can argue for the importance of such experience (as Merleau-Ponty did perhaps even better than Dewey) so that it will not be merely acknowledged to exist but will be more vigorously explored as a legitimate object of research and of personal cultivation. Overcoming its *parti pris* against the nonlinguistic, philosophy can lend support and analytic skills to scientific inquiries into the nondiscursive features of human experience (e.g., Daniel Stern's groundbreaking work on the prelinguistic understanding of infants).[28] It might even launch its own inquiries into the role of nonverbal experience in aesthetics, ethics, and other domains.

Secondly, contemporary popular culture displays an intense preoccupation with the body. Apart from the proliferation of gyms and centers for aerobics, massage, and body building, there is a growing number of somatic therapies that promise not merely relief from physical ailments but improved psychosomatic integration, or, more simply, better harmony of lived experience. Since the work of Alexander, we have been offered Rolfing, bioenergetics, eutony, Feldenkrais Method, and Ideokinesis, to name just a few. There is also greatly heightened interest in older practices such yoga and *taijiquan*. We philosophers are prone to dismiss these things as New Age quackery or simply ignore them as none of our business. But Dewey's attention to Alexander should give us pause. If philosophy sees itself most broadly as culture criticism, then somatics is an increasingly significant dimension of our culture that is ripe for philosophical critique. Philosophy here can have the role of critically examining such body practices and their attendant ideologies to see what sense they make, what good or harm they do, and whether they could profit from a better formulation of aims and methods.[29] It might helpfully disentangle useful technique from misguided theory so as to make these practices more convincing and effective.

Finally, the most radical and interesting way for philosophy to engage somatic practice is to integrate such bodily disciplines into the very practice of philosophy. This means practicing philosophy not simply as a discursive genre, a form of writing, but as a discipline of embodied life. One's philosophical work, one's search for truth and wisdom, would not be pursued only through texts but also through somatic exploration and experiment. By acute attention to the soma and its nonverbal messages, by the practice of body disciplines that heighten somatic awareness and transform how one feels and functions, one discovers and expands self-knowledge by remaking one's self. This quest for self-knowledge and self-transformation can constitute a philosophical life of increasing embodied enrichment that has irresistible aesthetic appeal.

Though alien to today's academy, the idea of philosophy as an embodied, aesthetically engaging way of life was important to the *logos*-loving Greeks and Romans. It was also shared by Emerson and advocated by Thoreau, who affirmed that philosophy "is admirable to profess because it was once admirable to live," and that "life is not [mere] dialectics. . . . Intellectual tasting of life will not supersede muscular activity."[30] Such a vision of philosophy as a thoughtfully disciplined, somatically centered way of life was powerfully revived by Foucault in his very last lectures at the Collège de France, inspired in large part by the example of Diogenes the Cynic. "The *bios philosophikos*," Foucault explains, "is the human being's animality taken up as a challenge, practiced as an exercise, and thrown in the face of others as a scandal."[31] But the somatically focused, aesthetically potent philosophical life need not be as scandalous as Foucault preferred to see it. Thoreau's exercises in simple living, labor, and purity of diet—or Dewey's explorations through the Alexander Technique (to which he attributed his improved capacities for attention and awareness, and even his longevity)—present alternative models of embodied philosophical life that may prove equally informative, transformative, and aesthetically enriching, though less dramatically spectacular than either Diogenes's exhibitionist primitivism or Foucault's transgressive experiments in drugs and S/M.[32]

Philosophy needs to pay more critical attention to the variety of somatic practices through which we can pursue our quest for self-knowledge and self-creation; for beauty, potency, and pleasure; for the reconstruction of immediate experience into improved living. The discipline that would treat this embodied pursuit I call "somaesthetics." Experience, in this somatic sense, should belong to the practice of philosophy.

Chapter Three

Organic Unity

Analysis and Deconstruction

I

Dating back to the Greeks (and even implicit in their very idea of the cosmos), the notion of organic unity finds significant application in a host of philosophical enterprises: ethics, aesthetics, and political theory, philosophy of mind, cosmology, and, of course, the philosophy of biology, with whose central concept of organism it is clearly, etymologically connected. Just as organic unity provides one of the two classical goals of art (the other being *mimesis*), so it furnishes one of the two most fundamental models of truth and knowledge—that of a systematic unity or coherence of beliefs. Here again, the other major epistemological model is that of representational correspondence to the real. It is intriguing that, for all their apparent differences, aesthetics and epistemology share the same basic alternative strategies: representation or unity.

Since mimetic theories of art have long been discredited by twentieth-century artistic developments, it would be nice to find reassurance in organic unity. Certainly, most contemporary Anglo-American aesthetics has sought its ultimate principles in such a notion, whether it located that unity in the external art object or its aesthetic experience.[1] But organic unity has been radically challenged by recent developments in postmodern aesthetics, and not without reason. For this notion can become fetishized and frozen into a repressively rigid ideal that stifles creativity and formal experiment, and that can induce in us an overly facile and complacent sense of harmony in the world. Coupled with postmodern art's emphasis on fragmentation and decentering, there has been an intense theoretical attack on the whole idea of unity, where not merely its value but its grounding and even its coherence are questioned. Foucault, of course, provides a wide-ranging challenge to presumed structures of unity and continuity in our thinking, including the unities of the genre, the book, and the author's oeuvre. Pierre Macherey, from his Marxist perspective, similarly lashes out against the traditional presumption of unity in aesthetics: "The postulated unity of the work which, more or less explicitly, has always haunted the enterprise of criticism, must now be denounced. . . . Rather than that *sufficiency*, that ideal consistency, we must stress that determinate insufficiency, that incompleteness which actually shapes the work."[2] But probably the most rigorous attempts to discredit and overthrow the notion of organic unity in aesthetic theory come from deconstruction.

One of Jacques Derrida's central aims is to challenge and dismantle the traditional idea of structure as a centered and complete organic whole, limiting the field of "freeplay." This field, through the inescapable medium of language, must always be "a field of infinite substitutions," and through its infinite play of substitutions "excludes totalization" and overruns all putatively fixed limits of structural closure.[3] Such a vision of decentered, unlimitable freedom and substitution clearly conflicts with our most familiar (originally Aristotelian) understanding of organic unity as a complete whole having a definite "beginning, a middle, and an end" and having parts so integrally connected "that if any one of them is displaced or removed, the whole will be disjointed and disturbed."[4]

In Paul de Man, the deconstructionist attack on organic unity is aimed more directly at Anglo-American aesthetics as represented by the New Criticism, whose celebration of semantic richness in the unity of a text is said to end up by revealing "a plurality of significations that can be radically opposed to each other." But this, according to de Man, "explodes" the very idea of any organic unity in poetry, of any unity analogous to "the coherence of the natural world." "This unitarian criticism finally becomes a criticism of ambiguity, an ironic reflection on the absence of the unity it had postulated."[5] De Man's argument begs two very crucial and dubious premises (which for him are perhaps ultimately the same): namely, that organic unity can never embrace any radical oppositions and that the unities or coherences of "the natural world" (which de Man equates with "the organic world") involve no similar oppositions or conflicting forces. Yet a whole skein of thinkers stretching back to Heraclitus insist on the possibility that such unity not only contains but is sustained and enhanced by the tension of the opposites it embraces;[6] and modern science seems to reveal that radical opposition inhabits the unities of nature right down to the positive and negative charges of the atom. De Man's unwarranted and unconvincing assumptions are never argued for. They appeal to a univocal, monolithic concept of organic unity that is never articulated, and their problematic character points to the need for a more careful and rigorous study of this concept to see what, if anything, can be redeemed from it for contemporary thought.

I will do so by mapping the oppositional relations in which deconstructionist and analytic theories of organic unity are deeply interlocked. Although deconstruction opposes organic unity in aesthetics, we shall see that at a much deeper *logical* level, it is fundamentally committed and inextricably wedded to one central (originally Hegelian) sense of organic unity. Indeed, its attack on aesthetic unity relies precisely and essentially on this organic principle. Conversely, analytic philosophy, while advocating some form of organic unity as an aesthetic principle, vigorously denies the more radical logical principle of organic unity that forms the crucial foundation of deconstruction's assault not simply on aesthetic unity but on the very possibility of reference and individuation—the foundational core of the analytic project. From the agonistic deadlock between these rival philosophies, pragmatism emerges as the most likely option for recuperating the advantages of each. To chart these oppositional reversals and the pragmatist alternative, we first need to distinguish the various senses of organic unity; and the best place to begin is with its tripartite analysis by G. E. Moore, who, together with Bertrand Russell, established analytic philosophy at the beginning of the twentieth century through their common revolt against the then prevailing Hegelian idealism.

II

Moore's treatment of organic unity is complex because complexly motivated. This notion plays a central role in his two major philosophical projects of defending realism and the objectivity of intrinsic value. In the former it is a demon of idealist thinking that must be exorcised, while in the latter it plays a crucial positive role in explaining how the intrinsic value of something can be dependent on its parts (themselves of possibly negligible value) but still not be reducible to the sum of the values of its parts. This organic principle by which wholes can have intrinsic value even if their necessary constitutive parts have none greatly widens the range of possible intrinsic goods and hence the opportunities for realizing the good life. It is thus crucial to Moore's ethics. Moore sought to resolve the conflicting valencies that organic unity had for his ontological and ethical projects by clearly distinguishing different senses of the notion to which the conflicting valencies could then be allocated. He thus moves from a virulent blanket rejection of organic unity in "The Refutation of Idealism" to a more careful and balanced tripartite analysis in *Principia Ethica.*[7]

For Moore's realism, organic unity is an inimical principle to be savaged, since it supplies his idealist opponents with a weapon for denying the force of the distinction between "a sensation or idea and . . . its object," a distinction crucial to Moore's argument that there is some real object beyond or distinct from what is perceived. According to Moore, although idealists would in some sense grant that green and the sensation of green can be distinguished, they would counter that "the things distinguished form an 'organic unity' . . . [such that] each would not be what it is *apart from its relation to the other.*" Hence to consider them as "separable" or independent from each other is an "illegitimate abstraction," and thus any apparent distinction between them cannot be used to argue for the reality of green or green objects outside our ideational experiencing of green. Moore describes the principle of organic unity as asserting "that whenever you try to assert *anything whatever* of that which is a *part* of an organic whole, what you assert can only be true of the whole"; and he roundly condemns this as absurdly implying (given the premise that true universal substitutivity entails identity) that the whole is absolutely identical with the part while at the same time presuming them somehow distinct by contrasting them (RI 14–15).

This summary rejection of organic unity is accompanied by a derisive denunciation of its Hegelian source. "The principle of organic unities . . . is mainly used to defend the practice of holding both of two contradictory propositions, wherever this may seem convenient. In this, as in other matters, Hegel's main service to philosophy has consisted in giving a name to and erecting into a principle, a type of fallacy to which experience had shown philosophers, along with the rest of mankind to be addicted. No wonder that he has followers and admirers" (RI 16). The critique of Hegelian organic unity gains detail and rigor in *Principia Ethica*, where Moore distinguishes between three senses of "organic unity" or "organic whole," two of which he endorses. The first is where the parts of a whole are so related "that the continued existence of . . . one [part] is a necessary condition for the continued existence of the other [parts]; while the continued existence of . . . [the] latter is also a necessary condition for the continued existence of the former" (*PE* 31). This conception is more than the mere assertion that an organic whole could not exist precisely as it does if its parts were not precisely what they were. For that will hold for any whole rather than mark a specifically organic one. It seems a trivial logical truth that any change of a whole's parts must change to some extent that whole, which then, *ex hypothesi*, would have different parts and thus be a different whole.[8]

What Moore's first sense of organic unity instead asserts is that not simply the whole but its constituent parts as well could not survive the destruction of other constituent parts. In such an organic whole the constituent parts (or at least some of them) have "a relation of mutual causal dependence on one another" (*PE* 32), the sort of relation once thought (before recent advances in medical technology) to exist between the various vital organs of the body. One's heart would not simply stop being a part of the same body if one's lungs and liver were removed; it would soon stop existing altogether. But, as Moore implies (*PE* 32), such reciprocal dependence of parts can exist also in nonliving structures. Though Moore accepts this first, "causal" sense of organic unity, it is not the sense he finds indispensably useful to his ethics and aesthetics. That crucial organic phenomenon is rather that a whole can have emergent properties that are not reducible or even proportionate to the properties of its constituent parts. Moore typically expresses this principle of holistic organicist emergence in terms of value: that an organic whole "has an intrinsic value different in amount from the sum of the values of its parts"; indeed "that *the value of such a whole bears no regular proportion to the sum of the values of its parts*" (*PE* 27, 36). But since he clearly recognizes that there is no difference in value without difference in properties (*PE* 35), this sense of organic unity can be more generally regarded as a unity where the properties of the whole are different from the sum of the properties of its individual parts and not reducible to them.

This sense differs from the first by allowing no inference from the existence of one part to the existence of the others without which that part could not exist. Here the organic relation is not a matter of the parts' reciprocal dependence for their existence but of the whole's dependence on the parts for its qualities and value. Of course, this second organic unity applies to living organisms, where the bodily system as a whole has special properties and value absent from its specific parts. Yet such unity is considered especially characteristic of works of art (which are not ordinarily organic in the first sense), and Moore thus illustrates it aesthetically: "All the parts of a picture do not have that relation of mutual causal dependence, which certain parts of the body have, and yet the existence of those which do not have it may be absolutely essential to the value of the whole" (*PE* 33). But again, such unity can easily be found outside living organisms and artworks, as any salad- or sandwich-maker knows.

Moore then contrasts these two notions of organic unity to the Hegelian one condemned in "The Refutation of Idealism." That suspect unity claims to be one where "just as the whole would not be what it is but for the existence of its parts, so the parts would not be what they are but for the existence of the whole." Therefore, "any particular part could not exist unless the others existed too" (*PE* 33). However, this is not the mere causal dependence of the first sense. It is rather a logical dependence, where the very essence or identity of the part involves the whole to which it is related, so that without the whole it would not strictly be the same part. The idea is that when a thing forms a part of such a whole, it possesses properties it would otherwise not possess—not merely the property of being part of the whole but also more substantial emergent properties acquired through its participation in the whole. A hand when part of an organically whole human being has powers and properties different from that hand as a detached member. Things with different properties cannot be identical, so the hand as an organic part must be essentially different from that same hand cut off from the whole. Its different identity clearly seems due to or constituted by the whole to which it belongs. Since the whole allegedly forms part of its part's identity, that part cannot be what it is and loses its very "meaning or significance apart from its whole." Hence such "parts are inconceivable except as parts of that whole" (*PE* 34, 36).

Moore repudiates this form of organic unity as both confused and self-contradictory. It confuses emergent properties belonging properly only to the whole with intrinsic defining properties of the part itself. Secondly, it asserts, in effect, that any part of such a whole necessarily has that whole as part of that part itself; but this is inconsistent with the part's being a distinguishable part of that whole. The first point is that for a part to display an emergent property or value in conjunction with the whole's other parts but not to display it by itself in isolation means that it itself (i.e., the part) does not really have this property as part of its identity. For to display a property *only* as part of a whole, only together with other parts, is not to have the property at all but rather to be part of that (i.e., the whole) that does have it. This idea, that emergent properties and values belong only to the organic wholes as *wholes* and not properly to the parts whose conjunction in the whole produce them, is the crucial point for Moore, and he shrewdly employs it in questions of ethical valuation. But it is easy enough to apply in aesthetics. We may, for example, point to a part of an artistic whole (say, a line in the picture of a face) and assert that this part is a silly or sly smile but wouldn't be one if not for the arrangement of the other lines of the face. But the silliness or slyness of the smile is, strictly speaking, a property of the whole face, not just of the single line; even though we may just point to that line, a single part of the whole, in order to focus perception so that this emergent expressive property of the whole is better grasped. Moore makes this point nonaesthetically in arguing against investing the human arm with the emergent properties it displays when connected with the living body:

> We may easily come to say that *as* a part of the body, it [the arm] has great value, whereas *by itself* it would have none; and thus its whole "meaning" lies in its relation to the body. But in fact the value in question does not belong to *it* at all. To have value merely as a part is equivalent to having no value at all, but merely being part of that which has it. Owing, however, to neglect of this distinction, the assertion that a part has value, *as a part*, which it would not otherwise have, easily leads to the assumption that it is also different, *as a part*, from what it would otherwise be; for it is, in fact, true that two things which have a different value must also differ in other respects. (*PE* 35)

Moore brings the further charge of self-contradiction. At the same time that this organic principle asserts there is a part (*P*), which helps to form a whole (*W*) and is therefore logically distinguishable from *W*, it denies that *P* has any such independent or distinguishable nature of its own, but rather that its very identity involves the whole (*W*) and its system of interrelations of which it is a part. Thus, while P is originally identified as being distinct from *W*, as being a mere part of *W*, it is then contradictorily taken as analytically including *W* as part of itself, since it itself is constituted by the whole set of *W*'s interrelations of parts. In other words, the radical notion of organic unity requires that any individual part we distinguish as contributing to form the whole cannot be so distinguished. It cannot be the same part in itself and as part of the whole, because as part of the whole it has different essential or constitutive properties (viz., those of its emergent interrelations and value with the other parts in the whole). Thus, we are led to the contradiction that P is and is not part of the whole, W; or alternatively that P is not P (since it is not the same thing when it is part of the whole and when it is isolated). As Moore sums it up, "The assumption that one and the same thing, because it is a part of a more valuable whole at one time than at another, therefore has more intrinsic value at one time than at another, has encouraged the self-contradictory belief that one and the same thing may be two different things, and that only in one of its forms is it truly what it is" (*PE* 35).

III

Moore's critique of organic unity derives its power from such deeply entrenched principles as the laws of identity and contradiction and the reality of self-identical particulars or logically independent individuals. But it is not immune to criticism. In the first place, his tripartite analysis does not exhaust the senses of organic unity that have been influential in intellectual history. What is most clearly lacking in Moore is any awareness of the temporal, vitalistic, developmental sense of organic unity, which was very important in romanticism and in Dewey.[9] For Dewey and the romantics, an organic whole was a dynamic unity whose parts evolve and unfold into the whole they form by some process of natural growth or ordered development.

There is good reason why Moore's account of organic unity ignores temporality and vitalistic development. For to admit such fluidity to his account might suggest that what his commonsense understanding grasps firmly as the particular, logically independent, and stable parts of a whole are not fixedly given in the nature of things. And if what counts as a part can change with time, if parts can simply be differently constituted by different temporal interpretations of an array into parts and wholes, then the whole idea of the logically durable self-identity of parts becomes more problematic, while the Moorean commonsense argument from contradiction that relies on it becomes much less compelling. From a Hegelian perspective, one might say that in ignoring the temporal aspect and the formative play of the mind in its shifting interpretive constitution of what the parts and whole are, Moore locks himself into the secure but philosophically jejune level of commonsense understanding. This level naively thinks that the objects, parts, and wholes with which we deal are fixed, autonomous realities, while the Hegelian and deconstructionist will instead regard them as but the flexible abstractions and constructed products of the activity of mind or of language's play of differences. Pragmatism also regards them as largely products of human practices and purposes; but it insists that our common-sense objects, parts, and wholes can still be quite firm and reliable, given the adamant durability of some of those objects and some of our practices.

Not only does deconstruction challenge Moore's analytic commitment to the fixed self-identity of parts, but it attacks the analytically endorsed *aesthetics* of organic unity by relying precisely on the radical logical sense of this notion that Moore put in question. The best way to show this is by showing how deconstruction's critique of aesthetic unity relies on the notion of *différance* and by showing how *différance* is essentially a version or corollary or application of the older notion of radical organic unity. I start from the second point.

Derrida's concept of *différance* is based on the Saussurian structuralist idea that in the linguistic system "there are only differences, *without positive terms*."[10] For example, the identity of any particular phoneme is not constituted by any positive essence, any real distinctive acoustic sound (for it is realizable in a multitude of qualitatively different sounds), but instead by its differential relations with other phonemes in the system. Building on Saussure and recognizing further that all the objects and concepts of our world are linguistically mediated, Derrida asserts that all the objects, elements, or categories of discourse are also differentially constituted and do not rest on foundationally real, positive essences beyond the differential network of language. They "do not have as their cause a subject or substance, a thing in general, or a being that is somewhere present and itself escapes the play of difference"; and he warns against the metaphysical response to supply such positive elements, "to respond with a definition of essence, of quiddity, to reconstitute a system of essential predicates."[11]

Différance, then, is "a structure and a movement . . . of . . . the systematic play of differences, of traces of differences, of the *spacing* by which elements are related to each other . . . without which the 'full' terms would not signify, would not function" (*Pos* 27). In other words, since any thing or element depends for its individuation and meaning on its differential interrelations with other elements, it follows that what any thing is, is essentially a function of what it is not. Because it is thus constituted by its differential relations with elements that, as different, are neither simply present *in* it nor necessarily simultaneously or contiguously present *with* it (and here the deferring sense of *différance* is displayed), any thing or element is never fully present in itself or constituted simply by (or for) itself.

> The play of differences supposes . . . syntheses and referrals which
> forbid at any moment, or in any sense, that a simple element be
> present in and of itself, referring only to itself . . . no element
> can function . . . without referring to another element which
> itself is not simply present. This interweaving results in each
> "element" . . . being constituted on the basis of the trace within
> it of the other elements of the chain or system. . . . Nothing,
> neither among the elements nor within the system, is anywhere
> ever simply present or absent. There are only, everywhere, dif-
> ferences and traces of traces. (*Pos* 26)

That the notion of *différance* and the radical concept of organic unity
are essentially the same should now be obvious, especially if we take the
notion of whole as representing the system or structure of linguistic differences. For, as we saw, radical organicism asserts that any part or element
"can have no meaning or significance apart from its whole," that no individual part can be a self-identical, self-sufficient "distinct object of thought,"
because all "the parts would not be what they are but for the existence of
the whole," "are inconceivable except as parts of that whole," for each part
derives its meaning from its relations to the whole's other parts (*PE* 33, 34,
36). Now since any object that we ordinarily conceive as a whole can itself
be seen as part of a larger whole, structure, or system (at the very least in
the minimal, vague sense that it is part of the world), we can apply this
principle of organic, differential identity to any object. From this logical
principle of organic unity or *différance*, it then follows that what any object
is, is essentially a function of what it is not; it is essentially constituted by
its differential relations with other objects from which it is distinguished
but without whose associative, relational distinctions it could not be, or be
distinguished as, what it is.

As Moore recognized, this idea can be traced back to Hegel, that philosopher of the whole so often repudiated by analytic thinkers: "Everything
that exists stands in correlation, and this correlation is the veritable nature
of every existence. The existent thing in this way has no being of its own,
but only in something else."[12] But the same idea is also salient in Nietzsche
(another Teutonic protodeconstructor and analytic anathema), where it forms
the logical core of his central doctrines of the will to power and the eternal
recurrence. "'Things that have a constitution in themselves'—a dogmatic
idea with which one must break absolutely," exhorts Nietzsche. "In the
actual world . . . everything is bound to and conditioned by everything

else." Thus "no things remain but only dynamic quanta, in a relation of tension to all other dynamic quanta: their essence lies in their relation to all other quanta."[13]

IV

How is this organicist logic of *différance* deployed in deconstructing organic unity as an aesthetic notion? It provides the structuring logical foundation for the two major arguments aimed at undermining the very coherence of the notion of an artwork's unity. Typical of deconstructive reasoning, both arguments start with assumptions of aesthetic unity but then work through them to reveal aporia or internal contradictions within the very idea of such unity and necessarily violating it.

The first argument concerns the sense of wholeness and integrity contained in the idea of a work's organic unity. We regard the work as a distinct integral whole, composed of the parts belonging to it and complete in itself as constituted by those and only those parts. But such unity, it is argued, is constituted only on the basis of distinguishing and excluding something outside it, elements not part of or constitutive of the unified whole. If we hold with Aristotle that an organically unified work must have a beginning, middle, and end (or even just a beginning and end), we must recognize that it cannot have them without having something before the beginning and beyond its end in order to mark them and shape or frame the work they enclose. Thus, what is alleged to be outside, apart from, or irrelevant to the self-sufficient work as a whole becomes essential to it and constitutive of it. What seems to lie outside the work and beyond it is as much a part of what makes the work as the constitutive parts inside the work. The whole distinction between inside and outside the work, on which the notion of integral unity rests, becomes problematized when what lies outside the work becomes essential to its inside. The very possibility of the work as a distinct organic unity composed only of its parts is voided when the work is seen to be equally constituted by what are not its parts but rather that which frames them. Its unity of parts, constituted by what is foreign and contrastively opposed to this unity, is thus fundamentally and ineluctably self-divided rather than unified.

Jonathan Culler employs this line of argument, asserting "that the 'organic unity' of works of art is the product of framing," which relies on "the distinction between inside and outside [that] evades precise formulation," a distinction between an external background or supplementary frame and the unified totality of the work this frames. But then "this marginal supplement" or outside is therefore "essential, constituting, enshrining"; for "framing is what creates the aesthetic object." Although outside the work's intrinsic structure, "the frame is what gives us an object that can have an intrinsic content or structure." So for Culler, the external or marginal to the work "becomes central by virtue of its very marginality" (*OD* 195–99). Culler's dialectical argument of the frame (elaborated both in terms of criticism as a framing discourse of literature and in terms of the framing metalinguistic devices in the literary work itself) is taken from Derrida's analysis of the frame as *parergon*. Their formulations may seem somewhat more complex than the organicist argument I outlined above. But this is only because the frame itself, as they see it, is not clearly identified with the outside of the work. Rather, in Derrida's words, "It is a *parergon*, a composite of inside and outside, but a composite which is not an amalgam or half-and-half but an outside which is called inside the inside to constitute it as inside."[14] Nonetheless, we have here the same essential argument. For it is the frame's being outside that makes it be summoned and drawn into the inside to make the inside an inside, just as it is the excluded external nonparts in the logical principle of organic unity that are ineluctably reinscribed as essential and constitutive of the internal parts.

The second argument against the work of art as a unified whole concerns not the work's distinction from what is outside it but rather a distinction within the work itself. To constitute the work as a unity of parts, we need to distinguish some coherent structure of parts in the whole, a structure that is in some sense privileging or hierarchical. We therefore typically speak of what is central as opposed to marginal in a work; and analytic aestheticians often distinguish the work's "hard core of essential features" from "the surrounding penumbra of inessential ones," or in Nelson Goodman's terms its "constitutive" from its "contingent" properties.[15] We are all familiar with the conventions of literary competence by which we disregard some features of the text as ancillary, inessential, or accidental in order to concentrate on what really counts in the text. Apparently insignificant words or punctuation, the text's visual shape and color,[16] the homonymic meanings or alternative uses of its words, distant associations that they might raise in other fields but that are plainly out of place in the given literary context—all these we standardly dismiss as being beside the point and as obstructing, if we focus on them, the real meaning and unity of the work.

However, the deconstructors ask, if these irrelevant aspects belong to the text, what justification is there for branding them irrelevant or inessential vis-à-vis some contrasting essence of the text? For by the logical principle of organicism, the essential properties or meanings could neither be nor be distinguished as essential if not for the so-called irrelevant and inessential ones that frame them. And if the inessential is thus revealed as essential to the essential, this would undermine the privileging structure of parts and meanings that constitutes the work as a unity. It would moreover suggest that the inessential (as essential) deserves our attention as critics and appreciators; but such attention would seem to disrupt the psychologically experienced unity of the work. Unity is thus undone both objectively and subjectively.

This argument, clearly reflected in Derrida's logic of marginality or supplementarity and in deconstruction's interpretive practice of focusing on textual "irrelevancies," is articulated by Culler. "Interpretation generally relies on distinctions between the central and the marginal, the essential and the inessential: to interpret is to discover what is central to a text or group of texts." But since marginality is not something ontologically given but a product of interpretational framing, "what has been relegated to the margins or set aside by previous interpreters may be important for precisely those reasons." Yet the fact that we can "reverse a hierarchy to show that . . . [the] marginal is in fact central" does not lead "to the identification of a new center . . . but to a subversion of the distinctions between essential and inessential, inside and outside. What is a center if the marginal can become central" (*OD* 140)? Moreover, building on de Man's suggested reversal of the traditional "ethos of explication" by attempting "a reading that would no longer blindly submit to the teleology of controlled meaning,"[17] Culler repudiates "our inclination to use notions of unity and thematic coherence to exclude possibilities" of meaning that would pose a problem for a coherent interpretation of the text "because they would disrupt the focus or continuity" of such a reading (*OD* 246–47).

This further twist of the argument is important, since a defender of unity might concede the point that the marginal or inessential is logically essential for framing but then go on to argue that we must not confuse such essentiality with aesthetic centrality or worthiness for aesthetic attention. In rejoinder, Culler would first point out that our standard for judging what in a text is central or appropriate for aesthetic appreciation is the criterion of its fit or contribution to the postulated unity of the text. But this, he would then insist, is precisely to beg the question that the text is unified. We cannot appeal to the text's disputed organic unity to prove that unity. Nor do we have the right to posit as a metaphysical axiom that literary works are organic unities by virtue of some special ontological status, irrespective of the intentional acts of authors and interpreters. De Man's critique of New Criticism for reifying the literary work into an autonomously organic form is compellingly correct here. The postulated unity of a text (like the text's meaning) is at most an intentional structure, hermeneutically and contextually constructed; it is not a foundational and unchanging given.

But before we deconstructively scrap the idea of unity, pragmatism intervenes to recover it. For without foundational unity, there remains pragmatic justification for postulating unity in the work as a strategy of reading and an interpretive criterion of relevance and centrality: rich unity and the satisfactions it affords are what we primarily seek in reading literary texts. Culler is quick to reject this aim as reflecting a narrowly formalist hedonism, as falsely relegating literary works to the realm of play and pleasure, devoid of the cognitive rigor, seriousness, and powers of mastery that proper reading of literature should involve. Besides reflecting a perverse puritanism, this attitude presumes a false dichotomy between reading for pleasure and reading for cognitive empowerment. If our human need to perceive and experience satisfying unities in the disordered flux of experience is what motivates our interest in art, this need should not be rejected. What we should reject is the repressive limitation of art to the expression of only such unity, the prohibition of jarring fragmentation and incoherencies that can have their own stimulating aesthetic (and cognitive) effect, and that can result in more complex forms of coherence. Similarly, we should not fetishize art's objects as if they were independently valuable unities in themselves, apart from their work in experience. Nor should the unity of aesthetic experience be fetishistically embalmed or reified into something static, permanent, and isolated from the changing flow of life. Pragmatism's insistence on these provisos does not gainsay its recognition of unity's value.

Culler might dismiss our presumptive bias for unity as merely a cultural "convention" of literary competence, and therefore arbitrary and dispensable. But such a move falsely assumes that all our cultural conventions are indeed superficially arbitrary, an assumption based on an uncritical acceptance of the natural/conventional distinction. As I elsewhere argued, there is no sharp line to be drawn between natural and culturally informed or "conventional" human interests and practices. Many of our so-called conventions are so deeply entrenched that we naturally employ them (as second nature) and take them as basic to our form of life. Doing without them, if indeed feasible, would be doing most poorly, alienating ourselves from what constitutes our very forms of thinking, action, and experience.[18] With respect to our conventional aesthetic prejudice toward unity, Culler is honest enough to admit that "the critical writings that most vigorously proclaim their celebration of heterogeneity are likely to reveal, under exegetical scrutiny, their reliance on notions of organic unity which are not easy to banish" (*OD* 200). This indeed is precisely what we have seen in Derrida and Culler's own celebration of the philosophical heterogeneity of *différance*.

There is another pragmatic justification for the interpretive presumption of a work's unity. It is the Heideggerian-Gadamerian idea that interpretive understanding is the working out of a partial fore-understanding based on "the fore-conception of completion," the presumption "that only what really constitutes a unity of meaning is intelligible." The very same pragmatic linkage of unity with intelligibility underlies Dewey's definition of inquiry as the transformation of a confusing problem-situation into a unified whole. We always expect a text (or action) to issue in some coherent whole when it is worked out and understood. Thus, when it seems incoherent, either in itself or in its relation to our views on what it concerns, we need to interpret it so that some "unified meaning can be realized," as Gadamer states.[19] We typically do this either by interpreting the text as more coherent with itself and with our beliefs or by interpreting its incoherencies within a coherent explanatory account (e.g., its author's different cultural or psychological context or his desire to express incoherence so as to shock us); in other words, understanding incoherence and disunity within a larger coherent totality of meaning. Even de Man, while criticizing organic unity as a naturalistic reification, still recognized its hermeneutic reality: the undeniable "intent at totality of the interpretative process," "the necessary presence of a totalizing principle as the guiding impulse of the critical process."[20]

However, this principle of interpretive holism, the idea that intelligibility somehow relies on some idea of unity, has been denounced by Derrida as the pervasive error of "the axiomatic structure of metaphysics, insofar as *metaphysics itself* desires, or dreams, or imagines its own unity." "Since Aristotle, and at least up until Bergson, 'it' (metaphysics) has constantly repeated and assumed that to think and to say must mean to think and to say something that would be a *one*, one *matter*."[21] Analytic philosophy expresses this assumption in the view that all intelligible thought and language rely on "individuating reference" and that anything we can refer to (hence speak about) must be self-identical. As the once popular dictum put it, "no entity without identity." But to what extent is this assumption of unity and identity really necessary, valid, or even possible? Are there "ones" that we can refer to and distinguish as really independent from others? Must we at least presume that there are, and in what way must these "ones" be unified?[22] We are thus led back to organic unity at its most fundamental and challenging level—as a principle of logic, metaphysics, and philosophy of language, a principle that perhaps most sharply divides analysis and deconstruction, yet binds them in an unavoidable and perhaps interminable agon of confrontation.

V

We should recall that Moore first attacks organic unity for mistaking the emergent relational properties of the whole for defining properties of a given part, and then second for self-contradictorily holding that a part is logically distinct from the whole and the whole's other parts, and yet essentially includes them all as part of its own nature. The force of both these criticisms clearly depends on the assumption that we can really talk about a part and its intrinsic nature. Yet it is precisely this assumption that radical organic unity is challenging when it asserts that everything (hence any part) lacks intrinsic features of its own but is constituted solely through its interrelations with and differences from everything else—relations that (as Nietzsche and Hegel would urge) are not foundationally fixed but the product of (possibly changing) interpretation. Any identification of a part depends on what other parts it is interpreted as being related to and distinguished from. In other words, there are no parts, like no facts, without interpretation.[23] But if there is no identity apart from interpretation, we can dismiss the charge that the part's identity is misdescribed or self-contradictorily construed. Parts simply become different parts by being differently interpreted in terms of different interrelations. Moore's logic-chopping argument has lost its blade.

To this differential, interpretive account of identity the analyst might respond in two related ways. He could argue that the whole notion of differences or interrelations presupposes that there are entities differentiated or interrelated and that we cannot speak of an entity without identity. Difference relies conceptually on identity as much as identity seems to presuppose the idea of difference. The inseparability of these notions seems to be William James's pragmatist point in listing "the same or different" as *one* of our most important commonsense concepts.[24] But the deconstructor and pragmatist could cogently reply that this need not entail foundational self-identical substances, since sufficient identity for differentiation is provided in the idea of "identity according to a particular interpretation." Similarly, the analytic argument that we need real particulars as the individual referents necessary for thought and discourse can be answered by indicating that such referents could simply be individuals according to some interpretation.

The analyst might press further by questioning more specifically the basic differential terms or Nietzschean "dynamic quanta" that deconstruction sees as entering into the interrelational interpretations that constitute all objects. What are these interpretational elements? If they are basic atoms, then some things that enter into the interpretive constitution of objects are not themselves so constituted. If, instead, these basic elements are themselves the product of interpreting still more basic elements in *their* interrelations, then we can and should ask the same question about those more basic ones. Recursively applying this analytic strategy (the essential strategy of logical atomism), we must either end in atomic elements of some sort or instead "never end" in an infinite regress or circle of interpretations where ultimately there is nothing beyond interpretations to interpret. This is not simply a question of the independent world collapsing into the texts that represent it. Here the very idea of text itself dissolves into interpretations without any independent "interpretation-free" text or object that they are interpretations of.[25]

Derrida would hardly flinch at such consequences, and he would certainly repudiate the analytic argument (with its reductive quest for original foundations) as a paradigm symptom of that onto-theological metaphysics that has so long dominated our thought. In responding to John Searle, he warned that the analytic "enterprise of returning 'strategically,' ideally, to an origin or to a 'priority' held to be simple, intact, normal, pure, standard, self-identical . . . is not just *one* metaphysical gesture among others; it is *the* metaphysical exigency."[26] Pragmatism would also reject the metaphysical strategy of infinite regress, insisting that in actual life and thinking there is always a point where it is pointless or even meaningless to go back further in regressive analysis or explanation.

The metaphysical roots of traditional analysis are surely clear.[27] What is far from clear, however, is whether deconstruction, in its very critique of analysis, is not itself ensnared by a metaphysics that it desperately seeks to avoid. For the notion of organic unity that underlies its critique reflects a potent and pervasive metaphysical gesture of its own. The deconstructive idea that everything is a product of its interrelations and differences from other things, that nothing has an independent or intrinsic nature, rests at bottom on the idea that all things are indeed ineluctably interconnected. This idea of the world as an organic totality or system of terms, whose relationality undermines the existence of independent substances, is explicit in Hegel and Nietzsche, where it saliently looms as a metaphysical thesis. To recall, in Hegel: "Everything that exists stands in correlation, and this correlation is the veritable nature of every existence. The existent thing in this way has no being of its own, but only in something else." Similarly with Nietzsche, who is probably closest to Derrida: "In the actual world . . . everything is bound to and conditioned by everything else." There is nothing "but dynamic quanta, in a relation of tension to all other dynamic quanta: their essence lies in their relation to all other quanta." "Every atom affects the whole of being."[28]

This view of the world as a totality of interrelated and reciprocally defined elements, a world whose apparently independent individual objects are simply interpretive constructs of such internal systemic relations—is this not a metaphysical view? And why should we accept it as the true one? Derrida himself has condemned the idea of "a totality of beings" as a dangerous metaphysical idea, one from which he would like to extricate Nietzsche (and ultimately, if unknowingly, himself).[29] Perhaps the best way to effect this escape would be to regard Nietzschean cosmological organicism not as a foundational metaphysical view but simply as one more interpretive perspective on the world. The problem, then, is that mere perspectival status seems to rob organic unity of its power to refute the "atomist" or ordinary perspective that sees the world as having things with definite properties or constitutions of their own. As merely another perspective on the world, what does radical organicism have to offer? It surely does not provide a view either congenial to or practical for our entrenched logocentric ways of speaking, thinking, and acting; and its advocates quite openly and cheerily admit this. Is it then offered on more aesthetic than pragmatic grounds? There is nothing wrong with assessing ontological perspectives also aesthetically; and perhaps no essential dichotomy between their aesthetic and pragmatic justification. Quine's ontological minimalism was simultaneously linked both to pragmatism and to "a taste for desert landscapes."[30]

Radical organicism might provide a metaphysical aesthetic gratification in presenting the chaotic and unfathomable congeries of our world as ultimately (or, at least, best construable as) an organic whole of essentially interrelated elements that have no life or meaning apart from their interconnections and that can be differently arranged, shaped, and manipulated by intervening interpretation. We can therefore look through the shattered and disjointed fragments of our postmodern wasteland and see them all as one vast sum and unity of essentially interrelated objects. Besides the satisfying, reassuring consolation of this comprehensive unity, there is the comforting promise that any disturbing fact or object in the world can simply be transfigured or deconstructed by reinterpretation of the differential elements into more pleasing interpretive constructions.

This unity will strike many (the analyst, the pragmatist, and the layman) as too remote and metaphysical to be of real comfort. It seems an unsatisfying substitute for the loss of the traditionally entrenched unities we are accustomed to regard as the individual objects or beautiful artworks of our ordinary world, things that deconstructive organic unity asks us to question or abandon. But if our faith in those unities has already been lost—if, as marginalized intellectuals in the humanities, we have become disenchanted with both the ideology of facts and the facts themselves and even with the works of art through which we hoped to escape the cruel facts—then the principle of organic unity offers some solace of unification. For not only is everything essentially connected, but all facts dissolve into interpretations.

Pragmatism, the best mediator and option between analysis and deconstruction, can also see things as being in some sense (or at some time) interpretations, but interpretations so inextricably entrenched in our actual thinking that they take the status of fact or reality. However, it need not rush from the unavailability of foundational facts to the totalizing conclusion that all understanding is interpretation, that in the free and fluid play of intelligible experience there is nothing to distinguish them. This would be giving up a frequently useful distinction between understanding and interpretation, between what we grasp without requiring further elucidation and what needs to be interpreted for us to handle it satisfactorily. Because reality for the pragmatist is basically what has "coerciveness, in the long run, over thought," while truth is roughly "whatever proves itself to be good in the way of belief" and "expedient in the way of our thinking," "in the long run and on the whole," pragmatism will be closer than deconstruction to the world view of common sense, with its particular objects and independent things having properties of their own.[31] But it will not want to proceed from this way of taking the world to a fundamental metaphysical inference regarding what ultimately there is. It will want to leave that ontological question open or perhaps simply leave it as unhelpful.

Derrida would deny that his version of organic unity is caught up with the metaphysics of totality, which he explicitly repudiates. For does he not explicitly repudiate the idea of totality? But it is hard to see how we can make sense of the systematic differential production of meaning without presupposing the idea of at least a provisional (and possibly ever expanding) totality of interrelated terms. In any case, the very presumption that *all* the elements or objects of our world are essentially differentially interconnected and reciprocally constitutive of each other (however un-totaled or un-totalizable they may be) clearly suggests a metaphysical perspective predisposed to ultimate, albeit differential, cosmic unity.

Confronting traditional analytic philosophy with deconstruction on the deepest ontological level, we are confronted with a choice: Russell's and Wittgenstein's atomistic metaphysics of foundationally independent and self-identical entities that form the structure of facts through their external relations versus the Hegelian-Nietzschean deconstructive picture in which there are no such separate individual entities or unities, but only because there is a much vaster differential unity of all there is, an all-embracing unity whose internal differential relations are what constitute that which the analyst takes as individual things. What the pragmatist sees on this ontological level is neither: neither a world of autonomous atoms nor one solely of integrated interrelations and their essentially connected, reciprocally constituted terms. What she instead sees is "a world imperfectly unified still," largely "the common-sense world, in which we find things partly joined and partly disjoined," things that are self-identical but whose individuation depends on our practices and purposes.[32]

And what does the pragmatist want with respect to organic unity? James provides a handy declaration that suggests an answer while weaving some themes and catchwords of analysis and deconstruction: "Provided you grant *some* separation among things, some tremor of independence, some free play of parts on one another, some real novelty and chance, however minute, she is amply satisfied, and will allow you any amount, however great, of real union."[33] Though deeply appreciative of unity, pragmatism should equally respect difference; and this respect goes beyond ontology and aesthetics—to ethics, politics, and race and gender issues. Organic unity, at least in those versions where the different parts enjoy some relative autonomy, can perhaps provide a model for non-repressive unity or harmony in difference.

Finally, where should pragmatism stand on the question of essence? Clearly, it must reject the foundationalist idea of immutable essences that permanently define the different identities of our objects and concepts. Like hermeneutics and deconstruction, pragmatism recognizes that such identities are the product of perspectival grasping and revisable linguistic practices, and thus are always subject to reinterpretation. This insight can kindle a radical anti-essentialism that insists not only on the ubiquity of interpretation but also on the absolute contingency and arbitrary particularity of everything. Such a pragmatism, advocated by Richard Rorty, however, turns into an inverted essentialism of anti-essentialism that asserts "the universality and necessity of the individual and contingent."[34]

Of course, in the sense of logical necessity, everything may be contingent. But some things are clearly more contingent than others, and failure to distinguish between these differing sorts of contingencies simply reflects our bad philosophical habit of absolutist thinking. If there are no logical necessities in our world, there remain probabilities that constitute practical certainty; if there are no foundational essences, there remain historical norms (alterable and contestable as they are) that structure and regulate our linguistic and other social practices, thus serving, so to speak, as relative historicized essences. A post-Rortyan pragmatism needs to recognize this more moderate yet more liberated option. For once we really break free of foundationalist metaphysics, the notion of essential properties (and the distinction between essential and inessential) can be pragmatically reinterpreted and redeemed for use. Similarly, a true break with foundationalist epistemology allows the pragmatist to reinterpret the nature and role of interpretation itself.

Chapter Four

Affective Cognition

From Pragmatism to Somaesthetics

I

Pragmatist philosophy was not an attractive option for cognitive science when that new interdisciplinary field began to surge and flourish in the 1950s and 1960s. First, pragmatism was in serious decline, professionally eclipsed and demonized by analytic philosophy as too woolly and insufficiently scientific. Second, cognitive science was very much concerned with formal logics or models of computation and information processing that were largely isolated from real-world social contexts and independent of living human bodies but that could be equally instantiated in artificial intelligence systems, whereas pragmatism tended to insist on the essentially contextual, embodied, and social nature of all meaning and knowledge. Third, pragmatism was identified as a philosophy based on ideas of human action, practice, or conduct rather than on the concept of mental representations. Related to this emphasis is pragmatism's strongly empirical stance toward inquiry, the primacy of observation and experimentation rather than formal deductions. This apparent privileging of action, practice, and conduct along with observation might make pragmatism seem a natural ally with behaviorism, which eschewed ideas of inner mental life and internal representations. As midcentury cognitive science was much concerned with internal representations and keen to challenge the then dominant behaviorist paradigm (for instance, Chomsky's critique of Skinner's behaviorism), pragmatism must have seemed an unhelpful if not an inimical orientation.[1]

Fortunately, things have greatly changed. Recent cognitive science displays an increasingly robust trend to insist that cognition is embodied and enactive but also embedded in a contextual, environmental, and social matrix and that it extends beyond the individual brain and particular body into that larger context that includes cognitive tools and affordances and established meanings and knowledge forms. This "4E" variety of cognitive science has obvious affinities with classical pragmatism. In this chapter, I suggest two other important dimensions of cognition found in classical pragmatism and developed in somaesthetics. These are the affective and aesthetic dimensions of cognition. To integrate them more neatly into the already established notion of the 4E cognitive science model, we could call them instead "emotive" and "esthetic" and speak rather of a "6E" approach. I focus here primarily on the affective dimension because it provides a way of resolving an apparent paradox in the very notion of pragmatism as a philosophy essentially defined through the concept of action and cognate notions such as conduct, practice, and the practical. I therefore begin by noting how action, practice, and conduct formed the defining essence of classical pragmatism, but then show the centrality of affect in its formative theories.

Claiming that its name's "history will show you . . . what pragmatism means," William James explains that "the term derives from the same Greek word πράγμα, meaning action, from which our words practice and practical come"; and he rightly credits C. S. Peirce for having first introduced it to philosophy by reasoning that since "our beliefs are really rules for action," then "to develop a thought's meaning, we need only determine what conduct it is fitted to produce: that conduct for us is its sole significance."[2] Peirce first formulated his pragmatic principle in terms of practical import: "Consider what effects, that might conceivably have practical bearings, we conceive the object of our conception to have. Then, our conception of these effects is the whole of our conception of the object."[3] But he later expressed the principle in terms of conduct: "The entire intellectual purport of any symbol consists in the total of all general modes of rational conduct which, conditionally upon all the possible different circumstances and desires, would ensue upon the acceptance of the symbol" (*CP* 5.438). (And still later, when differentiating his pragmatism from James's by emphasizing its less individualistic character, Peirce again characterizes his view of the pragmatic principle in terms of "action" and "practical results" but of a kind suitable to "generalization, such action as tends toward regularization, and the actualization of the thought without which action remains unthought" [*CP* 8:250].)

Practical bearings for conduct are likewise central to an equally famous pragmatist maxim that James authored: to accept no theoretical difference that could not make a possible difference in practice. "There can be no difference which doesn't make a difference, no difference in abstract truth which does not express itself in a difference of concrete fact, and of conduct consequent upon the fact, imposed on somebody, somehow, somewhere, and somewhen." In other words, "If there were any part of a thought that made no difference in the thought's practical consequences, then that part would be no proper element of the thought's significance. . . . The ultimate test for us of what a truth means is indeed the conduct it dictates or inspires."[4] Pragmatism's view that action (rather than reason) is the ultimate structuring ground for all thought and meaning has roots in the Darwinian insight that humans are living organisms whose struggle to survive requires that action take priority over thought and that thought's essential role is to provide better action. Our human essence is more vitally active than rationally reflective.

But there is a problematic paradox for a philosophy that advocates the primacy of action over thought: namely, philosophy's image as an essentially contemplative activity whose reflective, deliberative stance requires a certain critical distance from action and indeed a certain inhibiting of it. Maurice Merleau-Ponty notes this problem in explaining why "philosophy limps." "Since it is expression in act, it comes to itself only by ceasing to coincide with what is expressed, and by taking its distance in order to see its meaning. . . . Hence it can be tragic, since it has its own contrary within itself. It is never a serious occupation. . . . The philosopher of action is perhaps the farthest removed from action, for to speak of action with depth and rigor is to say that one does not desire to act."[5] The inhibiting opposition of thought to action is a familiar topos whose most famous literary expression may be Hamlet's complaint (III.i) that "conscience does make cowards of us all,/ And thus the native hue of resolution is sicklied o'er with the pale cast of thought," so that our "enterprises . . . lose the name of action." Even when it does not entirely repress action, thought's reflective deliberation tends to delay it, slow it down, or make it more hesitant. As the third of pragmatism's great patriarchs, John Dewey, remarked, "All thinking exercises by its very nature an inhibitory effect. It delays the operation of desire, and tends to call up new considerations which alter the nature of the action to which one felt originally impelled."[6]

II

Where, then, do we get our psychic energy for action if thought is not its effective motor? Affect is the pragmatist answer I suggest: our passionate nature, our feelings, emotions, or mood provide the dynamic spur or trigger for action, including the action involved in cognition and inquiry. James provides pragmatism's most vehement advocacy of affect's crucial role in action and thought. He strikingly characterizes pragmatism in affective terms as a philosophy of "the strenuous mood," a mood whose defining affect is that of vigorous active energy toward robust effort or impassioned strength longing to break forth into action. Distinguishing this mood from the "easy" or "easy-going" mood, James explains how it pushes us toward decisive action; and he explains how its "emotional excitability is exceedingly important in the composition of the energetic character" because of "its peculiarly destructive power over inhibitions" that so often impede our action.[7] For James, affect was not just the motor for action but also a generator of belief and of value. We believe in something, he argues in *The Principles of Psychology*, when "the belief chimes in with an emotional mood that currently dominates our consciousness" (*PP* 924). And in a much later essay he claims: "Our judgments concerning the worth of things, big or little, depend on the *feelings* the things arouse in us. . . . If we were radically feelingless, and if ideas were the only things our mind could entertain, we should lose all our likes and dislikes at a stroke, and be unable to point to any one situation or experience in life more valuable or significant than any other."[8]

Dewey follows James in recognizing that our mental life—including our beliefs, perceptions, values, and recollections—are significantly shaped by our moods and feelings, "strained through the mesh of imagination so as to suit the demands of the emotions." He therefore asserts that "Time and memory are true artists; they remold reality nearer to the heart's desire."[9] In contrast to "the traditional theory of a pure intellect," Dewey insists our cognitive processes are shaped by our organic needs and feelings, intimately linked "with affectivities, with cravings and desires" that are "deep-seated in the organism." In acknowledging thought's inhibitory effect on action, Dewey likewise posits the affectivity of desire as action's stimulus, since action's goals are also "set by the needs of our affective nature."[10]

Even C. S. Peirce, the most rationalist and logically oriented of the classical pragmatists, defends the cognitive and practical importance of sentiment. Not only affirming that inquiry, "which terminates in action, must begin in emotion," Peirce also "put forward three sentiments, namely interest in an indefinite community, recognition of the possibility of this interest being made supreme, and the hope in the unlimited continuance of intellectual activity, as indispensable requirements of logic" (*CP* 2.655). He boldly defended the core idea of sentimentalism, arguing (on evolutionary grounds) "that great respect should be paid to the natural judgments of the sensible heart," and further claiming that his own "strong feeling" of conviction for the theory of evolutionary love "is in itself . . . an argument of some weight in favor of the agapistic theory of evolution," insofar as his own "passionate predilection" for it "may be presumed to bespeak the normal judgment of the Sensible Heart" (*CP* 6.292).

For classical pragmatism, then, the heart was not a mere organ that pumped out blood and metaphorically pumped up feeling to trigger action, it denoted an affective dimension that was important and productive in shaping thought and judgment. After examining the crucial cognitive roles that affect plays in pragmatism's three founding fathers, I will explore how somaesthetics develops this appreciation of affect in the pragmatist aim of enhancing both action and thought. In doing so, as an auxiliary line of argument, I explain pragmatism's insistence on the aesthetic dimension of cognition, which is closely related yet distinguishable from the affective dimension.

III

Classical pragmatism's appreciation of the cognitive roles of feeling and aesthetic quality recalls an important earlier moment in American thought from which it could draw considerable power: the religious philosophy of Jonathan Edwards (1703–1758) and the valorization of sentiment in religion's Great Awakening, in which Edwards participated. Pragmatism's insistence on the role of affect and aesthetics in cognition constitutes a naturalization of Edwards's spiritual doctrines. Peirce's invocation of "the Sensible Heart" echoes the famous doctrine of "the sense of the heart" promulgated by Edwards.[11] Enchanted as a Yale student by John Locke's enlightenment philosophy, Edwards sought to balance the claims of Calvinist theology with logical reasoning and empirical evidence. In the same way, he tried to balance the claims of established theological doctrine with the rising wave of impassioned religious experience that was sweeping across the New England community in the Great Awakening, partly through Edwards's own powerful sermonizing.

Recognizing the dangers of emotion for encouraging superficial or fraudulent forms of religiosity, Edwards nonetheless insisted that "true religion . . . lies very much in the affection of the heart" (*E* 116) and that holy individuals were blessed with a special form of cognitive power (at once spiritual and affective) that he identified as "the sense of the heart" (*E* 272). He describes it as a new way of perceiving, given by God's grace to certain individuals and comparable to "a new sense" (*E* 32, 220) because it is so direct, immediate, and experiential. As its source is God, so its focus is the appreciation of the divine beauty of holy things. The sense of the heart "is some spiritual sense, taste or relish they have of the divine" (*E* 220), a special sense involving the "love of divine things," based on an appreciative understanding of the "beauty or loveliness" of such things, which is "the proper and immediate object" of that sense of the heart. "And therefore that kind of understanding or knowledge, which is the proper foundation of true religion, must be the knowledge of the loveliness of divine things" (*E* 271).

The sense of the heart is thus also a distinctively aesthetic sense, which underlies, shapes, and enlightens true spiritual understanding precisely by appreciating the beauty of holiness. "Spiritual understanding consists primarily in a sense of heart of that spiritual beauty. . . . There is a distinction to be made between a mere notional understanding, wherein the mind only beholds things in the exercise of a speculative faculty; and the sense of the heart, wherein the mind don't [*sic*] only speculate and behold, but relishes and feels" (*E* 272). Thus true "spiritual understanding does not consist in any new doctrinal knowledge, or in having suggested to the mind any new proposition" (*E* 278), but is rather affectively experiential, involving a direct perception of the divine that has "a new taste or relish of beauty and sweetness" (*E* 278). This experience has the cognitive power "to convince the mind of the truth of the gospel" (*E* 301) in an immediate way but also aids our conviction of holy truths indirectly by removing false prejudices against the holy and by energizing the mind with an intensity of focus that makes religious doctrine much more lively and compelling. As what is powerfully experienced "convinces the soul," so, more particularly, it is the aesthetic feeling of experienced beauty, harmony, and sweetness that attracts, compels, and satisfies the mind.

As the sense of the heart's aesthetic affect enhances our spiritual cognition, its emotional energy likewise motivates action. Edwards explicitly articulates the point I made earlier: a convincing philosophy of action or practice requires an essential affective dimension to motivate action and overcome reflection's typical inhibitory effects on acting. "The Author of the human nature has not only given affections to men, but has made 'em very much the spring of men's actions. . . . These affections we see to be the springs that set men agoing, in all the affairs of life, and engage them in all their pursuits." And Edwards applies this insight to religious practice as well: "In religious matters, the spring of their actions are very much religious affections," so no "change . . . of a religious nature" will come about in a person's mind "that had not his affections moved" (E 100–101). Consequently, we should do as much as possible to stimulate the affections, provided they are genuinely religious affections and not a false or superficial emotionalism. If what stimulates our religious feelings involve "just apprehensions, and a right judgment of them; the more they have a tendency to move the affections, the better" (E 122). But if true religious practice (like true religious understanding) depends on true religious affections, then the evidence for such genuine religious affections reciprocally depends primarily on practice.

Here Edwards clearly anticipates James's use of experiential fruits of practice as a cognitive criterion of truth, while invoking Christ's authoritative epistemic criterion (in Matthew 7:16) "to guide us in our judging of others' sincerity; viz. that we should judge of the tree chiefly by the fruit" (E 185). In other words, the best assurance of genuine religious feeling is not by words or even "by self-examination" but rather "by action" (E 195). As "the fruit of holy practice is the chief evidence of the truth of grace" (E 449) so, Edwards insists, "Christian practice is the chief of all the signs of saving grace" (E 450) or "the true and saving knowledge of God" (E 444). James, in *The Varieties of Religious Experience*,[12] explicitly cites this argument of Edwards, but Peirce (5.402n2) also alludes to the Matthew text when explaining his views on judgment by the fruits of practice. Rather than pursuing the complex question of historical influence any further, we should turn to the uses of affect (and aesthetic appreciation) in classical pragmatism's account of cognition and then in somaesthetics.

IV

The classical pragmatists used a variety of terms to denote affect ("emotion," "mood," "feeling," "sentiment," "passion," "heart," and others, including "affect" itself) but without distinguishing clearly between them. The current usage of these terms remains rather vague, not only in everyday discourse but even among academic specialists.[13] Nonetheless, it is helpful to note the more common ways they are distinguished. "Affect" typically serves as a global term that subsumes the others, while contemporary distinctions between "emotion," "feeling," and "mood" (the affective terms most significantly deployed by classical pragmatism) are often drawn as follows: Moods are more pervasive, enduring, and general than emotions or feelings.[14] Moreover, while emotions and feelings are typically regarded as intentional (in the sense of essentially being about something), moods "have no essential intentionality" in that they can exist without being about anything in particular but merely providing "the tone or color" for conscious states that do have an intentional object, such as an emotion of anger (or anxiety) at being slighted or a feeling of shame (or humor) at one's gaffe. Emotions are often thought to be clearer, more defined, and more intense than moods, but also more volatile in appearing and disappearing more suddenly. Finally, emotions and feelings are often regarded as more somatic or physiological in expression than moods, which by contrast are considered more cognitive and psychological, more a function of mind than body. This last proposed distinction would be problematic for classical pragmatism, which sees moods as significantly embodied. Moreover, the terms for mood in Romance languages (such as *humeur* or *humor*) clearly suggest embodiment because they derive from the ancient theory of the four bodily fluids (or humors) as determining our personality, outlook, and attitude.[15] Rather than trying to distinguish, classify, and define these different forms of affect, it is better to focus on the diverse pragmatist roles of affect in cognition. Consider the following seven ways, which I distinguish for clarity of exposition, but which clearly overlap.

1. Mood colors our sensibility, giving experience its basic tonality. James notes how mood shapes our perception and alters our appreciation of what we perceive. We experience things differently "when we are in different organic moods. What was bright and exciting becomes weary, flat, and unprofitable" (*PP* 226). This function of tonal quality is so basic that Peirce uses the notion of mood to characterize the most fundamental principles of experience: his "trichotomy" of first, second, and third that he ingeniously and systematically applies to the manifold fields of inquiry that he studied. In explaining his extensive "use of threefold divisions" he claims that "the ideas of first, second, third . . . [are] so broad that they may be looked upon rather as moods or tones of thought" (*CP* 1.355). Firstness is defined most basically as "presentness" in the most concrete sense of immediacy, of immediate "quality of feeling" without any conceptual or relational overlay (*CP* 1.304). To explain this notion, Peirce invokes the idea of "the poetic

mood which approaches the state in which the present appears as it is present" in itself, "regardless of the absent, regardless of past and future" (*CP* 5.44). If firstness is a feeling of presentness, then secondness is characterized by "the element of Struggle," the notion of resistance that reality poses to our immediate feelings, including our desires (*CP* 5.45). To get a sense of this strenuous effort or struggle, Peirce says, "Imagine yourself making a strong muscular effort, say that of pressing with all your might against a half-open door." This sense of "effort cannot exist without the experience of resistance," an experience that will have the affective tonality of resistance and struggle, which suggests the affectivity of the Jamesian strenuous mood (*CP* 5.45; *CP* 8.330).

2. A second crucial cognitive function of mood is to structure thought by felt affinity with the mood. This structuring involves not only the selection of elements for thinking but also their articulation, distinction, direction, sequencing, and unification in our experience. What guides the direction of our association of ideas in the stream of consciousness? What keeps our thought going in the desired route and sustains our focus on the chosen topic and its purpose? For James it is a background felt quality, "a mood of interest" with "a felt fringe of relations," and "however vague the mood, it will still act in the same way, throwing a mantle of felt affinity over such representations, entering the mind, as suit it, and tingeing with the feeling of tediousness or discord all those with which it has no concern" (*PP* 250). The mood welcomes ideas that harmonize with its tone and felt tendency, that give a "sense of furtherance" of its interest or concern, while it resists ideas that instead bring "discord" or "hindrance of the topic," that are uncongenial to the mood's "fringe of felt affinity." The most influential aspect of these fringes in structuring thought is not cognitive but rather affective and aesthetic, "the mere feeling of harmony or discord, of a right or wrong direction" (*PP* 250–51).

Dewey follows James closely on this point, making the immediate qualitative feeling of background mood not only the foundation of his aesthetics but also of his entire theory of experience and coherent thought. Mood provides the *felt quality* that unifies the diversity of our sensory input into a coherent experiential whole by selecting what fits that mood, just as it provides the directional tendency, focus, and energy for thought's progress toward its conclusion "Any predominant mood automatically excludes all that is uncongenial with it. . . . It reaches out tentacles for that which is cognate, for things which feed it and carry it to completion. Only when emotion dies or is broken to dispersed fragments can materials to which it is alien enter consciousness."[16] In affirming mood's structuring by selection, Dewey emphasizes its crucial role in providing unity to thought and experience, a unity whose paradigmatic expression is the enriching wholeness of artworks. Mood is the affective background that shapes the creation and appreciation of art: "Artist and perceiver alike begin with what may be called a total seizure, an inclusive qualitative whole," which (citing Friedrich Schiller) he describes as "a peculiar musical mood of mind" that precedes "the poetical idea" and its articulation into the concrete parts of the poem. Dewey moreover insists that not only does the mood "come first, but it persists as the substratum after distinctions [of the parts] emerge; in fact they emerge as its distinctions" (AE 195–96). In short, Dewey sees mood as providing the structuring background that contemporary philosophy of mind increasingly recognizes as necessary to our making sense of what is foregrounded as the content of our thought.

Mood's pervasive enveloping quality gives a felt sense of what elements of our experience should be articulated or foregrounded as the focal objects of consciousness; for example, what words or images should be selected as appropriate in creating a poem or highlighted in our attention of reading it, and what ideas in the work should be individuated and how they should be sequentially organized. "The undefined pervasive quality of an experience is that which binds together all the defined elements, the objects of which we are focally aware, making them whole" (AE 198). Our evidence for this, Dewey argues, "is our constant sense of things as belonging or not belonging to the work, of relevancy, a sense which is immediate" rather than "a product of reflection," even though reflection may be used to formulate and judge the value of that thing perceived as "pertinent" or not (AE 198). For such reflection itself needs to be guided, and what guides it must be the background mood-structured unifying quality of which we have an "immediate" sense (AE 198).

Although its enriching, enlivening, unifying power is particularly evident in artworks and essentially defines aesthetic experience, Dewey sees mood's unifying background quality as necessary for all coherent thought and experience. This is why he distinctively elevates aesthetic experience as the key to understanding experience as a whole (AE 278). In art, this qualitative feeling likewise provides the animating energy and emotional color to the different elements and phases of aesthetic experience as well as its unifying direction: "It enlivens and animates, it is the spirit of the work of art" (AE 197). As a "vague and undefined" background, this qualitative feeling cannot be named or articulated as a specific part of the work, though it shapes, selects, unifies, and animates all those parts; and as the soul or spirit "in which the particular work is composed and expressed," it is what "stamps [the work] with individuality." Like the firstness of Peirce, for Dewey, this "penetrating quality that runs through all the parts of a work of art and binds them into an individualized whole can only be emotionally 'intuited,'" that is, "can only be felt" or "immediately experienced" rather than properly known (*AE* 196–97).

3. By selecting ideas in terms of their harmony with its affect, mood shapes both intellectual content and emotional reactions. This explains mood's power to endure. It selects ideas with emotional associations that suit and sustain it. "The same objects do not recall the same associates when we are cheerful as when we are melancholy," writes James. "Nothing, in fact, is more striking than our utter inability to keep up trains of joyous imagery when we are depressed in spirits. Storm, darkness, war, images of disease, poverty, and perishing afflict unremittingly the imaginations of melancholiacs." In contrast, "those of sanguine temperament," find that their thought "association [immediately] dances off to flowers and sunshine." Even the same person will react with different feelings to the same object if she encounters it in a very different mood. James confesses how his emotional reaction to *The Three Guardsmen* changed radically when he read it while "depressed with seasickness" and thus unable to appreciate its "joyous animal spirits" (*PP* 543).

Dewey follows James not only in noting how "mood automatically excludes all that is uncongenial with it," but also in recognizing the problem this poses for the will (*AE* 73). Pragmatism recognizes that humans are more essentially active than rational creatures (as survival requires more action than thought), so consciousness is implicitly impulsive, and our natural tendency is to act on what comes to mind. If mood's affect selects ideas in terms of their congeniality and reinforcement of the mood's tonality and direction, then to break the hold of that mood by introducing a thought of opposing, uncongenial tonality requires a special effort, one involving a feeling capable of holding that opposing idea in consciousness and breaking through the formerly dominant mood. Thus, in contrast to the classical view of the will as using reason to overcome feeling and desire, the pragmatist recognizes that will power involves generating enough feeling or desire to keep "the idea of the wise action to stay before the mind" when the prevailing mood is uncongenial to it and seeks to dismiss or smother it (*PP* 1167).

4. Affect shapes not only our ideas and emotions but also our beliefs, the ideas that we hold true and that guide our action. This is because

feeling, more than reason, makes us believe; our basic sense of reality, James argues, is a more affective than reflective affair. In the ordinary sense "in which one thing is said to have more reality than another, and to be more believed, reality means simply relation to our emotional and active life" (*PP* 924). Generally, we believe in something when "the belief chimes in with an emotional mood that currently dominates our consciousness," and even unreasonable beliefs can be held tenaciously when their emotional appeal is very powerful. For most people, "To conceive with passion is *eo ipso* to affirm," and to resist this emotional pull by critically holding back assent "is the highest result of education" and self-discipline (*PP* 936–37). Here again Dewey echoes his mentor: "The standard used to measure the value of the suggestions that spring to mind is not congruity with fact but emotional congeniality. . . . Are they consonant with the prevailing mood?"[17] James, however, remains the most radical pragmatist champion of affect's power of conviction, even claiming (wrongly in my opinion) that "wherever there is a conflict of opinion and difference of vision, we are bound to believe that the truer side is the side that feels the more, and not the side that feels the less."[18]

5. Feeling, for James, not only trumps rationality in our habits of belief; it even underlies our very sense of the rational and our power to reason. A thinker knows when he has found a rational solution "as he recognizes everything else, by certain subjective marks with which it affects him," by a certain feeling that James calls "the sentiment of rationality." It involves "a strong feeling of ease, peace, rest," deriving from achieving a desired simplification, order, unity, and clarity. "The transition from a state of puzzle and perplexity to rational comprehension is full of lively relief and pleasure," and James identifies this pleasure with "the two great aesthetic needs of our logical nature, the need of unity and the need of clearness."[19] In its role as the engine of thought, feeling provides the necessary energy and focus for reasoning: "If focalization of brain activity is the fundamental fact of reasonable thought, we see why intense interest or concentrated passion makes us think so much more truly and profoundly. . . . When not 'focalized,' we are scatter-brained; but when thoroughly impassioned, we never wander from the point. None but congruous and relevant images arise" (*PP* 989–90).

Contemporary neuroscience confirms this view. Since there is no "Cartesian theater" where all brain input meets together for simultaneous processing, human thinking works "by synchronizing sets of neural activity in separate brain regions" through "time binding" of images in different places "within approximately the same window of time." But this requires "maintaining focused activity at different [brain] sites for as long as necessary for meaningful combinations to be made and for reasoning and decision making to take place."[20] The affective energy of our emotions, feelings, and moods not only serves "as a booster for continued working memory and attention" but also facilitates "deliberation by highlighting some options" while eliminating others in terms of their fit with our background mood and its sense of direction as expressed in vaguely felt bodily feelings or "somatic markers" (*DE* 174, 198). As Antonio Damasio argues, pure rationalist cold-bloodedness, like the cold-bloodedness of his brain-damaged patients, would make the "mental landscape" of working memory not only "hopelessly flat" but also "too shifty and unsustained for the time required . . . of the reasoning process," so we would "lose track" or direction and fail to achieve an effective rational result (*DE* 51, 172–73).

6. Affect, as noted earlier, functions as a dynamic force to stimulate action. The mere thought of an action is not enough to produce it. Reflection, deliberation, and reasoning instead inhibit action. If James famously asserts that "consciousness is in its very nature impulsive" and naturally leads to action, then this is because he identifies consciousness with feeling rather than mere thought and identifies feeling as the dynamic motor. He adds the proviso that the feeling of consciousness "must be sufficiently intense . . . to excite movement," noting that the "intensity of some feelings is practically apt to be below the "discharging point" for action (*PP* 1134, 1142). Promoting strong enough feeling for a thought to generate action, the strenuous mood also enhances will power; this is because "true strength of will," Dewey argues, works not by simply repressing desire with critical thought's inhibitory effect. Rather it "brings thought and desire together" by attaching desire to a "better end which thought discloses," thus guiding action with "thoughtful desire." The feeling of desire "provides the drive" or motor, since "mere thinking would not lead to action; thinking must be taken up into vital impulse and desire in order to have body and weight in action" (*E* 190).

7. As thought is essentially affective, there is no dichotomy between thought and action. For pragmatism, cognitive life is fundamentally active and not merely reactive as the traditional stimulus-response model suggests. Long before enactive theories became popular, Dewey argued that perception of a stimulus always already involves actions of attention (that in turn always involve somatic movements or adjustments, even if only very subtle ones) as well as actions (such as locomotion or reaching) that bring us to encounter

that stimulus and shape it as a stimulus. For pragmatism, then, action must not be narrowly construed in terms of practical tasks. All inquiry (whether scientific or ordinary problem solving) is itself a form of action that needs the energy of affect as a dynamic motor. In fact, pragmatism's defining account of inquiry, as formulated by Peirce, portrays inquiry in affective terms as a struggle to remove the troubling irritation of doubt, though not the Cartesian methodological doubt that abstractly questions everything we do not know with certainty. "There must be a real and living doubt," Peirce insists, for us to engage in active inquiry (*CP* 5.376). This "real and living doubt" has a distinctive affective, sensory dimension that is rooted in our Darwinian somatic heritage, as is our need to resolve doubt with belief to guide our action. Because we need to act in order to survive and we need beliefs to direct our action, we cannot long remain in a state of real doubt. Doubt is therefore experienced on a sensory, somatic level as a disturbing irritation that the organism must remove by reaching a belief that ends the irritating, paralyzing state of doubt and brings relief by removing an obstacle for action. As Peirce puts it, "Doubt is an uneasy and dissatisfied state from which we struggle to free ourselves and pass into the state of belief; while the latter is a calm and satisfactory state which we do not wish to avoid, or to change," because it brings a feeling of relief and thus affectively soothes us while providing guidance for action. Doubt "stimulates us to inquiry until it is destroyed. . . . The irritation of doubt causes a struggle to attain a state of belief. I shall term this struggle Inquiry" (*CP* 5.373–74).

Rather than firm knowledge, our primary goal in inquiry is achieving an improved feeling: namely, the calmer pleasanter mood of belief. "The irritation of doubt is the only immediate motive for the struggle to attain belief. It is certainly best for us that our beliefs should be such as may truly guide our actions so as to satisfy our desires; and this reflection will make us reject every belief which does not seem to have been so formed as to insure this result. But it will only do so by creating a doubt in the place of that belief. With the doubt, therefore, the struggle begins, and with the cessation of doubt it ends" (*CP* 5.375). In short, affect guides inquiry not only by stimulating it through unsatisfying irritation but also by marking its conclusion with the positive, satisfactory feeling of belief.

V

Aesthetic considerations crucially contribute to the satisfactory affect of belief, where such satisfying affect is not simply an accompanying product of belief but part of its generating cause. Among classical pragmatists, James and Dewey seem to be the most explicitly insistent on the role of aesthetic considerations in cognition. Recall James's notion of "the sentiment of rationality," defined as the "strong feeling of ease, peace, rest" that is "full of lively relief and pleasure" and that is explained aesthetically in terms of "the two great aesthetic needs of our logical nature, the need of unity and the need of clearness."[21] In *The Principles of Psychology*, he reaffirms the multifaceted cognitive role of the aesthetic. The basic desire to classify that is so essential to logical and scientific thinking stems from "a great aesthetic delight" in order and patterns (*PP* 1242). At a higher level, the aesthetic plays a central role along with affect in theory choice. "That theory will be most generally believed which, besides offering us objects able to account satisfactorily for our sensible experience, also offers those which are most interesting, those which appeal most urgently to our aesthetic, emotional, and active needs" (*PP* 940). Thus, James continues, "The two great aesthetic principles, of richness and of ease, dominate our intellectual as well as our sensuous life" (*PP* 943). What we want are theories that are "rich, simple, and harmonious," which sounds like the classic definition of beauty as unity in variety. "The richness," James argues, "is got by including all the facts of sense in the scheme; the simplicity, by deducing them out of the smallest possible number of . . . primordial entities." Simplicity provides the aesthetic sense of ease because it tends to make things clearer and more "definite," whereas excessive complexity strains our limited powers of attention and memory (*PP* 943–44). Dewey similarly insists that both logical reasoning and science are guided aesthetically by "imagination, under the influence of desire, in re-creating the world into a more orderly place" through "the production of relations of consistency and order" like those that "operate in artistic structures" (*AE* 107). James explains the differences between rival philosophies as expressing different "tastes" or basic "aesthetic discords," while Dewey likewise describes philosophy as an "excursion of the imagination" whose meaning is "something comparable to the meaning of Athenian civilization or of a drama or a lyric."[22]

These pragmatists explain the structure of thinking in aesthetic terms. The selection and individuation of elements in our thought process, their relevant aspects, relational organization, associations, and the directional flow of our streams of thought are all claimed to depend on whether they harmonize nicely with the prevailing mood or pervasive unifying quality that governs the thinking. Insisting that this immediate unifying quality is essentially aesthetic in character, Dewey asserts that all coherent thought and experience must have a fundamentally aesthetic dimension.

James, for his part, brings the principle of aesthetic shaping into our most basic perceptions. From the vast array of incoming sensations, attention selects only "special groups of sensible qualities, which happen practically or aesthetically to interest us" and which we therefore identify as "things" and their properties. From all the shades of color or shapes of a thing we may perceive in different perceptions of an object, its real color, "its real size, its real shape, etc. are but optical sensations selected out of thousands of others, because they have aesthetic characteristics which appeal to our convenience or delight" (*PP* 274, 934). Cognition is inherently aesthetic as well as affective. If James and Dewey explain these matters naturalistically in terms of evolution and organic needs, they nonetheless share the basic thesis of Edwards: the sense of the heart, which perceives truth through affect, is also a sense of beauty whose experienced aesthetic delight commands our attentive focus and carries considerable power of conviction.[23]

VI

Somaesthetics, like cognitive science, is an interdisciplinary field. Briefly defined as the critical study and ameliorative cultivation of the experience and use of the body as a locus of sensory-aesthetic appreciation (aesthesis) and creative self-fashioning, somaesthetics embraces a wide variety of disciplines that structure somatic experience and can improve it, thus integrating theory and practice. If analytic somaesthetics involves the descriptive inquiry into the nature of bodily perceptions and somatic practices (and their various cognitive, social, and cultural uses and values), the other two main branches of the field are distinctively oriented toward practice. Pragmatic somaesthetics involves the normative inquiry into methods of somatic improvement and their comparative critique (including a critique of the values embedded in those methods), and practical somaesthetics is the actual practice of these meliorative somatic methods or disciplines. Along with these three interrelated branches, somaesthetics involves three somewhat overlapping dimensions: experiential (focusing on inner somatic experience), representational (focused on outer bodily form or appearance), and performative (focused on successful somatic performance).

Recognizing the essentially embodied nature of affect, somaesthetics argues that if affect shapes our actions (including those actions that serve the acquisition of knowledge), then enhanced awareness of our affect can provide better understanding of our actions, which in turn can help improve our conduct and knowledge. Key to this somaesthetic argument is that affect is essentially embodied and therefore that a heightened, cultivated body consciousness—one more aware of our bodily feelings—can provide reliable evidence of affect that we might not otherwise notice although we may be in the very grip of it. Consciousness of our breathing can help us become aware we are angry or anxious when we were previously unaware of these feelings and thus vulnerable to their misdirection in hasty conclusions or misguided action. Similarly, a cultivated sense of proprioception can help us recognize that our body posture and tonus express aggressive tenseness that we may not otherwise notice but would wish to conceal. If improved somatic sensibility augments our emotional knowledge, then it can likewise improve the conduct that emotion shapes. The somaesthetically trained individual who notices her nervousness from her rapid, shallow respiration can alter her breathing pattern to induce tranquility, giving her a steadier hand in action or a more judicious process of thinking or speaking. Similarly, somaesthetic mastery, by enabling an individual to relax an undesired postural tension, can also correct the undesirable affect it expresses and therefore avoid the undesirable conduct that such affect would tend to induce. The reciprocal causal connections between affect and action does not imply a vicious circle, because our affective consciousness is not monolithic. Somaesthetic sensitivity can discern strands of feeling or elements of desire that lie outside our current affective focus and that could alter that mood if we bring our attentive focus toward those currently marginal affective elements.

How does the somaesthetic quest for improved experience involve a distinctively aesthetic dimension? One notable way is by using our felt sense of beauty, harmony, grace, and pleasure to assess the quality and ease of our movements, and thus the efficiency or efficacy of actions performed through those movements. Kinetically efficient movements feel graceful, unified, easy, and harmonious rather than jerky, effortful, and discontinuous. We have a pleasurable aesthetic sense of ease and grace when our movements are very smooth, fluid, and agile; just as we feel a certain uneasy, awkward feeling when we perform a movement very clumsily or ineptly. Part of the pleasure in watching dance, figure skating, diving, and other athletic activities is that we empathetically experience (allegedly though mirror-neuron networks) something like the proprioceptive pleasure of performing these aesthetically demanding yet elegantly executed movements. People with enhanced somaesthetic awareness can be more penetrating and subtle in their perceptions of grace and awkwardness in movement. Even in a generally graceful arc of movement, such people can proprioceptively notice the particular points where its smooth fluidity is slightly flawed through some jerkiness, hesitation, trembling or forced effort (which is sometimes noticeable by its effect on one's respiration, by a momentary holding of one's breath because of effort). Once we discern the points where a movement is awkwardly performed, we can more effectively work on smoothing those rough edges to render the movement both more aesthetically enjoyable and more kinetically efficient. Cultivated somaesthetic awareness, moreover, enables us to try out the feel of different ways of performing the same action (e.g., deploying slightly different postures or initiating the movement from different body parts, such as reaching for an object by first shifting the pelvis rather than first extending the arm) and then feeling which of these different ways of performing the movement feels and works best.

Although somaesthetics was most strongly inspired by my personal experimentations in somatic disciplines and my professional training as a somatic educator/therapist in the Feldenkrais Method, pragmatist philosophy (along with the ancient idea of philosophy as an embodied art of living) was a key resource for its theoretical development. Even somaesthetics' insistence on actual bodily training found encouragement in the classical pragmatist tradition, for all three pragmatist patriarchs seemed to affirm the importance of somatic cultivation (including disciplines of heightened body consciousness) for the practice of philosophy, though they affirmed it in different ways. Dewey offers the most explicit advocacy of heightened somatic awareness through disciplined training in critical reflective body consciousness, which he learned to appreciate through his extensive study of the Alexander Technique. Dewey not only prefaced and celebrated F. M. Alexander's books, he also received countless therapeutic training sessions with this technique (from Alexander and others), attributing even his own healthy longevity to Alexander's lessons. Like Alexander, Dewey argued that somaesthetic training was necessary for overcoming our bad habits and "debauched kinaesthetic systems" that give "defective registrations" of our actual somatic "feeling-tones," and that such training in reflective body consciousness could help provide the "art of conscious control" needed for successful behavior and true freedom in practical life.[24]

Although James sharply warned against reflective attention to bodily feelings in practical life, he was a fierce advocate and master of reflective somatic introspection for research in psychology, demonstrating the formative somatic dimensions of our emotions, stream of thought, and sense of self, time, and space. Though he recognized the scientific limits of introspection, it formed (along with physiology) a major pillar of his psychological research. Though "difficult and fallible" as "all observation of whatever kind" is, James insists (with his unfortunately typical overstatement) that "Introspective Observation is what we have to rely on first and foremost and always" in studying mental life (*PP* 185, 191). In defending the significant role of bodily feelings in our mental life against critics who challenged their effective presence, James argued that those critics were simply insufficiently aware or inadequately skilled in somatic introspection to notice those feelings. He concluded that we cognitive researchers must therefore "sharpen our introspection" to improve our acuity in body consciousness and should collect such improved introspective observations to advance our inquiries (*PP* 357, 360–62, 1070).

Peirce, the first American to publish a paper in the new science of experimental psychology, strongly criticized the introspective approach when it was construed as reflectively analyzing our "immediate feelings" by "direct observations of the operations of the mind," which Peirce argued was "pure delusion" precisely because "immediate consciousness" as an immediate present cannot be the genuine object of report or analysis, which are always necessarily mediated through language and in time (*CP* 1.310; *CP* 7.376; *CP* 7.465). But when introspection is understood as mediated retrospection on the immediate past (or what James called "the specious present"), then Peirce argued that such introspective self-questioning "on what seems to have been present from the standpoint of subsequent reflection," though often "mendacious," is also often "the only witness there is" on many psychological questions. Thus, on many psychological topics, we must "rely entirely" on it, while still seeking "here and there perhaps some secondary aid" from impersonal experimentation (*CP* 7.420; *CP* 7.584; *CP* 1.579–80).

Like James, Peirce insists that to sharpen our capacities for such introspective cognitive research, we must sharpen our acuity in observing our feelings. In the context of a discussion of aesthetic qualities and their associated feelings, Peirce recommends a systematic training in discriminating and sharpening one's perception of feelings, much in the spirit of somaesthetic training: "I have gone through a systematic course of training in recognizing my feelings. I have worked with intensity for so many hours a day every day for long years to train myself to this; and it is a training which I would recommend to all of you. The artist has such a training; but most of his effort goes to reproducing in one form or another what he sees or hears, which is in every art a very complicated trade; while I have striven simply to see what it is that I see" (*CP* 5.12).[25]

Somaesthetics' project of cultivating heightened skills of body awareness to improve our understanding of mental life clearly finds support in classical pragmatism, but how can it be applied to contemporary research in cognitive science? We conclude with three brief suggestions. First, cognitive science should not simply tolerate but also welcome first-person introspective testimonies in its scientific investigations, and somaesthetics can make those testimonies more accurate or precise. There is already growing interest in integrating "third-person data about behavior and first-person data about subjective experience" and increased exploration of different first-person methodologies to do so.[26] But since the value of first-person testimony depends on its quality of accuracy and clarity, we must explore and cultivate the best methods for making such testimonies more acute by developing heightened skills of self-observation. Francisco Varela and his disciples, for example, propose neurophenomenology as one such method, deriving it from the phenomenological tradition of Husserl and Merleau-Ponty. Somaesthetics draws on phenomenology but builds heavily on the embodied pragmatist tradition while deploying a variety of techniques to cultivate such improved skills of somatic awareness, including interactive digital technologies.[27] Although experimental techniques today are far superior and far more wide-ranging than they were when the classical pragmatists trained their skills of somatic self-observation, there remain many issues that are technically too difficult to successfully test with our currently available techniques and instruments and where we may have to rely on first-person introspective accounts of consciousness.

Second, somaesthetic training in skills of somatic awareness could be useful for cognitive science not only in preparing better experimental subjects to provide more accurate testimony of first-person experiences. It could also provide researchers new tools and insights for designing and interpreting experiments that deploy somatic awareness for exploring questions concerning our mental life and modes of action. Third, if we understand science in the broad sense, as going into fields of knowledge beyond the realm of controlled laboratory experiment, then heightened skills of somaesthetic awareness and reflection can enrich our knowledge of cognitive functioning in everyday, real-life situations where mental life is often significantly different (and significantly more important to understand) than it is in the very limited sphere of experience and action found in controlled laboratory experiments. Pragmatism should be most concerned with such real-life situations because they are what its meliorist agenda seeks to improve through a better understanding of them. Somaesthetics can in turn improve such understanding by sharpening our somatic perceptions and knowledge of how we experience those situations.

II

Ethics and Politics

Chapter Five

Postmodern Ethics and the Art of Living

I

In a brief and bracketed interjection in proposition 6.421 of his *Tractatus Logico-Philosophicus*, Wittgenstein asserts that "ethics and aesthetics are one."[1] The message appears as cryptic as it is bold, pronounced parenthetically with no further clarification or justification, in that austere economy of pregnant minimalist expression so characteristic of the modernist style. What the young Wittgenstein meant can best be surmised by looking not only at the *Tractarian* context but at his earlier *Notebooks*,[2] where the dictum originally appeared along with some sketchy elucidation. Apparently, he wished to convey the idea that ethics and aesthetics were fundamentally the same in at least three significant respects. First, both involve seeing things *sub specie aeternitatis*—that is, transcendentally, "from outside," in "such a way [that] they have the whole world as background." In aesthetics, "the work of art is the object seen *sub specie aeternitatis*; . . . [while in ethics] the good life is the world seen *sub specie aeternitatis*. This is the connection between art and ethics" (*N* 83). Second, both ethics and aesthetics concern the realm of "the mystical," not only because their statements (being neither empirical nor logical propositions) belong to the unsayable, but also because both employ that transcendental global perspective he associates with the mystical and with "absolute value."[3] Third, both are essentially concerned with happiness. As "the artistic way of looking at things . . . looks at the world with a happy eye," since "art is gay," so ethics amounts to the question of being "either happy or unhappy; that is all. It can be said: good or evil do not exist" (*N* 74, 86).

Whatever sense and cogency we find in these three connections, they hardly establish the utter unity of ethics and aesthetics. Moreover, though the doctrine is not repudiated (as so many *Tractarian* doctrines are) in Wittgenstein's later philosophy, neither is it explicitly affirmed or developed. Indeed, one might argue that his later, decentered, nontranscendental, and pluralistic philosophy of language games, which Jean-François Lyotard claims as a major source of postmodernist thought,[4] would be hostile to any homogenizing unification of the ethical and aesthetic domains. For these domains surely appear to involve somewhat different language games.[5] On the other hand, the substantial underlying connection of ethics and aesthetics is strongly implied in Wittgenstein's later account of aesthetic appreciation. For such appreciation is seen as not reducible to isolated, formulizable critical rules and expressions of approval, but rather as deeply and necessarily situated in a complex cultural background, entwined in and shaped by ways of living that cannot but include an ethical dimension.[6] If we had to assign Wittgenstein a final position on the "oneness" of ethics and aesthetics, it would probably be the balanced if uninspiring view that they are neither fully united and identical nor completely distinct.

Having paid our exegetical dues for appropriating his language, we now turn to why Wittgenstein's parenthetical phrase is today so meaningful. The answer, I believe, is that the dictum "ethics and aesthetics are one" gives pointed expression to important insights and problems of both aesthetic and ethical theorizing in our postmodern age. It denies modernism's aesthetic ideology of artistic purism, common to modernist poetry and to the formalist and abstract movements in plastic art. Instead, it implies that such isolationist ideology is no longer viable now that the traditional compartmentalizations of knowledge and culture threaten to disintegrate into manifold forms of interdisciplinary activity. In such conditions, there is not only room, but also need, for a criticism of art that is morally, socially, and politically motivated, just as there is need for art itself to be so motivated. I devote this essay not to the ethico-political in art but rather to its no less significant converse, the aestheticization of the ethical. The idea here, to adumbrate its more salient aspects in a phrase, is that aesthetic considerations are or should be crucial and ultimately perhaps paramount in determining how we choose to lead or shape our lives and how we assess what a good life is. It fleshes out Wittgenstein's ambiguous dictum that ethics and aesthetics are one by erecting the aesthetic as the proper ethical ideal, the preferred model and criterion of assessment for the good life. Such aestheticization is understandably directed primarily at what might be called the private ethical realm, the question of how the individual should shape her life to fulfill herself as a person. But it can be very naturally extended to the public realm, to questions of what a good society should be like. At the very least, one could argue that a good society must be such as to ensure the possibility, if not the productive fostering, of an aesthetically satisfying life for its constituent individuals. Moreover, good societies have often been characterized in aesthetic terms, conceiving such societies as organic unities with an optimal balance of unity in variety—that classic and still potent definition of the beautiful.

If the aestheticization of the ethical is a dominant (though hardly unprecedented)[7] current in our postmodern age, it is perhaps more evident in our everyday lives and the popular imagination of our culture than in academic philosophy. We find it in our culture's preoccupation with glamour and gratification, with personal appearance and enrichment. The celebrated figures of our time are not men of valor or women of virtue but those significantly called the "beautiful people." We are less inclined to the imitation of Christ than to imitating the cosmetics and fashion of the pop celebrity Madonna; no one today reads the lives of the saints for edification and example, but the biographies of film stars and the success stories of corporate billionaires are perennial bestsellers. However, the postmodernist ethics of taste is not without philosophical apologists. It finds clear support in Michel Foucault (with his ideal of "an aesthetics of existence") and in other continental thinkers in the Nietzschean tradition. But I will concentrate primarily on its expression in recent Anglo-American philosophy. My major focus is Richard Rorty, perhaps the most outspoken and outrageous philosophical exponent of America's popular imagination and one who explicitly advocates "the aesthetic life" as the good life. For Rorty, "this aesthetic life" is one of "private perfection" and "self-creation," a life motivated by the "desire to enlarge oneself," "the desire to embrace more and more possibilities" and escape the limiting "inherited descriptions" of oneself—a desire expressed in "the aesthetic search for novel experiences and novel language."[8] In other words, aesthetic gratification, self-enrichment, and self-creation are sought not only through actual experiments in living but also through the more timid option of employing "new vocabularies of moral reflection" so as to characterize our actions and self-image in a more freshly appealing and richer way (R 11).

Rorty's aestheticized ethic of private perfection is coupled with an affirmation of liberalism (with its tolerance of individuality, distaste for cruelty, and its procedural justice that "aims at human equality" [*CIS* 88]) as the best form of public morality and social solidarity. But he does not think that these private and public ideals can be fused in one theory or quest; and it is clearly the aestheticized private ethic that he privileges as giving real content to life, while liberalism merely provides the necessary stable framework of social organization for us to pursue in peace and comfort our individual aesthetic goals. For Rorty explicitly urges us to see the prime value and "aim of a just and free society as letting its citizens be as privatistic, 'irrationalist,' and aestheticist as they please so long as they do it on their own time—causing no harm to others and using no resources needed by those less advantaged" (*CIS* xiv). Rorty's aestheticization of the ethical presents, I believe, a promising direction, even if it needs to be criticized and modified in important ways. To assess it, we also need to set it in the context of other arguments for and visions of the aesthetic life.

II

Why should postmodern philosophy aestheticize the ethical? The rise of the ethics of taste can be largely explained as the result of the fall of more traditional models of the ethical. Just as, once born, we have to live our lives in some fashion, so once we start reflecting ethically on how to live we must reflect in some fashion. Erosion of faith in traditional ethical theories left an ethical horror vacui that the ethics of taste naturally rushed to fill. Rorty seems close to saying this when he argues that after Galileo, Darwin, and Freud "neither the religious nor the secular and liberal morality seems possible, and no third alternative has emerged"—except, it would seem, for the aesthetic one that he goes on to advocate.[9] The most powerful reasons impelling contemporary philosophers to reject traditional ethics appear to derive from two general philosophical attitudes. The first is a historicist and pluralist anti-essentialism as to human nature, while the second perceives severe limitations in morality that make it clearly inadequate for a full-blown satisfying ethic. We can describe this second view as the underdetermination of ethics by morality. Each of these attitudes involves a few aspects that merit attention.

1. Traditionally, ethical theories have sought to justify not only themselves but the whole ethical enterprise from what Bernard Williams calls "an Archimedean point: something to which even the amoralist or skeptic is committed but which, properly thought through, will show us that he is irrational, or unreasonable, or at any rate mistaken."[10] Typically,

such foundationalist theories base themselves on general theories of human nature, trying to derive what life is essentially good for humans from what is essential to or essential in humankind, and recognizing that any ethical "ought" depends on some nonethical "can." The desire for pleasure or happiness and the capacity for and exercise of rational thought and action have been the most familiar and compelling candidates for such essential features. In synthesizing the two, as well as in giving a much more concrete and substantial picture of what constitutes the good life for man (though not for women and slaves), the ethical theory of Aristotle enjoys an advantage over that of Kant. For while Kant's epistemology fully recognizes both the sensuous and the rational character of human nature, his distinctive ethic rests on a very purified concept of man as rational agent. Such an agent, to realize his rational essence, requires some freedom of choice in action, and he properly exercises it ethically by choosing on the basis of rational, universalizable principles without regard to contingent considerations of prudential expediency and sentiment.

The particular problems with the Aristotelian and Kantian enterprises, many of which Williams neatly outlines, need not concern us here. The more basic problem that pervades these and similar attempts to ground ethics in an account of a person's intrinsic or essential nature is our strong postmodern suspicion that there really is no such thing. We have an even stronger suspicion that there is no ahistorical essence that is both universally found and ontologically fixed in humankind and yet is also determinate and substantial enough to generate or justify, by mere logical derivation or elaboration, a definite ethical theory. We have come to see that even our best candidates for essential status, like rationality and happiness, seem promising only as long as we don't probe too deeply into the culturally and historically divergent accounts of what in fact really constitutes these things.

The lack of an ahistorical, ontologically given human essence does not, however, foreclose all possibility of deriving an ethical theory from essential human nature. For that project could perhaps get by with some nonontological but still transhistorical, cross-cultural human essence; some sort of amalgam of linguistic, cultural, and biological universals found to be present in and necessary to human life whenever and wherever it has flourished, and one from which could be projected a definite and coherent picture of what constitutes the good life. But skepticism here is no less potent in the face of obvious historical and cultural divergence. Even in what we conceive as the same cultural tradition—say, that which T. S. Eliot once personified as "the mind of Europe"[11]—we find very different answers to the question of what is essential to or desirable for a properly human life. Moreover, given what Lyotard diagnosed as our postmodern suspicion of grand legitimating narratives,[12] we cannot try to explain away such divergence by appeal to the variant but progressive manifestation of the human spirit in search of liberation and/or perfection.

Yet, though we may reject both ahistorical and transhistorical human essence as a ground for some universal ethic there still remains the more modest option of generating an essential ethical theory for our own specific age and culture. This "limited" aim is surely what we most want, since what we want to know is how to live our own lives rather than those of our ancestors or descendants, which are obviously not ours to live. But even drastically narrowing the focus to contemporary American society, we find there is just too much significant variety to talk confidently of any formative essence that could tell us what to seek in seeking the good life. We are perhaps unified in a commitment to freedom and opportunity for the pursuit of happiness. But such notions, as communitarian critics of liberalism frequently complain, are helplessly vague and abstract; and the unity they apparently provide quickly disintegrates into rival visions of what freedom, happiness, and opportunity really mean.

There are at least two good reasons why not even such localized human essences can be found. First, not only in America but in any advanced civilization, there is a very high order of division of labor, a division of occupational roles. The notion of a general functional essence of man such as Aristotle and other ethical theorists assumed and built on seems no longer viable when men *and women* have so many different functional occupations that are so difficult to reconcile. How do we reconcile the functional essence of the farmer and the stockbroker, the creative artist and the factory hand, the priest and the cosmetician, the scientist and the casino operator? More disturbing is the fact that we not only collectively experience a conflict of divergent functional essences, we feel it just as powerfully within our individual selves. The conflict between a woman's functional essence as defined by her profession and that defined by her role as mother is perhaps the most familiar and acute of such contemporary problems of identity. But there are countless other examples of how our professional roles or self-definitions sharply conflict or simply do not coherently mesh with our self-definition as friends, family, or political agents, thus making it seem impossible to find a functional essence for the individual in some coherent amalgam of his or her social roles. To say that a postmodern cannot generate a general or even a personal ethic from his or her specific functional role because we all inhabit collectively and individually a plurality of inadequately integrated roles is to say with Wittgenstein and Lyotard that we inhabit such a motley variety of language games and are shaped by so many forms of discourse that we no longer can say definitively who we are. We cannot tell what is the good life for us, because the nature of us is so questionable and unsteady with our changing roles and self-representations. It is questionable, Rorty would argue, because it is not definitively there to be discovered, but instead open to be made and shaped, and should therefore be shaped aesthetically.

Moreover, according to Rorty, not only is it pointless to try to penetrate our social roles to find a common human essence that is not there, but even the idea of an underlying coherent individual essence of particular personhood (one's own true self) is a myth that Freud effectively exploded. One's own self or personality is instead revealed as an uneasy combination of a number of conflicting (conscious and unconscious) "quasi persons" formed through historical contingencies and composed of "incompatible systems of belief and desire," a view that discredits the whole idea of a person's one "true self" (R 5, 9, 19). Rather than something unified and consistent emerging from an autonomous, stable, and rational core, the self is "centerless," a collection of "quasi selves," the product of "random assemblages of contingent and idiosyncratic needs," shaped and modified by "a host of idiosyncratic, accidental episodes" transformed by distorting memory and multiple vocabularies (R 4, 12, 14). "Anything from the sound of a word through the color of a leaf to the feel of a piece of skin can, as Freud showed us, serve to dramatize and crystallize a human being's sense of self-identity. . . . Any seemingly random constellation of such things can set the tone of a life" (CIS 37).

For Rorty, this Freudian decentering, multiplication, and randomization of the self "opened up new possibilities for the aesthetic life" as an ethic. For if there is no true self to discover and conform to, then the most promising models of "moral reflection and sophistication" become "self-creation" and "self-enlargement" rather than "self-knowledge" and "purification" (R 11–12). Anti-essentialism as to human nature thus leads to an ethics of taste. It would be wrong, however, to see this as a logical derivation. If human nature's absence of essence means it implies no determinate ethic, it therefore cannot imply an aesthetic one. But it still can lead to an ethics of taste, since in the absence of any intrinsic foundation to justify an ethic, we may reasonably be encouraged to choose the one that most appeals to us; and it is plausible to think that such appeal is ultimately an aesthetic matter, a question of what strikes us as most attractive or most perfect.

2. I now turn from anti-essentialism to the second general attitude that works to undermine traditional ethical theories and thereby promote an aestheticized ethics of taste. This attitude, "the underdetermination of ethics by morality," has two aspects, which respectively concern the extension and dominance of moral considerations in ethical thought. The first aspect finds its most general expression in contemporary philosophy's increasing recognition that morality as traditionally conceived does not really cover the full gamut of ethical concern. For the ethical involves a very wide range of considerations of value and goodness in respect to how one should live. Many of these considerations are clearly personal and egoistic, or at least not universalized (e.g., special concern for one's own interests or one's family's), and many are nonobligational (e.g., munificence and uncalled-for acts of kindness or heroism). But the traditional project of morality, as Bernard Williams and Richard Wollheim maintain, constitutes a much narrower special "subsystem" of the ethical, governed by obligation and universalizability. Taking "morality in the narrow sense . . . to be that which has obligation as its core," Wollheim contrasts it sharply with the realm of value and goodness in terms of their differing psychological genealogy and consequent potential for human satisfaction. "One (morality) derives from introjection [of a menacing figure], the other (value) derives from projection ['of archaic bliss, of love satisfied']. One is in its origins largely defensive and largely coercive, the other is neither. One tries to guard against fear, the other to perpetuate love."[13] And if Wollheim's account of morality emphasizes its menacing beginnings and baneful aspects, Williams is still more explicit (and perhaps more extreme) in asserting with insouciant bluntness that "we would be better off without it" (*ELP* 174).

Williams's critique of "morality, the peculiar institution" or "special system" (*ELP* 174) concentrates less on its distressing psychological sources and effects than on its logical peculiarities and insufficiency in accounting for our ethical thinking. What makes this insufficiency so vitiating is that while morality clearly underdetermines ethics, it constitutes and sees itself as a system that is globally exhaustive in its determinations. It presents itself as a consistent system of obligations (and consequent rights) that can tell us what we should do in any instance. The fact that we should or ought to do something implies that we can do it, and therefore these obligations will be hierarchically ordered so as to prevent their conflicting in any final or irresolvable sense, since they cannot be allowed to issue in contradictory actions, which, as incompatible, cannot be performed. "Moral obligation is inescapable," and whether you want to subscribe to the system or not, it includes you in its categorical universalizing logic and imputes you moral blame if you do not act according to its comprehensive system of obligations (*ELP* 177–78). Williams is chiefly occupied with challenging two of morality's globally categorical presumptions: its claim to exhaustive extension of application and its supreme, overriding potency wherever applied. He shows how morality cannot defend the first claim against obvious cases of kindness and generosity that are nonobligatory or even in clear conflict with some prior definite obligation. And he exposes the failures of philosophical efforts to salvage the claim through the unconvincing positing of an elaborate hypothetical system of differently ordered obligations (particular obligations, general obligations, negative obligations, prima facie obligations, obligations to self, to others, etc.) so that any action we might look upon with favor or distaste will be seen as deriving or deviating from some relevant (or ordered complex of) obligation.

Closely connected with morality's assumption that it exhausts all ethical action and choice, that any worthy act can ultimately be justified only in terms of some obligation, is the presumption that in any ethical question moral considerations should always override all others and determine how one should act or live. Thus, if the performance of a noble unobliged act of kindness prevents me from meeting a trivial obligation, say arriving to dinner on time, then a vague general obligation relating to kindness must be posited to justify my act's obvious worth. The idea that certain things can be good regardless of obligation and can even outweigh obligation in ethical deliberation is utterly foreign and intolerable to the system of morality. Williams calls this morality's maxim "that only an obligation can beat an obligation" (*ELP* 187), and its perceived falsity constitutes the second part of the postmodern case for the underdetermination of ethics by morality. Ethics, as distinguished from morality, recognizes that there is more to the good life than the fulfillment of obligations and even "can see that things other than itself are important . . . [to life] as part of what make it worth living" (*ELP* 184). This does not mean that ethics need reject moral considerations entirely, only that it must reject their claim to entirety and overridingness. What is denied (and this time in Wollheim's words) is "the view that morality is ultimate or overruling" (*TL* 225).

Demoting moral obligation to merely one significant factor in ethical deliberation on how to live the good life makes such deliberation much more like aesthetic judgement and justification than syllogistic or legalistic discourse. Finding what is right becomes a matter of finding the most fitting and appealing gestalt, of perceiving the most attractive and harmonious constellation of various and variously weighted features in a given situation or life. It is no longer the deduction of one obligation from another more general obligation or group of obligations; nor is it the outcome of a logical calculation based on a clear hierarchical order of obligations. Likewise, ethical justification comes to resemble aesthetic explanation in appealing not to syllogism or algorithm but to perceptually persuasive argument (through well-wrought narrative, tendentious rhetoric, and imaginative examples) in its attempt to convince. Such justification relies on and aims to sustain and extend some basic consensus (a vague *sensus communis*) on the bounds of appropriate action, yet it also recognizes and serves to promote a tolerance of difference of perception or taste within these (revisable) bounds. As with aesthetic interpretation and evaluation, we want our interlocutors to understand our ethical perspectives and choices and to see them as reasonable; but no longer is it so crucial that they accept them as universally right and valid for all. Ethical judgements can no more be demonstratively proved categorically true through unexceptionable principles than can aesthetic ones. For ethical decisions, like artistic ones, should not be the outcome of strict application of rules but the product of creative and critical imagination. Ethics and aesthetics become one in this meaningful and sensible sense; and the project of an ethical life becomes an exercise in living aesthetically. Perhaps this is what Wollheim has in mind when for one brief moment he very vaguely and tentatively suggests that ethics be viewed "like art" (*TL* 198).[14]

III

This aestheticization of the ethical seems a solid step in the right direction, but Rorty's explicit advocacy of the aesthetic life is far more radical and substantive. Rejecting traditional moral theory on the grounds that we have no common essence but are products of random and idiosyncratic contingencies, Rorty urges the conclusion that we must create ourselves and must do so by self-enriching aesthetic redescription. One might argue that a self could be created by one's choice of even the most traditional or ascetic of moralities, so the necessity of self-creation in no way entails or prescribes the pursuit of a distinctively rich aesthetic life. But, as we shall see, Rorty insists on identifying the life of self-creation as an aesthetic life; even if the specific life he urges does not do justice to the varieties of aesthetic life advocated by philosophers over the ages and even in modern times.

What then is Rorty's vision of the aesthetic life, and how does it compare to others? It rejects any "search for purity" and focused simplicity based on stable self-knowledge, and affirms instead "a search for self-enlargement," "self-enrichment," and "self-creation" (R 11, 15; *CIS* 41). "The desire to enlarge oneself," says Rorty, "is the desire to embrace more and more possibilities, to be constantly learning, to give oneself over entirely to curiosity, to end by having envisaged all the possibilities of the past and of the future," an end which is obviously endless (R 11). This quest for self-enrichment and self-creation involves a dual "aesthetic search for novel experiences and [for] novel language" to redescribe and thereby enrich those experiences and their experiencer (R 15). Similarly, "the development of richer, fuller ways of formulating one's desires and hopes" makes "those desires and hopes themselves—and thereby oneself—richer and fuller" (R 11). The aesthetic aim is no longer to "see things steadily and see them whole" but to see them and ourselves through ever new "alternative narratives and alternative vocabularies [designed] as instruments for change" (R 9). Those "exceptional individuals" who can take the breathless pace and confusion of producing and inhabiting these multiple vocabularies bent on continuous change will be able "to make their lives works of art," where such works of self-creation must be strongly original, neither a "copy or replica of something which has already been identified" nor even "elegant variations" on previous creations (R 11; *CIS* 28).

Rorty identifies such masters of the aesthetic life in the different figures of the curious intellectual "ironist" (perhaps best personified as the skeptical, wide-ranging literary critic) and "the strong poet." Yet he wants to assimilate the two as essentially the same in their ethico-aesthetic quest, as both adventurously aiming at self-enrichment and self-creation through the use of novel language to redescribe the self. But the aims of self-creation and of enrichment through endlessly curious self-redescription are not at all identical. Not only could we achieve one without the other, but the two goals can be in deep tension. Boundless seeking for change can threaten the concentration necessary for creating oneself in a strong and satisfying way. The curious ironist and the self-creating strong poet represent two quite different forms of aesthetic life that Rorty unfortunately runs together as the aesthetic life he advocates. Besides being problematically conflated, each genre presents difficulties in its Rortian formulation.

The aesthetic life of "the curious intellectual" or "ironist" is "the life of unending curiosity, the life that seeks to extend its own bound rather than to find its center." Its "desire to embrace more and more possibilities" by embracing more and more different vocabularies for self-redescription comes with the injunction to be "increasingly ironic, playful, free, and inventive" with regard to whatever vocabulary one currently chooses or regards as determining one's self-description and ethical identity (R 11, 12). Rorty calls this determining vocabulary one's "final vocabulary," and he defines the ironist as one who "has radical and continuing doubts about the final vocabulary she currently uses" and is thus constantly looking for new and better ones through wide reading. "Ironists are afraid that they will get stuck in the vocabulary in which they were brought up" or indeed in any single vocabulary. Having abandoned the idea of any essential self, final vocabulary, or grand narrative on which they should converge, they are bent on "diversification and novelty" of self-description, continuously enlarging their "own moral identity by revising [their] own final vocabulary." The ever curious, self-enriching ironist "reminds herself of her rootlessness" as she restlessly tries to take the most tricks in as many new language games as she can learn to play (*CIS* 73, 75, 77, 80).

By contrast, the strong poet must know and respect limitation in order to create herself as a distinctive individual. She cannot give herself "over entirely to curiosity" to embrace as many narratives and vocabularies as possible, ideally experimenting with "all the possibilities of the past and of the future." For to do so would risk losing the focus necessary to fix and firmly imprint a sense of what is special and distinctive to her life and language; and this is the very core of Rorty's poetic life of self-creation. The strong poet's fear is that, even if her words survive, "nobody will find anything distinctive in them." "One will not have impressed one's mark upon the language but, rather, will have spent one's life shoving about already coined pieces. So one will not really have had an I at all" (*CIS* 24). Yet this fear implies a powerful critique of the ironist's aesthetic life of self-enrichment. That life is essentially romantic picaresque in genre, a tireless, insatiable, Faustian quest for enriching titillation through curiosity and novelty, a quest that is as wide-ranging as it is unstructured through the lack of center it so celebrates.

However, the absence of any structuring center (which need not be universally human, statically permanent, nor given rather than made) prevents it from being the sort of *Bildungsroman* it seems to want to be. For the maximized spawning of alternative and often inconsistent vocabularies and narratives of the self, which aims to deconstruct any stable self into a changing, growing multiplicity of selves or self-descriptions, makes the whole prospect of an integral enduring self seem altogether empty and suspect. But without such a self that is capable of identity through change or changing description, there can be no self that is capable of self-enrichment or enlargement, and this would nullify the Rortian aesthetic life of self-enrichment by rendering it meaningless. Similarly, to abandon the notion of a firmly distinctive self, one that is not continuously supplanted by endless redescription in new vocabularies acquired from others, is to render the prospect of distinctive self-creation problematic at the least. This need for self-centering, self-distinguishing limitation—the very opposite of the quest for all possibilities—is forcefully expressed in the lines from Philip Larkin that Rorty uses to introduce the aesthetic ideal of self-creation:

And once you have walked the length of your mind, what
You command is as clear as a lading-list.
Anything else must not, for you, be thought
To exist.
And what's the profit? Only that, in time
We half-identify the blind impress
All our behavings bear, may trace it home.

The argument for self-limiting self-definition is not an appeal to an essential self that exists at the foundational core of every one of us, but rather an appeal to unity and coherence. For, having rightly abandoned essentialism, we can constitute the self only in terms of narrative about it. It follows that the unity and coherence of the self will depend on the unity and coherence of its narratives. Thus, though he rejects Alisdair MacIntyre's nostalgia for Aristotelian narratives, Rorty cannot quarrel with his insistence on "a concept of a self whose unity resides in the unity of a narrative."[15] For without any unity and coherence of narrative, there is no intelligible self for the aesthetic ironist to enrich, enlarge, or perfect. If we abandon the aim of a unified, coherent self-narrative for Rorty's chorus of inconsistent "quasi selves" constituted by alternative, constantly changing, and often incommensurable narratives and vocabularies, with no complex narrative "able to make them all hang together" (R 5, 8), then the project of self-enrichment becomes mythical and incoherent with the myth and incoherence of a single self collecting these riches together.

The self-unity needed to speak meaningfully of self-enrichment or perfection is, however, something pragmatically and often painfully forged or constructed, rather than foundationally given. It surely involves developmental change and multiplicity, as all narrative unity must, and it can display conflict in its unity, just as interesting narratives do. A unified self is not a uniform self; but neither can it be an unordered collection of incompatible "quasi selves" inhabiting the same corporeal machine. Rorty seems to recognize the necessity for self-unity when he asserts that the only post-Freudian version of human dignity is "a coherent self-image" and when he tries to appropriate MacIntyre's unifying virtue of "integrity or constancy" as part of his aesthetic life's "search for perfection" (R 17, 19). But he implicitly denies coherence in advocating a self composed of "a plurality of persons . . . [constituted by] incompatible systems of belief and desire" (R 19); and the only constancy that he in fact prescribes for the ironist aesthete is the constancy of change, of novel alternative self-descriptions and narrations, the constancy of inconstancy, which essentially nullifies the coherence of the self.

In learning so much from Freud, Rorty might have probed why Freud seemed much less eager to dispense with a unified, integrated self. Why, for example, did he prefer to posit a dominated unconscious rather than simply multiple consciousnesses or personalities residing in the same body? Why did he never portray our psychological constituents in Rortian fashion as ideally "egalitarian," as "rational" quasi-persons engaging in free conversation (R 7–9), unordered by repression and censorship, which of course imply some organizational hierarchy? One reason may be that Freud realized what a pricelessly important yet fragile achievement the unity of self is, how difficult and painful such a unified self or self-narration is to construct, and yet how necessary it is for leading any plausible version of a good, satisfying life in human society. It is certainly presupposed in Rorty's ideal of the ironist's aesthetic life, no matter how much his theory of multiple selves claims to reject it. In fact, what makes his portrayal of this life seem not only coherent but perhaps attractive to us is that it in fact centers around one kind of self-vocabulary and narrative, that of the curious intellectual and her quest.

The other strand of Rortian aesthetic life, that of self-creation as personified by the strong poet, is free from the theoretically self-vitiating denial of self-coherence. We already saw how this life requires focusing limitation. It also implies some sort of central narrative or unifying pattern—contingent, idiosyncratic, developing, and actively shaped as it may be—which organizes the crazy congeries of experience into "the drama of an individual human life . . . as a whole," so that it is not an endlessly expanding hodgepodge of incompatible narratives in incommensurable vocabularies (*CIS* 29).

Thus, in the words of Larkin's poem, "all our behavings" may come to be understood and structured in terms of that pattern that may become "clear as a lading-list," even though it be based on "the blind impress" of certain contingent factors in our lives that we can only "half-identify." Moreover, while the blind impress is irrevocably given, the pattern is not; and Rorty rightly insists on self-creation as the felicitous reweaving of the pattern, the artistic construction of a narrative that will render our lives and selves more satisfying. Rorty, however, gives us too narrow a picture of what constitutes aesthetically satisfying life and self-creation. For even when the ideal of the endlessly changing ironist is supplemented by the ideal of the strong poet who creates a firm and distinctively original identity, the possibilities of aesthetic life remain too limited. We can see these limitations by noting two other versions of aesthetic life that found cultural expression and philosophical advocacy.

IV

Perhaps the most familiar one is a life devoted to the enjoyment of beauty: beautiful objects of nature and of art, as well as those hybrid products of nature and art we are loath to regard as objects of either—beautiful people. This aesthetic life was very influential in the early part of the twentieth century through the fashionable Bloomsbury coterie who confess to having imbibed it from G. E. Moore's account of the ideal in human life. For Moore (who, like Rorty, repudiates any ethics based on the idea of an essential "true self"), the ideal consists of "certain states of consciousness, which may be roughly described as the pleasures of human intercourse and the enjoyment of beautiful objects." This is because "personal affections and aesthetic enjoyments include *all* the greatest, and *by far* the greatest, goods we can imagine."[16] Both these components of the aesthetic life are constituted by very complex and rewarding organic unities (composed of countless and changing variables) that cannot be reduced to algorithmic prescription. However, Moore does affirm that the highest pleasures of personal affection require "that the object must be not only truly beautiful, but also truly good in a high degree," and that a proper appreciation of human beauty must include appreciation of its "purely material" form and the "corporeal expression" of its mental qualities (*PE* 203–4).

If this Moorean-Bloomsbury aesthetic life strikes us as distinctively and even chicly contemporary in engaging with our hedonistic penchant for beautiful things and beautiful people, we should remember that it represents (like Rorty's ironist quest) a familiar romantic genre, more particularly a late romantic ideal of aestheticism. Unwilling to accept the universal dominance of the mechanized world picture, unable to accept the traditional religious and moral claims to spirituality, and unready to be sullied by philistine politics and the grubby toil of social reform, the aesthetes sought individual salvation through the satisfying gemlike flame of art and sensuous plaeasure rather than through God or State. Their ideal of the aesthetic life differs from Rorty's not only in being less preoccupied with the ceaseless strivings of intellectual curiosity and the strenuous struggle of original self-creation but also in being more appreciative of beauty, pleasurable sensation, and the leisurely luxury of satisfaction. It is essentially the ethic of Walter Pater and Oscar Wilde, an exquisite flower of aestheticist decadence that remains undeniably and captivatingly sweet, and may be the only flower still capable of growing in our postmodern wasteland of social hope.

However, as versions of the aesthetic life tend somewhat to overlap and be compounded, we find in Wilde's Nietzschean maxim that "life itself is an art" a clear suggestion of another form of aesthetic life, which can be called, for contrast, the classical.[17] The idea here is not so much a life of aesthetic consumption but a life that is itself a product worthy of aesthetic appreciation for its structure and design as an organic unity. Like many old ideas, it is reclaimed and recycled in postmodern thought. Foucault, for example, returns to it through an analysis of ancient Greek culture, whose "ethics . . . was an aesthetics of existence," the expression of "the will to live a beautiful life, and to leave to others memories of a beautiful existence."[18] The Greeks, as Williams and Wollheim both note in discussing ethical reflection, were strongly inclined to conceive and assess the good life holistically, as a unified whole. The idea that an individual's life needs to be seen, organized, and evaluated in terms of such an organic (rather than merely aggregative) unity gave Solon's famous injunction to "call no man happy until he is dead" its special force. For a disastrously inappropriate end could distort beyond repair the satisfying unity of the life led thus far. One of the basic projects of Greek ethics was to try to find a satisfyingly well-structured life that is maximally free from the threat of disunifying misfortune; and one general strategy to achieve such unity is to establish a center and contours for life by a kind of overarching aim or interlocking set of aims, a limiting concentration on a narrower range of goods (naturally those less susceptible to misfortune).

This kind of slimmed-down, centered, limit-respecting life of unity is labeled by Rorty "the ascetic life" (R 11) in unfavorable contrast to "the aesthetic life" he advocates. But such characterization is misleading and unfair. It is simply wrong to assume that a life emphasizing strong unity and thus adopting the limits this requires cannot be an aesthetic life, that it cannot be enjoyed and praised as aesthetically satisfying or even recommended for its aesthetic appeal. One could well choose the life of an earth-rooted, family-bound farmer over a jet-hopping, spouse-swapping academic simply in terms of its aesthetic joys of order, coherence, and harmony, which stem from a centrally structured and limited project of development, whose unity is both enhanced and largely constituted by cyclical and developmental variations on its central theme or narrative. As Foucault realized in his study of Greek ethics, one can pursue still greater simplicity and purity of life in order to stylize oneself as an extraordinary individual through a distinctively unified concentration on a narrow project. Even real asceticism can be recommended as aesthetically effective, not simply through a style of minimalist distinction where less becomes more since it is beyond the taste of the masses, but also because of the positive pleasures of self-limiting self-mastery.[19]

While the classical perspective on aesthetic living can accommodate asceticism, it is not confined to ascetic narrowness. It instead embodies the classical definition of beauty as unity in variety and thus is far from opposed to richness and diversity. What it maintains is that variety must not be maximized beyond the limit it can be coherently held together in some satisfying unity. An ascetic aims at a very narrow focus of unity through the unavoidable variety of life's vicissitudes. But the classical ideal of aesthetic life can endorse a rich variety of experience, if our aesthetic taste, psychological needs, and material and social conditions allow the forging of more complex and looser unities. Such unity would be neither foundationally given nor static. It could even be the sort of genealogical, self-constituted, and self-projected unity in variety that Nietzsche (surely a classically steeped romantic) seems to be offering us as the ideal life or character.[20] Such unity can even accommodate a self of multiple narratives, as long as these can be made somehow to hang together as a higher unity from the right narrative perspective, one that makes that self more compellingly rich and powerful as an aesthetic character.

Just as one need not be a rootless ironist to live the aesthetic life, so one need not take the path of the strong poet to create oneself aesthetically. Here, too, Rorty confuses the aesthetic with the radically novel, just as he conflates artistic creation with unique originality, and autonomy with distinction. Aesthetic self-creation, for Rorty's strong poet, must be strikingly novel and distinctive. Her goal is "to make something that never had been dreamed of before," highlighting her idiosyncrasy and describing herself "in a new language," "in words never used before," so as to create "a self to be which her predecessors never knew was possible." We fail in this aesthetic quest if our creations and our selves are simply "better or worse instances of familiar types," even "elegant variations on previously written poems" (*CIS* 13, 24, 28–29). But even if the ethical goal of narrative self-creation be modeled on the creation of an aesthetic work of art, it still does not follow that such creation must be radically novel and altogether unique. For neither do artworks require such radical and idiosyncratic originality in order to be aesthetically satisfying, as we can see most clearly in classical and medieval art. To think that true artistic creation precludes established types and variations on familiar formulas is to confuse art with the artistic ideology of romantic individualism and the modernist avant-garde, a historically parochial confusion to which Rorty falls victim. One can style oneself aesthetically, create one's life as a work of art, by adopting and adapting familiar roles and lifestyles, adjusting these generic forms to one's individual contingent circumstances.

This, as Foucault recognized, was the Greek manner of the aesthetic construction of life, a stylized construction of the ethical subject not in terms of categorical moral prescriptions but through a sense of the art of living based on certain generic formulas and ideals already socially entrenched as appropriate. There was no need to invent an entirely new formula; there was nothing inartistic about elegant variations on the familiar. Today, of course, we find a much wider range of recommended lifestyles and much less consensus on the most appropriate. But this merely provides us with more materials and models for artistic self-fashioning; and if we still suffer from the modernist, high-culture habit of identifying art too narrowly with radical originality and individualistic uniqueness, postmodernism and popular art are increasingly putting that aesthetic into question.

As Rorty's notion of the strong poet conflates artistic creation with innovative uniqueness, it similarly confuses between autonomy and original self-definition, freedom and uniqueness. The only way Rorty thinks we can define ourselves as free individuals is to escape from inherited self-descriptions by redescribing and thus reconstituting the self in new ways and new language that "the past never knew." But why can't our autonomy be expressed in the freedom to define ourselves through an already existing lifestyle or language? There is no reason why the freedom to be oneself should be incompatible with being like others, unless we conflate autonomy with radical individualism. Indeed, the Rortian compulsion to create oneself in novel fashion can itself be seen as a form of nonautonomy, a bondage to the new and individualistic. Its motivating fear of being a replica suggests, in fact, a very tenuous sense of self, one desperately needing to assert itself by unique individuality and concentration on personal distinction. Its vision of self and self-perfection as "standing out" in one's private dimension rather than as being expressed and enriched through enveloping folds of social solidarity seems a very one-sided and phallocentric concept of selfhood.[21]

Moreover, it is a form of autonomy and aesthetic living that is limited to a narrow elite. "It is something which certain particular human beings hope to attain by self-creation, and which a few actually do" (*CIS* 65). Given its elitist distinction, the project of radically innovative self-creation is difficult to recommend as a general model for aesthetic living, as a direction that all should take in their search for private perfection and happiness. But instead of taking the promising pluralist option of recognizing a variety of forms of aesthetic life, some not requiring original distinction,[22] Rorty tries to universalize and democratize the strong poet's quest by making everyone an innovative and ambitiously individualistic strong poet in their unconscious. Building on Freud, he argues that since even the most prosaic person has an imaginative fantasy life that seeks expression, we should "see the conscious need of the strong poet to *demonstrate* that [she] is not a copy or replica as merely a special form of an unconscious need everyone has" (*CIS* 35–36, 43). But the fact that everyone's idiosyncratic unconscious seeks expression does not mean that what it seeks is the expression of one's idiosyncrasy, one's self-presentation as something distinctively original and innovative.

V

Rorty's emphasis on personal distinction reflects his view of the aesthetic life as a distinctly private ethic, essentially independent of the public ethics of social life; and he indeed claims that no philosophy or theory can synthesize the "private" goal of self-creation with the public one of social solidarity (*CIS* xiii–xiv). This claim could be challenged as the misguided product of our deeply entrenched liberal ideology and romantic aesthetics. Only when the former defines the self as essentially private and the latter regards aesthetic creation as, by necessity, radically individualistic do the making of self and society seem inherently at odds. We must be careful not to interpret a given sociocultural structure of division into an intrinsic philosophical divide. Still, as long as our society shares these liberal and romantic commitments, Rorty may be right about the impossibility of a satisfactory synthesis.

To construct an aesthetic life that unites private and public would require rethinking not only our ethics and politics but also the nature of artistic creation and its demand for radical originality. The shape of such a synthesis is at present hard to envisage, but liberating our concept of art from its bondage to the ideal of avant-garde individualist genius would seem a propitious preparation for its exploration. Even granting that liberal society does not allow the goals of self-perfection and social solidarity to be fused in a single ethical vision, we should still criticize Rorty's vision of the aesthetic life for its excessively privatized character. It rests "on a firm distinction between the private and public" (*CIS* 83) that occludes the latter's formative influence on the former. For, given the familiar dialectic of self and other, the private self that Rorty wants to create and perfect is always largely the product of a public field; it is always already social and must be so as soon as it has a language for its private thoughts. Indeed, Rorty's particular private morality as well as his privatization of morality are obviously reflective of the particular public and wider society that shape his thinking—the intellectual field and the consumerist world of late-capitalist liberalism.

Consider the essential public dimension of the strong poet's putatively private quest. First, as Rorty admits, her new language must borrow from the shared language of the past to develop and highlight its novelty, just as it depends on the shared language of the future if it is to remain comprehensible. Moreover, the success of her putatively private quest depends essentially on public recognition; for this is what makes the difference between original "genius" and mere aberrational "eccentricity" (*CIS* 29, 37). In fact the very ideal of private self-creation, the desire for individual distinction and originality, is itself the product of the pressures of a given public field: the field of artistic and intellectual competition, whose social logic of increasing individuation to secure legitimation, distinction, and marketability has been closely analyzed by Pierre Bourdieu.[23] One is not a genuine thinker or artist unless one succeeds in producing one's own particular brand of thought or art; so there are pressures to distinguish one's position by marking, affirming, and highlighting one's differences within the shared field of endeavor. The fact that these social pressures have been internalized by individual agents does not render them essentially private in character, and the so-called private ethical project they structure cannot be said to swing clear of public influences and consequences.

The privatized quest of the ironist aesthete is no less informed by public pressures and ethos. One does not need a very penetrating or subversive eye to see in its glorification and quest of the new, in its "aesthetic search for novel experience and novel language," precisely that old worship of the new that fuels the rapid and relentless pace of commodity consumption in our late-capitalist consumer society. As critics of commodity aesthetics have shown, the demand for constant aesthetic innovation, urged in the noble names of creativity and progress, is also a cunningly systematic program to increase exchange value by masking or distorting use value, by making the already purchased and still very much usable item seem outdated and in need of change, thereby stimulating new purchasing.[24] This programmatic, profit-driven innovation pervades our whole consumer society and thus, inevitably, its ethical thinking. The ironist's quest to acquire more and more new vocabularies is the philosophical counterpart of the consumer's quest to maximize consumption. Both seem narcotic dreams of happiness induced by capitalism's master dream (a grimly real one) of greater sales and greater profits.

Moreover, the very privatization of morality into a matter of mere personal enrichment clearly reflects the public morality whose privileging of the autonomous private individual (property owner or consumer) was so central to the collective rise of capitalism and liberalism. Yet this autonomy of self is precisely what is stricken and undermined by late capitalism's fragmented society. Competitive individualism and its attendant societal deformations have dissolved the stable and interlocking social roles that once afforded some solid structure to the self. In this socioethical void and in the absence of serious thinking as to how best to structure life aesthetically, the shaping of the self and its career is simply left to the whims of market forces. We are abandoned to the changing sway of well-advertised, profit-motivated notions of self-fulfillment and gratification, while lacking any stable sense of a self to fulfil. The advertised idea that everyone should fashion himself as a unique individual through the free personal choice of lifestyles cannot hide the fact that not only the range of viable lifestyle options but also the individual's very awareness and choice are severely constrained and relentlessly programmed by societal forces that are usually far beyond his power (as individual) to resist, let alone control.

This late-capitalist paradox of the privatized quest for self-fulfillment issuing in the loss of real autonomy and integrity of self is perfectly reflected in Rorty's deep contradiction of exhorting the ironist's self-enrichment while effectively denying her the existence of a self to be enriched. The Rortian nonself of incompatible "quasi selves" intent on multiple shifting vocabularies is indeed the ideal self for the powers governing a consumer society:

a fragmented, confused self, hungrily acquiring as many new commodities as it can but lacking the disciplined integrity to challenge either its habits of consumption or the system that manipulates and profits from them. In its extreme privatization of morality, in failing to recognize how deeply and ineluctably the public ethos structures the very conception of our diverse quests for private perfection, Rorty's vision of the aesthetic life needs to be expanded to embrace more of the social. It needs a similar expansion to embrace a wider variety of genres of aesthetic living and self-creation. I conclude my critique by examining another dimension where Rorty's vision of human nature and self-fulfillment seems much too narrow—his reductive linguistic essentialism.

Although Rorty is vehemently outspoken in repudiating essentialism, and though he specifically denies we share a human essence by sharing a common thing called language, his view of the self as nothing but a complex web of vocabularies and narratives seems uncomfortably close to an essentialist view of human nature as exclusively linguistic. All that seems to matter for selfhood and human being-in-the-world is language: "human beings are simply incarnated vocabularies"; it is simply "words which . . . made us what we are" (*CIS* 88, 117). Thus, Nietzsche is praised as one who "by describing himself in his own terms . . . created himself, [since] he . . . created the only part of himself that mattered by constructing his own mind. To create one's mind is to create one's own language" (*CIS* 27). For humans are "nothing more than sentential attitudes—nothing more than the presence or absence of dispositions toward the use of sentences phrased in some historically conditioned vocabulary" (*CIS* 88).

Such remarks clearly suggest that man is essentially mind and that mind is essentially linguistic. More puzzling than their apparent essentialism is the fact that they endorse a fundamentally mentalistic view of human nature against Nietzsche's own emphasis on the formative role and value of the body, even in the shaping of the mind. This linguistic mentalism and dismissive neglect of the body is particularly counterproductive in a philosopher intent on advancing the aesthetic life. For aesthetics' connection with bodily senses and pleasures and with nonlinguistic perceptions should be obvious were it not for the rationalizing bias that has enthralled so much traditional aesthetic theory and that still ensnares Rorty's.

Although he strives to exclude the subsentential from the significantly human and aesthetic, when Rorty turns to expounding his notion of liberalism as the "desire to avoid cruelty and pain," the nondiscursive returns with a vengeance in the form of pain, which "is non-linguistic" and all but threatens to oust language as the most common human factor. "What unites . . . [an individual] with the rest of the species is not a common language but *just* susceptibility to pain, and in particular that special sort of pain which the brutes do not share with the humans—humiliation," a pain that Rorty identifies, however, as the loss of language (*CIS* 65, 92, 94, 177–78). Indeed, pain, together with brute power, seems to constitute for Rorty the fundamental unchangeable reality of the world that cannot be vanquished by our transformative narratives:

> For our relation to the world, to brute power and to naked pain, is not the sort of relation we have to persons. Faced with the nonhuman, the nonlinguistic, we no longer have an ability to overcome contingency and pain by appropriation and transformation [of language], but only the ability to *recognize* contingency and pain. The final victory of poetry in its ancient quarrel with philosophy—the final victory of metaphors of self-creation over metaphors of discovery—would consist in our becoming reconciled to the thought that this is the only sort of power over the world which we can hope to have. For that would be the final abjuration of the notion that truth, and not just power and pain, is to be found "out there." (*CIS* 40)

That the bottom-line, untransformable reality is "just power and pain" seems a sweepingly metaphysical statement rather out of character with Rorty's repudiation of metaphysics. But whether we read this as a regressive slip to bad metaphysics (through a metaphysics of badness) or instead as just an empirical generalization about our nonlinguistic experience, it betrays a deep and particularly troubling deficiency in the Rortian vision of aesthetic life. It is a very sad and unsatisfying aestheticism that affirms the pervasive presence of nonlinguistic pain but ignores the sensuous bodily pleasures. Such pleasures are "out there" too; and not only do they form a large part of what makes life worth living, but they can be cultivated to make life more aesthetically rich and rewarding. Rorty's neglect of such pleasures makes his aestheticism unsatisfyingly eviscerate and tame. It remains too much the product of a puritan and capitalist America; for it is aimed not at rich sensual satisfaction or even more generally at pleasure (a notion he hardly mentions), but rather at the breathless production and accumulation of new vocabularies and new narratives. It is more a poetics, a theory of industrious making, than an aesthetics of full-bodied enjoying.

The aesthetic life should also cultivate the pleasures and disciplines of the body. Although such somatic experience may be irreducible to linguistic formulation, its contribution to the formation of mind and selfhood cannot be denied and indeed reveals the fundamental wrongheadedness of considering mind and body as separate entities and of identifying the self narrowly with the former. Though Rorty correctly insists that the self is structured by the vocabulary it inherits, Foucault is equally right in stressing that it is also the product of disciplinary practices inscribed on the body. And if we can emancipate the self through new language, we can also transform and liberate it through new bodily practices.

I do not want to suggest that working through the body provides an altogether autonomous route to private perfection and self-creation. Like the language of the strong poet, the body is not a wholly private affair. Significantly shaped and repressively scarred by history's dominant social practices and ideologies, it is also not free from linguistic markings. But the fact that the somatic has been structured by body-punishing ideologies and discourse does not mean that it cannot serve as a source to challenge them through the use of alternative body practices and greater somatic awareness. We may have to read and listen to the body more attentively; we may even have to overcome the language-bound metaphorics of reading and listening, and improve our attentive capacities of somatic feeling. Of course, working on one's self through one's body is not in itself a very serious challenge to the sociopolitical structures that shape the self and the language of its description. But it can instill attitudes and behavioral patterns that would favor and support social transformation.

Ideally, pursuit of the aesthetic life would involve enrichment of self and society through combined somatic, linguistic, cognitive, psychological, and social change that would be mutually supportive if not collaborative. Some fear, however, that social reform can only be stymied by attention to the body because this focus must be narrowly individualistic. As Fredric Jameson argues, attention to the body only concerns "my individual relationship with my own body . . . and not that very different relationship between myself or my body and other people," and it therefore can only promote the pernicious privatism on which unhappy bourgeois society rests.[25] But viewing the somatic as essentially private is itself a problematic piece of bourgeois ideology. Not only is the body shaped by the social, it contributes to the social. We can share our bodies and bodily pleasures as much as we share our minds, and they can be as public as our thoughts.

Talk of self-transformation through body practices is likely to evoke some dangerously simplistic and standardized images: the callow confidence acquired by the ninety-pound weakling through muscles developed in a body-building program or the fragile self-esteem that the formerly flabby achieve through aerobic slimming and toning. The idea that somatic self-transformation must fit the paradigm of top models and body builders is a very pernicious presumption that reflects the poverty of thinking on the aesthetics of the body. For when it is assumed that the body is not a proper locus for seriously critical and imaginative aesthetic thinking, the pursuit of somatic well-being is left to the domination of market forces plying standardized ideals of superficially impressive body contours.

Advocating a more embodied pragmatist aesthetic does not mean confining aesthetic fulfillment to lean, tan, athletic youth. This is not simply because it recognizes other dimensions of aesthetic achievement, but because the aesthetics of the body is not limited, to its surface form and ornamental cosmetics; it also concerns how the body moves and experiences itself. If our rationalist aesthetic tradition privileged firm external forms and distanced appreciation, a more experiential somatic approach is needed. Such an approach would consider how factors like better-balanced breathing and posture, greater kinesthetic harmony, and, more generally, greater somatic consciousness can aesthetically enrich our lives in terms of an enhanced quality and awareness of felt experience. It would also explore the ways in which bodily practices that achieve these effects can help transform the self emotionally, cognitively, and ethically by instilling greater psychological balance, perceptual receptivity, and open, patient tolerance.

If all this sounds excessively "New Age," it must be remembered that many of these ideas can trace themselves back to ancient Asian traditions like yoga and *taijiquan*. That is why, I borrowed James's description of pragmatism to introduce the project of somaesthetics—as "a new name for some old ways of thinking."[26]

Chapter Six

Self-Knowledge and Its Discontents

I. Introduction

On Apollo's ancient temple at Delphi, three Greek maxims were inscribed whose importance was reaffirmed in Roman times, by preserving their inscription in gilt letters. The most famous of these maxims—Γνώθι σεαυτόν (*Gnothi seauton* or "Know thyself")—has been, by far, the most philosophically influential and forms the focus of this chapter, though my argument will ultimately converge with a second of these maxims that is also rich in historical significance.[1] Heraclitus gave the injunction to self-knowledge its earliest enduring philosophical application when he affirmed, "I dived into myself" because "All men have the capacity to come to know themselves and to have self-control" (whose Greek term is *sophronein*, sometimes translated as "temperance").[2] The next known Greek usage of the maxim is more artistic yet less cryptic. In his play *Prometheus*, Aeschylus gives self-knowledge its crucial meaning of knowing one's level or limitations. When the punished but still proudly defiant Prometheus is approached by the Titan god Oceanus, who offers to help him effect a reconciliation with Zeus, Oceanus urges: "Know thyself: change thy course" because Zeus now rules "o'er the Gods."[3]

Socrates, however, is the ancient thinker most strongly associated with the maxim of self-knowledge and the one who established it at the core of philosophy. Acclaimed as the wisest of all men by the Delphic oracle of Apollo (the God of Truth), Socrates claimed his main wisdom was the self-knowledge of his ignorance. In contrast to the many recognized experts who wrongly believed themselves full of wisdom concerning things they did not really know, Socrates at least knew himself well enough to know he did not know what others claimed to know; his wisdom was appreciating the limits of his knowledge. Indeed, he argues that the oracle declared him the wisest so as to prompt his critical search for wiser men and thus show that the most reputed "human wisdom is worth little or nothing" (*Apology*, 23b).[4] Asserting his lack of interest in lofty speculations, he explains (in *Phaedrus*, 229e–230a), "I am still unable, as the Delphic inscription orders, to know myself; and it really seems to me ridiculous to look into other things before I have understood that." Deploying the injunction of self-knowledge to chide the arrogant Alcibiades to recognize that his "good looks, height, birth, wealth, and native intelligence" are far from enough to put him in a class with Spartan and Persian kings, Socrates affirms such knowledge of current limitations as the necessary spur for cultivating oneself for the political leadership his ambitious young lover seeks. "Trust in me and in the Delphic inscription and 'know thyself,'" Socrates tells him, for "every human being needs self-cultivation, but *especially* . . . us" (*Alcibiades I*, 124b–d).

But what, exactly, is the self to be known and cultivated? After some dialogical sleight of hand, Plato's Socrates leads Alcibiades to the conclusion "that the soul is the man" and "nothing other than his soul," so "the command that we should know ourselves means that we should know our souls" (130c–d) and make them the object of our self-cultivation. Hence, a man's knowing or caring for his body is merely knowing or "caring for something that belongs to him, and not [knowing or caring] for himself." As the soul is the true governing self, so Socrates claims that "being self-controlled is knowing yourself" (131b); and this association of self-knowledge with the self-control of moderate behavior is reinforced in the *Charmides*, where we read "that 'know thyself' and 'be temperate' [*sophrosyne*] are the same" (164d–165a). The connection of self-knowledge with *sophrosyne*—a Greek term of virtue implying more than our notion of temperance by including a sense of modesty in knowing one's place and respecting one's superiors—confirms the primary ancient sense of "know thyself" as an awareness of one's vulnerability, shortcomings, mortality, or inferior stature (vis-à-vis the gods or others).

If the dominant thrust of the Socratic demand for self-knowledge is critical recognition of our limitations and deficiencies, such fault-finding analysis can certainly stimulate and guide our efforts at self-improvement. But if rigorously pursued, it also risks disheartening bouts of self-doubt and self-loathing that can generate depression. In its long history, Western philosophy (including the Christian theology it helped shape) has developed more positive interpretations of self-knowledge. While briefly tracing them, this chapter also shows how the original deprecatory implication of the maxim continues to resurface, often accompanied by sharp criticism of the ideal of self-examination—including complaints that real self-knowledge is impossible and that rigorous, critical self-reflection can be psychologically devastating. From these historical lessons, complemented by some contemporary findings in experimental psychology, I argue for the need to distinguish more clearly the different varieties of self-examination whose diversity can help explain the often radically differing assessments of its value, and provide a better appreciation of the most philosophically scorned form of self-examination and self-cultivation—that of our bodies and somatic self-consciousness.

II. Historical Interpretations

Acknowledging the traditional humbling sense of "know thyself" but introducing a more positive interpretation, Cicero writes (in encouraging his brother's rhetorical talents), "Don't suppose that the old maxim γνῶθι σεαυτόν was made only to reduce conceit; it also tells us to know our strong points."[5] Like Plato, Cicero interprets the Delphic injunction as "know your soul," while underlining the positive nature of the soul through its divine source: "For he who knows himself will realize, in the first place, that he has a divine element within him, and will think of his own inner nature as a kind of consecrated image of God; and so he will always act and think in a way worthy of so great a gift of the gods."[6] Developing the idea of knowing the self as soul, Neoplatonists like Plotinus urge us to focus self-study on the soul's highest dimension—that is, *Nous*—which we share with higher, purer, divine spirits. "Remove all stains from yourself and examine yourself, and you will have faith in your immortality," Plotinus explains, for "the self-knowledge of the *Nous* of the soul consists in knowing itself no longer as man but as having become altogether different, in hastening to unite itself with the Higher alone."[7] Proclus likewise explains the Delphic injunction as an "ascent to the divine and the most effective path towards purification."[8]

This logic of self-knowledge as a preparatory, purgational step toward the higher contemplation and union with God is often taken up by Christian mystics. Saint Catherine of Siena urges the individual "to abide forever in the cell of self-knowledge" so as to recognize one's sins and cut them off from one's better, truer self in the continuous quest for God, who provides a mirror of holiness to regard one's flaws and lead one to higher purity and divine communion. "As a man more readily sees spots on his face when he looks in a mirror, so the soul who with true knowledge of self rises with desire and gazes with the eye of the intellect at herself in the sweet mirror of God, knows better the stains of her own face by the purity which she sees in him."[9] Affirming the holiness of one's true self as soul, St. Juan d'Avila later expresses the same basic argument that "knowledge of one's self, which is certainly a holy thing, is also the path to the Holy of Holies, which is knowledge of God."[10]

We can appreciate the spiritual uplift expressed here. But is there not a risk that rigorously examining one's sins and weaknesses in the "cell of self-knowledge" could constitute a stifling and psychologically devastating form of mental self-flagellation? If the mystic's firm faith in God's saving power of grace is what ensures that such self-critical askesis leads not to the perdition of depression and despair but rather to the elevating contemplation and union with the divine, what happens when one's faith is less than supremely certain? While Socrates had already questioned whether one could indeed truly know oneself, Renaissance thinkers increasingly expressed worries about the health and wisdom of intense self-study, recognizing the need to look away or get away from oneself.

That Michel de Montaigne makes the quest for self-knowledge the core of his life and masterwork of *Essays* ("I study myself more than any other subject") does not prevent him from asserting that the task is not only unachievable but also devastating if taken to extremes.[11] Asserting that Socrates, by seeking "to know himself . . . had come to despise himself" (*M* 275), Montaigne argues more generally that the Delphic maxim is "a paradoxical command," as Nature wisely directs us to look beyond ourselves. This not only helps us find resources and escape dangers from the outside but also avoids predatory problems from within, since rigorous self-study must be a depressing, difficult, and dangerous exercise for creatures so full of folly, flaws, and misery as we are. "This common attitude and habit of looking elsewhere than at ourselves has been very useful for our business. We are an object that fills us with discontent; we see nothing in us but misery and vanity. In order not to dishearten us, Nature has very appropriately thrown the action of our vision outward" (*M* 766). Hence Montaigne also insists on the essential restorative value of entertainment and pleasures of diversion that both relieve and strengthen the mind through alternative exercise and focus (*M* 621–38).[12] In the next century, Blaise Pascal—whose brief, unhappy life was plagued with greater physical infirmity and hypochondriac fears—confirms Montaigne's thesis that we desperately need diversion from self-reflection because of our self-wretchedness: "The only good thing for men therefore is to be diverted from thinking of what they are," since even a king "becomes unhappy as soon as he thinks about himself."[13]

If despite such worries, Montaigne could still affirm the philosophical quest for self-knowledge as the key to better self-care and self-cultivation, then it is not surprising that the centrality of self-study continues into modern philosophy through Descartes's striking method of building the entire edifice of knowledge from the foundations of his mental introspection in his influential *Meditations on First Philosophy*, which has shaped so much of the modern philosophical agenda. "There is no more fruitful exercise than attempting to know ourselves," he elsewhere argues, where he even asserts the value of knowing our bodily constitution. But by ontologically separating body from mind and locating the substance of self within the mind alone (which, he claims, unlike the body could be known directly through introspection), Descartes furthers the Platonistic trend of identifying self-study as knowing one's mind or soul with the aim to "acquire an absolute power over its passions."[14]

The contrast of mind and body allows for two radically different approaches to the project of self-examination and self-knowledge: one including introspection of our bodily feelings, habits, and comportments; the other essentially confined to our distinctively mental life of thought. With but few exceptions, modern Western philosophy has preferred the more narrowly mentalistic approach, either ignoring or repudiating somatic introspection. Immanuel Kant is exemplary in this regard. In his *Metaphysics of Morals*, he claims that "the First Command of All Duties to Oneself" is to "'*know* (scrutinize, fathom) *yourself*,' not in terms of your physical perfection (your fitness or unfitness for all sorts of . . . ends) but rather in terms of your moral perfection in relation to your duty. That is, know your heart—whether it is good or evil, whether the source of your actions is pure or impure." Recognizing that such moral self-examination "into the depths (abysses) of one's heart" is not only cognitively difficult but could also generate self-loathing or self-contempt, Kant counters by arguing that the very effort to critically examine one's moral stature provides comforting evidence of the individual's "noble predisposition to the good" that is "worthy of respect" and can lead to self-improvement. "Only the descent into the hell of self-cognition can pave the way to godliness," Kant concludes, echoing the ancient Christian logic that purgational self-criticism provides the path to divine illumination and union.[15]

In contrast to the duty to examine one's moral consciousness, Kant repudiates the project of reflecting on bodily feelings, claiming that it leads to the madness of hypochondria and morbid despondence. In *The Conflict of the Faculties*, Kant describes hypochondria as a "sort of melancholia" (*Grillenkrankheit*) defined by "the weakness of abandoning oneself despondently to general morbid feelings" that do not point to a definite bodily malfunction but are usually associated with or produced by anxious attention to bodily sensations of unease or unhealthy discomfort. Noting constipation and flatulence as such somatic conditions of discomfort, he confesses his own "natural disposition to hypochondria because of [his] flat and narrow chest, which leaves little room for the movement of the heart and lungs," thus engendering an oppressive feeling in the chest. But insisting on "the mind's power to master its pathological feelings" through a firm resolution of will, Kant claims he was able to cure this morbidity by simply refusing to pay attention to the discomforting somatic feeling that promoted it, "by diverting [his] attention from this feeling."[16] Noting more generally how hypochondria is expressed in compulsive attention to bodily feeling, Kant concludes, "Turning reflection away from the body leads to health."[17] In short, introspective somatic self-study is harmful to both mind and body; and the best way to treat one's body is to ignore as much as possible the self-knowledge of how it feels, while using it actively in work and exercise.

In the economy of mind/body dualism, mind could signify a soul of immortal power and divine purity, while the body—already deeply associated with vulnerability, sin, and limitation (not only by its aging and mortality but also by its spatial boundaries and personal particularities)—could be ignored as bearing all the negative connotations of self-knowledge and self-examination. G. W. F. Hegel's affirmation of the Delphic maxim reflects this logic: knowing oneself is construed emphatically as knowing *Geist* (i.e., mind or spirit) and not "the particular capacities, character, propensities, and foibles of the single self." Self-knowledge "means that of man's genuine reality—of what is essentially and ultimately true and real—of mind as the true and essential being."[18] Moreover, Hegel's idea of self-knowledge as knowledge of mind is given universal historical scope, in which all history is seen as mind's "revelation of itself from its first superficial, enshrouded consciousness [to] the attainment of this standpoint of its free self-consciousness, in order that the absolute command of mind 'Know thyself,' may be fulfilled."[19]

Through its active spirituality, the mind or soul represents the self's divine, transcendent element, ensuring that careful self-examination does not degenerate into stifling immanence, narrow self-absorption, or morbid self-loathing and despair at the self's limitations, symbolized by the body's weakness and mortality. Such fear of despair through self-knowledge without a grounding of the self in the divine finds literary expression in a well-known eighteenth-century poem by Edward Young, "Night Thoughts," where the poet contemplates the depression that self-knowledge would bring without the faith in a divine immortal soul that God both creates and inspires in us:

> To *know myself*, true wisdom? No, to shun,
> That shocking science, Parent of despair!
> Avert thy mirror: if I see, I die."
> . . .
> The man is dead, who for the body lives. . . .
> Thyself, first, know; then love: a self there is
> Of Virtue fond, that kindles at her charms.
> . . .
> Who looks on that, and sees not in himself.
> An awful stranger, a terrestrial God?
> A glorious partner with the Deity
> In that high attribute, immortal life.[20]

Coleridge's advocacy of self-reflection for self-knowledge is similarly grounded in the transcendence of the soul: "There is one art of which every man should be master—the art of reflection. . . . There is one knowledge which it is every man's interest and duty to acquire, namely, self-knowledge."[21] Inspired both by Neoplatonism and Christianity, the poet-philosopher writes, "We begin with the *I Know Myself* in order to end with the absolute *I Am*."[22] If paganism gave us the Delphic maxim, Coleridge continues, Christian "Revelation has provided . . . new subjects for reflection and new treasures of knowledge, never to be unlocked by him who remains self-ignorant. Self-knowledge is the key to this casket: and by reflection alone can it be obtained."[23] Other English intellectuals of faith could affirm self-knowledge by emphasizing the maxim's sense of knowing our humbler place as human creatures blessed by a far superior divinity but incapable of truly understanding God's ways. As Alexander Pope poetically proclaims, "Know then thyself: presume not God to scan. The proper study of mankind is man," so John Ruskin insists that man's self-knowledge is "to recognize his everlasting inferiority, and his everlasting greatness; to know himself and his place; to be content to submit to God without understanding Him; and to rule the lower creation with sympathy and kindness."[24]

Leo Tolstoy's *Confession* is a moving account of the novelist's midlife crisis, in which rational self-examination led to morbid, self-questioning despair and thoughts of suicide, whose only remedy was religious conversion. Without regained faith in God's infinitude and his own God-given soul (a faith born not of rational but emotional conviction), Tolstoy claims, "It is possible to live only as long as life intoxicates us; once we are sober we cannot help seeing that it is all a delusion, a stupid delusion." The sole secure solution to nihilistic depression, Tolstoy concludes, is by believing in and "seeking God, for there can be no life without God."[25] Earlier, Kierkegaard's classic study of despair likewise insists that the only remedy is recognition of the self's divine grounding that inspires the self to elevate itself toward the vision of God. "The self is in sound health and free from despair only when, precisely by having been in despair, it is grounded transparently in God." Without such grounding, he argues, self-reflection only intensifies the morbidity: "the more consciousness, the more intense the despair." Yet Kierkegaard affirms self-reflection (even if painful); for without it the self can never properly realize its essential spirit and relationship to God, and thus permanently escape from despair.[26] "The depressed person is a radical, sullen atheist," concurs our contemporary Julia Kristeva in her book on melancholia, but for very different (psychoanalytic) reasons.[27]

III. Modern Critiques

Modern intellectuals less committed to traditional Christian or idealist doctrines of the soul's transcendent immortality and divine connection have been more prone to question the value of self-knowledge through self-examination. Johan Wolfgang van Goethe's critique is exemplary and influential. Fearful that the Delphic maxim confines the mind to a stifling isolation that promotes ignorance, inaction, morbidity, and "psychological self-torture," he insists that the only way to approve the command to "know thyself" is to interpret it as knowing the world in which one lives and acts. This includes knowing one's relations to other selves who provide enlightening reflections that help one to know one's own self. "We mustn't interpret it," Goethe warns, in what he calls the ascetic sense of "our modern hypochondriacs, humorists . . . and *Heautontimorumenen* [self-torturers], but [it] quite simply means: pay attention to yourself, watch what you are doing so that you come to realize how you stand *vis-à-vis* your fellows and the world in general."[28] Elsewhere, he elaborates: "That great and important-sounding phrase *erkenne dich selbst* merits the suspicion that it was a device of secretly bound priests, who confused men with unattainable requirements and wanted to lead them away from the activities of the outer world to an inner false contemplation. Man knows himself only in so far as he knows the world, . . . and he becomes aware of himself only in it. Each new object, if looked at well, opens up in us a new way to see [ourselves]."[29]

Rigorous self-examination is especially unwise and unhealthy because it is perversely unnatural and its goal of self-knowledge impossible. The command "that man should strive to know himself . . . is a singular requisition, with which no one complies or indeed ever will comply. Man is by all his senses and efforts directed to externals—to the world around him, and he has to know this so far, and to make it so far serviceable, as he requires for his own ends. . . . Altogether, man is a darkened being; he knows not whence he comes, nor whither he goes; he knows little of the world, and least of himself."[30]

Goethe's argument recalls Montaigne's image of our natural outward gaze but also looks forward to William James's critique of self-reflection in terms of what he calls the "law of parsimony" in consciousness.[31] Because we must economize our attention, the pressing demands of life and action will not allow us to focus long and intently on ourselves. Even if we succeed in grasping ourselves, we must immediately forget ourselves to direct attention to ever-new elements in the changing flux of experience. As Goethe's pithy couplet puts this point: "*Erkenne dich!—was hab'ich da für Lohn?/Erkenne ich mich, muss ich gleich davon.*"[32] Thomas Carlyle, who translated Goethe and greatly admired him, likewise rejects "the folly of that impossible Precept *Know Thyself* . . . till it be translated into this partially possible one, *Know what thou canst work at.*"[33] Convinced that the Delphic maxim implies the passivity and self-torture of introspective contemplation, Carlyle rejects this "tormented" project and instead advocates the alternative of external action through which one more productively knows oneself through one's deeds and works. "Think it not thy business, this of knowing thyself; thou art an unknowable individual: know what thou canst work at; and work at it, like a Hercules! That will be thy better plan."[34]

Given Friedrich Nietzsche's notorious "death of God" thesis, his mordant skepticism toward idealist notions of mind or soul, and his ferocious critique of the self-flagellation of Christian conscience, it is not surprising that he challenges the traditional injunction to self-knowledge as psychologically unhealthy, unnatural, and indeed impossible. "This digging into one's self, this straight, violent descent into the pit of one's being, is a painful and dangerous undertaking. A man who does it may easily take such hurt that no physician can heal him," Nietzsche writes in "Schopenhauer as Educator."[35] "What indeed does a man know about himself?" he continues in his essay "Truth and Lies in an Extra-moral Sense." "Nature keeps secret from him most things, even about his body . . . so as to banish and lock him into a proud, delusional consciousness!" Echoing Montaigne's idea that such self-ignorance is a beneficial gift of nature's providence, Nietzsche cautions, "Woe to the fateful curiosity which might be able for a moment to look out and down through a crevice in the chamber of consciousness, and discover that man, indifferent to his own ignorance, is resting on the pitiless, the greedy, the insatiable, the murderous, as if hanging in dreams on the back of a tiger."[36] Moving here beyond the familiar worries that self-examination brings painful, paralyzing consciousness of limitation or sin, Nietzsche prefigures the Freudian idea of a far more vicious and unruly unconscious dwelling within us but from which we are helpfully protected by ignorance of self.

Like Goethe and Carlyle, Nietzsche prefers the projective activity of self-cultivation to the introspective immanence of self-examination, hence his famous injunction "to become what one is." Rejecting the very idea of a fixed essential self to be known, Nietzsche instead advocates a self that emerges through a process of perfectionist becoming: "Active, successful natures act, not according to the dictum 'know thyself,' but as if there hovered before them the commandment: 'will a self and thou shalt *become* a self' . . . whereas the inactive and contemplative cogitate on what they *have* already chosen."[37] For the bold and willful spirit of "self-cultivation," he thus concludes, "*nosce te ipsum* [i.e., know thyself] would be the recipe for destruction."[38]

Twentieth-century thinkers as different as Ludwig Wittgenstein, William James, and Michel Foucault adapt this notion of a malleable, constructed self that is always in the making together with the perfectionist ideal to become a different, better self. James's epoch-making *The Principles of Psychology* (1890) radically dispenses with the idea of a transcendental ego, while defining the self as a bundle of habits and then instructing how habits could be changed. His meliorist ideal of self-development advocates a "strenuous mood" heroically exercising "active will" toward the "character of progress."[39] By his own confession, Wittgenstein went to war in 1914 not for the sake of country but through an intense desire "to turn into a different person," and his continuous striving to improve himself and his philosophical positions helps explain why most of his works were published posthumously and why his notebooks include the injunction: "You must change the way you live."[40]

Self-transformation rather than self-knowledge, Foucault insists, is the guiding goal of the philosophical life: "The main interest in life and work is to become someone else that you were not in the beginning."[41] As Wittgenstein acknowledges that self-examination can be painfully difficult ("The folds of my heart always want to stick together, and to open it I must always tear them apart"), so Foucault highlights the tormenting interrogational practices of our culture that have been inspired by the traditional ideal of self-knowledge, and he instead privileges self-cultivation as the higher ideal.[42] Knowing the dolors of depression, both philosophers seriously contemplated suicide. It had been the solution for two of Wittgenstein's impressive older brothers, and it so fascinated Foucault that he not only attempted it but also studied it and publicly advocated for its legitimation.[43]

William James, who suffered from repeated attacks of melancholy and related psychosomatic ailments, confessed to his brother Henry that he welcomed a university teaching job because it would divert him from "those introspective studies which had bred a sort of philosophical hypochondria."[44] Although his trailblazing *Principles of Psychology* urges and indeed demonstrates exquisite expertise of introspective analysis, James nevertheless vigorously warns against its use in practical life, arguing the case more explicitly than Foucault or Wittgenstein ever did. Intense self-examination, James writes, involves

> *strong feeling about one's self* [that] *tends to arrest the free association of one's objective ideas and motor processes.* We get the extreme example of this in the mental disease called melancholia. A melancholic patient is filled through and through with intensely painful emotion about himself. He is threatened, he is guilty, he is doomed, he is annihilated, he is lost. His mind is fixed, as if in a cramp on these feelings of his own situation, and in all the books on insanity you may read that the usual varied flow of his thoughts has ceased. His associative processes, to use the technical phrase, are inhibited; and his ideas stand stock-still, shut up to their one monotonous function of reiterating inwardly the fact of the man's desperate estate. And this inhibitive influence is not due to the mere fact that his emotion is *painful.*[45]

We must, James continues, free our selves—our thoughts, volitions, and actions—"from the inhibitive influence of reflection upon them, of egoistic preoccupation about their results," of "the over-active conscience" and self-consciousness. Recall his maxim for effective action and self-expression: "Trust your spontaneity and fling away all further care."[46]

IV. Contemporary Psychology and Varieties of Self-Reflection

James could find his view widely supported by recent psychological literature on self-examination. Current studies that analyze this behavior under the notion of rumination not only point to its negative psychological affects but also link it in particular to the morbidity of creative people. As novelist William Styron notes in his own memoir of melancholia:

> Despite depression's eclectic reach, it has been demonstrated with fair convincingness that artistic types (especially poets) are particularly vulnerable to the disorder—which, in its graver, clinical manifestation takes upward of twenty percent of its victims by way of suicide. Just a few of these fallen artists, all modern, make up a sad but scintillating roll call: Hart Crane, Vincent van Gogh, Virginia Woolf, Arshile Gorky, Cesare Pavese, Romain Gary, Vachel Lindsay, Sylvia Plath, Henry de Montherlant, Mark Rothko, John Berryman, Jack London, Ernest Hemingway, William Inge, Diane Arbus, Tadeusz Borowski, Paul Celan, Anne Sexton, Sergei Esenin, Vladimir Mayakovsky—the list goes on.[47]

In linking creativity with depression, recent psychological research suggests that self-reflection is the underlying root of the connection. Findings indicate not only that "negative affect leads to increased self-reflective rumination and . . . that inducing self-reflective rumination leads to increased negative affect," but also that self-reflecting people tend to be both more creative and more prone to morbidity. Just as the causal link with depressive feelings is usually explained through the negative judgments of imperfections that rigorous self-examination typically yields, so increased creativity is explained as resulting from the fact that self-examiners take themselves more seriously and thus have greater motivation for distinctive creative expression. Moreover, their sustained practice of reflecting on themselves develops greater fluency of thought (such fluency being measured in quantity of new ideas within a given time span), which in turn promotes creativity.[48]

Although the arguments linking self-examination and self-knowledge with depression are empirically supported, I would defend the value of self-reflection by suggesting that we need a more careful parsing of its modes and uses than its detractors (or its advocates) have provided. First, we should recognize, with Plato, that any viable program of self-cultivation and transformation needs to start with some grasp of what one is so that one can have some sense of what one wants to change and whether or how one is changing. To get to where one wants to go, it helps to know where one is starting from. The first step to correcting a bad habit is to recognize what that habit actually is. If, as James argues, the self is a malleable bundle of habits,[49] a crucial first step to self-improvement is probing the present limits of one's self and habits in order to grasp the needed dimensions and directions of change. As Wittgenstein advocates, "If anyone is unwilling to descend into himself, because this is too painful, he will remain superficial."[50]

Looking more carefully at Nietzsche, we see he does not fully repudiate self-reflection because a certain degree of it is implied in his ideal of self-cultivation. "Each of us bears a productive uniqueness within him as the core of his being; and when he becomes aware of it, there appears around him a strange penumbra which is the mark of his singularity," he writes in "Schopenhauer as Educator." Recognition of this uniqueness is crucial for spurring efforts of self-cultivation toward a higher self with the aid of exemplary authors who both inspire you toward realizing this higher self (that Nietzsche calls "your own true self" or "your true nature") and help keep you from becoming "depressed and melancholic" from this labor of focus on the self.[51] Even when describing self-cultivation in terms of self-fashioning through deceptive fabrications and concealments, Nietzsche recognizes that such artful stylizing requires self-observation and self-knowledge. One must "survey all the strengths and weaknesses of [one's] nature and then fit them into an artistic plan until every one of them appears as art and reason and even weaknesses delight the eye. Here a large mass of second nature has been added; there a piece of original nature has been removed—both times through long practice and daily work at it. Here the ugly that could not be removed is concealed; there it has been reinterpreted and made sublime."[52] If self-transformation must begin with clear, explicit recognition of what one already is, we can understand why Wittgenstein insists, "A confession has to be part of your new life," for "a man will never be great if he misjudges himself."[53]

Second, since many practicing advocates of self-reflection have not suffered from melancholia to any significant extent, there does not seem to be a necessary link between self-reflection and depression. So we need to inquire more precisely about the conditions or modes in which self-examination becomes morbidly depressing. One such condition seems to be an unrelenting, uncontrollable focus on the negative—negative judgments, negative affects, hypochondriac fears of negative futures, and a general negativity of the meaninglessness of one's life. Positive dimensions and hopes are totally eclipsed or obliterated in the obsessive gloom radiating from melancholy's scorching black sun. Negativity itself may not be the most depressing aspect of melancholic self-reflection; the uncontrollable, compulsive nature of such rumination could be worse. Kant defines the melancholia of hypochondria or the hypochondria of melancholia (the two terms, as Styron notes, being used interchangeably until the nineteenth century) precisely in terms of the mind's lack of "power to master its pathological feelings" by willfully diverting attention from its "brooding" about "fictitious disease" and imagined "ills."[54] The core problem, then, is the mind's weakness of will that is powerless to stop us from unwillingly "paying attention to mental and bodily phenomena" that trouble us.[55] The inability to control one's direction of thought and stem its passive repetitive feeding on morbidity creates, in turn, a strong negative feeling of impotence that heightens one's already negative mood and passive inertia, thus making it ever harder to divert one's attention to positive thoughts and action that could remedy the situation.

Contemporary psychological literature describes this passive, uncontrollable dimension of melancholic self-reflection as rumination. Susan Noelen-Hoeksema, a leading researcher in connecting depression and rumination (and in documenting their particularly frequent and strong combination in women), defines "rumination" as "passively and repetitively focusing on one's symptoms of distress," and argues that women are more likely to exhibit this uncontrolled, excessive focus because they tend to have a more diminished sense of mastery and control than men as well as a more limited scope for remedial action in the world.[56] But must self-reflection be passive and uncontrollable? Aren't there forms of self-observation that instead display and encourage active, disciplined, and heightened control of mental focus? Doesn't such sharpening of mental concentration, acuity, and willpower constitute part of the traditional philosophical argument for self-examination and self-knowledge?

Self-reflective meditative disciplines in both Asian and Western traditions have long justified and sustained themselves by providing their diligent practitioners with enhanced mental focus, strength of will, spiritual peace, psychic happiness, and somatic well-being (including great pleasure). Recent psychological research is also beginning to realize that self-examination or "personal self-consciousness" includes a wide variety of motives, styles, and foci, so that it should not be narrowly identified with passive, obsessive, depression-promoting rumination. One study shows a clear distinction between neurotic self-attentiveness (or *rumination*) and intellectually curious self-attentiveness (or *reflection*). If the former seems clearly linked to depression and motivations of fear and anxiety, the latter is instead essentially motivated by active, positive curiosity that is not significantly correlated with bad feelings but instead saliently linked to "self-control" and "conscientiousness" that imply willpower and mental mastery.[57]

Other recent studies in experimental psychology and neurophysiology have demonstrated that meditation training (including disciplines of self-examination) can effectively reduce symptoms of anxiety, depression, and panic, thus generating more positive affect in the meditating subjects.[58] Further experiments have established the neurological basis of this positive power. Having determined that positive feelings and a "resilient affective style" are associated with high levels of left prefrontal activation in the brain and high levels of antibody titers to influenza vaccine, scientists have shown that subjects introduced to an eight-week meditation training program display not only significantly higher levels of left-sided anterior activation than the control group of nonmeditators but also significant increases in antibody titers.[59] Such studies clearly suggest that disciplined forms of meditative self-monitoring can improve our mental health and powers. Identifying the obsessiveness of rumination as the key to its morbidity helps us see that condemnations of self-knowledge as detrimental to mental health wrongly equate such knowledge with relentless, disproportionate overuse of self-conscious self-examination. Too much of any good thing can be bad, and that is the case for self-reflection, whose value depends on using it in the appropriate circumstances and measures. Here it is worth recalling that alongside the maxim to "know thyself," Apollo's Delphic temple inscribed the maxim "nothing too much," as if to insist on the need for appropriate moderation in understanding and applying the first maxim.

V. Somatic Self-Consciousness

Besides the different styles, motives, quantities, contexts, and levels of self-control in self-examining consciousness, there are also different foci to distinguish. One useful distinction is between attending to one's own experience in contrast to thinking about how one appears to others (whether in terms of bodily appearance, character, social status, or overall identity). And within one's own experience, some would distinguish examining one's mind, character, or soul from examining one's somatic feelings. Recall how Kant and the Neoplatonists contrasted the uplifting duty to reflect on one's soul with the unhealthy degeneracy of somatic reflection. As someone who has been advocating and practicing the discipline of somatic reflection for more than two decades—not only as a philosopher engaged in somaesthetics but also as a professional somatic educator in the Feldenkrais Method, I have a stake in defending somatic self-awareness and reflection against the familiar condemnations of asocial selfishness, morbid passivity, obsessive weakness of will, melancholic hypochondria, and ruination of effective action. My general arguments in its defense are outlined elsewhere, but here I conclude by relating somatic self-awareness specifically to the tradition of self-knowledge and the issue of melancholia.

First, we could highlight advocates of reflective body consciousness, among them Montaigne, Nietzsche, and Dewey, who all, in different ways, inspired my work in somaesthetics. Celebrating its use for magnifying our sensuous pleasures through "the greater . . . attention that we lend" them, Montaigne urges us to "meditate on any satisfaction" so that it reverberates beyond the "senses" (*M* 853, 854). Nietzsche's critique of self-examining consciousness as fruitless and unhealthy is superseded by his recommendation to increase our self-knowledge with respect to corporeal matters. Complaining that "man has not known himself physiologically," Nietzsche recommends taking "the body . . . [as] the starting point," since "the body, as our most personal possession, our most certain being, in short our ego," inspires more faith and more promising possibilities of self-knowledge than the ethereal notions of the spirit or soul.[60] Affirming the body as "an unknown sage" within you that has "more reason than in your best wisdom," he urges us to "listen . . . to the voice of the healthy body."[61] John Dewey, though well aware of the dangers of ruminating introspection, advocated and practiced the Alexander Technique of "conscious constructive control" that involves intense focusing on certain aspects of one's body posture and movement in order to understand more clearly our habitual modes of action (and thought) and thus provide a better cognitive basis for improving them.[62]

Moreover, the meditation techniques used in recent psychological research to demonstrate the salutary benefits of disciplined self-examination for reducing anxiety, panic, and depression while promoting better affective resilience include techniques that rely on deploying focused body consciousness: namely, yoga, body scanning, and seated meditation. This should not surprise us, since *if* yoga, zazen, and other systematic disciplines of somaesthetic introspection did indeed lead to the mental weakness, morbid introversion, and hypochondria that Kant and James feared, they would never have thrived for so many centuries and in such different cultures. My Zen training in Japan taught me how methodical somaesthetic reflection can strengthen one's powers of mind and will by directing intensely focused consciousness to one's breathing or to other somatic feelings (such as the contact of one's feet with the floor in walking meditation). Willpower, as James insists, involves keeping attention firmly fixed on an idea and resisting the mind's natural tendency to wander. Our evolutionary instincts as well as our habits and interests prompt us to devote attention to the outside world of flux and the ever-changing perceptions that it stimulates, not to the constant and imminent experience of breathing. Even if we momentarily focus on our breathing, our attention very quickly turns to other things. It is thus extremely difficult to compel one's attention to remain focused wholly on the experience of breathing itself. Disciplines of sustained somaesthetic focusing can strengthen our will by training our attention to sustain concentration and resist the inclination to wander. Breathing and the body are ideal targets for such exercises of focusing attention because they are always there to focus on, while the mind typically ignores them in running off to more interesting or demanding objects. One's increased powers of concentration can then be shifted beyond one's breathing or other somatic focus and applied more generally to better govern our thoughts and steer them away from morbid compulsive directions.

I close by confronting a lingering worry about the morbidity of somatic reflection. Christian, Platonist, and idealist arguments against the body are often based on its essential vulnerability and imperfection. In contrast to the inspiring nobility, alleged immortality, or even divinity of the soul, reflective focus on one's corporeal self would promote self-diminishment and self-loathing whose only value would be to compel us to look higher to a sacred soul. But even without invoking such a soul, should not somatic self-focus necessarily tend to depress us by reminding us of the mortal flaws and limitations of our flesh? Only, I would argue, if we unrealistically expect a kind of purity and perfection that we have no right to expect and whose absence should not therefore be a depressing disappointment. Without the presumption of divinely perfect bodies (immortally invincible and free from all pain, fatigue, or blemish), there is every reason to regard our somatic selves with grateful wonder and enthusiastic curiosity for the vulnerable yet astoundingly complex and well-functioning organization of biological, social, psychological, and cultural materials that we indeed are.

Not only poets, but even philosophers as staid as John Dewey have waxed lyrical over the somatic self, describing the living, sentient human body as "the most wonderful of all the structures of the vast universe" and condemning the fallacy that serious somatic attention "would somehow involve disloyalty to man's higher life." Praising F. M. Alexander's method of intensely focused somatic self-reflection for improved self-use, Dewey concludes that when such an attitude becomes more general, not only individuals but the societies which they compose will be healthier through greater self-knowledge and self-control, as even one's will and thought is necessarily embodied.[63]

There is a more radical and paradoxical way to counter the fear of somatic reflection revealing deficiencies that diminish self-worth and lead to melancholy. It is the Buddhist option of using such reflection for denying the ultimate reality of a substantial, autonomous individual self whose imperfections could be a cause for deep depression. In this strategy, the self's apparent permanence and individuality is—through focused body consciousness—mindfully dissolved into a porous, messy welter of different elements (liquids, solids, and gases) whose transitory and changing collaboration gives rise to the temporary, fragile construct we identify as the bodily self and falsely oppose to the rest of the world from which it is temporally constructed and without whose materials and energies it could never be. Let me close with a passage from one of the Buddha's sermons advocating heightened mindfulness of the body:

> A bhikkhu reflects on this very body enveloped by the skin and full of manifold impurity, from the sole up and the hair down, thinking thus: "There are in this body hair of the head, hair of the body, nails, teeth, skin, flesh, sinews, bones, marrow, kidneys, heart, liver, midriff, spleen, lungs, intestines, mesentery, stomach, faeces, bile, phlegm, pus, blood, sweat, fat, tears, grease, saliva, nasal mucus, synovial fluid, urine." . . . Thus, he lives observing the body.[64]

So concludes the Buddha, knowing that such self-knowledge is far from a recipe for melancholia but instead a release from ultimately depressing illusions of the self's substantial permanence that make us take our individual selves with too much of the wrong kind of seriousness and selfishness.[65] Nothing too much, echoes the second Delphic maxim.

Chapter Seven

Dialectics of Multiculturalism

Ethics and Politics

I

As the new medias of cyberspace command our technological imagination, so multiculturalism seems to have captured our sociopolitical and cultural concerns. One of the noisiest buzzwords of recent times, it expresses (almost in the cybernetic sense of noise) less a clear message than a confusing, if positive, disturbance. Like its sister notion of globalization, multiculturalism is ambiguous and contested. Both notions are widely exalted as the twin keys to a new, rainbow-rich world community, but they are also frequently deplored as a virulent threat to the very roots and life of true community and culture. In bringing a wealth of new consumers and inexpensive goods from foreign markets, globalization threatens the stability of our local economy, inflicting not only chronic social anxiety but frequent tremors in our labor force through factory closures and mass layoffs. Reciprocal fears of losing sales to cheaper foreign manufacture have eroded some of the hard-earned, state-protected social benefits of workers in the nations of the still imperfectly unified European Union. Celebrated as an end to cruel centuries of nationalist wars of imperialism, globalization is now brandished to promote the imperialist aims of multinational conglomerates by undermining the protective statutes of national welfare states (that are accused, in turn, of being obsolete vestiges of narrow chauvinism). Nonetheless, right-wing nationalists conversely wield the notion of globalization to inspire a racist hate of foreign workers and resident immigrants.[1] In bringing Western contract law and business practices to the farthest corners of the world, globalization claims to be redeeming human rights and individual freedom from the tyranny of traditional social bonds. But it often seems to be simply destroying these traditional cultures (with their difference of values) in order to erect the universal tyranny of the dollar. Is globalization really establishing the intrinsic value of the Person or simply the market function of the Consumer? If anything is clear about globalization, it is its complexity, ambiguity, and conflicting valuations.

Multiculturalism, as I experience it, incorporates similar perplexities and mixed emotions. As a binational whose philosophical career spans three continents and four languages, I am sometimes urged to take pride in my multicultural education. But just as often I am made to feel anxious and ashamed of therefore having no fixed cultural training at all; of constituting precisely the sort of rootless Jewish intellectual that T. S. Eliot once condemned as a menace to Western civilization. And when I fell in love with a Japanese beauty, I did not know whether to congratulate myself on being open to an interracial relationship or instead to despise myself as a postcolonial white predator pursuing an exploitative erotic fascination for the exotic other. Was it perhaps wrong to think of her in ethnic terms at all? Most readers, I expect, have their own anecdotes of multicultural malaise. And whatever our specific "subject-positions" and personal partisanship in the culture wars, we cannot fail to see that multiculturalism evokes a confusing tangle of ambiguities and ambivalence. Its different meanings and shifting uses (perhaps too diverse and conflicted to make the concept entirely satisfactory) engender a host of controversies. Just consider the following five points of contention.

1. Praised for promoting the expression of difference in the face of society's strong homogenizing pressures, multiculturalism affirms the rights of cultural otherness against the established privilege of dominant ethnic identities. But its radical emphasis on diversity, critics allege, spawns an unhealthy fragmentation of the social body into opposing fractions, thus robbing our country of a wider sense of national identity whose unifying power is required for effective political action, even for ensuring the advancement of multiculturalism's own aims of achieving fuller freedom and flourishing for all.

2. Affirmed for boosting the self-respect of ethnic minorities by recognizing the legitimacy of the cultures to which they belong, multiculturalism is condemned for distracting public attention from deeper problems of poverty and political injustice that frame the issues of cultural recognition but that

cannot be resolved through merely cultural means. I, too, have had to face this charge. My (early 1990s) case for the artistic legitimacy of rap music has sometimes been accused of assuming that aesthetic recognition will somehow eventually assure (or compensate for) full economic and political freedom, that rap's artistic value somehow dissolves or indemnifies the evils of ghetto crime and poverty. Though pleading not guilty, I recognize the dangers of confusing cultural acceptance with social empowerment, even if I also insist on the limited (but still valuable) power of aesthetics for politics.

3. Vaunted for protecting the established cultural traditions of minority ethnic groups from erosion by the assimilating pressures of more powerful cultures, multiculturalism is conversely condemned for violating the individual's most basic rights to freedom. While some extol the multicultural ideal of cherishing French Quebecer culture by requiring its natives and new immigrants to be educated in French-speaking schools, others denounce it as a repressive violation of personal liberty and a reactionary refusal of a broader, more progressive transculturalism through new cultural affiliations and productive mixing.

4. Touted for bringing new cultural richness by introducing the diversity of non-European aesthetic traditions, multiculturalism is contrastingly chided for impoverishing our culture through loss of pedagogic focus rooted in a coherent canon. More means less, say the critics, when it is mere dilettante dipping in the cultural inkwells of ethnic otherness. Still worse, it seems a disrespectful plundering of the cultural goods of disadvantaged others. For champions of the traditional canon, multicultural eclecticism also presents a threat. By ushering in so many new works, new styles, and new standards in such wholesale fashion, it risks radically reshaping our artistic tradition, threatening the value of what we already have by challenging the integrity of the structure of tradition through which artworks acquire their meaning. Moreover, by introducing its new works and styles more on the basis of universal claims of ethical fairness than through concrete aesthetic justification, multiculturalism sometimes seems to challenge the very legitimacy of aesthetic discriminations of good and bad. Nothing could be worse for the cause of culture and the appreciation of difference.

5. Finally, while multiculturalism claims to underline the diversity of cultures, critics argue that it in fact obscures real cultural diversity by confusing culture with superficial fictions of race and individuating cultures by the surface criterion of skin color. In affirming the multicultural rights of Native Americans, there seems to be less respect for the specific differences between Navaho, Seminole, Cherokee, and Apache cultures than a general

concern to assimilate them all as common victims of political injustice. The same might be said for the differing African-rooted cultures that exist in American diaspora and that are grossly lumped together under the concept of African-American. The monocultural blurring of multiculturalist concepts is still more evident in the category of Asian-American, which ignores the enormous differences between Japanese, Chinese, Korean, Indian, and other Asian cultures. All this suggests that today's idea of multiculturalism is not really based on respect for coherent cultures at all but rather on a sad recognition of grave social injustices that Americans (and Europeans) have systematically committed along racial lines, the term "culture" euphemistically substituting for "race." Indeed, if terms get their meaning through contrast, one wonders what is the defining contrast of multiculturalism? Rather than "monoculturalism" (a term rarely used or defended), its usual opposite is "Eurocentrism"; yet this term belies the great cultural diversity in Europe itself.

That multiculturalism is a confused and contested concept does not mean it is a useless one. Vague terms still signify; they even serve better as political rallying calls precisely because of their encompassing vagueness. But in deploying the concept for philosophical work, we need to recognize how its precise meaning shifts according to the specific contexts of multicultural debate, from nation to nation, discipline to discipline, from one historical context to another. In the United States—a country with a nonethnic ideology that separates church from state and that prides itself as a country of immigration from different cultures and races yet has a history marked by a dominant Anglo culture—the pressing issues of multicultural debate will differ from those in a country like Germany. For German national ideology still maintains (despite demographic facts and recent legislature to the contrary) that it "is not a land of immigration" and instead insists on linking its national identity to the romantic idea of a special *Kulturnation* based on a deeply shared language, tradition, and ancestry. Germany is also the place where an enlightened postwar population still struggles with the living Nazi memory of state-orchestrated genocide of foreign ethnicities.[2]

So while German multicultural debate has focused on the problem of citizenship, social integration, and safety from violence for the vast population of (primarily Turkish) foreign workers and their families, multiculturalism in the United States concentrates on other issues: How much distinctive cultural recognition and compensatory advantages should be given to the different minority cultures resulting from immigration (including the forced immigration from the African slave trade but also the cultures of Native

Americans, who became a minority through the immigration of others)? How can a unified core American culture be sustained in this diversity? And if this country is just a container for the multiple, hyphenated identities of African-American, Asian-American, Hispanic-American, Italian-American, Jewish-American, Polish-American, and so on, how can we maintain sufficient unity to guarantee effective political process for our national interests? Countries (like Canada or Finland) that have rival linguistic communities and more than one official language face their own special multicultural issues. In France—which combines a large immigrant population from its colonial past with an ideology of republican egalitarianism through French acculturation orchestrated by a powerfully centralized education system—multicultural battles have focused most prominently on the dress-code infraction of the Muslim schoolgirl's *foulard* and on the violation of personal rights in religiously motivated rituals of clitoridectomy.

Even in the same country, the precise meaning of multiculturalism can differ from one historical age to another, often because of changes in the ways the different cultures are individuated. Thus the "cultural pluralism" that Horace Kallen advocated for the United States in the 1910s and 1920s was far more concerned with different European cultures of minority immigrants facing the established hegemony of Anglo culture. Like later pluralist movements before the present multicultural boom, it also gave far more weight to religious factors than American multiculturalism does today.[3] Finally, the meaning of multicultural discourse shifts greatly from discipline to discipline. If literature departments treat multiculturalism as a question of revising the artistic canon to redress the oppressive blindness of cultural hegemony (including patriarchal, sexist culture), constitutional theory and political philosophy see the issue in very different terms—as a conflict between group rights and individual rights, or in terms of the familiar paradoxes of toleration endemic to liberal democracy: Does freedom of speech entail the right to hate speech? To what extent should we tolerate views and practices that themselves seem intolerant?

In emphasizing the multiple meanings of multicultural discourse, my aim is not to deny that this diversity is rooted in a commonality of overlapping problems but simply to insist that when exploring the idea of multiculturalism, we should be clear about the sort of philosophical issue that shapes the context of our concern. Neither the constitutional issue of group versus individual rights nor the paradoxes of liberal tolerance is what motivates me here. My prime concern is how the idea of multicultural understanding can be integrated into the ethical project of self-transformation where philosophy is conceived and practiced as a critical, meliorative art of living within determinate sociopolitical cultural contexts.

II

Charles Taylor has influentially argued that multiculturalism's political issues of group rights, tolerance, and recognition of difference all grow out of the deeper problem of the individual's need for distinctive self-expression and self-fashioning.[4] With the collapse of traditional social hierarchies of honor based on inequalities of distinction, modernity developed a universalist and egalitarian sense of dignity rooted in human personhood. But by the end of the eighteenth century, and stimulated by Rousseau's notion that moral judgments were properly rooted in the intuitions of our sentiments, the idea of realizing one's personhood took a less abstract, more individualized turn. Then, in Taylor's view, Johann Herder's notion that "every person has his own measure and mood" finally introduces original self-expression as "the modern ideal of authenticity." Taylor explains: "There is a certain way of being human that is my way. I am called upon to live my life in this way, and not in imitation of anyone else's life" (*PR* 30). To live a full and authentic life, Taylor argues, has thus come to mean expressing one's individuality.

But authenticity's "goals of self-fulfillment and self-realization" require more than the individual's own resources. For the self is essentially social and dialogical in character, constructed from our interaction with other selves, who give us a sense of our own qualities, roles, limits, and worth. Even the meaning of our most private thoughts derives from a language that depends on, and is acquired through, dialogue with others. So if we fail to gain the recognition of others for what we are, our own sense of self is somehow diminished and impaired. These others who help constitute our identity and whose recognition is crucial for our own self-affirmation include not only those intimates whom we care most about, those "significant others" (in George Herbert Mead's phrase) who introduce us to our values and set our models, expectations, and horizons for self-realization. Beyond this crucial intimate circle, we need recognition from wider social groups with which we interact and against which we measure ourselves.

If the modern self demands expression not of a universal human essence but of its own particular authentic identity, then we need more than simple recognition of our basic, equal dignity as human beings; we need a recognition of the *distinctive* people we are. But since part of our distinctiveness depends on the distinct ethnic, gender, or social group of which we are members (groups whose cultural resources form the individual's tools for self-expression and self-creation), then our right to distinctive dignity of self seems to require a right for the distinctive dignity of these groups to which we belong. Particularly with groups that have suffered humiliating oppression, self-dignity requires a recognition of the special worth and dignity of one's group, not just the consolation of being recognized, at bottom, as sharing essential human personhood with individuals of more dignified social categories. In this way, "the politics of difference grows organically out of the politics of universal dignity," while opposing its universalizing tendency to level cultural differences (*PR* 39).

Taylor therefore argues for the rights of distinctive cultural groups to sustain and protect their distinctive identities, even to the point of imposing limits on the freedom of their members (as, for example, in requiring French Quebecers to educate their children in Francophone schools). Such group rights, he maintains, paradoxically grow out of the individual's rights to express her distinctive identity and to preserve the distinctive cultural resources for continuing to express this distinctiveness. For the individual's "rights to cultural membership"[5] cannot mean much when that culture lacks the political means to preserve itself. Hence Taylor accepts the legitimacy, in certain circumstances, of collective goals overriding one's individual freedoms in order to ensure the survival of an endangered cultural species (such as, presumably, the French Quebecers). Defenders of our dominant, procedural liberalism retort that individual rights always come first and have "absolute precedence over collective goods," unless those collective goals are themselves adequately justified by more important, fundamental rights of individuals. These liberal critics, who doubt whether the rights Taylor alleges are sufficiently fundamental, are also quick to emphasize the political dangers of full respect for cultural otherness. Pointing to the dilemma of tolerating intolerant claims of cultural expression, they cite cases such as the fundamentalism of the Rushdie death *fatwah* threat and the racism of hate speech.

I now turn from these important political issues in order to probe more deeply the basic multicultural issue of expressive self-realization from which they seem to stem. Taylor's helpful account needs to be refined by looking more closely at the intricate dialectics that complicate the assertion of identity through multicultural recognition. It especially needs to be complemented by an altogether different perspective on multicultural identity that Taylor and other philosophers tend to ignore. Taylor argues that our demand for distinctive self-expression to realize our identity emerges from two modern phenomena: the loss of a secure (if not always flattering) identity guaranteed by fixed social hierarchies, and a new desire for a more "*individualized* identity" (*PR* 28) than that expressed by something universal like human reason. This desire, which Taylor traces to the late-eighteenth-century advocacy of intuitive moral sense guided by feeling, as against an overly rational ethics of "dry calculation" (*PR* 28), suggests a third complex reason for the growing demand for individual self-fashioning in the past two centuries. A diminishing faith in traditional moral codes and in the very possibility of deriving any universal ethical principles from a presumed human essence has made the conduct of life increasingly a matter of taste and style.

As ethics melts into aesthetics, so art replaces religion as the most credible core of spiritual value. The artistic genius (a positive power beyond the fixity of traditional laws) replaces the saint (and even the scientist) as the spiritual hero of our culture. Yet the waxing power of democratic ideology (reinforced no doubt by a profit-hungry economy keen to market lifestyles) calls upon all of us to become the artists of our individual lives. "Everyone is special," paradoxically intones the familiar mantra of advertising, as it perplexingly implores us to affirm our distinctive uniqueness through the purchase of mass-produced commodities. Taylor sees the need for distinctive self-expression as entailing a need for recognition of the distinctive culture of the social group through which our identity was forged, because culture provides us with far greater resources for meaningful self-expression than we could ever achieve on our own. Our lives become larger and more significant when seen as part of the greater group and history to which we belong. But in taking the artist as exemplar of authentic individuality, Taylor unwittingly introduces a problem for his view, since the modern paradigm of the artist's self-expression involves critical distance and an oppositional stance toward the society that shaped her.[6] Likewise, the most potent moments of artistic creativity more often seem the product of adventures in cultural traveling than narrowly inbred expressions of ethnic patriotism.

There is another puzzling wrinkle in multiculturalism's affirmation of self-expression through advocacy of cultural difference. Taylor and others justify this politics of difference by arguing that the distinctiveness of the minority cultures must be emphasized to counteract the tendency to assimilate them to the dominant culture. This assimilation is often done implicitly by ignoring their specificity and subsuming them under a universal humanism, so that these minority cultures are taken to express the very same core human essence that the dominant culture does, although less clearly or familiarly. Such essentialism, it is claimed, robs the dominated cultures of their specific worth and content. But the politics of difference courts its own damaging dialectic of essentialism. In denying traditional universal humanism as an oppressive myth disguising Eurocentric-phallocentric hegemony, multiculturalism affirms an anti-essentialist emphasis on cultural difference that recognizes the historical construction and complexities of human identities. But, given the practical stakes of cultural struggle and the problematic way in which our history of oppression has individuated minority cultures, the politics of difference quickly falls into its own form of essentialism that often seems especially self-serving. In a competitive society whose ideology of equality demands compensatory favoring of disadvantaged ethnic groups that have been somehow exploited or persecuted, individuals seek to promote themselves by affiliation with such victimized cultures. A common cultural essence is thus presumed and projected in ways that often seem arbitrary and opportunistic. This presumed common essence obscures the valuable distinctiveness of the different cultures lumped together in terms of this essence and instead perpetuates the same primitive categories of race and color that generated these cultures' history of oppression. The multicultural category of Asian-American (which did not originally include Asians from the Indian subcontinent and still often ignores them in practice) looks more like a racist essentialism of "yellow people" than a politics of recognition of difference; for it brutally homogenizes the important cultural differences between (and within) the Chinese, Japanese, Korean, Thai, Vietnamese, and other East Asian–rooted cultures that exist in America.[7]

To ensure the presumed distinctive essence of a culture (especially when that essence seems vulnerable or dubious), its borders must be protectively policed. Insisting that American society should open itself up to include specific minority cultures, multicultural advocates often exercise their own separatist strategy of purist exclusion, even when they know the distinctive culture they champion is far from pure and even owes its distinction to its hybrid mixing. Rap culture provides a good example of this phenomenon. Celebrating the aesthetic of the mix through its signature technique of sampling, rap is the product of blending different cultures of African diaspora with American pop culture in the volatile crucible of urban life. But despite its affirmation of hybridity and its aspiration to embrace a rainbow coalition of hip-hop enthusiasts from all over the world, rap still needed to affirm itself distinctively, and sometimes even exclusively, as black ghetto music. In a dialectic of exclusion where rejected cultures affirm their intrinsic worth by rejecting those who rejected them, rap separatists repeated the proud but wayward strategy of the Jews: the more that Jews were scorned, persecuted, and excluded in ghettos, the more they insisted on their special status as the "chosen people" and the higher they raised the bar of conversion for those who wanted to identify with their culture.[8]

Such turns toward essentialism and separatist exclusion plague the logic of multicultural difference. In eschewing the notion of a universal human essence so as to insist on the claims of cultural difference, multiculturalism threatens to erect such differences into rigid distinctions between a set of impermeable cultures. In defining one's cultural group by sharply contrasting it to rival groups, one multiplies the barriers to mutual understanding within the multicultural spectrum. Yet isn't the goal of multicultural recognition to have one's self and culture understood, not just stridently asserted as different? The advocacy of difference seems crucial, however, to resist the cultural imperialism of liberalism's standard formula for recognizing people of other cultures: simply assimilate them into us and ignore their differences. Thus Richard Rorty's neoliberal ideal of multicultural understanding is "to extend our sense of 'we' to people whom we previously thought of as 'they.'"[9] But such an imperially patronizing attitude does not really credit the foreign culture with any integrity or value of its own. If, as Taylor insists, a people's "identity is partly shaped by recognition or . . . the misrecognition of others" (*PR* 13), then they need recognition not simply as an assimilated "us" but as a respected "they." By homogenizing or ignoring their difference in our aim of inclusive understanding, we are robbing them of the "external recognition" of their "equal value" that Taylor sensibly sees as necessary for self-respect (*PR* 64). But if true recognition demands understanding a different culture on its own terms rather than ours, how can this be achieved? How do we get beyond this apparent conflict between recognition of otherness and shared understanding?

Part of the problem, I think, is a one-sided stress on affirming one's culture vis-à-vis the culture of others.[10] This attitude clearly underlies Rorty's presumption that assimilation to our own culture is the only way minorities can gain our recognition. But this self-affirming stance is also evident in Taylor's pluralist counterclaim that minority cultures should proudly demand from mainstream culture an "external recognition" of their distinctive yet equal worth. Beyond this simple logic of self-assertion, I propose a different approach: a self-challenging exploration of the culture of others in order to test, deepen, and enrich our own sense of self.

III

Even when most sincere, the quest for a better understanding of the culturally other often contains the further (sometimes even dominant) desire of better understanding oneself.[11] To seek self-understanding through the medium of others reflects the Delphic injunction "to know oneself" that set the entire course of Western philosophy when Socrates pursued it for himself by engaging others in dialogue. Exploring the self through comprehension of the other proceeds not simply by confrontational contrast but also by way of integrative participation. We learn to understand ourselves better by discovering the cultural others in us. Sometimes these others are already deeply present and just need to be uncovered, but sometimes they lurk more in the margins as potential dimensions waiting to be incorporated into the self. The self can incorporate them because it is neither a fixed universal essence nor an immutable personal one. Shaped through change and interaction, it derives its unity not from a permanent core but from its stability and coherence in transformation and narrative.

We should begin by recognizing the productive value of simple contrast expressed in the conceptual interdependence of self and other. In the logic of complementarity—whose importance in Western philosophy can be traced back to Heraclitus and whose modern champion is Hegel—anything or everything is defined by its others.[12] The limits of any entity, hence its individuation, are determined by what lies outside those limits, by what constitutes the environing field in which these limits can be constructed and the entity individuated from the rest of the field. To understand oneself as a self implies a knowledge that there is something outside the self, an *other* in contrast to which the self can be defined and distinguished. Since our environing fields are social and cultural as well as spatiotemporal, we need a sense of the culturally other against whose background our own culture and self can be defined. Beyond the bare logical point that self-understanding requires the other because the very definition of self does, the other provides a medium or dialogical partner through which the self can see and test its limits. Insisted on by many post-Hegelians but already evident in the dialogical and epistolary philosophical traditions of antiquity, this theme of contrast is also prominent in the fictional literature of diverse cultures. In order to find himself (or herself), the protagonist must venture into foreign lands or into the wilderness (a *natural* otherness that by differing from one's indigenous culture and requiring quite a different way of life amounts to a *cultural* otherness as well).

Encountering the culturally other not only prompts us to self-awareness but spurs us toward a deeper probing of who we really are. Hans-Georg Gadamer makes this point in his famous discussion of prejudice, which he treats as cognitively enabling because it is limiting: "It is impossible to make ourselves aware of [our prejudice] while it is constantly operating unnoticed, but only when it is, so to speak, stimulated" by something that challenges its limits. An encounter with a culturally other, even if it is merely "the encounter with a text from the past, can provide this stimulus" and so "make conscious the prejudices governing our own understanding" and constituting our own culture and self.[13] But in using other cultures as a contrast to help us better grasp our own, we must not forget the danger of stressing differences rather than shared appreciation and empathetic interchange. How can we avoid erecting such cultural contrasts into a divisive arena of oppositional self-assertion between cultural identities that seek to define themselves by presuming their essential, irremediable difference? This question is extremely difficult to answer, not only because it is nested in the tangled dialectic between multicultural difference and shared understanding (which dialectically includes the understanding of difference), but also because multicultural recognition enfolds a complex web of varied and often conflicting motivations: social acceptance, cultural distinction, economic advantages for disfavored difference, et cetera. Those who struggle to fit in, sometimes (in other contexts or for other motives) prefer to stand out.

One strategy to deploy cultural contrast while avoiding the unbridgeable barrier of essentialist difference would be to loosen the fixity of cultural identities by recognizing their contextual character, given their constitution in terms of contrasts in their environing sociocultural fields. Such identities can be neither very precisely nor rigidly defined but must change with the changing elements in the given sociocultural field, where the field is as much a construction of its elements and their varying positions as those elements are a function of their place in the field. The result is that one's self-definition and sense of self are differently constructed in different contexts in light of the kind of others who constitute the self's field. One is more conscious of being a white man when one suddenly finds oneself surrounded by a large group of Japanese women. By the same logic of contextual complementarity, a patriotic Breton is apt to feel his cultural difference from France more in Paris than in Beijing, which provides a far more dramatic range of contrasts.

As an American-Israeli binational, I know the vagaries of cultural identity from personal experience. Since English was my mother tongue, I was defined by Israelis as being an "Anglo-Saxon," while in America I am defined as Jewish in contrast to Anglo-Saxon ethnicity. As an Israeli, one is geographically Asian, though culturally very close to Europe. Hebrew, however, is far from a European language; and Israel has not been admitted to the European Union, though it belongs to European sports associations (having been thrown out of Asian sports!). In the East/West division of culture—a division as false as most binary oppositions—Israeli culture seems to inhabit (and suffer) the punctuating slash. When I studied at Oxford, I would vacillate between presenting myself as an Israeli and as an American, though a close Sikh friend of mind had a third view of my ethnic identity. As my father and all my grandparents came from Eastern Europe, I was neither American nor Israeli but essentially of East European ethnic heritage. Since the fields that define the self can thus be differently drawn through different narrative contexts and from different historical perspectives, even at the same time, the variety of identity-changing contexts can be greatly multiplied. And in a world where increasing speed of physical transit and information flow makes us shift our contextual fields quite rapidly, it is not surprising that our sense of identity has become more problematic. If this fuels the postmodern idea of the disintegration of the subject, it also promotes today's passion for multicultural identity politics as a tool to sharpen our vague sense of identity by self-affirming, contradistinctive ethnic affiliations, even though (or perhaps because) our different cultures are becoming more porous and mixed.

Encounter with the culturally other fosters self-understanding in a second way: not by mere contrast but through accretion or absorption. In other words, in defining ourselves by addressing another culture, we can revise and enrich ourselves by assimilating aspects of that other and by integrating the complex consequences of this cultural interchange. Through this process of self-definition and development by self-transformational absorption of the other, an individual (in Friedrich Nietzsche's phrase) "becomes what one is."[14] T. S. Eliot provides good testimony of how one's self is defined and transformed through wide reading in alien cultural worlds. To understand the literary works of another culture, one must to some extent accept their structures of meaning and belief. As Eliot describes it, "You have to give yourself up, and then recover yourself," "but the self recovered is never the same as the self before it was given."[15] When we are immature and read a powerful author, Eliot explains, "what happens is a kind of inundation, of invasion of the underdeveloped personality by the stronger personality" of the author. But the more experience and wider reading we assimilate, the more well-rounded, tempered, and sturdy our belief structures become, and thus the less likely we are to be one-sidedly possessed by any one author or foreign culture.

Moreover, since different cultural views are often in conflict, digesting a variety of them makes us compare them critically. And this stimulates a clearer formation and expression of our own selfhood through our comparative assessment of the different views. As Eliot explains, wide reading and experience of the culturally other are valuable, therefore, "not as a kind of hoarding" or accumulation of information, but "because in the process of being affected by one powerful . . . [author or culture] after another, we cease to be dominated by any one or by any small number. The very different views of life, cohabiting in our minds, affect each other, and our own personality asserts itself and finds each a place in some arrangement peculiar to ourself."[16] Hence Eliot urges that "we make the effort to enter those worlds of poetry in which we are alien" so that we can better understand the world and culture we identify as most our own, but do so without falling into a parochial cultural chauvinism.

Eliot practiced what he preached. A native of St. Louis, Missouri, he absorbed himself deeply in French and Indian culture before thoroughly projecting himself into the English culture that he eventually made his own, even to the point of naturalization as a British subject and conversion to Anglicanism. Eliot's early fascination with Indian philosophy is particularly instructive on this issue of self-understanding and self-fashioning through projection into the culturally alien. His example suggests there are practical limits beyond which one's understanding and absorption of the other threatens to destroy one's stable, familiar sense of self. Though he originally hoped to make it his prime topic of doctoral research, Eliot confessed to have abandoned his study of Indian philosophy because the task of bringing himself to understand it in its utmost depth would have involved transforming himself into a very different person, which for practical and personal reasons he did not wish to become. Self-expanding, self-testing encounters with the other are enriching but can be dangerously destabilizing. What seems easy and limitless in theory is often painfully stressful and incapacitating in practice, as we could learn from refugees who are forced to settle in alien cultures. My conclusion is not to reject cultural travel but simply to recognize its risks and limits, so as to make it more fruitful. That is a pragmatic way of putting what can also be aesthetically formulated. We should seek cultural variety for enriching and defining the self but only to the extent that such variety can be held in a satisfying unity. As with other aesthetic questions, no fixed rules can be prescribed for the ideal balance. Critical taste and intelligence will be required to find this optimum.

Besides contrast and assimilation, there is a third way in which understanding the culturally other can promote a better understanding of the self. This is in cases where our cultural selves are, in fact, composed of elements of the culturally other that we have so far failed to recognize and thus have not fully understood. Here, by coming to understand the other we improve our self-understanding by understanding that other in ourselves. Typically, we take the "selfhood" of our cultural self for granted; we presume the unity and autonomy of our culture, ignoring that our cultural self is often partly constituted by elements from cultures that we all too simplistically regard as radically other. We fail to realize the cultural others in ourselves in two different ways: either by simply failing to recognize the culturally other dimension of these elements or by failing to reclaim the richness of this dimension even when we recognize its otherness.

Take two examples. Western philosophy tends to distinguish itself sharply from both Asian philosophy and from African philosophy (to the meager extent that it is even ready to acknowledge and respect the latter). Yet it can be argued that Western philosophy is deeply indebted to Asian and African philosophical traditions, and thus has already incorporated these presumed radical philosophical others. We do not need to enter the "Black Athena" debate and engage the more radical Afrocentric claims that Egypt is the prime source of Greek philosophy. For whatever the truth about ultimate origins, it is clear that ancient Greek thought was deeply influenced by Asian and African sources. Even Diogenes Laertius, the patriotic chronicler of the early Greek philosophers, who zealously insists philosophy was a Greek invention, nonetheless is ready to admit that several of the most important Greek thinkers (such as Democritus) learned significantly from the Indian "Gymnosophists" and Egyptians.[17] It is also clear that modern continental philosophy (in Schopenhauer and others) has been partly influenced by Asian thought, which has also marked American philosophy through its seminal impact on Emerson. Failure to recognize these cultural others in our own Western philosophical tradition is not just an insult to these others, a failure of external recognition; it also constitutes a failure of self-recognition, a lack in our own cultural understanding.

For an example far outside the realm of philosophical culture, consider the case of American country music. Frequently expressing the most patriotic and chauvinistic sentiments, it regards itself as an "all-American" music and has sharply distinguished itself from African-American music and other ethnic music. Yet country music is in fact deeply rooted in the black musical tradition of the United States; country's first and most formative stars, such as Jimmie Rodgers and Hank Williams, learned their skills and style from black performers. This influence was originally so evident that country music was first classified (in record stores and in the professional music magazines) along with black music. The steel string guitar sound, regarded by fans as characteristic of "pure country," was in fact imported from Hawaii as late as the 1940s. These foreign ethnic roots have been quickly forgotten by today's country fans who see themselves as the protectors of the country tradition. They have been erased in popular consciousness not simply by the passage of time but also by the drive to sustain a model of authenticity based on an imaginary cultural pureness, rather than pursuing an alternative model of authenticity based on the fruitful facts of cultural mixing.[18] Underlying this drive for pureness is the false assumption that cultural identity is inherently diminished or violated by the inclusion of elements from another culture. Such an assumption must deny the obvious fact that most cultures are hybrid and historically constructed through dialogical exchange with each other and that cultural traditions seem for the most part stronger and richer through their synthesis of multicultural sources.

The English language gained its rich range and power by absorbing both French and German elements. If American culture seems today more potent than the English culture from which it stems, this is largely the product of its integration of many different vibrant cultures through successive waves of immigration (not all of them voluntary or happy). Even Jewish culture, despite its tenaciously separatist ideology of the "chosen people," actually derives its longevity and richness more from its skills of cultural adaptation and importation from more dominant environing cultures: Hellenistic, Arabic, and European. Cultural syncretism is already evident in the Hebrew culture of the Old Testament.

If our self-understanding as Western philosophers (or as country music fans) requires the realization of the foreign roots or elements that helped form our tradition, what does such realization actually amount to? Two levels can be distinguished. Realizing the other in our cultural selves can simply mean recognizing the historical fact of these other elements. Such bare recognition, however, does not seem sufficient for a deep understanding of the other in ourselves; hence it cannot give us a full self-understanding. More than simply acknowledging that inner other, we need to learn and incorporate it for ourselves, to grasp and reclaim consciously what previously belonged only blindly and implicitly to us. This calls for a personal discipline of cross-cultural study whose limits and rewards seem ever expanding but whose "trans-world" travel risks are far from negligible.

I know this from personal experience, since my own philosophical life has been structured by such a transcultural quest for self-realization, long before I ever thought of it as such. If leaving my native American home to settle in Israel at the age of sixteen gave me a much deeper realization of my Jewish identity through a life of work, study, and military service in the Jewish state, it also deeply alienated me from the American culture that had formed me. My Israeli life paradoxically made it more difficult to reintegrate myself into the American Jewish community when I finally returned to the United States.[19] After being back for more than thirty years, it is still hard to feel that I have entirely come home. Perhaps I never shall. Like most binationals, wherever I go (even if back to Israel), home has also been, will always have been, a very different place. Grateful for the enrichment of my Israeli experience, I am nonetheless sometimes saddened by the loss of an undiluted, unequivocal American identity, particularly when I think of how strongly I identify myself with American pragmatism.

But the same desire to deepen my identity by reclaiming a cultural other buried in myself led me to leave America again in the mid-1990s and make Berlin my home for eighteen months, an experience that shaped my writings on urban aesthetics and other themes.[20] As a pragmatist philosopher, I recognized how deeply classical American pragmatism drew from German philosophical culture and how closely it relates to the work of the Frankfurt School. As a secular Jewish intellectual, I recognized how profoundly this cultural identity has been informed by German culture. Even my family name bears a German imprint, though I have no known German ancestors. While I long regarded German culture as not only foreign but hostile (hence I never studied its language and literature in my student days in Jerusalem and Oxford), it had undeniably marked my identity in many ways, even in something as personal as my surname. To give these marks a clearer meaning I needed a fuller knowledge of the culture and language that marked them; and knowing the woeful limits of my skills in learning from books, I knew I had to transplant myself to Germany to learn the language by living in it for at least a year. If to know myself meant learning that culturally other, this in turn meant distancing myself, once again, from the things most dear to me in American life, including its cultural, ethnic, and racial diversity. Of course, philosophy's quest for self-knowledge has never been perceived as effortless and trouble-free, even if its end is often seen as peace and tranquility. But, for me in Germany, it was not always easy to distinguish between the healthy asceticism of philosophical self-improvement and the twisted psychological self-torture of pushing oneself beyond where one should go.

In the cosmic economy, our gains always seem to involve some loss. But my experience suggests that philosophers risk losing more by a stolid refusal to recognize and integrate the cultural other in ourselves. This plea for greater openness could be expanded to include more integration of personal experience and testimony as a rhetorical "other" in academic philosophical discourse. Although the personal witness of the last two paragraphs makes me somewhat uncomfortable, I feel uneasy for stylistic rather than philosophical reasons. I am worried about the limits of good taste, not logical relevance. We cannot outlaw the use of autobiographical details here by arguing that they are contingent while philosophy should only concern the necessary. That argument may work for certain topics of philosophy but not for those that involve understanding our contingent selves. Even if banished on the level of explicit discourse, the personal will always motivate us beneath the surface. Why philosophize about our understanding of self and other, if not out of the personal experience of its inadequacies and the desire to improve our understanding not only in theory but in our own concrete practice?

Chapter Eight

The Ethics of Democracy

I

Two of America's most prominent contemporary philosophers, Hilary Putnam and Stanley Cavell, address the question of democracy by studying the arguments for its justification and reconciling its defense with the claims of individual self-perfection. Both Putnam and Cavell explore democracy not in terms of its concrete rules and political institutions but rather as an ethical ideal that is central to what they regard as the primal philosophical question "How to live?" Thus Cavell advocates "the life of philosophy" for its "power to change people" by teaching them to live better; while Putnam declares that "the role of philosophical reflection at its best" is "to change both our lives and the way we see our lives," since "we all have the potential of thinking for ourselves with respect to the question of How to Live."[1]

This, of course, was the burning question for nineteenth-century Harvard-bred thinkers like Emerson and Thoreau, who avidly pursued it not only theory but also through adventurous experiments in living (such as Thoreau's life in Walden). Faithful to this tradition of construing life as the central philosophical project, Cavell and Putnam chide professional philosophers for ignoring it to concentrate narrowly on metaphysical issues that have virtually no impact on how one lives. By affirming philosophy's practical orientation to the problems of life, Putnam and Cavell are likewise true to the spirit of pragmatism. Both are especially inspired by Dewey's ethics of democracy and self-realization.[2] But by criticizing its alleged limitations, each attempts a better theory of the democratic philosophical life. To continue this project of reconstructive pragmatist meliorism, I hope to show where their own theories, as well as Dewey's, require revision and amplification. I begin with Putnam, who, unlike Cavell, firmly identifies himself with pragmatism.

Putnam's defense of democracy is explicitly built on two Deweyan lines of argument that he characterizes as *social* and *epistemological*. The social line of argument helps combat the kind of skepticism about democracy that derives from a demand for "absolute" justification, one that would justify democracy in terms of "the world as it is independent of our experience" (*RP* 81).[3] Dewey's pragmatism—with its insistence that knowledge is always situated and has impact on the plastic, changing universe—rejects the very idea of such an absolute point of view. There is thus no possibility and no need to justify democracy in terms of something beyond the experience and values that situated members of a community already share. Justification of democracy is always already social, addressed to a community and based on its values. It aims at "giving reason to people already disposed to hear it, to help in continually creating a community held together by that same disposition." It is, as Putnam says, "addressed to *us* as opposed to being addressed to each 'me'" (*RP* 183). Moreover, the values to which it appeals are essentially social in a further sense: being values of shared intelligent discourse and action, rather than mere values of physical or psychic fitness (metaphorically described by Bernard Williams as the "ethological standard of the bright eye and the gleaming coat" *RP* 182).

Complementing this "social justification" is what Putnam calls Dewey's "*epistemological justification of democracy*," a line of argument that similarly issues from pragmatism's insistence that knowledge (along with the very notion of reality) depends on a community of inquirers.[4] Putnam formulates the claim like this: "Democracy is not just one form of social life among other workable forms of social life; it is the precondition for the full application of intelligence to the solution of social problems" (*RP* 180). How is this strong claim supported? The argument's first premise, Putnam maintains, is that "*epistemology is hypothesis*." Experience has shown that knowledge of the world, including its realm of values, is best achieved not through *apriorism* or acceptance of authority but through "intelligently conducted inquiry," which includes the formation of hypotheses and their testing in experimentation (*RP* 186). Second, the social condition that promotes the fullest capacities for forming and testing hypotheses is surely a free collaborative community of inquirers exchanging their different points of view and results. Hence "the need for such fundamental democratic institutions as freedom of thought and speech follows from requirements of procedure in general: the unimpeded flow of information and the freedom to offer and to criticize hypotheses" (*RP* 188). For Dewey such freedom means *positive* freedom or real empowerment to apply one's thought to the government of self and society. Democracy means active participation rather than simply leaving questions of governance to experts who are entrusted with the job of ensuring the freedoms and benefits that we enjoy from society.

Dewey can defend his participationist model of democracy over the consumerist one of expert-governance by again employing his epistemological justification. Despite their specialist knowledge, experts do not know everything relevant to the direction of society. Good government, therefore, needs the participation of all members of society, because all these different members, through their diverse situations, possess differently situated knowledge that needs to be heard so as to ensure not only a wider range of hypotheses about how to direct society but also a wider range of criticisms of those hypotheses that are actually tested. As Putnam states Dewey's argument, because the materials used to assess and improve democracy "cannot be circumscribed in advance," it follows that "there is no one field of experience [or one class of people] from which all the considerations relevant to the evaluation of democracy come" (*RP* 189).

Dewey was particularly suspicious of the "cognitive distortion" produced by the privilege of experts: "A class of experts is inevitably so removed from common interests as to become a class with private interests and private knowledge, which in social matters is not knowledge at all," since it fails to see the experience and interests of other sections of society (*PIP* 319). "All special privilege narrows the outlook of those who possess it" (*E* 347). The argument that experts rule best gets its power by assuming that they *know* best, that they possess more than *all* others all the necessary knowledge for governing society. But this in turn assumes that we know what that necessary knowledge is, that we know, for example, what our essential human nature, needs, and capabilities are. "In contrast," Putnam asserts with Dewey, "we don't know what our interests and needs are or what we are capable of until we actually engage in politics. A corollary of this view is that there can be no final answer to the question of how we should live, and therefore we should always leave it open to further discussion and experimentation. That is precisely why we need democracy" (*RP* 189; *WL* 217).

II

While endorsing Dewey's "social philosophy" of democracy as "overwhelmingly right," Putnam finds his "moral philosophy" inadequate for treating "problems of individual choice" that are central to the core ethical issue of how to live (*RP* 190). The problems Putnam has in mind are those "individual existential choices" of the kind evoked by Jean-Paul Sartre's famous character Pierre (described in *Existentialism and Humanism*), who confronts the agonizing choice between joining the Resistance (and thus leaving his aged mother alone on the farm) or remaining with his mother (and forsaking the Resistance). Such "problems of individual choice" cannot simply be handled like "social problems" of collaborative empirical problem-solving, where we aim "to 'maximize' the good" by choosing the best solution in terms of "estimated utilities." For it is not a question here of obtaining general social consequences that are good but rather of what is good or "right" for the individual (*RP* 190).[5] Such decisions cannot be determined by scientific method but instead require an "existential" act of freedom or leap of faith beyond any available evidence. As Putnam forcefully puts it:

> Someone who acts only when the "estimated utilities" are favorable does not live a meaningful human life. Even if I choose to do something of whose ethical and social value there is absolutely no doubt, say, to devote my life to comforting the dying, or helping the mentally ill, or curing the sick, or relieving poverty, I still have to decide not whether it is good that someone should do that thing, but whether it is good that I, Hilary Putnam, do that thing. The answer to that question cannot be a matter of well-established scientific fact, in however generous a sense of "scientific." (*RP* 194)

Putnam therefore turns to William James, who famously argued that with crucial, pressing personal questions (such as religious faith) one has the right to exercise the will to believe "in advance of the evidence" (*RP* 192). Seeing this Jamesian voluntarist idea reflected in Sartre's and Kierkegaard's views of existentialist self-creation, of "becoming who [one] . . . is," Putnam endorses it as the best model for addressing the personal ethics of how to live (*RP* 191).[6] Dewey's failure to recognize such individual ethics is explained as resulting from a "dualistic conception of human goods" that divides between a social-ethical dimension expressed in terms of rational collaboration and, on the other hand, an aesthetic dimension where the individual finally finds expression but only through her private "consummatory experience." Putnam continues,

For Dewey there are fundamentally two, and only two, dominant dimensions to life: the social dimension, which for Dewey
meant the struggle for a better society, the release of human
potential; and the aesthetic dimension. To the criticism that
he fundamentally saw all of life as social action, Dewey could
and did always reply that, on the contrary, in the last analysis
he saw all "consummatory experience" as aesthetic. The trouble
with this answer is that a bifurcation of goods into social goods
which are attained through the use of instrumental rationality
and consummatory experiences which are ultimately aesthetic
is too close to the positivist or empiricist division of life into
the prediction and control of experiences and the enjoyment of
experiences to be adequate. (*RP* 196)

That Dewey's "conception of human goods" involves a rigid dualism between
the social and the aesthetic—the one concerned with improving society
through scientific rationality while the other concerned simply with private
consummatory experience—is a very troubling charge. It is particularly
troubling since Dewey's declared pragmatist agenda was to overcome such
divisions between science and culture, society and the self, instrumentality
and art. But any such social/aesthetic dualism can be refuted by looking more
carefully at Dewey's ethics and aesthetics and by elaborating an important
argument for democracy that Putnam ignores, one I shall call the *aesthetic
justification* for democracy. Before taking this up, we should appreciate the
full force of Putnam's claim that neglecting the individual ethics of how to
live is not merely a minor omission in a theory of democracy but a central
gap that would undermine the whole democratic project of modernity.

III

Putnam draws a useful distinction between three basic conceptions of
equality in premodern Western culture (all seen to be inspired by "the
Jerusalem-based religions") and the modern conception established by Kant.
The former three Putnam formulates as follows:

(I) There is something about human beings, some aspect which
is of incomparable moral significance, with respect to which all

human beings are equal, no matter how unequal they may be in talents, achievements, social contribution, etc.

(II) Even those who are least talented, or whose achievements are the least, or whose contribution to society is the least, are deserving of respect.

(III) Everyone's happiness or suffering is of equal prima facie moral importance. (*MFR* 45)

In all three of these traditional conceptions, Putnam notes, "the value of equality does not have much to do with individual *freedom*" and "can be reconciled with various sorts of totalitarianism" (*MFR* 46, 51). One can easily imagine a totalitarian theocracy urging and interpreting these equalities in terms of "divine human nature" and then repressively limiting freedom so that this divine nature and its promise of eternal happiness and salvation are not perverted by ungodly temptations. One can imagine secular totalitarianisms making similar moves to ensure "equality."

In contrast, Putnam argues, Kant gives a radically new "content to the notion of equality . . . that builds liberty into equality." Human autonomy, for Kant, means more than free will and our capacity for reason. It is also "the idea that we have the further freedom that we have no knowledge of a fixed end of what human happiness is," since abstract reason cannot determine the content of "an inclusive human end that we should all seek (unless it be morality itself, and this is not an end that can determine the *content* of morality")" (*MFR* 46, 49). Our choice of how to live is therefore not predetermined or constrained by any knowledge of the essence of human nature, function, or happiness.

Consequently, as Foucault also noted,[7] Kant urged the enlightenment maxim *Aude sapere*: dare to know by daring to think for yourself. And this need to think for ourselves is likewise where we find a particularly modern democratic conception of equality that also implies freedom. Since we all have to think for ourselves without prior knowledge of what human essence and happiness are, this ability to think becomes "itself the most valuable fact about our lives. *That* is the characteristic with respect to which we are all equals. We are all in the same predicament, and we all have the potential of thinking for ourselves with respect to the question of How to Live" (*MFR* 50). This "is not just a virtue but . . . the most significant moral capacity that we have," one whose denial in an individual would mean that the denied "has failed to live a fully human life" (*MFR* 61–62).

If equality is defined in such terms of free thinking about how to live, then constraints on that freedom would threaten democracy's claim to equality as well as to liberty. And if ethics were simply a question of social planning in which collaborative inquiry by the group provides the knowledge that determines all decisions about how to live, then there would no longer be freedom for the individual to choose how to become who she is. Such an ethics would be inconsistent with modern democracy. These are the deep worries that spur Putnam to attack Dewey for refusing individual ethics through a bifurcation of the social and aesthetic. But we can dispel such fears and allegations by recognizing an aesthetic justification for democracy that we can elaborate on the basis of Deweyan ideas, a justification based on the strongly personal yet social aesthetic satisfactions that democracy provides when pursued as "a *personal* way of individual life" (*LW* 14: 226).

We should first remember that Dewey's aesthetics denies any dichotomy between social instrumentality and aesthetic consummatory experience. I explain his arguments in *Pragmatist Aesthetics*, but let me briefly recall them here. In contrast to the dominant Kantian tradition that defines the aesthetic in opposition to practical interest, Dewey celebrates the embodied interest and wide-ranging "instrumental function" of aesthetic experience, whose stimulating energy both enriches present activity and overflows into tasks (*AE* 140, 144). Moreover, in contrast to a privatistic aesthetic, he insists that art's experience is essentially social and communicative: "Since it is constituted . . . by the common qualities of the public world," art is a communicative "remaking of the experience of the community in the direction of greater order and unity" (*AE* 87, 275). Finally, Dewey insists on the ethical dimension of aesthetics, claiming that "art is more moral than moralities" (*AE* 350). Aesthetic imagination is always suggesting ideals higher than those of conventional morality, evoking new visions or models of life beyond those the individual has encountered in real life but to which she can aspire in addressing the question of how to live. As if to answer Putnam's worry about the need to go "in advance of the evidence," Dewey declares that art fosters our "sense of purposes that outrun evidence and of meanings that transcend indurated habit," such purposes and meanings enriching the experiencing self both aesthetically and ethically (*AE* 350).

If aesthetics is not in opposition to the social, instrumental, and ethically personal, we can develop an aesthetic justification for democracy based on the idea of enriched experience and self-realization. It involves three related lines of argument. The first is this: Any individual of a community is a social individual who has needs, habits, and desires associated with and affected by communal life. Therefore, the individual's free and active participation in democratic life—in the social business of directing associated life as well as in the protection and government of her own personal freedom—will make her experience and self aesthetically much richer and more interesting than if she had no opportunity to participate in the government of self and society. Since democracy provides better opportunities for the free and equal participation of more individuals in government, it can provide them a richer life and is thus superior. As Dewey puts it: "Only by participating in the common intelligence and sharing in the common purpose as it works for the common good can individual human beings realize their true individualities," and the "self which is formed through action which is faithful to relations with others will be a fuller and broader self than one which is cultivated in isolation" from them (*LSA* 20; *E* 302). The second aesthetic justification is closely related. If nothing is "as fulfilling and as rewarding as is concerted consensus of action," then since participatory democracy promotes such action, it should be valued and pursued for the experiential satisfactions such action brings. Democracy is based on communication, which "is consummatory as well as instrumental," and fosters "shared experience [which] is the greatest of human goods" (*EN* 145, 157).

The third argument appeals again to the aesthetic idea of personal, experiential enrichment but develops it through democracy's respect for difference and the right of every individual to have and develop her distinctive perspective on life. Democracy's advocacy of the free and equal (though not necessarily identical) participation of all different types of people in the direction of community life greatly enriches the experience of them all. It not only provides the spice of variety and novelty but gives the individual a heightened sense of her own distinct perspective and identity. "To cooperate by giving differences a chance to show themselves because of the belief that the expression of difference is not only a right of the other persons but is a means of enriching one's own life-experience, is inherent in the democratic personal way of life" (*LW* 14: 228).

In defining democracy by the aim that "further experience will grow in ordered richness," and in recognizing that this pursuit will be guided by "need and desire" that go "beyond knowledge, beyond science," Dewey can be seen as offering not only an aesthetic justification but also an aesthetic ideal of democracy that affirms the role of personal ethics and life choices in advance of the evidence. "Democracy, as a personal, an individual, way of life," demands "a working faith in the possibilities of human nature," the same sort of will to believe that Putnam appeals to in James (*LW* 14: 226, 229). It also requires faith in one's (and others') aesthetic sense regarding which existential choices will make a richer but still unified self. These choices of the self, Dewey insists, cannot be legislated by the group for the individual on the basis of scientific findings about social utilities; they are rather a function of one's particular needs and desires. Explicitly linking democratic theory to aesthetics, Dewey claims that just as significant aesthetic wholes must be "constituted by parts that are themselves significant," so "no significant community can exist save as it is composed of individuals who are significant" (*AE* 207–8).

Blind to this aesthetic justification of democracy, Putnam falsely condemns Dewey for a bifurcation of the social and the aesthetic that leaves no room for a personal ethics of self-creation. Like Richard Rorty, he wrongly identifies Dewey's democratic project with the procedural, institutional democratic theory of John Rawls. But while Rorty finds such a public-democratic/private-aesthetic dualism convenient for his privatized aestheticist ethics of self,[8] Putnam resists this aestheticism and instead looks to James and existentialism to find a place for an individual ethics that defies the alleged Deweyan dichotomy of the social and aesthetic. However, just as the aesthetic/social, aesthetic/ethical, and aesthetic/instrumental dualisms are false, so is the dualism of social/individual. The individual, as Dewey insisted, is always already social. Even one's most private thoughts and personal dilemmas reflect the voices of society one has internalized, which does not, for all that, preclude one's freedom.[9]

Putnam may have overlooked the individual dimension of Deweyan democratic ethics, because Dewey *does* tend to highlight the social—insisting not only on the social construction of the self but also on the essentially social nature of its self-realization. Although advocating individual "self-realization as the moral ideal," he argued that the individual self is best fulfilled not by consciously attending to its individuality but by instead attending to the social relations and shared concerns that shape and enrich the self in forming its interacting environment. "Self-realization may be the end," but preoccupation with self is not the way to achieve it. For "to make self-realization a conscious aim might and probably would prevent full attention to those very relationships which bring about the wider development of the self" (*E* 302). Hence Dewey's recommendation for individual fulfillment in democracy is not to cultivate consciously one's distinctive self but to enrich it by concentrating on shared interests and "objects that contribute to the enrichment of the lives of all" (*E* 302–3). This does not deny individual expression in lifestyles, since differences in our talents, situations, and inclinations will make for distinctive contributions to the society and values we share. Nor does it mean that every life must be devoted to politics, since the realm of shared interests is much wider. But it does militate against extreme concentration on the self's personal distinction and private gratifications.

Dewey practiced the ethic he preached, translating his personal quest for self-fulfillment into the social struggle for a more democratic society and systematically sublimating (perhaps even repressing) his more private concerns and desires. If his life proved that distinctive self-realization is consistent with selfless social action, it fails to entail that this is the best or only way for self-perfection today. Nor does it really prove that democratic self-realization must always eschew the focus on selfhood. If contemporary society is more fragmented, selfish, and privatistic than in Dewey's day, then self-realization may more likely succeed by taking a more privatist turn. This is Rorty's conclusion, reinforced by the fear that attempts to force a unity of social and personal good will lead either to repressive self-denial or oppressive imposition of one's personal authority on others. Forsaking Dewey's union of democracy and the ethics of self, Rorty consigns democracy to the merely external role of protecting our freedom to pursue private, aesthetic self-fulfillment.

Sharing Rorty's concern for individualism and failing to see it satisfied in Dewey's democratic theory, Putnam instead seeks a way to connect the projects of self-creation and democracy. He does so by seeing self-creation as expressing the basic equality that modern democracy must guarantee: freedom of thought about how to live. However, given the basic tensions between freedom and equality that Putnam (like Dewey) recognizes, this strategy seems far too thin to unite the quests for democracy and self-fulfillment. The value of thinking *for* oneself does not entail the value of thinking largely *about* one's distinctive self. Dewey's worry remains: preoccupation with distinctive selfhood not only impoverishes the self but also deprives others of care and weakens the social bonds of democracy. To relieve this worry we could turn to Stanley Cavell's ingenious ethics of democracy, whose arguments share Dewey's strategies but surpass them.

IV

Cavell's 1988 Carus Lectures on Emersonian perfectionism seek to reconcile the ideals of self-realization and democracy that together constitute the core of the American dream. Emerson's advocacy of independent, nonconformist, self-perfection (one that inspired Friedrich Nietzsche's elitist *Übermensch*) must therefore be shown to be consistent with democracy's egalitarian concern for the good and justice for all. But Cavell (like Dewey and Putnam) wants more than mere consistency through compartmentalization. He wants the deep, essential integration of democracy and self-realization. In defending the conscious cultivation of distinctive self-perfection, his ambitious goal "is not simply to show that it is tolerable to the life of justice in a constitutional democracy but to show how it is essential to that life" (*CH* 56). How, then?

Put most briefly, perfectionism is "essential to the criticism of democracy from within" by providing the sort of caring, demanding, critical, self-improving individuals who can best guarantee that the institutions and practitioners of democracy will not rest content with the always imperfect justice and improvable good they provide. Cavell develops his argument through a critique of Rawls's seminal account of democracy as essentially a matter of institutional rules and procedures for administering justice. Praising Rawls's formulation of the general principles by which constitutional democracy can both administer justice and criticize its failures to do so "from within" its principled framework, Cavell nonetheless insists that perfectionism is also "essential to the criticism of democracy from within," and he contests Rawls's rejection of perfectionism as "inherently undemocratic, or elitist" (*CH* 3).

Formulated in his distinctive writerly style, Cavell's arguments resist clear summary. Yet the main lines are these. First, perfectionism is necessary because institutions and principles are only as strong, just, and effective as the individuals who animate, apply, and criticize them. Only perfectionism can build the "character to keep the democratic hope alive in the face of disappointment with it" (*CH* 56). This is precisely Dewey's argument about why democracy must be practiced as a personal, individual way of life: "Democratic *institutions* are no guarantee for the existence of democratic individuals . . . [while] individuals who are democratic in thought and action are the sole final warrant for the existence and endurance of democratic institutions" (*LW* 14: 92).

Second, to rely simply on institutional principles of justice allows us to become complacent about the injustices, brutalities, and waste of human opportunities that, given the existing complexities and scarcities of our world, are not excluded by mere compliance to the general principles of justice. Cavell thus contests Rawls's idea that by correctly following these principles we could live "above reproach" (*CH* 18).[10] The perfectionist will never be satisfied with herself or with the system as long as any injustice or misery exists. Reproaching herself and the system for not doing better, she will constantly struggle to better herself and others. Democracy, if it is to realize the best justice possible, needs this vigilance and supererogation.

Finally, Rawls sees perfectionism as a fixed teleological principle "directing society to arrange institutions and to define the duties and obligations of individuals so as to maximize the achievement of human excellence" in some particular set of valued domains.[11] But Emersonian perfectionism, Cavell argues, is no institutional principle promoting some fixed hierarchy of ends; it is rather an individual ethical injunction to strive to be better and do so by being always open to exploring the claims of different ends.

These critiques of Rawls's institutionalism are clearly in line with Dewey's democratic ethics of the self, whose ideal of continual growth and self-perfection spurns complacency as intrinsically immoral and refuses the very notion a fixed set of final ends that would set a limit to growth. Like Dewey, though clearly more inspired by Emerson, Cavell advocates a dynamic self that is directed at self-improvement and (through this) at the improvement of society. Constantly in the making, the self should always be striving toward a higher "unattained yet attainable self." "To recognize the unattained self . . . is a step in attaining it," but the process of striving is never completed: not because we never reach the next or higher self, but because in reaching it, we always see yet another next, still higher self to reach for (*CH* 12).

Self-perfection, as "a process of moving to, and from, nexts," demands real courage. Not only must it overcome habit and fear's "resistance to internal change," but it must also face the unpleasant fact that we *need* radical improvement (*CH* 12, 16). For Cavell, this borders on self-loathing: "Emersonian Perfectionism requires that we become ashamed in a particular way of ourselves" so as to consecrate ourselves to our next selves and a better society. It involves "an expression of disgust with or a disdain for the present state of things so complete as to require not merely reform, but a call for a transformation of things, and before all a transformation of the self—a call that seems so self-absorbed and obscure as to make morality impossible." Replying to the apparent immorality of such self-perfecting self-absorption, Cavell questions: "What is the moral life apart from acting beyond the self and making oneself intelligible to those beyond it?" (*CH* 16, 46).

In linking self-transcendence with intelligibility to others, Cavell deploys a Deweyan strategy for countering the radical opposition of self and society. The self must be seen as essentially dialogical and structured by the society it shares. Informed not only by society's shared language but also by the different voices it has heard and internalized, the self cannot fulfill and understand itself without regard for others. "Becoming intelligible to oneself may accordingly present itself as discovering which among the voices contending to express your nature are ones for you to own here, now" (*CH* xxxvi). Moreover, the self can define its own distinctiveness only by its relations of contrast and connection with others. Hence perfectionism's preoccupation with self, its demand for "absolute responsibility of the self to itself," is not aimed at narcissistic isolation. It instead calls for "responsibility of the self to itself, by way of others," "through endless specification [of the self], by way of exemplification, in the world (of and with others)." Cavell calls this "the absolute responsibility of the self to make itself intelligible, without falsifying itself" (*CH* xxvii).

Such general arguments for the conceptual interdependence of self and society hardly dissolve all conflict between individual-focused perfectionist cultivation and the claims of democratic community. They could not dispel Dewey's fear that democratic self-realization will only be stunted by taking one's own self (rather than one's environing community) as the conscious end-in-view. Yet, by applying Dewey's own epistemological and aesthetic arguments, Cavell can make a strong case that democracy is excellently served by self-absorbed perfectionism. The idea, in a nutshell, is that the struggle to perfect one's individuality and exemplify it in the social world will provide our democratic community with attractive models that recommend both why democracy is worth having and how it may be improved or enriched.

Epistemologically, perfectionism serves the democratic search for better life and greater justice by offering three related resources: an inspiring example of untiring meliorism, specific hypotheses about how best to live, and the critique of such hypotheses. Perfectionism's relentless demand for self-improvement gives an exemplary standard and spur to improving the society in which the self is found. Not only does it build the "character to keep the democratic hope alive" in the face of disappointment, but it offers a potent way of recognizing the value of other selves by its privileging of the unattained, next self who is, as yet, another. Thus "recognizing my differences from others [is] a function of recognizing my differences from myself" (*CH* 53). Since self-growth and intelligibility require properly acknowledging others, self-perfection should promote social change toward a more democratic "human" order. Perfectionism means being "open to the further self, in oneself and in others; which means, holding oneself in knowledge of the need for change; which means, being one who lives in promise, as a sign, or representative human, which in turn means expecting oneself to be, making oneself, intelligible as an inhabitant now also of a further realm . . . , call this the realm of the human—and to show oneself prepared to recognize others as belonging there" (*CH* 125).

Cultivation of individualistic self-realization also serves democracy by providing the community with a wealth of different life hypotheses of how to live. The democratic community is involved in a search for better ways to live and to provide greater justice. By refusing to conform to conventional ways of living but instead consciously cultivating one's individual distinction and exemplifying it in the world, perfectionists provide their fellow citizens with new models or experiments of good living, whose value is tested through their lives, thus advancing democracy's "conversation of justice" (*CH* 24–25).[12] Through her nonconformist, heightened sense of self, the perfectionist makes herself representative of a very particular way of life, developing her own special "partiality," since there are always different ways of living that might, for some, be better; and our human finitude means we can live only in some partial way. By presenting their distinctive lifestyles, perfectionists offer alternatives to conventional life that we might adapt and apply to our own conditions. Still better, they could inspire us "to let their foundings of partiality challenge us to find our own." Others thus stand for selves that we have not yet recognized or achieved; they represent "our beyond" (*CH* 58, 126).

Finally, perfectionism offers the democratic community an immanent critique of its various visions of the good life. Each partial life of self-perfection constitutes an implicit critique not only of any universal claim of other perfectionist partialities but *especially* of the necessity and value of conformity to the conventional. Such critique by exemplars of difference seems especially democratic since it works not by appeal to some absolute end or fixed standard that denies our freedom to choose the life we think more perfect. Instead, the exemplar's critical force derives from its aesthetic appeal, its attraction over other ways of living. The aim is not to refute the other's way of living "but to manifest for the other another way" (*CH* 31).

The manner of persuasion is similarly aesthetic; here discursive "moral justifications come to an end and something is to be shown"—the superior appeal of such a life (especially in contrast to the misery that complacent principles of "good enough justice" still allow). Here, ethical "constraint names, in the place of the Kantian 'ought,' a form of attraction, the relation to the friend [another or further self]; and judgement is backed not by a standard (a moral law, a principle of justice) but fronted by the character of the judger," whose power is the attraction of the life and self she both displays and strives for (*CH* xxix–xxx, 31, 124). As aesthetics figures centrally in our assessment and adoption of the best ways to live, so it affords an argument for encouraging individualistic self-cultivation in democracy. Besides a greater range of useful hypotheses for living, individualism offers self and society the pleasures of rich variety and distinctive difference: hence, "separateness of position is to be allowed its satisfactions" (CH 25).

Although employing these very arguments for individual self-realization, Dewey still cautioned against its conscious cultivation, advocating instead that self-realization should be sought in selflessly attending to other things. Emerson made the same case for indirection in self-perfection: "I like not the man who is thinking how to be good, but the man thinking how to accomplish his work."[13] Yet Cavell may have an argument why this indirect strategy will not succeed. If the motor for self-perfection is self-critique that results in deep shame or self-loathing, then *unless we examine ourselves closely and constantly*, this shame will not surface and constantly prod us toward perfection.

Cavell's argument why self-improvement requires self-absorption is presented as a categorical or universal claim, as true for the ancients as for our contemporaries. But even if historicized, it can still be effective and seems even more convincing.[14] For Dewey, who grew up with the Congregationalist ideal of selfless service and a deeply entrenched religious sense of guilt, the meliorative habit and sense of community may have seemed sufficiently strong to motivate self-perfection through social service. For us postmodern seculars steeped in social fragmentation and skepticism about progress, Cavell may be right that only intense concentration on oneself can generate a strong enough drive for continuous improvement. But whether this drive must be fueled by shame and self-loathing is not clear. Narcissism and heroism, which run deep in the history of philosophical life, are also strong motives for self-absorption, even if egalitarian democrats may not want to face this. Indeed, Cavell's perfectionism can be seen as a form of democratic heroism in which self-cultivation encourages us to ever greater efforts to respect the difference, claims, and suffering of others, even if these labors take the form of pursuit of our own further self who is represented in others as "our beyond."

V

Cavell's reconciliation of self-cultivation and democracy is extremely ingenious: self-focused perfectionism entails concerned respect for others since they are implied in the self's unattained but attainable further self. But will this strategy work? Does perfectionist self-cultivation really make us more democratic or is it, as Rorty thinks, indifferent to the question of democracy and therefore in need of relegation to the private sphere? Since neither conceptual inference nor controlled experimentation seem real options here, how indeed could we determine this issue? One is tempted to assess Cavell's theory by its own aesthetic standards of attraction, not simply as an abstract line of argument, but (as he puts it) by its "exemplification" in the philosophical life he leads. Has his own cultivation of individual perfection made him more democratic? Is Cavell an "exemplar" whose attraction constrains and inspires us to take a similar (though, given our own individuality, also a somewhat different) course of self-absorbed self-cultivation?

These questions clearly call for ad hominem arguments, which academic philosophy, as any freshman knows, has firmly dismissed as invalid. But if philosophy is viewed as recommending a way to live, such arguments cannot be dismissed; a philosopher's theory of living can surely be assessed in terms of the actual life it inspires. But if legitimate and important, how should ad hominem considerations be pursued? How available is a philosopher's actual life, and how far is it reasonable and moral to probe it? Do we need investigative reporters and private detectives to assess a philosophy of life?[15]

Although he never directly raises such questions, Cavell's account of philosophical living suggests an answer to them. It is embodied in his advocacy of a tool of democratic self-perfection that he rightly criticizes Dewey for neglecting: the transformative activities of writing and reading. Compelling us to go beyond what we already are by expressing something new, writing drives us toward our unattained but attainable self. And, in so showing the importance of this other self, it helps us to appreciate the value of others. Conversely, reading compels us to consider thoughts we had not previously attained, thus inducing not only recognition of the other selves who wrote them but also that of our own further self who, by embracing them, is enriched. Cavell thus makes writing and reading the essence of the philosophical life of self-perfection. Speaking as much for himself as for his heroes Emerson and Thoreau, Cavell insists that the philosopher's "writing is part of his living, an instance of the life of philosophy"; "his writing is this life." Or, since writing and reading are simply "variations" of each other, we can say "the interplay of writing and reading is what he claims as his philosophy" (QO 10, 18; CH 42).[16]

In highlighting philosophical textuality as a valuable means for democratic self-perfection, Cavell marks an advance on Dewey. But even if we regard textual activity as important as more overt democratic action, one should not take it as an adequate substitute for the latter. Otherwise, Cavell's textualist advance on Dewey would be a grave regression. It may, in any case, reflect philosophy's retreat from more robust praxis. Cavell's emphasis on textual activity conveys (as it atones for) the admission that philosophy's true target is the ideal "city of words" (*CH* 7–8) rather than the direction of actual community life. Dewey was not ready to concede this, but his confidence in philosophy's public leadership is now much harder to share, though perhaps not quixotic in all domains.[17]

Construing democratic self-perfection as an essentially textual way of life might help answer the ad hominem questions raised above. It suggests both a criterion for assessing the attraction of a philosophical life and a way of limiting what in that life should be relevant for such assessment. If the philosopher's life is expressed primarily in his writing, then the attraction of that exemplified life must also be exemplified in that writing. So if the persuasiveness of a philosophy of life is in the attraction of the life lived, this in turn is in the appeal of the life as written. No wonder Cavell has turned to "autobiographical exercises" as in *A Pitch of Philosophy* and more recently in *Little Did I Know*.[18]

But there is danger of grave confusion here, because the notions of writing and its attraction have a very distinctive meaning for Cavell. Writing, for him, is not merely the formulation of texts and ideas but a deeply personal, ethical work of self-critique and self-transformation. It is (in Pierre Hadot's sense) a spiritual exercise or *askesis* on one's actual self.[19] If one's writings genuinely transform one's self, it is only because they transcend it by moving toward a higher self toward which they also bring the actual, living self. It is *not* because they constitute a higher, merely textual *persona* that is only causally connected with the concrete, embodied person who writes. Similarly, for Cavell, the attraction of writing cannot mean the easy charm of an appealing writing style like, say, that of William James. Otherwise, Cavell's philosophy would stand condemned by its own criterion. In contrast, the self-conscious difficulty of Cavell's writing aims not to flatter the reader's taste (or Cavell's own) but rather to challenge it and thus engage both self and reader more deeply so as to effect the aim of self-transformation. If one challenged his "aversive," difficult style as an obstacle to democracy's egalitarian aims, Cavell could counter that an easy style would be false to the struggle for self-knowledge and transcendence that is equally central to democracy's project. He might further argue that even apparently obscure and difficult texts (like Wittgenstein's) can eventually reach a wide audience and be effective on various levels of understanding.

Indeed, despite its uncompromising, often tortured style, Cavell's own work has enjoyed a rather wide reception, even outside academic philosophy.

The idea of simply perfecting and presenting oneself as a beautifully written text would be condemned by Cavell as a debased perfectionism. But such a vision of philosophical life has indeed been proposed, most explicitly in Alexander Nehamas's *Nietzsche: Life as Literature*. Here "Nietzsche himself . . . is none other than the character [his] very texts constitute." His philosophical life has nothing to do "with the miserable little man who wrote them but with the philosopher who emerges through them, the magnificent character those texts constitute and manifest."[20] The whole life of philosophy, the philosopher's very substance, becomes a merely literary affair—no doubt a seductively flattering and cozy conclusion for academic philosophers after the linguistic turn, especially for those with literary pretensions. But Nietzsche himself can be invoked against this. In attacking the modern neglect of philosophical living, he complains: "The only critique of philosophy that is possible and that proves anything, namely trying to see whether one can live in accordance with it, has never been taught at universities: all that has ever been taught is a critique of words by means of other words."[21] In scorning the academic textualism of the universities, Nietzsche reverts here to an ancient Hellenistic distinction between real philosophical living and mere philosophical words. The beauty of a life should be in the former and not merely in the latter.

Although Cavell's ethics of democracy is not reducible to a mere textual aestheticism, it leaves itself too vulnerable to such an interpretation through its extreme emphasis on writing and neglect of other important dimensions of democratic philosophical life. For isn't there more to knowing how to live than knowing how to write and read, even in the special, more demanding, perfectionist sense that Cavell gives these textual terms? If the philosophical life is really taken seriously—that is, with the full-blooded rich concreteness that life entails, we need to go not only beyond a fictive textual persona but also beyond the ideal "city of words" and idealistic dimensions of self-transformation that Cavell emphasizes. We want to know not only how attractively a philosophy of life was pursued and formulated in words but also how attractively it was embodied in concrete deeds, in ethical and political praxis. Socrates's appeal derives not simply from its linguistic expression (for that is mostly Plato's) and from its sense of inner struggle for self-betterment but largely from the heroic public actions of his exemplary life and death. If Dewey's philosophical life attracts us, this is not due to his expansive good will and melioristic industry as exemplified in the persistent reformulations of his ideas in prose (that is often dull and prolix); it is because his actual life embodied tireless democratic praxis.

An attractive ethics of democracy must be concretely lived as well as written. In distinguishing between mere professors of philosophy and true philosophers, Thoreau insists on this point: "To be a philosopher is not merely to have subtle thoughts, nor even to found a school, but so to love wisdom as to live according to its dictates, a life of simplicity, independence, magnanimity, and trust. It is to solve some of the problems of life, not only theoretically, but practically."[22] No one knows this better than Cavell, who first reclaimed Thoreau and Emerson precisely to criticize academic philosophy's retreat from the practical task of philosophical living. Yet by emphasizing philosophy as writing and reading, while saying nothing about other forms of self-perfection, Cavell does not do enough to prevent philosophy's reappropriation as a merely textual activity.

There are, of course, problems in going beyond a philosopher's texts. If we assess a philosophy of life by its real-life embodiment, philosophical criticism then converges with biography. Heidegger's contemptible Nazi collaboration becomes relevant to his philosophy of authenticity, as Foucault's concrete acts of political rebellion and experiments with drugs and sadomasochism become relevant to his philosophy of transgressive truth. Their writing on these topics does not suffice. What, then, is the range of biographical details that can be relevant? Any that can be shown relevant by a good critic who understands a philosopher by interpreting both writings and life in light of each other. Such philosophical criticism requires not only analytic power but also historical skills and psychological insight.

If embodiment puts additional demands on the critic, it is still more demanding on the philosopher who must exemplify his way of life as attractively as he can, not only through exemplary writing and ethico-political praxis but also through the appeal of his own personal appearance and style. "The philosopher," Thoreau urges, should be "in advance of his age even in the outward form of his life" (W 270). The quest for attractive philosophical embodiment must therefore not neglect the philosopher's own body, whose shape and functioning express the nature and quality of his life: "Every man is the builder of a temple, called his body, to the god he worships, after a style purely his own, nor can he get off by hammering marble instead. We are all sculptors and painters, and our material is our own flesh and blood and bones" (W 468).

What sort of body makes an attractive exemplar for a democratic philosophical life? This may seem a ridiculous question, but it simply extends

Putnam and Cavell's concern with "how to live" to a crucial dimension of life they neglect. The soma is a site where we can really "change both our lives and the way we see our lives" (*RP* 200) by literally reshaping ourselves and our relationship to our bodies.[23] Independent self-realization in this dimension can also contribute to the democratic discussion of how to live by offering and testing new hypotheses about which somatic forms and practices are most rewarding and emancipatory. The conformist oppression of our highly advertised standards of bodily appearance, behavior, and functioning can and should be challenged.[24] These issues of somatic care and improvement belong to the field of "somaesthetics," an important but much neglected task for philosophical critique through both words and embodied practice. Both are integral to the fullest life of philosophy.

III

Aesthetics

Chapter Nine

The End of Aesthetic Experience

I

Experience, quipped Oscar Wilde, is the name one gives to one's mistakes. Does aesthetic experience then name the central blunder of modern aesthetics? Though long considered among the most essential aesthetic concepts, as including but also surpassing the realm of art, aesthetic experience has in the last half century come under increasing critique. Not only its value but its very existence has been questioned. How has this once vital concept lost its appeal? Does it still offer anything of value? The ambiguous title "The End of Aesthetic Experience" suggests this chapter's two goals: a reasoned account of its demise, and an argument for reconceiving and thus redeeming its purpose.[1] Though briefly noting the continental critique of this concept, I mostly focus on its progressive decline in twentieth-century Anglo-American philosophy, where its descent is most extreme and in whose tradition (of John Dewey, Monroe Beardsley, Nelson Goodman, and Arthur Danto) I situate my own aesthetic work. While Dewey celebrated aesthetic experience, making it the very center of his philosophy of art, Danto virtually shuns the concept, warning (after Duchamp) that its "aesthetic delectation is a danger to be avoided."[2] The decline of aesthetic experience from Dewey to Danto reflects, I shall argue, deep confusion about this concept's diverse forms and theoretical functions. But it also reflects a growing preoccupation with the *anaesthetic* thrust of this century's artistic avant-garde, itself symptomatic of much larger transformations in our basic sensibility as we move increasingly from an experiential to an informational culture.

To appreciate the decline of the concept of aesthetic experience, we must first recall its prime importance. Some see it as playing a major role, avant la lettre and in diverse guises, in premodern aesthetics (e.g., in Plato's, Aristotle's, and Aquinas's accounts of the experience of beauty, and in Alberti's and Gravina's concepts of *lentezza* and *delirio*).[3] But there can be no doubt that its dominance was established in modernity, when the term "aesthetic" was officially established. Once modern science and philosophy had destroyed the classical, medieval, and Renaissance faith that properties such as beauty were objective features of the world, modern aesthetics turned to subjective experience to explain and ground them. Even when seeking an intersubjective consensus or standard that would do the critical job of realist objectivism, philosophy typically identified the aesthetic not only *through* but also *with* subjective experience.

"Beauty," said David Hume in arguing for a standard of taste, "is no quality in things themselves; it exists merely in the mind which contemplates them," though some minds are more judicious and authoritative than others. Immanuel Kant explicitly identified the subject's experience "of pleasure or displeasure" as "the determining ground" of aesthetic judgment.[4] The notion of aesthetic experience moreover helped provide an umbrella concept for diverse qualities that were distinguished from beauty but still closely related to taste and art: concepts such as the sublime and the picturesque.

In the nineteenth and early twentieth centuries, aesthetic experience gained still greater importance through the general celebration of experience by influential *Lebensphilosophies* aimed at combating the threat of mechanistic determinism (seen not merely in science but also in the ravages of industrialization). In these philosophies, experience replaced atomistic sensation as the basic epistemological concept, and its link to vividly felt life is clear not only from the German term "*Erlebnis*" but also from the vitalistic experiential theories of Henri Bergson, William James, and John Dewey. As art subsumed religion's role by providing a nonsupernatural spirituality in the material world, so experience emerged as the naturalistic yet nonmechanistic expression of mind. The union of art and experience engendered a notion of aesthetic experience that achieved, through the turn of the century's great aestheticist movement, enormous cultural importance and almost religious intensity. Aesthetic experience became the island of freedom, beauty, and idealistic meaning in an otherwise coldly materialistic and law-determined world. It was not only the locus of the highest pleasures but also a means of spiritual conversion and transcendence; it accordingly became the central concept for explaining the distinctive nature and value of art, which had itself become increasingly autonomous and isolated from the mainstream of material life and praxis. The doctrine of *art for art's sake* could only mean that art was for the sake of its own experience. And seeking to expand art's dominion, its adherents argued that anything could be rendered art if it could engender the appropriate experience.

This hasty genealogy of aesthetic experience does not do justice to the complex development of this concept, nor to the variety of theories and conceptions it embraces. But it should at least highlight four features that are central to the tradition of aesthetic experience and whose interplay shapes yet confuses twentieth-century accounts of this concept. First, aesthetic experience is essentially valuable and enjoyable; call this its *evaluative dimension*. Second, it is something vividly felt and subjectively savored, affectively absorbing us and focusing our attention on its immediate presence and thus standing out from the ordinary flow of routine experience; call this its *phenomenological dimension*. Third, it is meaningful experience, not mere sensation; call this its *semantic dimension*. (Its affective power and meaning together explain how aesthetic experience can be so transfigurative.) Fourth, it is a distinctive experience closely identified with the distinction of fine art and representing art's essential aim; call this its *demarcational-definitional dimension*. These features of aesthetic experience do not seem, prima facie, collectively inconsistent. Yet, as we shall see, they generate theoretical tensions that propel recent analytic philosophy toward growing marginalization of this concept and have even inspired some analysts (most notably George Dickie) to deny its very existence.[5] Before concentrating on the Anglo-American scene, we would do well to note the major lines of contemporary continental critique. For only by comparison can we grasp the full measure of the analytic depreciation of aesthetic experience.

II

From critical theory and hermeneutics to deconstruction and genealogical analysis, the continental critique of aesthetic experience has mostly focused on challenging its phenomenological immediacy and its radical differentiation. Although Theodor Adorno rejects its claim to pleasure as the ideological contamination of bourgeois hedonism, he joins the virtually unanimous continental verdict that aesthetic experience is not only valuable and meaningful but that the concept of experience is crucial for philosophy of art. Unlike the facile pleasure of the subject, "real aesthetic experience," for Adorno, "requires self-abnegation" and submission to "the objective constitution of the artwork itself."[6] This can transform the subject, thereby suggesting new avenues of emancipation and a renewed *promesse de bonheur* more potent than simple pleasure. Here we see the transformational, passional aspect of aesthetic experience; it is something undergone or suffered. Although the experiencing subject is dynamic, not inert, she is far from a fully controlling agent and so remains captive and blind to the ideological features structuring the artwork she follows. Hence a proper, emancipatory understanding of art requires going beyond immediate experience, beyond immanent *Verstehen*, to external critique ("secondary reflection") of the work's ideological meaning and the sociohistorical conditions that shaped it. "Experience is essential," Adorno dialectically concludes, "but so is thought, for no work in its immediate facticity portrays its meaning adequately or can be understood in itself" (*AT* 479). In the same dialectical manner, while affirming aesthetic experience's marked differentiation from "ungodly reality," Adorno recognizes that such apparent autonomy is itself only the product of social forces that ultimately condition the nature of aesthetic experience by constraining both the structure of artworks and our mode of responding to them (*AT* 320–22, 478–79). Since changes in the nonaesthetic world affect our very sensibilities and capacity for experience, aesthetic experience cannot be a fixed natural kind.

This is a central theme in Walter Benjamin's critique of the immediate meaning of *Erlebnis* privileged by phenomenology. Through the fragmentation and shocks of modern life, the mechanical repetition of assembly-line labor, and the haphazardly juxtaposed information and raw sensationalism of the mass media, our immediate experience of things no longer forms a meaningful, coherent whole but is rather a welter of fragmentary, unintegrated sensations—something simply lived through (*erlebt*) rather than meaningfully experienced. Benjamin instead advocated a notion of experience (*Erfahrung*) that requires the mediated, temporally cumulative accretion of coherent, transmittable wisdom, though he doubted whether it could still be achieved in modern society.[7] Modernization and technology, he likewise argued, have eroded aesthetic experience's identification with the transcendent autonomy of art. Such experience once had what Benjamin called *aura*, a cultic quality resulting from the artwork's uniqueness and distance from the ordinary world of experience. But with the advent of mechanical modes of reproduction such as photography, art's distinctive aura has been lost, and aesthetic experience comes to pervade the everyday world of popular culture and even politics. Aesthetic experience can no longer be used to define and delimit the realm of high art. Unlike Adorno, Benjamin saw this loss of aura and differentiation as potentially emancipatory (although he condemned its deadly results in the aesthetics of fascist politics). In any case, Benjamin's critique does not deny the continuing importance of aesthetic experience, but only its romantic conceptualization as pure immediacy of meaning and isolation from the rest of life.

Clearly inspired by Martin Heidegger's critique of aesthetic experience,[8] Hans-Georg Gadamer attacks the same two features of immediacy and differentiation. By radically differentiating the artwork from the socio-historical world in which it is created and received, by treating it as an object purely of direct aesthetic delight, aesthetic consciousness reduces the work's meaning to what is immediately experienced. But, Gadamer argues, this attitude simply cannot do justice to art's meaning and lasting impact on our lives and world:

> The pantheon of art is not a timeless presence which offers itself to pure aesthetic consciousness but the assembled achievements of the human mind as it has realized itself historically. . . . Inasmuch as we encounter the work of art in the world, . . . it is necessary to adopt an attitude to the beautiful and to art that does not lay claim to immediacy, but corresponds to the historical reality of man. The appeal to immediacy, to the genius of the moment, to the significance of the "experience," cannot withstand the claim of human existence to continuity and unity of self-understanding.[9]

To take the work as merely experienced immediacy is to rob it of enduring wholeness and cumulative meaning through communicative tradition, disintegrating "the unity of the aesthetic object into the multiplicity of experiences" (*TM* 85) and ignoring art's relation to the world and its claims to truth.

Such critique of immediate, differentiated aesthetic consciousness does not, however, constitute a repudiation of the central importance of experience for aesthetics. Indeed, Gadamer claims it is undertaken "in order to do justice to the experience of art" by insisting that this experience "includes understanding," which must exceed the immediacy of pure presence (*TM* 89, 90).[10] Rather than identifying art with its objects as in typical analytic philosophy, Gadamer insists "that the work of art has its true being in the fact that it becomes an experience changing the person experiencing it"; this experience "is not the subjectivity of the person who experiences it, but the work itself" (*TM* 92), which, as a game plays its players, submits those who wish to understand the work to the rigors of its structures.

Although it rejects Gadamer's faith in experiential unity and stability, the deconstructionism of Jacques Derrida and Roland Barthes takes a roughly similar stand: its radical critique of firm disciplinary boundaries and the "myth of presence" challenges the radical differentiation and immediacy of aesthetic experience without dismissing its importance and power of *jouissance*. From the quite different perspective of sociologically informed genealogical critique, Pierre Bourdieu attacks the very same two targets: "The experience of the work of art as being immediately endowed with meaning and value" that are pure and autonomous is an essentialist fallacy. Aesthetic experience is "itself an institution which is the product of historical invention," the result of the reciprocally reinforcing dimensions of art's institutional field and inculcated habits of aesthetic contemplation.[11] Both factors take considerable time to get established, not only in the general social field but also in the course of each individual's aesthetic apprenticeship. Moreover, their establishment in both cases depends on the wider social field that determines an institution's conditions of possibility, power, and attraction, as well as the options of the individual's involvement in it.

What shall we make of the two main thrusts of the continental critique? Aesthetic experience cannot be conceived as an unchanging concept narrowly identified with fine art's purely autonomous reception, for it clearly extends beyond fine art (to nature, for example). Moreover, aesthetic experience is conditioned by changes in the nonartistic world that affect not only the field of art but our very capacities for experience in general. The second charge, that aesthetic experience requires more than mere phenomenological immediacy to achieve its full meaning, is equally convincing. Immediate reactions are often poor and mistaken, so interpretation is generally needed to enhance our experience. Moreover, prior assumptions and habits of perception, including prior acts of interpretation, are necessary for the shaping of appropriate responses that are experienced as immediate. This insistence on interpretation is also the crux of the Goodman-Danto critique of aesthetic experience. So when Gadamer urges that "aesthetics must be absorbed into hermeneutics" (*TM* 146), he is expressing precisely the dominant analytic line.

However, the claim that aesthetic experience must involve *more* than phenomenological immediacy and vivid feeling does not entail that such immediate feeling is not crucial to aesthetic experience. Likewise, Bourdieu's convincing claim that aesthetic experience requires cultural mediation does not entail that its content cannot be experienced as immediate. Though it surely took some time for English to become a language and for me to learn it, I can still experience its meanings as immediate, grasping them as immediately as the smell of a rose (which itself may require the mediation of gardening and complex cognitive processes of sense and individuation).[12]

The decline of aesthetic experience in analytic philosophy partly reflects such false inferences. But it also stems from confusions arising from the changing role of this concept in Anglo-American philosophy from Dewey to Danto, and especially from the fact that this diversity of roles has not been adequately recognized. Viewed as a univocal concept, aesthetic experience seems too confused to be redeemed as useful; so the first task is to articulate its contrasting conceptions.

III

The contrasting conceptions of aesthetic experience are best mapped in terms of three different axes of contrast whose opposing poles capture all four of its already noted dimensions. First, we can ask whether the concept of aesthetic experience is intrinsically honorific or instead descriptively neutral. Second, is it robustly phenomenological or simply semantic? In other words, are affect and subjective intentionality essential dimensions of this experience, or is it rather only a certain kind of meaning or style of symbolization that renders an experience aesthetic? Third, is this concept's primary theoretical function transformational, aiming to revise or enlarge the aesthetic field, or is it instead demarcational, that is, to define, delimit, and explain the aesthetic status quo?

My claim is that, after Dewey, Anglo-American theories of aesthetic experience have moved steadily from the former to the latter poles, resulting eventually in the concept's loss of power and interest. In other words, Dewey's essentially evaluative, phenomenological, and transformational notion of aesthetic experience has been gradually replaced by a purely descriptive, semantic one whose chief purpose is to explain and thus support the established demarcation of art from other human domains. Such changes generate tensions that make the concept suspicious. Moreover, when aesthetic experience proves unable to supply this definition, as Danto concludes, the whole concept is abandoned for one that promises to do so—interpretation. That aesthetic experience may nonetheless be fruitful for other purposes is simply, but I think wrongly, ignored. To substantiate this line of narrative and argument, we must examine the theories of Dewey, Beardsley, Goodman, and Danto.

Dewey's prime use of aesthetic experience is aimed not at distinguishing art from the rest of life but rather at "recovering the continuity of its esthetic experience with the normal processes of living," so that both art and life will be improved by their greater integration.[13] His goal was to break the stifling hold of what he called "the museum conception of art," which compartmentalizes the aesthetic from real life, remitting it to a separate realm remote from the vital interests of ordinary men and women. This "esoteric idea of fine art" gains power from the sacralization of art objects sequestered in museums and private collections. Dewey therefore insisted on privileging dynamic aesthetic experience over the physical objects that conventional dogma identifies and then fetishizes as art. For Dewey, the essence and value of art are not in such artifacts per se but in the dynamic and developing experiential activity through which they are created and perceived. He therefore distinguished between the physical "art product" that, once created, can exist "apart from human experience" and "the actual work of art [which] is what the product does with and in experience" (*AE* 9, 167, 329). This primacy of aesthetic experience frees art not only from object fetishism but also from its confinement to the traditional domain of fine art. For aesthetic experience clearly exceeds the limits of fine art, as, for example, in the appreciation of nature.[14] Dewey insisted that aesthetic experience could likewise occur in the pursuit of science and philosophy, in sport, and in haute cuisine, contributing much to the appeal of these practices. Indeed, it could be achieved in virtually any domain of action, since all experience, to be coherent and meaningful, requires the germ of aesthetic unity and development. By rethinking art in terms of aesthetic experience, Dewey hoped we could radically enlarge and democratize the domain of art, integrating it more fully into the real world, which would be greatly improved by the pursuit of such manifold arts of living.

The pervasiveness of aesthetic experience did not mean that it could not be distinguished from ordinary experience. Its distinction, however, is essentially qualitative. From the humdrum flow of routine experience, it stands out, says Dewey, as a distinctly memorable, rewarding whole—as not just experience but "*an* experience"—because in it we feel "most alive" and fulfilled through the active, satisfying engagement of all our human faculties (sensual, emotive, and cognitive) that contribute to this integrated whole. Aesthetic experience is differentiated not by its unique possession of some specific element or its unique focus on some particular dimension but by its more zestful integration of all the elements of ordinary experience into an absorbing, developing whole that provides "a satisfyingly emotional quality" of some sort and so exceeds the threshold of perception that it can be appreciated for its own sake (*AE* 42, 45, 63).[15] An essential part of that appreciation is the immediate, phenomenological feel of aesthetic experience, whose sense of unity, affect, and value is "directly fulfilling" rather than deferred for some other time or end.

The transformational, phenomenological, and evaluative thrust of Deweyan aesthetic experience should now be clear. So should its usefulness for provoking recognition of artistic potentialities and aesthetic satisfactions in pursuits previously considered nonaesthetic. It is further useful in reminding us that, even in fine art, directly fulfilling experience rather than collecting or scholarly criticism is the primary value. Nor does this emphasis on phenomenological immediacy and affect preclude the semantic dimension of aesthetic experience. Meaning is not incompatible with qualia and affect. Unfortunately, Dewey does not confine himself to transformational provocation but also proposes aesthetic experience as a theoretical definition of art. By standard philosophical criteria, this definition is hopelessly inadequate, grossly misrepresenting our current concept of art. Much art, particularly bad art, fails to engender Deweyan aesthetic experience, which, on the other hand, often arises outside art's institutional limits. Moreover, though the concept of art (as a historically determined concept) can be somewhat reshaped, it cannot be convincingly defined in such a global way so as to be coextensive with aesthetic experience. No matter how powerful and universal is the aesthetic experience of sunsets, we are hardly going to reclassify them as art.[16] By employing the concept of aesthetic experience both to define what art in fact is and to transform it into something quite different, Dewey creates considerable confusion. Hence analytic philosophers typically dismissed his whole idea of aesthetic experience as a disastrous muddle.

The major exception is Monroe Beardsley, who reconstructs this concept as the core of his own analytic philosophy of art, which, like most analytic aesthetics, is preoccupied with projects of differentiation. Instead of Dewey's quest to unite art with the rest of life, Beardsley's aim is to clearly distinguish art and the aesthetic from other practices. This means renouncing the transformational use of aesthetic experience. Instead, this concept serves to define what is distinctive of works of art and what is constitutive of their value (issuing in what Beardsley calls a "persuasive analysis of artistic goodness," *APV* 79). Beardsley's strategy is to argue that art can be defined as a distinctive function class if there is a particular function that works of art "can do that other things cannot do, or do as completely or fully" (*A* 526). The production of aesthetic experience is claimed as this function, so he explains both the general value of art and the differing value of its particular works through the basic value and intrinsic pleasure of that experience; better works, for Beardsley, are those capable of producing "aesthetic experiences of a greater magnitude" (*A* 531). Beardsley thus retains the Deweyan evaluative, affective, and phenomenological features of aesthetic experience. It is, he says, an "intrinsically enjoyable" "experience of some intensity" where "attention" and "the succession of one's mental states" is focused on and directed by some phenomenal field in a way that generates a satisfying "feeling" of coherence or "wholeness" and "a sense of actively exercising constructive powers of the mind" (*A* 527; *APV* 287–89). And he clarifies such defining characteristics of this experience in considerable detail.[17]

Analytic aesthetics rejected Beardsley's theory on three major grounds. One is skepticism about its phenomenological validity. George Dickie, an influential advocate of this line of critique, offers two principal arguments.[18] First, Beardsley must be wrong to describe the aesthetic experience as unified, coherent, et cetera, because doing so is simply a category mistake—treating the term "experience" as if it denoted a real thing that could bear such descriptions instead of recognizing that it is merely an empty term denoting nothing real. Talk about aesthetic experience is just a roundabout and ontologically inflationary way of talking about the aesthetic object as perceived or experienced. Beardsley's claim of the "unity of experience" is simply a misleading way of describing the experienced, phenomenal unity of the artwork. It alone can have such properties of coherence or wholeness. Particular subjective affects resulting from the work cannot have these properties, and the global aesthetic experience that purports to have them is just a linguistically constructed metaphysical phantom. Secondly, Dickie argues, even what is wrongly identified as aesthetic experience does not always have the affective content that Beardsley claims; and this critique can be extended to traditional claims that aesthetic experience is always pleasurable or unified.

What should one make of these two arguments? To the first, we can reply that empirical psychologists *do* accept the reality of experiences (including aesthetic ones) and the validity of describing them in terms of predicates (like unity, intensity, etc.) that, admittedly, are more often used to describe the objects of such experiences.[19] Of course, one could challenge this response by dismissing it as confused folk psychology and adopting philosophy of mind's once fashionable trend of dismissing the role of consciousness or first-person experience. For many reasons (including aesthetic ones), I think this trend should be resisted, and consciousness has made a strong comeback in recent philosophy of mind.[20]

The argument that Beardsley's phenomenological ascriptions of affect, unity, and pleasure are in fact phenomenologically incorrect can be assessed together with the second major criticism of his theory: that (the capacity to produce) aesthetic experience as Beardsley's phenomenology describes it cannot properly serve to identify and individuate works of art. Here the standard strategy is to show that such a definition would be both too wide and too narrow. It has been charged, for instance, that by Beardsley's criteria of aesthetic experience, good sexual experience would be falsely included as art, a conclusion that a Deweyan aesthetics could have welcomed but that runs against Beardsley's analytic aim of explaining established classifications.[21]

However, Beardsley's definition is most often attacked for being too narrow. It wrongly excludes all the many artworks that are not capable of producing enjoyable experiences of unity and positive affect. Certain good works neither produce nor even try to produce such experiences, but clearly the problem is most severe with bad works of art. Since Beardsley's concept of aesthetic experience is essentially honorific and definitional, it cannot accommodate bad artworks as art, and yet clearly this is how we analytically oriented philosophers think they must be classified. The concepts of art and aesthetic must allow for bad instances. Being a work of art cannot entail being a good work of art, otherwise negative evaluations of artworks would be impossible. This leads to the third major difficulty: the inadequacy of Beardsley's theory of aesthetic experience to explain our judgments of value. Because this experience is by definition enjoyable or positive, it can in no way account for strongly negative aesthetic judgments (e.g., of hideousness, repulsion, etc.), which cannot be explained by the mere absence of a positive aesthetic experience. Yet negative verdicts are central to the field of aesthetics, and any concept that claims to define this field must be able to account for bad as well as good art.[22]

Two conclusions emerge from all this critique. If aesthetic experience is to do the job of demarcating the entire realm of art, then its essentially evaluative content must be abandoned. Moreover, if one is suspicious of subjectivity and immediate feeling, then one must find a notion of aesthetic experience not centered on first-person phenomenology but rather on nonsubjective accounts of meaning. These two inferences determine the new semantic direction of Nelson Goodman's theory of aesthetic experience.

Though he shares Beardsley's analytic goal of demarcational definition, of "distinguishing in general between aesthetic and nonaesthetic objects and experience" (*LA* 243), he insists that such distinction must be "independent of all consideration of aesthetic value," since the existence of bad art means "being aesthetic does not exclude being . . . aesthetically bad" (*LA* 244, 255). Aesthetic experience must also be defined independently of phenomenological accounts of mental states or immediate feelings and meanings, as Goodman rejects such intentional entities. He insists on explaining all meaning in terms of varieties of reference, just as he renounces the very idea of an immediate given before or apart from its symbolic representation. Nor can aesthetic experience be distinguished by its peculiarly emotive character, since "some works of art have little or no emotive content." Even when emotion *is* present, its role, Goodman argues, is simply the cognitive one "of discerning what properties a work has and expresses" by providing "a mode of sensitivity" to it (*LA* 248, 250, 251). But such cognitive use of emotion (as Dewey also tirelessly urged) is equally present in science. Goodman concludes that while emotion is not an aesthetic constant, cognition of some sort is. He therefore defines aesthetic experience as "cognitive experience distinguished [from science and other domains] by the dominance of certain symbolic characteristics" (*LA* 262).[23]

Goodman calls these features "symptoms of the aesthetic" and individuates five of them:

> (1) syntactic density, where the finest differences in certain respects constitute a difference between symbols—for example, an ungraded mercury thermometer as contrasted with an electronic digital-read-out instrument; (2) semantic density, where symbols are provided for things distinguished by the finest differences in certain respects (not only the ungraduated thermometer again but also ordinary English, though it is not syntactically dense); (3) relative repleteness, where comparatively many aspects of a symbol are significant—for example a single-line drawing of a mountain by Hokusai where every feature of shape, line, thickness, etc. counts, in contrast with perhaps the same line as a chart of daily stock market averages, where all that counts is the height of the line above the base; (4) exemplification, where a symbol, whether or not it denotes, symbolizes by serving as a sample of properties it literally or metaphorically possesses; and finally (5)

multiple and complex reference, where a symbol performs several
integrated and interacting referential functions, some direct and
some mediated through other symbols. (*WW* 67–68)

If an object's "functioning exhibits all these symptoms," Goodman claims,
"then very likely the object is a work of art. If it shows almost none, then
it probably isn't" (*OMM* 199). Although these symptoms may fall short
of being disjunctively necessary and conjunctively sufficient conditions for
defining our concept of art, Goodman blames this on the fact that ordinary usage of this concept is too "vague and vagrant" to allow any clear
definition and thus requires reform (*WW* 69). His symptoms are therefore
offered provisionally in the "search for a definition" that will achieve this
clarification (*OMM* 135).

Rather than focusing on these provisional symptoms, criticism of
Goodman's theory should be directed at the underlying premises that generate their proposal. Three problems seem most central. First is the premise
of radical aesthetic differentiation, with its consequent presumption that
the function of the concept of aesthetic experience is to explain art's compartmentalized distinction. Goodman's theory, like Beardsley's, is haunted
by this goal of clearly defining art from all other realms, of seeking (in his
words) "a way of distinguishing aesthetic from all other experience" (*LA*
251). Thus, though keen to emphasize the great affinities between art and
science, he feels compelled to seek a definition that will clearly mark off
aesthetic from scientific experience. Invoking his symbolic symptoms to
achieve this, he rightly worries that they cannot adequately do the job by
providing necessary and sufficient conditions. But such worries arise only
by presuming that the concept of aesthetic experience should be coextensive
with art, that aesthetic experience cannot occur in science or other standardly
nonartistic pursuits but must apply in all art no matter how bad. There is
ample testimony to challenge this presumption, but Goodman must ignore
it. Methodologically wedded to the project of demarcating art by aesthetic
experience, he cannot recognize a concept of aesthetic experience that cuts
across conventional classificatory boundaries while maintaining its evaluative
sense as enjoyably heightened, affective, and meaningful experience. Yet such
a concept is fruitfully employed in common usage, not only in Dewey.

A second problem with Goodman's definition of aesthetic experience
is that it seems to render the very notion of experience—the conscious,
phenomenological feel of things—entirely superfluous. If the aesthetic is

defined entirely in terms of the dominance of certain modes of symbolization, with no essential reference to sentience, immediate feeling, and affect, then what is the point of speaking about aesthetic experience at all? We might as well just talk about the semantic symptoms of art and aesthetics, and simply drop the term "experience" (as Goodman does in later discussions). But apart from the once chic suspicion of consciousness, is there any reason why the concept of aesthetic experience must omit this phenomenological dimension with its immediacy of quality and affect? Goodman's account suggests (though never fully articulates) the following argument: Aesthetic experience is essentially meaningful and cognitive through its use of symbols. Use of symbols implies mediation and dynamic processing of information, while phenomenological feeling and affect imply passivity and immediacy that cannot account for meaning. Hence, aesthetic experience cannot be essentially phenomenological, immediate, or affective.

This argument is very problematic. First, even assuming all its premises, what follows is only that aesthetic experience requires *more* than these phenomenological features, not that they are not central to such experience. Secondly, we can challenge the premises by arguing that phenomenological consciousness *is* active and *can* include immediate perceptions of meaning, even if such immediate understandings on the conscious level require unconscious mediated processing or rely on a background of past conscious mediation. Further, one can argue that phenomenological feeling involves more than immediacy, just as affect (on both psychological and physiological levels) involves more than passivity. Moreover, if Goodman brings the argument that affect is not central to aesthetic experience because it is not always present in the experience of artworks, we can counter by challenging the presumption that aesthetic experience can be understood only as an artistically demarcational concept, applying necessarily to our encounter with all (and only) artworks, no matter how feeble the encounter and the works may be.

Finally, Goodman's semiotic theory of aesthetic experience has a third grave problem. Not only does it neglect the phenomenology and nonartistic extension of that experience, it is also wholly inadequate for its designated role of demarcating the realm of art. For its use in this role requires that we already know whether or not we are dealing with artworks. Here is the argument. According to Goodman an object is an artwork when its symbolic functioning saliently employs the symptomatically aesthetic modes of symbolization. But an object does not wear its symbolic use on its sleeve; a visually identical sign may function differently in different symbolic systems.

For instance, as Goodman remarks, the same drawn line may be a "replete" character artistically representing a mountain or instead a nonreplete character merely representing profits in a chart. But we do not know which symbolic functioning the object has until we know whether the object is an artwork or just a chart. Hence symbolic functioning (and thus aesthetic experience as symbolic functioning) cannot be the basis for defining the artistic status of an object.

This argument is, of course, a variation of the argument from indiscernibles employed by Arthur Danto to argue that perceptual properties alone, including those involved in aesthetic experience, are insufficient for distinguishing between artworks and nonart, between Warhol's Brillo Boxes and their nonartistic counterparts. Our experience should differ, Danto says, "depending upon whether the response is to an artwork or to a mere real thing that cannot be told apart from it." But "we cannot appeal to [such differences] . . . in order to get our definition of art, inasmuch as we [first] need the definition of art in order to identify the sorts of aesthetic responses appropriate to works of art in contrast with mere real things" (TC 94–95). Aesthetic experience, Danto notes, has the further problem of being traditionally defined as inherently positive, while many artworks, being bad, induce negative responses (T 92).

Since aesthetic experience cannot adequately demarcate art, Danto virtually ignores it, subordinating it to another concept that he thinks can do the definitional job (and do it with the same semantic emphasis that Goodman advocated). This concept is interpretation. "There is," he says, "no appreciation without interpretation," since "interpretations are what constitute works"; and "interpretation consists in determining the relationship between a work of art and its material counterpart" (TC 113; PD 45). I think these claims are problematic. But even granting them does not nullify the idea of aesthetic experience. Its failure to provide a nonevaluative definition of our current concept of art does not entail that it has no important role to play in aesthetics, though we need, of course, to specify what role this could be. Danto, however, suggests an additional argument. The concept of aesthetic experience is not only useless but a "danger," because the very notion of the aesthetic intrinsically trivializes art by seeing it as "fit only for pleasure," rather than for meaning and truth (PD 13). This argument not only falsely equates the aesthetic per se with a caricature of the narrowest of hedonistic formalisms. It also wrongly suggests a divide between pleasure and meaning, feeling and cognition, enjoyment and understanding, when instead, they tend, in art, to constitute each other. As T. S. Eliot remarked,

"To understand a poem comes to the same thing as to enjoy it for the right reasons."[24]

We can reinforce this point and the centrality of aesthetic feeling by adopting Danto's argument from indiscernibles but applying it this time not to objects but to subjects. Imagine two visually identical art viewers who offer identical interpretations of the very powerful paintings and poems before them. One is a human who thrills to what he sees and interprets. The other, however, is only a robot who, experiencing no qualia, feels no pleasure, indeed no emotion at all, but merely mechanically processes the perceptual and artworld data to deliver his interpretive propositions. We would surely say here that the robot, in an important sense, doesn't really understand these works. He doesn't, in a big way, get the point of such art, even if he recognizes that some feeling he cannot feel is somehow appropriate. For much of the point is precisely to feel or savor art's qualia and meaning, not just compute an interpretive output from the work's signs and artworld context. For this reason, even if the robot's interpretive propositions were descriptively more accurate than the human being's, we would still say that the human's general response to art was superior, and that the robot, since he feels absolutely nothing, does not really grasp what art is all about. Now imagine further that aesthetic experience was entirely expunged from our civilization, since we were all transformed into such robots or exterminated by them. Art might linger on a bit through inertia, but could it continue to flourish and robustly survive? What would be the point of creating and attending to it, if it promised no enriching phenomenological feeling or pleasure?

The uncertainty of art's future in such a sci-fi scenario implies the centrality of aesthetic experience—in its evaluative and phenomenological sense—for the concept of art. Although surely neither a necessary nor sufficient condition for application of this concept, it might be regarded as a more general background condition for art. In other words, though many artworks fail to produce aesthetic experience—in the sense of satisfyingly heightened, absorbing, meaningful and affective experience—if such experience could never be had, and never had through the production of works, art could probably never have existed.[25] If artworks universally flouted this interest (and not just on occasion to make a radical point), art, as we know it, would disappear. In contrast to necessary and sufficient conditions that aim at mapping art's demarcational limits, such a background condition concerns the *point* rather than the *extension* of the concept of art. In naming and so marking this point, aesthetic experience is not a useless concept.[26]

My futuristic robot parables are not so hard to imagine because they reflect real developments in recent aesthetics and contemporary life. Rejecting what he calls the traditional "strong and cold" "grip of aestheticism on the philosophy of art" (*PD* 33), Danto joins Goodman and many others in what might be termed a radical anaestheticization of aesthetics. Felt experience is virtually ignored and entirely subordinated to third-person semantic theories of artistic symbolization and its interpretation. Once a potent embodiment of art's sense and value, aesthetic experience is now "hermeneutered." Forsaking such experience for semiotic definitions of art should not be seen as merely the arbitrary preference of linguistic philosophers addicted to semantic theory. Goodman and Danto were sensitively reflecting developments in the artworld, which required ever more interpretation as art became more cerebrally conceptual in pursuing what Danto describes as its Hegelian quest to become its own philosophy: art as theory of art. Goodman and Danto were also responsive to artworld realities in claiming against Beardsley and Dewey that much contemporary art neither evokes nor aims to evoke powerful experiences having enjoyable affect and coherent meaning.

So much the worse, one might say, for contemporary art, which, having completed its philosophical transformation and lost the financial prop of 1980s' speculation, now finds it has lost an experiential point and a public to fall back on. For the public retains a deep need for aesthetic experiences, and as these became artistically *dépassé*, it learned to satisfy this need outside the official realm of contemporary art, beyond the white cube of gallery space. So aesthetic interest is increasingly directed toward popular art, which has not yet learned to eschew the experiential goals of pleasure, affect, and meaningful coherence, even if it often fails to achieve them. Mourning the artworld's loss of public, the prominent artists Komar and Melamid, together with *The Nation*, engaged a scientific marketing survey of popular aesthetic taste in the (perhaps ironic) quest to develop a new plastic art that would engage people as broadly and as powerfully as popular music does. One point emerging from the polling statistics is the demand that art provide positive affective experience through coherence.[27]

Branding this demand as stiflingly conservative, we would insist that art should *not* be confined to supplying agreeable unities or emotions. We may rightly claim that today some of our most exciting and rewarding artistic encounters involve unpleasant shock and fragmentation. But can we make sense of art as a whole without admitting the traditional and still formative centrality of vivid, meaningful phenomenological experience that is directly felt as valuable, even if not always as pleasant and unified? Of course, the presence of such experience does not entail the presence of art; so it cannot in itself legitimize popular art as true art, just as it cannot alone justify the claim that a given work is good art. In all these cases, since experience itself is mute, critical discourse is needed. Still, the power of aesthetic experience impels one to undertake such legitimating discourse through its felt value, just as it impels the public toward the arts wherein it can be found. If the experience has this power, then the concept of such experience has value in reminding us of it and directing us toward its use.

If art is in extremis, deprived (through completion) of its sustaining narrative of progress and thus groping without direction in what Danto calls its "posthistory," where anything goes; if art's groping is as lonely as it is aimless, cut off from the popular currents of taste in a democratic culture, then the concept of aesthetic experience is worth recalling: not for formal definition but for art's reorientation toward values and populations that could restore its vitality and sense of purpose.[28]

Art's turn from the aesthetic experience of enjoyable affective unities is no more an act of perverse willfulness than Danto's and Goodman's semantic anaesthetics. Like them, contemporary artists are simply responding to changes in our lifeworld, as we move from a more unified experiential culture to an increasingly modular, informational one. This results in art that highlights fragmentation and complexities of information flow that are often too helter-skelter to provide the coherence needed for traditional aesthetic experience's pleasurable sense of focused, funded affect. Already in the 1930s Walter Benjamin drew a stark contrast between experience and information, expressing the fear that through the fragmentation of modern life and the disjointed sensationalism of the newspapers, we were losing the capacity for deep experience and feeling. We have since undergone a far more extensive series of informational revolutions—from television and facsimile to the Internet and newer interactive systems of cyberspace and virtual reality.

Given this informational overload, it is not surprising that "the waning of affect" (in Fredric Jameson's phrase) is diagnosed as a prime symptom of our postmodern condition.[29] There is growing concern, far beyond the academy, that we are being so thoroughly reshaped by our informational technology that our experiential, affective capacities are wearing thin, so thin that we risk assimilation to the mechanical information processors that are already our most intimate companions in work and play. This worry is expressed nowhere more clearly than in science fiction. The only way of distinguishing real human beings from their physically identical Terminators or Replicants is the human capacity to feel, which itself is continuously buffeted and jeopardized by the unmanageable flux and grind of futuristic living. In the story that inspired *Blade Runner* (though not present in the film) there is even a crucial device to reinforce these affective experiential capacities—an "empathy box" that produces through virtual reality a powerful aesthetico-religious experience of empathetic fusion with others likewise plugged in.[30]

It may seem very "retro" to suggest that aesthetic experience can function something like an empathy box, restoring both our ability and inclination for the sorts of vivid, moving, shared experience that were once sought in art. Perhaps our informational evolution has already gone too far, so that an evening of beauty at the Met can do nothing to counter a life on Wall Street's chaotic trading floor. Perhaps aesthetic experience, and not just the philosophical value of its concept, has almost reached its end. How could philosophy do anything to forestall its total loss? First, it can remind us of the variety this concept still embraces as heightened, meaningful, and valuable phenomenological experience. So the threatened loss of one traditional form does not entail its utter extinction. Second, in any of its rewarding forms, aesthetic experience will be strengthened and preserved the more it is experienced; it will be more experienced, the more we are directed to such experience; and one good way of directing us to such experience is fuller recognition of its importance and richness through greater attention to the concept of aesthetic experience.

We thus find at least one good use for philosophical recognition of this concept: its orientation toward having the experience it names. Rather than defining art or justifying critical verdicts, the concept is directional, reminding us of what is worth seeking in art and elsewhere in life. Wittgenstein said, "The work of the philosopher consists in assembling reminders for a particular purpose."[31] If the same holds for philosophical concepts, that of aesthetic experience should not go unemployed.[32]

Chapter Ten

Art as Dramatization

I

"Dramatise, dramatise!" was the insistent cry that haunted Henry James's artistic genius.[1] The celebrated novelist knew himself a failure in the theater; his plays were almost all rejected for production, and one of the only two produced was roundly booed on the London stage. Yet James realized, with brave honesty, that the basic principle of drama nonetheless held the key to artistic greatness. Distinguishing nicely between the terms "Theatre-stuff" and "Drama-stuff"—between concrete stage performance and what he called the deeper "divine principle of the Scenario" (equally realizable in novels, films, and television)—James turned that essential dramatic principle more consciously to work in composing the later works of fiction that crown his great career. "The scenic method," he wrote, "is my absolute, my imperative, my *only* salvation." That salvation is evident in his posthumous dramatic success, in the frequent adaptations of his fiction into TV dramas, films, and even into two operas by Benjamin Britten (*Owen Wingrave* and *The Turn of the Screw*).[2]

James's assertion of the drama's superiority could have rested on ancient philosophical authority; but it was also not uncommon in his own time, and after. Friedrich Nietzsche, for example, just a year younger than James, was quick to affirm Richard Wagner's recognition that "the greatest influence of all the arts could be exercised through the theatre").[3] Some generations later, James's native countryman and fellow Anglophile, T. S. Eliot, would reaffirm the supremacy of drama as "the ideal medium for poetry." Combining the power of meaningful action with the beauty of musical order, poetic drama could capture two exquisitely precious and different kinds of aesthetic value not easily synthesized in a single form. And through its theatrical performance, Eliot further argued, drama enabled the poet to reach "as large and as miscellaneous an audience as possible."[4] Eliot therefore made his own sustained efforts to write for the theater, where, however, he enjoyed only little more initial success than James. (The Broadway hit *Cats*, though based on Eliot's light verse, is a posthumous dramatization of poetry that he in fact never intended for theater, let alone musical theater.)

Considered from the point of view of practicing artists (rather than that of philosophers), drama's preeminence derives not only from its presumed ability to reach more people and move them more powerfully and completely than other arts (something that seems truer today for cinema than for theater). There is also (dare I say it as an American) the charm that a successful theater play could bring in the quickest—if not always, ultimately, the greatest—income to its author. We know from private correspondence that money was certainly one motive for James's interest in writing for the theater. But the presence of this motive in no way falsifies the sincerity of his adulation of drama, which he praised as "the noblest" of arts, long before he ever seriously thought of a career in play writing. James thought drama was noblest because the most challenging—combining the gravest formal demands of "masterly structure" with the highest requirement of significance of "subject."[5]

In this chapter, I want to go beyond these more familiar assertions of drama's preeminent influence and nobility in order to suggest that the concept of drama embodies and unites two of the deepest, most important conditions of art and may therefore hold the key to a useful definition of art as a whole. But what *is* a useful definition of art? We may never entirely agree what this is, but we should at least realize that it can be something very different from what is typically taken and sought as a formally valid and true definition of art. Such a true (or "real") definition of art is usually construed in terms of a set of essential properties that jointly belong to all artworks—and only to them—or in terms of conditions that are jointly necessary and sufficient for something to be an artwork.[6] The avowed purpose of such formal definitions is "to tell us what is the extension of 'art.' It implies no more."[7] In short, the definition aims to cover or demarcate all and only those entities that are artworks, not to illuminate what is (aesthetically or artistically) important about them or about art.

It remains controversial whether we could ever provide such a definition that not only accurately and decisively delineates the current extension of art but that will continue to hold for all future artworks. Recurrent dissatisfaction with the definitions offered, together with a recognition of art's volatile, contested history and irrepressible impulse to challenge defining limits in questing for radically new forms, have raised doubts as to whether it is possible to formulate such a true or real definition that will be satisfactory for all times.[8] Some aestheticians have therefore limited their definitional efforts to proposing procedures for identifying artworks and thus determining art's extension in that more modest way. Others, who remain committed to the project of real or true definition, ingeniously conjure up complex defining formulae that aim to be flexible, general, vague, and multioptional enough (e.g., in positing a disjunctive set of overarching functions, procedures, or historical relations of artworks and art practices) to cover all possible artworks of the future. But whether or not such "wrapper" definitions ever prove successful in perfect and permanent coverage of art's extension is not, for me, the key issue in defining art. I am more concerned with whether a definition of art is useful in improving our understanding and experience of art by illuminating what is important in art, by explaining how art achieves its effect, or by taking a stand in the controversial struggles over art's meaning, value, and future.

A definition can be useful for aesthetics without being true in the formal sense of accurately delimiting the current extension of art. For instance, an honorific definition of art that is confined to meritorious works would be obviously false to the accepted extension of the concept of art and would be logically problematic in apparently precluding the notion of bad art. But, if it were accurate in picking out what is good art (or what is good in good art), then such a faulty definition would be far more useful for aesthetic purposes than truer definitions of art that succeed better in the aim of faithful coverage by equally covering art that is bad or indifferent. From my pragmatist perspective, it is usually more important for definitions and beliefs in aesthetics to be useful than to be formally true (though the two may sometimes coincide). For this reason, in *Pragmatist Aesthetics* (chap. 2), although I criticized Dewey's definition of art as experience for being a hopelessly inaccurate definition of art, I also argued that his definition was aesthetically more useful than another pragmatist option of definition that seems eminently more accurate and valid in the sense of conceptual coverage—art as a historically defined and socially entrenched practice.

If, for pragmatism, the value of a definition of art is in its contribution to our understanding and experience of art, then there are several forms this service can take. Definitions can be useful for recommending evaluative standards for art. Morris Weitz argued that though real definitions of art were impossible or wrongheaded, "honorific definitions" could nonetheless be valuable as "recommendations to concentrate on certain criteria of exccl-lence in art."[9] I argue that nonhonorific definitions can also be useful, and not only for the "criteria of evaluation" that Weitz stresses. Such definitions can serve to emphasize certain features of art that may not be receiving enough attention and whose neglect may result in an impoverishing of aesthetic experience and understanding. Definitions may also help us bring together various aspects of art into a more perspicuous constellation by combining features or reconciling orientations that otherwise seem uncom-fortably unconnected or even in conflict. So if the value of a definition of art depends on its capacity to improve our understanding and appreciation of art, what use could there be in defining art as dramatization? I believe this definition could highlight some enduringly important and distinctive features of art. But I begin more modestly by arguing that this definition is at least useful in integrating and thus reconciling the two most potent general orientations that dominate and polarize contemporary aesthetics. We can call them naturalism and historicism.[10]

II

Naturalism defines art as something deeply rooted in human nature, which therefore finds expression, in one form or another, in virtually every culture. This view, which is at least as old as Aristotle, sees art as arising from natural human needs and drives: a natural inclination toward mimesis; a natural desire for balance, form, or meaningful expression; a thirst for a kind of enhanced, aesthetic experience that gives the live creature not only pleasure but also a more vivid, heightened sense of living.[11] Art, naturalism argues, is not only deeply grounded in natural forces, energies, and rhythms but is also an important tool for the survival and perfection of human nature. Hence, for many proponents of aesthetic naturalism, the highest art, the most compelling drama, is the art of living. Even when art is significantly shaped by the societies, cultures, and specialized frameworks in which it is situated, the naturalists insist that art—at its best, truest, and most potent—expresses the fullness and power of life.

This line of aesthetic naturalism made its mark in German philosophy through Friedrich Nietzsche. His study of drama's origins in ancient Greece argues that art was born of natural roots, an expression of "overflowing life" or "lively action" arising from "the innermost ground of man," "even from the very depths of Nature" and deriving its power "from an overflowing health" or "fullness of Being."[12] The heightened experience of aesthetic ecstasy, which Nietzsche traces from early Greek tragedy back to the religious frenzy of Dionysian cult, is championed as "the highest, namely Dionysian expression of Nature." In contrast, he condemns "the culture of Opera" and its "stilo rappresentativo" as "something so completely unnatural" (*DG* 63, 121; *BT* 57, 113–14). Emerging from the deepest wells of Nature, true art celebrates through its "aesthetic delight" the principle of "eternal life beyond all appearance and despite all destruction." For Nietzsche, then, "art is not simply an imitation of nature, but its metaphysical supplement," a "justification of the world as an aesthetic phenomenon" (*DG* 108, 152; *BT* 101–2, 142–43).

John Dewey's pragmatist aesthetics plies a similar doctrine of naturalism: "Art—the mode of activity charged with meaning capable of immediately enjoyed possession—is the culmination of nature," while " 'science' [itself an art of sorts] is properly a handmaiden that conducts natural events to this happy issue."[13] Dewey's *Art as Experience* begins with a chapter titled "The Live Creature," and the major aim of the entire book is at "recovering the continuity of aesthetic experience with normal processes of living" (*AE* 16). Aesthetic understanding, Dewey urges, must never forget that the roots of art and beauty lie in the "basic vital functions," "the biological common-places" man shares with "bird and beast" (*AE* 19–20). Even in our most sophisticated fine arts that seem most removed from nature, "the organic substratum remains as the quickening and deep foundation," the sustaining source of the emotional energies of art whose true aim "is to serve the whole creature in his unified vitality." Dewey concludes, "Underneath the rhythm of every art and of every work of art, there lies the basic pattern of relations of the live creature to his environment," so that "naturalism in the broadest and deepest sense of nature is a necessity of all great art" (*AE* 155–56).

The impassioned aesthetic naturalisms of both Nietzsche and Dewey share a common but insufficiently acknowledged source in Ralph Waldo Emerson, the transcendentalist prophet who ardently preached the gospel of nature in all its manifold forms, uses, and resplendent spirituality. Art is just one example. "Art" as Emerson defines it "is nature passed through the alembic of man."[14] Rather than serving art for art's sake, art's aim is to advance nature by enhancing the life of its human expression; thus "art should exhilarate" by engaging one's "whole energy" and serving fully "the functions of life." "There is higher work for Art than the arts," Emerson concludes. "Nothing less than the creation of man and nature is its end" (*RWE* 192–94). Praising nature's gifts of beauteous forms and useful symbols for both art and ordinary language, Emerson anticipates Dewey's argument that art takes its very forms and symbols from our natural environment: for example, the pointed style of Gothic architecture emulates the forest's towering trees. Emerson likewise prefigures the celebration of the intense sublimity of aesthetic experience that both Dewey and Nietzsche later emphasize as the highest achievement of culture, peak experiences that are more profoundly transformative and creatively insightful than any discursive truth of science. "The poet gives us the eminent experiences only—a god stepping from peak to peak." "Poetry," Emerson continues (in a phrase that Nietzsche made more famous), "is the *gai science* . . . and the poet a truer logician, one "who unlocks our chains and admits us to a new scene" (*RWE* 443, 455–56).

The aesthetic naturalism of these philosophers is more than romantic sentimentalism. Contemporary science lends it significant support. Evolutionary researchers now recognize that, by and large, the things that naturally give us pleasure are good for the survival and growth of our species, since we have survived and evolved not by conscious planning but by making the choices that natural pleasures have unreflectively drawn us to. The intense pleasures of sex, for example, impel us toward procreation, even if it is not in the individual's rational best interest to take the risks involved in such dangerously close encounters. Art's beauty and pleasures, it can be argued, have evolutionary value not only for sharpening our perception, manual skill, and sense of structure but also for creating meaningful images that help bind separate individuals into an organic community through their shared appreciation of symbolic forms. Finally, art's pleasures—by their very pleasure—have evolutionary value in that they make life seem worth living, which is the best guarantee that we will do our best to survive. The long survival of art itself, its passionate pursuit despite poverty and oppression, and its pervasively powerful transcultural presence can all be explained by such naturalistic roots. For, as Emerson, Nietzsche, Dewey, and other life-affirming aestheticians have realized, there is something in the vividness and intensity of art's aesthetic experience that heightens our natural vitality by responding to deeply embedded human needs.

The quickening, transformative power of aesthetic experience that the naturalists stress as the energizing core of art need not be confined to wholly positive experiences of unity and pleasure, as my quotes from Emerson, Nietzsche, and Dewey might suggest. Naturalism extends beyond happy affirmations of organic wholeness, since nature not only unifies but disturbs and divides. Fragmentation and vivid encounters with disagreeable resistance can also stimulate an invigorating, life-enhancing aesthetic experience, as theorists of the sublime have long recognized. If contemporary art's most intense experiences often belong to this disruptive yet vitally exciting kind, then an updated naturalism can accommodate such an aesthetics of resistance, one that sees art's value in its ability to disturb and oppose social conventions through its experiential power of defiance, even if that oppositional power also partly relies on social conventions.

In critical contrast to aesthetic naturalism, historicism defines the concept of art more narrowly as a particular historical cultural institution produced by the Western project of modernity. Partisans of this view construe earlier and non-Western artistic forms not as art proper but as objects of craft, ritual, or cultural tradition that at best are precursors or imperfect analogues of autonomous art. The historicists stress the point that our current concepts of fine art and aesthetic experience did not really begin to take definite shape until the eighteenth century,[15] and that they achieved their present "autonomous" form only through social developments of the nineteenth century that established the modern institution of fine art and that culminated in the notion of "art for art's sake." In the words of the French sociologist Pierre Bourdieu, the most rigorous and systematic of the aesthetic historicists, it is not at all in nature that "the foundation of the aesthetic attitude and of the work of art . . . is truly located [but rather] . . . in the *history* of the artistic institution" that creates the very "*social conditions of possibility*" for art and aesthetic experience. Thus, "although appearing to be a gift from nature, the eye of the twentieth-century art lover is really a product of history."[16]

Twentieth-century art, the historicist argument continues, has taken this autonomy and turned art into its own preeminent purpose and its own prime subject matter. Just as art is held to be the product of its sociohistorical differentiation from real-world contexts, so art's meaning and value are seen as constituted simply by the social, institutional setting that distinguishes art from the rest of life. It is, of course, the sociohistorical institutional setting that makes a readymade object into a work of art and distinguishes it from its ordinary nonartistic counterpart. Museums, galleries, and other art institutions do not, therefore, simply display art, they help create the social space without which art cannot even be properly constituted as such.

Bourdieu is joined by the analytic philosophers Arthur Danto and George Dickie in stressing this point. These and like-minded historicists therefore conclude that it is only through the historically changing social framework of the artworld that an object becomes an artwork; its status as such, therefore, depends not at all on beauty, satisfying form, or pleasurable aesthetic experience, which contemporary art has shown to be inessential, if not altogether *dépassé*. Some historicists further insist that even the seemingly wider notions of aesthetic object and aesthetic enjoyment (without the further, more distinctive claim of *artistic* status) are likewise determined by the historical institution of art, because that institution is held to have determined the general form that any aesthetic appreciation should take by having defined the very meaning of the aesthetic.

How, then, should we choose between naturalism and historicism? It seems folly to simply choose one of these polarized views, since each has severe limitations.[17] If the naturalistic view does not sufficiently account for the social institutions and historical conventions that structure art's practice and govern its reception, then the sociohistorical view cannot adequately explain the ends for which art practices and institutions were developed, what human goods they are meant to serve, and why non-Western, non-modern cultures also pursue what seem to be artistic endeavors. To define art simply as the product of modernity puts in question the deep historical continuities that constitute the tradition of Western art from Greek and Roman times through medieval and Renaissance art into the modern period where art is said to originate. Another reason why we should not simply choose between aesthetic naturalism and historicist conventionalism, between lived experience and social institutions, is that these notions are as much interdependent as they are opposed. Our very notion of a natural language, which is nonetheless constituted by social conventions and history, shows the folly of the natural/sociohistorical dichotomy. Natural life without history is meaningless, just as history without life is impossible.

But if it seems foolish to choose between viewing art as natural and viewing it as nonnatural (since sociohistorical), a troubling tension remains between the two approaches. On the one hand, naturalism sees art's most valuable essence in the vivid intensity of its lived experience of beauty and meaning, in how it directly affects and stimulates by engaging themes that appeal most deeply to our human nature and interests. On the other hand, there is the historicist insistence that art's crucially defining feature has nothing at all to do with the vital nature of its experience but rather resides in the historically constructed social framework that constitutes an object as art by presenting it as such and institutionally determining how it should be treated or experienced. On one side, we see the demand for experiential intensity and meaningful substance; on the other, the requirement of a social frame without which no artistic substance, hence no experience of art, seems possible.

III

The idea of art as dramatization provides a way of reconciling the residual sense of conflict between these poles of aesthetic naturalism and sociohistorical contextualism by combining both these moments within its single concept. In contemporary English and German, there are two main meanings for the verb "to dramatize" (or "*dramatisieren*"), which parallel the two moments of experiential intensity and social frame.[18] In its more technical meaning, to dramatize means to "put something on stage," to take some event or story and put it in the frame of a theatrical performance or in the form of a play or scenario. This sense of "dramatize" highlights the fact that art is the putting of something into a frame, a particular context or stage that sets the work apart from the ordinary stream of life and thus marks it as art. Art is the staging or framing of scenes. The familiar French synonym for this sense of dramatize is, of course, "*mise en scène*," a convenient term that Nietzsche himself used in *Ecce Homo* to praise the artistic genius of the Parisians: "Nowhere else does there exist such a passion in questions of form, this seriousness in *mise en scène*—it is the Parisian seriousness *par excellence*."[19]

Besides the idea of staging and framing, "dramatize" also has another main meaning that suggests intensity. To "dramatise," says the *Chambers 21st Century Dictionary* is "to treat something as, or make it seem, more exciting or important."[20] The *Duden Fremdwörterbuch* makes the same point for German: "*dramatisieren*" means "*etwas lebhafter, aufregender darstellen*." In this sense of art's dramatization, art distinguishes itself from ordinary reality not by its fictional frame of action but by its greater vividness of experience and action, through which art is opposed not to the concept of *life* but rather to that which is lifeless and humdrum. Etymologically, our concept of drama derives from the Greek word "drama" (δρᾶμα) whose primary meaning is a real deed or action, rather than a formal framing or staged performance. This suggests that drama's power derives, partly at least, not from the framing stage but from the stirring energy of intense action itself; for action is not only a necessity of life but a feature that invigorates it. But how can we make sense of any action without grasping it through its framing context or situation?

I shall return to explore this intimate connection of action and place, but first I should underline the point already made: that dramatization effectively captures both moments—active intensity and structural frame—that the naturalist and contextualist theories respectively and contestingly advocate in defining art. The idea of art as dramatization may therefore serve as a handy formula for fullness, synthesis, and reconciliation of this longstanding and, I think, futile aesthetic debate.

To ensure that we are not building too much philosophy on the meaning of the single word "dramatization," let us turn to the synonym that many in Germany prefer to use: "*Inszenierung*," a term that clearly echoes the French term "*mise en scène*." Both terms, of course, derive, from the Latin "scaena" (the stage or scene of the theater), which derives from the Greek "*skene*" (σκηνή), whose primary meanings were not initially theatrical but rather generic designations of place: a covered place, a tent, a dwelling place, a temple. The concept of *mise en scène* or *Inszenierung*, with its direct invocation of scene as stage or place, seems to emphasize art's moment of frame rather than intensity of action or experience.

But we should not conclude that it therefore ignores this other key moment that we found in the concept of drama. First, *mise en scène* implies that something significant is being framed or put in place; the scene of *mise en scène* is not a blandly neutral space, but the site where something important is happening. Even the very word "scene" has come to connote this sense of intensity. In colloquial speech, the "scene" denotes *not* just any random location but, as one says in English, "where the action is." It denotes the focus of the most exciting things that are happening, for example, in the cultural life or night life of a city. To make a scene, in colloquial speech, is not simply to do something in a particular place but to display or provoke an excessive display of emotion or active disturbance. In short, just as the action of drama implies the frame of place, so the place of scene implies something vivid, vital, and exciting that is framed. For similar reasons, the English word "situation" (in locutions like "We have a situation here") is now often used colloquially to suggest the heightened intensity of a disturbing problem (argument, accident, emergency, breakdown, etc.).

This reciprocity of heightened experience and specially significant place, we should emphasize, is not a mere superficial linguistic coincidence of English and German. The notion of scene as the locus of the most intense experience goes back to the deepest ancient sources. Tellingly used by Euripides to denote a temple, the word "*skene*" (along with its derivative "*skenoma*") also served as the ancient Greek term for the holy tabernacle of the Old Testament where God's presence was said to dwell. In the original Hebrew, the word for tabernacle is מִשְׁכָּן, which is derived from the word for divine presence, שְׁכִינָה, both sharing the trilittoral stem *skn* (שכנ) that means to dwell.[21] Thus, the scene of *skene* means not simply the place of a play but the dwelling of God, the sacred site of divine activity and experience, a locus of overwhelming exaltation. For, as the Bible repeatedly declares, "the glory of the Lord filled the tabernacle" (Exodus 40:34, 35), exuding so much divine intensity that even the steady Moses was overcome. This Hebrew *skene*, the *Mishkan*, was the theater that God commanded Moses to build for Him from the voluntary donations of precious metals, cloth, and jewels collected from all the Hebrew people. Its crucial, sacred importance is witnessed through the detailed description of its complex construction and ornamentation, which fills the final six chapters of the book of Exodus. Thus, the divine roots of drama or *mise en scène*, its role as a holy locus of intense experience, is vividly present also in ancient Hebrew culture, not just in the Greek cult of Dionysus to which Nietzsche (a minister's son, after all) later pays tribute.

IV

Drama, as Aristotle long ago described it, is the presentation of heightened action within a well-structured formal frame of "a certain, definite magnitude," involving "a well-constructed plot" with a clear "beginning, middle, and end."[22] If the deep drama that defines art in general is a complex play of heightened experience and formal frame, then good art should ignore neither of these moments. To concentrate solely on the frame will eventually degenerate into bare and barren formalism where art remains alienated from the inspiring interests and energies of life. But to dismiss art's concern for cultivation of its frame because of a frantic lust for experiential intensity would threaten a parallel artistic wasteland: the empty clutter of shallow sensationalism devoid of any enduring form, so that we might eventually lose the very capacity to distinguish particular artworks from each other and from other things. Even those genres (such as performance art and happenings) that most effectively challenged the rigidity of art's separating frame nonetheless rely on some sense of this frame in order to claim their artistic status and give themselves the meaning they intend.

But if good art must be fundamentally dramatic in the double sense we have identified, namely, as intense experience captured and shaped within a special formal frame, how then do these two dimensions of drama—intensity of experience (in action or feeling) and formal staging—fit together? How compatible can they be? They *seem* to pull in different directions, especially when we accept the popular presumptions that lived fervor cannot tolerate formal staging and that art's distancing frame conversely subverts real-life intensity of affect and action. Art's power, however, might be better understood by challenging these dogmas. So I shall conclude by arguing that the apparent tension between art's explosively vital life-feeling and its formal frame (a tension that underlies the conflict between aesthetic naturalism and artistic historicism) should be seen as no less productive and reciprocally reinforcing than the familiar tension between content and form to which it seems clearly related.

A frame is not simply an isolating barrier of what it encloses. Framing focuses its object, action, or feeling more clearly; and thus sharpens, highlights, and enlivens. Just as a magnifying glass heightens the sun's light and heat by the concentration of its refracting frame, so art's frames intensify the power its experienced content wields on our affective life, rendering that content far more vivid and significant. But, conversely, the intensity of feeling or heightened sense of action that is framed reciprocally justifies the act of framing. We do not frame just anything. A frame with nothing in it would be unsatisfying, so that when we find an empty frame or plain white canvas hanging on a gallery wall, we automatically project a significant content onto the apparent emptiness, even if it be the interpretive content that art need have no other content but itself and its essential aspect of framing. Other arts can provide their own similar examples. Think of composer John Cage's famous *4'33"* or choreographer Paul Taylor's *Duet* (two dancers motionless on stage).

In short, just as action makes no sense without the notion of a framing place where the action occurs, so our sense of frame, place, or stage has the prima facie implication that some significant activity (recalling the original Greek root of "drama") inhabits that frame. Great writers such as Henry James are therefore praised for rendering their fictional scenes so captivatingly vivid and real, not by providing intricately long descriptions of their physical setting (since such description can be tediously deadening), but instead through the compelling intensity of action that takes place within that setting, including the action of passionate thought and feeling. This lesson of aesthetic realism finds confirmation in the psychological theories of

Henry's famous brother, the philosopher William James, who argues that our immediate sense of reality "means simply relation to our emotional and active life . . . In this sense, whatever excites and stimulates our interest is real."[23]

Although art's dramatizing frame can heighten reality through its intensification of feeling, we must not forget the frame's other, contrasting, function that is far more familiar to our thinking about art. A frame not only concentrates but demarcates; it is thus simultaneously not just a focus but also a barrier that separates what is framed from the rest of life. This important bracketing effect, which tends to "derealize" what is framed, not only helps explain the long aesthetic tradition of sharply contrasting art to reality but also forms the fulcrum for influential theories of aesthetic distance. This bracketing aspect of the frame clearly inspires aesthetic historicism, which, we saw, defines art and the aesthetic by their social differentiation from other realms, entirely in terms of the special historically constructed institutional framework that makes an object an artwork or renders its appreciation a distinctively aesthetic experience.

In this knot of productive tension that binds art's heightened experience to its formal staging, another dialectical strand should be noted: precisely the bracketing off of art from the ordinary space of life is what affords art its feeling of lived intensity and heightened reality. Because art's experience is framed in a realm alleged to be apart from the worrisome stakes of what we call real life, we feel much more free and secure in giving ourselves up to the most intense and vital feelings. As Aristotle already adumbrated in his theory of catharsis, art's frame permits us to feel life's most disturbing passions more intensely, because we do so within a protected framework where the disruptive dangers of those passions can be contained and purged, so that neither the individual nor society will suffer serious damage.

Art's restraining frame thus paradoxically intensifies our passionate involvement by removing other inhibitions to lived intensity. Art's fictions are therefore often said to feel far more vividly real than much of what we commonly take as real life. It is as if the bracketed diversion of art from ordinary reality allows us an indirect route to appreciate the real far more fully or profoundly by putting us somehow in touch with a reality that is at least greater in its experiential depths of vivid feeling. This argument seems clearly prefigured in Nietzsche's famous praise of drama for piercing the everyday veil of solid, separate objects—an Apollonian dreamworld of clear forms and distinctive persons governed by the *"principio individua-tionis,"* so as to deliver our experience to the deeper Dionysian reality of frenzied "Oneness" and flux, the ground reality of "omnipotent will behind individuation, eternal life continuing beyond all appearance and in spite of all destruction" (*DG* 62–64, 108; *BT* 55–58, 101–2).

Some might protest that such arguments corrupt the very meaning of reality, which we should reserve for the world of ordinary life and science and keep absolutely distinct from the notion of art with its frame of staging—the sign of the unreal. To reply to such protests, one could invoke the constructed fictions and staged experiments that form the respected realities of science. But we should also note that the realities of everyday life are everywhere played out on the stages set by diverse institutional frames. Indeed, from certain lofty yet familiar perspectives, it seems that "All the world's a stage," as Shakespeare tells us, where life itself is but "a poor player that struts and frets his hour upon the stage, and then is heard no more."[24] In the ancient quarrel between philosophy and poetry, one wonders whether art has so often been denigrated as a staged imitation of life because real life itself is modeled on dramatic performance.

I will not venture here to resolve the question of the real nature of reality. It seems a hopeless task, partly because "reality" is an essentially contested concept but also because it is based on a grammatical substantive derived from the very flexible adjective "real," which, as J. L. Austin showed, is so peculiarly variable and complexly contextual in usage that any attempt to find a significant common core that constitutes what is real "is doomed to failure."[25] Instead, let me conclude by recalling the paradox that art's apparent diversion from real life may be a needed path of indirection that directs us back to experience life more fully through the infectious intensity of aesthetic experience and its release of affective inhibitions. This suggests that the long-established art/life dichotomy should not be taken too rigidly, that we have here at best a functional distinction that surely seems to dissolve with the idea of the art of living.

Chapter Eleven

Entertainment

A Question for Aesthetics

I. Introductory Remarks

One of the more important aesthetic debates of recent times concerns the artistic status and general cultural value of popular art. Because this is the art that is most enjoyed by most people in today's diverse societies, its status is crucial to the culture of democracy. Although some influential leftist thinkers (such as Mikhail Bakhtin and Antonio Gramsci) have defended such art, an army of cultural conservatives are joined by progressive intellectuals (such as Theodor Adorno, Hannah Arendt, and Pierre Bourdieu) in rejecting it and suggesting that the very notions of popular art, popular culture, and a popular aesthetic are essentially contradictions or category mistakes. Using the insights of pragmatism to challenge their critique, I defended popular art through a position I call meliorism, which acknowledges popular art's flaws and abuses but also recognizes its merit and potential. Meliorism holds that popular art needs improvement because of its many failings, but that it can be improved because it can and often does achieve real aesthetic merit and serve worthy social ends.[1]

Studying the many criticisms my arguments have provoked, I realized that resistance to popular art frequently stems from attitudes regarding more basic or general concepts. The specific term "popular art" is relatively modern and problematically ambiguous. Its English usage dates only from the nineteenth century, and it applies also to what might more aptly be called "folk art," not only to the modern mass-media arts of the entertainment industry, which today is its main meaning.[2] It is also contested by rival terms. Some theorists insist on using the more pejorative terms "mass culture," "mass art," or "mass entertainment" rather than the term "popular art."[3] One might even argue that simply using the term "popular art" already begs the key aesthetic question, since the term "art" itself already suggests aesthetic value, even if not every artwork demonstrates such value. Thus, critics often recognize the aesthetic worth of some of the popular music and films I discuss but argue that this is not proof of popular art's value, merely proof that the works in question transcend the realm of entertainment that defines popular culture. Other critics, who firmly refuse to grant aesthetic merit or artistic status to popular music and cinema, dodge the charge of stuffy snobbery by affirming that they actually like such things—but only as entertainment, not art.

This made me realize that underlying the stubborn hierarchical dichotomy between high and popular art there is a far more basic contrast at work: art versus entertainment. Yet the complex network of language games deploying these concepts reveals that entertainment is not simply contrasted to art but often identified with art as an allied or subsuming category. Newspapers frequently devote a single section to "Arts and Entertainment," and the arts are sometimes described as forms of entertainment. Because the concept of entertainment seems deeply and complexly related to the concept of art, and because it is also broader and older than the concept of popular art, its analysis could be illuminating not only for the question of popular art but also for aesthetics as a whole.

I begin with two general remarks about the cultural forces shaping our understanding of entertainment. First, such forces are typically hierarchical and contestatory in the struggle over culture. Like popular art, entertainment has been largely defined by its deprecatory contrast with what philosophy considered to be higher forms of culture, whether the contrast was with philosophy itself or (at a later stage) with forms of high art. As a result, theories of entertainment and popular art are typically caught between two strategies. The first conceives entertainment as a field entirely dependent, derivative, and subordinate to the field of high culture from which it borrows and that it corrupts. The second strategy defines entertainment as a realm apart, defiantly opposed to the world of high culture but with its own autonomous rules, values, principles, and aesthetic criteria.

Philosophy has generally favored the former strategy, ever since Plato condemned art for providing corruptive pleasures of entertainment through imitations of the real that pretend to truth and wisdom but lack cognitive legitimacy and promote moral degeneracy by stimulating the lower part of our souls. Art's entertainment value is thus completely subordinated to the ideals and criteria of truth, moral character, and political value that are imported from philosophy. A far less frequent approach regards popular art or entertainment as defiantly contrastive to high culture by offering its own oppositional pleasures and values, particularly those of self-consciously earthy, carnal, profane life that express the regenerative values of material nature. This strategy is probably best exemplified by Mikhail Bakhtin's theory of the carnivalesque. Neither of these approaches, when taken in its extreme form, seems fully adequate to treat the nature of entertainment and popular art. If the Platonic approach falsely subsumes all values to philosophical truth, failing to recognize any degree of relative autonomy for aesthetic values of form and pleasure, so the extreme autonomist approach to popular art and entertainment does not do justice to the complex, intimate relations between high culture and lower entertainments, nor to the lingering traces of hegemony that the former still wields on the latter. As meliorism plies a middle way between condemnation and celebration, so we need a theory of entertainment that steers between mere subservience to and sheer defiance of high culture.

My second prefatory point is that because the cultural forces shaping the concepts of popular art and entertainment are historically changing, so is the extension of these concepts and the boundary drawn between them and serious art. The popular entertainments of one culture (such as Greek or Elizabethan drama) often become the high art classics of a subsequent age. Novels by the Brontës and Charles Dickens were initially received as light popular fiction, not as the masterpieces of great literature we regard them today. Movies have undergone similar evolution of status. Indeed, even within the very same cultural period, a given work can function either as popular entertainment or as high art, depending on how it is presented or interpreted, and how appreciated by its public. In nineteenth-century America, Shakespeare's plays were both high theater and vaudeville.[4] Thus, the precise meaning of entertainment is highly contextual, depending on what it is being contrasted to. Increasingly in modern times, the contrast term has become "serious art." But in earlier times, entertainment or amusement was contrasted to philosophy and the serious business of life, while the fine arts as a whole were regarded as having the lower status of entertainment (even though one could still then distinguish between higher and lower entertainments). Something of this older contrast remains today, as when we distinguish between work and entertainment or between reading for instruction and reading for amusement.

II. Terminological Complexities

During its long philosophical history in the West, the concept of entertainment has been expressed through a variety of terms with slightly different but overlapping meanings. For brevity, I confine myself here to the three major European languages of modern philosophy: English, French, and German. Besides the term "entertainment," other English words used to express this concept include "amusement," "pastime," "distraction," "divertissement," and "recreation." But related words such as "play" and "game" are also sometimes used. The French mainly employ such terms as *"amusement," "divertissement,"* and *"distraction,"* but they also use such terms as *"rejouissance"* and *"passetemps."* In German, *"Unterhaltung"* is the most common term for entertainment, but the terms *"Zerstreuen," "Zeitvertreib,"* and *"Belustigung,"* and, occasionally, *"Ergötzlichkeit"* are also used. The English term "entertainment" derives ultimately from the Latin *"inter"* + *"tenere,"* meaning "to hold together," "to maintain," "to uphold." The earliest English usages of "entertainment" in the sixteenth century were indeed devoted to this sense of maintaining or sustaining: particularly the maintenance of persons (especially guests and soldiers) through material provisions and the maintaining, in one's behavior, of proper manners and treatment. Another early usage of "entertainment" (found in Shakespeare's *Love's Labours Lost*) is an "occupation" or "spending of time." From these earlier meanings, the principal aesthetic meaning of "entertainment"—"the action of occupying (a person's) attention agreeably," "that which affords interest or amusement," "a public performance or exhibition intended to interest or amuse"—seems to have derived. The German term *"Unterhaltung"* clearly parallels the English, moving from connotations of support or sustenance to the idea of occupying one's time pleasantly (as does *"Belustigung"*). The straightforward philosophical lesson implied by this etymology is that a good, if not necessary, way to maintain oneself is to occupy oneself pleasurably and with interest. The same idea is expressed in the term "recreation," where one sustains oneself by reviving or recreating our energy through pleasurable activity. That pleasure is an aid to survival and flourishing is a point reinforced by evolutionary biologists.

The philosophical lesson becomes more complex, however, when we consider the English and French terms of "amusement," "divertissement," and "distraction." Here instead of emphasizing the maintenance of one's self (or one's guests), the focus is diverted to some other, presumably far less important, matter that captures our attention. The English term "amusement" derives from the verb "to muse" whose early meanings include being absorbed in thought, to wonder, to be astonished or puzzled. But both English terms stem back to the French "*muser,*" meaning to waste time or trifle by idly attending to light matters. Amusements thus prompt us to stop the serious business of maintaining ourselves and others and instead lure us to meditate on other things. The terms "distraction," "diversion," and "divertissement" all suggest (through their root meaning of "tearing away" or "turning aside") that we are turned away from our focus of attention and instead directed to something else. The German "*Zerstreuen*" (which Walter Benjamin uses to describe the distraction of film and other popular entertainments) likewise suggests that in entertainment the attentive subject is dispersed or scattered, in contrast to the concentration of the self that high art demands and that Benjamin denotes as "*Sammlung*" (a term that conveys the notion of collecting oneself or self-composure).

There is also an important philosophical lesson in this etymology of distraction, but it is more paradoxical and dialectic: to maintain the self one needs also to forget it and look elsewhere. To sustain, refresh, and even deepen concentration, one also needs to distract it; otherwise, concentration fatigues itself and gets dulled through monotony. These lessons, one might say, are inscribed in our anatomy of vision: we succeed in securing our physical sustenance and refreshment for the self by looking outward, not inward. This paradoxical structure of entertainment that binds, in a productive dialectic, the seeming opposites of focused attention and diversion, concentration and distraction, serious maintenance and playful amusement, also finds potent expression in various moments of the concept's genealogy.

III. Genealogical Reflections

The conceptual history of entertainment is too complex to be presented in a short, neat narrative, so I shall focus only on the most influential moments to highlight some key points. We can begin with Plato's *Phaedrus* (276a–277a), where Socrates, in arguing against the idea of writing philosophy, draws a sharp contrast between philosophy and entertainment. Written speeches, even of philosophy, are only valuable "for the sake of amusement," in contrast to the truly "serious" philosophical "art of dialectic" through oral dialogue, which actively inseminates the mind "and renders the man who has it as happy as any human can be." Philosophy is thus superior to amusement not only in its education but in its pleasures. The Greek term used here for "amusement" is "*paidia,*" which is strikingly close to the

Greek word for education, *paideia*, since they both have the common root related to children, a point that Plato deploys in book 2 of *Laws*. Trivialized as childish "kidding around" or playing, entertainment is contrasted with true education, which should be serious and controlled.[5] The mimetic arts, with their strong entertainment function, are for Plato not only a childish diversion from the truth but a deceptive distortion of it and a corruption of the soul. Hence his *Republic* strongly condemns them, even to the point of urging their banishment in book 10.

Although Aristotle's *Poetics* introduced some independent criteria for assessing the aesthetic value of tragedies—the pleasures of formalist unity and cathartic release—his defense of the artistic entertainments of his time still depended on philosophy's high value of truth. Hence art's mimetic pleasures are defined as lower versions of philosophy's higher cognitive joys; and the way Aristotle chooses to praise poetry is for being "more philosophic and of graver import than history" because it describes not the mere contingent particulars of the past but rather universal things: "a kind of thing that might happen, i.e.[,] what is possible as being probable or necessary." Although poetry uses proper names of particulars, "its statements are of the nature rather of universals, whereas those of history are singulars."[6]

At the dawn of modern thought, Michel de Montaigne still observes the ancient distinction between entertainment and serious philosophical wisdom in his discussion of reading. However, he skeptically challenges the traditional hierarchy of serious thought over playful amusement by proudly affirming that he now reads primarily for pleasure.[7] In his essay "Of Books" (*M* II:10, 297), he writes: "I seek in books only to give myself pleasure by honest amusement; or if I study, I seek only the learning that treats of the knowledge of myself and instructs me in how to die well and live well." Montaigne confirms this preference in a much later essay, "Of Three Kinds of Association," where he explains that although he first read, as a youth, for ostentation and then later for wisdom, he now reads only "for recreation." Anticipating critique of this love of amusement, Montaigne counters: "If anyone tells me that it is degrading the Muses to use them only as a plaything and a pastime, he does not know as I do the value of pleasure, play, and pastime. I would almost say that any other aim is ridiculous" (*M* III:3, 629).

Montaigne must not be mistaken for a lightweight, frivolous mind; the gargantuan work of intense self-study that constitutes his massive *Essays* makes this clear. He insisted that this meditative activity "of entertaining one's own thoughts" was a form of entertainment that, in a strong mind, could rival all other activities in both intellectual demandingness and pleasure. Feeling, however, that prolonged, vigorous self-meditation could be dangerously exhausting and unsettling, Montaigne recognized his mind's need to divert itself with other pleasures in order to "settle down and rest." Books were his favorite form of distraction, since their amusement provided not only rest from the rigors of self-study but enabled the mind "to be diverted from a[ny] troublesome idea" that might haunt it, but he also relished friendly associations, especially with "beautiful and well-bred women" (*M* III:3, 621, 622, 628). Montaigne's account of entertainment contains three crucial points. First, entertainment can take also demanding, meditative forms that involve not merely pleasure but also the superior exercise of the mind, hence the pursuit of entertainment, pleasure, and serious intellectual activity should not be seen as inconsistent. Second, as pleasure is not a trivial value, entertainment's deep connection with pleasure should not demean but rather elevate it. Third, entertainment's diversion of the mind is not a necessarily negative feature that diminishes the mind by distracting its attention but rather, in dialectical fashion, strengthens the mind's powers by providing it with both relief and alternative exercise in changing the focus and style of its activity.

In the eighteenth century, the notion of entertainment begins to be contrasted not simply with the serious praxis of life and thought, but also with more serious forms of art. Thus Samuel Johnson, the key critical figure of eighteenth-century English neoclassicism, attributes to "entertainment" a specific application to "the lower comedy," and notes its growing use for denoting "an assemblage of performances of varied character, as when music is intermixed with recitations, feats of skill, etc."[8] In Diderot's *Encyclopedia*, the article "Divertissement" suggests a somewhat similar point. After noting the more technical meaning of "divertissement" in the arts of that time—designating "all the little poems put to music that one performs in the theatre or concert; and the dances, mixed with song, that one sometimes places at the end of comedies of two acts or one act," and "more particularly those dances and songs episodically introduced into the acts of opera"—the article more generally defines "divertissement" as "the generic term that includes particular amusements, recreations, and festivities [*rejouissances*]." Despite their somewhat different nuances, these terms are claimed to be "synonyms and have distraction [*dissipation*] or pleasure as their base." The article's closing caution that "all divertissements that do not take useful or necessary things as their goal are the fruit of idleness and love of pleasure" suggests a contrast of mere entertainment with true art, "whose supreme merit," Diderot elsewhere writes, "lies in combining the pleasant with the useful." Of course, this neither implies that art itself is not a form of entertainment nor that entertainment must be confined to idle matters of useless pleasure.[9]

In Immanuel Kant's *Critique of Judgement*, the notion of entertainment is used with both low and high connotations. Although applied to the sensual, "interested" pleasures that distinguish the merely agreeable from the beautiful (book 1, para. 7), it is later used for the disinterested (that is, purposeless) free entertainment of the mental faculties ("freie und unbestimmt-zweckmäßige Unterhaltung der Gemütskräfte") that mark our experience of beauty.[10] Friedrich Schiller's appreciative identification of the aesthetic with the realm of play and appearance recognizes the positive human need of entertainment as expressed through the concept of play: "Man plays only when he is a human being in the fullest sense of the term, and he is only fully a human being when he plays."[11] Schiller likewise insists on the ennobling value of play as both an expression of human freedom and a noncoercive, effective form of moral edification. The concept of *Schein* (appearance), which is clearly related to that of *Spiel* (play) and to the spectacle sense of entertainment, is similarly valorized by Schiller as a locus and instrument of freedom. As the notion of entertainment in Kant's *Critique of Judgment* maintained a fragile balance between interested and free pursuits (and thus a consequent bivalence of the term between the lower realm of the merely agreeable and the higher cognitive realm of the beautiful), so Schiller's ideal of play suggests that entertainment (in its nobler forms) itself provides and symbolizes the perfect equilibrium of ideal form and material life.

But this balanced view of entertainment is decisively disturbed by Hegel's influential aesthetics, with its fateful spiritualizing turn toward the ideal. With Hegel, entertainment seems unequivocally identified with what is unworthy of the name of art. In his initial remarks to affirm the worthiness of art in his *Vorlesungen über die Ästhetik*, Hegel feels he must sharply distinguish between "true art" and the "servile" artistic distractions that are merely "a fleeting game in the service of pleasure and entertainment" and of other "external" ends of "life-related pleasantness." Entertainment thus marks the inferior realm of servitude to pleasure and its external ends. In contrast, the fine arts become true art only when they are free from this subservience. Here we already see the strong contrast between art and entertainment that still dominates contemporary debate about the popular arts. However, despite his explicit claims for what he calls the *"freie Kunst"* of the fine arts, Hegel does not really leave these fine arts free. For he imperiously assigns to them their "*highest* task": "as simply a mode of revealing to consciousness and bringing to utterance the Divine, the deepest interests of humanity and the most comprehensive truths of the mind."[12] Hegel thus both confirms and confuses the rigid contrast between entertainment—defined as "servile" by its aim of pleasure through appearances—and real art, whose freedom is paradoxically defined by its servitude to God, truth, and the ideal. This Hegelian attitude still dominates contemporary aesthetics, whose idealist turn has privileged truth over beauty and pleasure, while also aesthetically privileging the realm of art high over the splendors of nature.

Nietzsche presents a more complex and salutary view of entertainment and its relationship to art and thought. He can deploy the term very pejoratively to denote a trivial concern with shallow pleasure and the passing of time to alleviate boredom. Indeed, he uses the term "entertainment" not only to condemn such trivialities in the realm of artistic expression but also in the realm of knowledge and philosophy itself. In "Schopenhauer as Educator" (§6), he complains how scholarly books and their trivial truths serve as mere "means of entertainment or fly-swatters against boredom" or as "play" or "amusement." His essay "Richard Wagner in Bayreuth" contrasts true art and culture (whose aim should be genius) to what he calls the "corrupt" "art-entertainments" of the art of his time. But this "poorly concealed addiction for amusement, for entertainment at any price," is not identified with the popular arts but rather with the official high art of "the cultivated people" and "scholars," and is indeed contrasted with Wagner's recognition of the common people as "the poetic folk."[13]

On the other hand, in *Ecce Homo* ("Why I Am so Clever," §3), Nietzsche expresses the positive power of entertainment through the notion of "recreation" ("*Erholung*"), which he regards, along with choice of climate and nourishment, as essential to self-care, as what allows him to escape himself and his own self-demanding "seriousness": "Every kind of reading belongs among my recreations."[14] An intense practitioner of self-meditation like Montaigne, Nietzsche affirms the productive paradox of entertainment's distraction that we earlier gleaned from etymology and from Montaigne—that the self is sustained and strengthened by being freed from attention to itself, that serious self-care also entails amusing distraction from oneself. And this paradox, I think, implies a further dialectical lesson: that the self is enlarged and improved by forgetting itself and plunging its interest into the wider world. Real growth means letting go of what one already is in order to embrace something greater. This lesson might also be extended to contemporary art, whose intense and often narrow concentration on itself (on its own internal history, theory, masterpieces, and presumed essence rather than on the wider world of nature and human life in which it is situated) has resulted in a loss of power and appeal.

As Montaigne and Nietzsche urge the value of entertainment for dialectically strengthening our mental power through diversionary play and restorative relaxation, we could suggest a further hypothesis concerning the cognitive contribution of entertainment: its relaxing function not only provides relief or diversion that can restore concentration, but it can also sharpen sensitivity of perception by lowering the sensory interference caused by surplus tensions of muscular contraction resulting from excessive effort or straining. This hypothesis finds support in the psychophysics embodied in the famous Weber–Fechner Law and recognized in common experience: a smaller stimulus can be noticed more clearly and easily if the already preexisting stimulation experienced by the stimulated organ is small, whereas the stimulus, if it is to be noticed, must be so much the larger, the greater the preexisting stimulation is.[15] For instance, the light of a cigarette may be barely visible from a short distance in blazing sunlight but will be visible from afar in the dark of night; sounds of wind-blown leaves that we hear in the silence of the woods at midnight are inaudible in the city's noise of day. In the same way, a hand that is hardened into a fist or tightly extended fingers will not be as sensitive to fine discriminations of touch and texture as would a soft hand free from muscular strain. Entertainment's function of relaxation may thus provide not mere restorative relief but finer sensibility for new insights.

Unfortunately, after Nietzsche, the dominant trend in German philosophy to denigrate the entertainment function of art reasserts itself. Martin Heidegger insists that artworks are not truly presented when they "are offered for merely artistic enjoyment," since art's defining essence is not pleasure or entertainment but "the becoming and happening of truth." Even Hans-Georg Gadamer, whose aesthetics features the notion of play, emphasizes art's ontological and interpretive revelations while largely neglecting its function of entertainment, and he cautions against the seductive dangers of "aesthetic immediacy" and "*Erlebnis*."[16] The Hegelian trend in German aesthetics to privilege truth over pleasure and even over beauty is still more strikingly dominant in Adorno, who together with Max Horkheimer introduced the disparaging notion of "the culture industry" to denigrate the entertainments of popular art, whose allegedly passive and mindless pleasures "fill empty time with more emptiness." For Adorno, it almost seems that the entertaining pleasures of art are starkly opposed to cognition: "People enjoy works of art the less, the more they know about them, and vice versa." In the contest of artistic values, Adorno is clear that pleasure must be sacrificed to truth. "In a false world, all hedone is false. This goes for artistic pleasure too. . . . In short, the very idea that enjoyment is of the essence of art needs to be thrown overboard. . . . What works of art really demand from us is knowledge or, better, a cognitive faculty of judging justly."[17]

But why should it be assumed that there is an essential opposition between truth and entertainment, knowledge and pleasure? Note how one influential Anglo-American poet-critic-theorist wisely maintained the fruitful interconnection of these terms and therefore could affirm art's entertainment without denying its cognitive import. T. S. Eliot, inspired by the ideas of Remy de Gourmont, famously defined poetry as "a superior amusement," while immediately cautioning that this does "not mean an amusement for superior people." The arts constitute a superior amusement, Eliot argues, because their pleasure appeals not just to the senses but to the understanding.

> To understand a poem comes to the same thing as to enjoy it for the right reasons. One might say that it means getting from the poem such enjoyment as it is capable of giving; to enjoy a poem under a misunderstanding as to what it is, is to enjoy what is merely a projection of our own mind. . . . It is certain that we do not fully enjoy a poem unless we understand it; and, on the other hand, it is equally true that we do not fully understand a poem unless we enjoy it. And that means, enjoying it to the right degree and in the right way, relative to other poems.[18]

By deconstructing the opposition between aesthetic pleasure and cognition, Eliot also sought to challenge the dichotomy between high art—presumably devoted (in Hegelian fashion) to sublime truth—and, on the other hand, vulgar popular entertainments that presumably pander to mere pleasure. Seeing instead a continuum between high art and entertainment, Eliot insists that the good poet "would like to be something of a popular entertainer . . . would like to convey the pleasures of poetry." In mordant demystification of Romanticist notions of the poet as prophetic genius and perceiver of deep truths, Eliot says he would be pleased to secure for the poet "a part to play in society as worthy as that of the music-hall comedian," and he deliberately turned his poetic efforts to the theater in his quest to reach a wider audience. An avid fan of music hall, Eliot realized that it is naïve to speak of the audiences of high and popular art as if they were disjoint publics, just as it is wrong to think that works of high art cannot acquire a broad popularity or that works stemming from vernacular popular culture cannot achieve high aesthetic value.[19]

Most cultural critics, nonetheless, sharply contrast art and entertainment, identifying the latter with idle pleasure-seeking and lower-class vulgarity. Many factors of cultural and conceptual economy have made this identification seductive. As the notion of pleasure centrally includes pleasures of the flesh, so idealist philosophy and otherworldly Christianity conspired to distance their realms of value from such low, corporeal taints. The protestant ethic of work and thrift, long entrenched in North America and Northern Europe, has also given pleasure a bad name. Moreover, the intellectual asceticism that constitutes the typical *habitus* of theorists prompts them to resist full recognition of pleasure's rich values. With modernity's secularization of the natural world and the loss of traditional religious faith, art increasingly came to function as a locus for our habits of sacralization. Even if the sacred aura of art has been challenged by the mechanical reproduction of artworks, the desire to sustain art as a transcendental, spiritual value remains. In secular society, the classics of literature have become our sacred texts while museums have replaced churches as the place where one visits on the weekend for one's spiritual edification. But if art is to be sacralized, it must be sharply distinguished from entertainment, since entertainment is associated with earthy pleasures that serve to refresh embodied human life rather than wholly devoting itself to the realm of transcendental spirituality celebrated by romantic "theologies" of art. Pleasure and life—two of the crucial values that pragmatist aesthetics sees in art—are paradoxically two of the cardinal sins for which entertainment is condemned. I therefore conclude with arguments in their defense, although common sense would think that none are needed.

IV. Pleasure and Life

I begin with pleasure, as my aesthetics has been criticized for hedonism, even though I never claim that pleasure is the only or the highest value in art and life.[20] I do, however, think that post-Kantian aesthetics wrongly tends to dismiss the importance of pleasure by failing to realize the complexity of its logic and the diversity of its forms and uses. This diversity is even suggested in the vast vocabulary of pleasure that far exceeds the single word. Besides the traditional contrast between sensual voluptuousness (*voluptas*) and the

sacred heights of religious joy (*gaudium*), there is delight, pleasantness, gratification, gladness, elation, titillation, fun, exhilaration, enjoyment, exultation,
bliss, rapture, ecstasy, and more. While fun and pleasantness convey a sense
of lightness that could suggest triviality, the notions of rapture, bliss, and
ecstasy clearly evoke just how profound and potently meaningful pleasures
can be. Such pleasures, as much as truth, help constitute our sense of the
sacred and can establish or reinforce our deepest values.[21]

    Conventional empiricism sees pleasure (and experience more generally)
in terms of passive sensations existing only in the private mental world of
the experiencing subject. So conceived, pleasure might seem trivial. But
pleasure is not such an isolated passive sensation, it is rather, as Aristotle
recognized, a quality of any activity that "completes" or enhances that activity
by making the activity more zestful or rewarding and thus promoting it by
intensifying our interest in it. Pleasure is thus inseparable from the activity
in which it is experienced. To enjoy tennis is not to experience intensely
agreeable feelings in one's sweating racket hand or running feet (feelings
that would distract us from the game); it is rather to play the game with
gusto and absorbed attention. Likewise, to enjoy art is not to have certain
pleasant sensations that we might obtain from something else, like a good
espresso or a steam bath; enjoying an artwork is rather taking pleasure in
perceiving and understanding the particular work's qualities and meanings,
where such pleasure tends to intensify our attention to the work in a way
that aids our perception and understanding of it. This Aristotelian conception lies behind Eliot's view of the essential connection of poetic enjoyment
and understanding.

    By strengthening our activity, pleasure contributes to the perfection
of life. Far from a radical voluptuary, Spinoza actually defines pleasure "as
the transition of man from a less to a greater perfection," "the greater the
pleasure whereby we are affected, the greater the perfection to which we
pass." And the sober Aristotle similarly insists: "Whether we choose life for
the sake of pleasure or pleasure for the sake of life, they seem to be bound
up together and not admit of separation, since without activity pleasure
does not arise and every activity is completed by the attendant pleasure."[22]
Contemporary evolutionary theory confirms this linkage of life and pleasure.
Some of life's most powerful pleasures are closely linked to the activities
of nourishment and procreation that have been necessary for the survival
of the species. Pleasure's logic of desire guides us to what we need more
quickly and powerfully than deliberative reason can. Besides making life
sweet, pleasure makes continued life more possible by offering the promise

that it is worth living. Aesthetic entertainment certainly contributes to these life-fulfilling pleasures.

Although a powerful Kantian tradition insists on a very specific type of aesthetic pleasure, narrowly defined as the intellectual pleasure of pure form arising from the harmonious play of our cognitive faculties, the pragmatist tradition construes aesthetic pleasure more generously. First and most simply, there are the variegated pleasures of sense—rich qualities of color, shape, sound, movement, touch, and so on. The pleasures of heightened perception, stirred by an artwork's appealing sensory qualities, are part of what makes it stand out from the ordinary flow of perception as a special aesthetic experience worthy of the name of art, an experience that so absorbs our attention that it also constitutes an entertaining distraction from the humdrum routine of life. Indeed, aesthetic pleasures are often so intensely delightful that they suggest metaphysical or religious transcendence to a higher realm of reality. Indian philosophy claims the aesthetic pleasure of *rasa* (the special emotion expressed in art, most paradigmatically in drama) is "transcendental" or "unworldly" in its power and quality of "bliss."[23] The sense of divine pleasure is also clear in the original meaning of the Japanese term for entertainment ("*goraku*"), which indicates the receiving of hospitality from a heavenly maiden.[24] Besides intense yet well-ordered feelings, aesthetic pleasures include the satisfactions of meaning and expression. Such pleasures motivate not only the creative artist or entertainer but also the critic and the broader public who engage in interpretation to communicate and explain the pleasures they experience and to deepen them through enriching analysis.

The pleasures of meaning and expression imply another aspect of aesthetic pleasure that is often obscured: its social dimension. Too often we assume the enjoyment of art or entertainment is simply subjective, hence essentially private and narrowly individualistic. But there is a radiating feature in pleasure that takes it beyond mere individual satisfaction. Pleasures are contagious; when we see a child enjoying a song, we will be inclined to take pleasure in her pleasure, even if we do not know the child and do not think that the song is especially beautiful. When we experience joy, we typically want to share it with others; and we *can* share our aesthetic pleasures in the same way we share an aesthetic experience. Although every one of us attending an art show, or a movie, or a rock concert will feel aesthetic pleasure through one's own consciousness, this does not deny the shared character of our enjoyment, nor the fact that our enjoyment is heightened by our sense of its being shared. Aesthetic experience gains intensity from a sense of sharing something meaningful and valuable together, and this includes the feeling of shared pleasures. Art's power to unite society through its enchanting pleasures of communication is a theme that resounds from Schiller to John Dewey, yet the unifying power of mass-media entertainment is likewise recognized, though vilified, by the critics of popular art.[25]

I have been arguing that we should not trivialize the aesthetic pleasures of art and entertainment because they contribute in many significant ways to the maintenance, meaning, and enrichment of life. But this service to life is precisely the reason why some philosophers denigrate entertainment as trivial, low, and devoid of cultural value. Combining Kant's idea of the aesthetic as disinterested and purposeless perception with Hegel's idealist notion of the freedom and spiritual transcendence of fine art, this line of argument sharply contrasts art and entertainment by asserting that only the latter has practical functionality in serving life, while true works of art eschew this petty role of means or function and indeed transcend the realm of mortal life. Hannah Arendt offers a powerful example of this approach.

Entertainment, she admits, has real utility for "the life process of society" because it relaxingly fills "vacant time" in "the biologically conditioned cycle of labor" with enjoyable commodities for experiential consumption. But Arendt still scorns "the noisy futility of mass entertainment" by contrast to art's creation of permanent things that she sees as belonging to the special enduring world of culture, which stands entirely outside the realm and necessities of "biological life" and whose beauty and value are beyond all needs and function, inhabiting an immortal realm of freedom.[26] "Culture relates to objects and is a phenomenon of the world; entertainment relates to people and is a phenomenon of life" (CC 208). Although "we all stand in need of entertainment and amusement in some form or other, because we are all subject to life's great cycle," we must not confuse it for an aesthetic or cultural pursuit. "Entertainment, like labor and sleep, is irrevocably part of the biological life process," which is "a metabolism" of consumption. Entertainment thus provides mere "commodities" for experiential consumption, functional "consumer goods" to be used and "used up" (CC 205, 206, 208). "They serve . . . to while away time . . . which . . . is biological in nature, left over after labor and sleep have received their due" (CC 205). In contrast, works of art are not used but appreciated through a purely "disinterested" contemplation; their "durability is the very opposite of functionality" or use in the process of life (since, for Arendt, such use implies being "used up"). "They are the only things without any function in the life process of society; strictly speaking, they are fabricated not for men, but for the world which is meant to outlast the life-span of mortals"

(CC 208, 209, 210). In short, whereas entertainment is a "means" that serves to sustain and improve human life, artworks are pure ends, things of "intrinsic, independent worth," "things which exist independently of all utilitarian and functional references, and whose quality remains always the same" (CC 215–16). For Arendt, art's "beauty is the very manifestation of imperishability," while "the entertainment industry" is a danger that threatens to pillage and corrupt the permanent, imperishable beautiful things of art, turning them into disposable commodities of human consumption (CC 207, 218).

Arendt's position has a sense of noble grandeur and disinterested selfless purity that may strike us as initially attractive. Surely art is more than a mere means for the smooth functioning of life's biological processes of consumption. But why should we identify life and functionality with such a narrow physiological conception? Human life is always more than biological; it intrinsically involves meaning, making, and conduct. And what would the world of culture be without human life and the experience of mortal people to animate it? A collection of things that are lifeless rather than immortal. Functions and means need not be low and menial. Is the study of philosophy or art a slavish pursuit because it serves the end of wisdom or beauty? Underlying Arendt's theory is an aristocratic attitude that philosophy inherited from the Athenian class system, an attitude that associated all means and acts of making with the lower class of laboring servants and that contrasted this "banausic" work with the pure contemplation of "the most noble group of the free-born men." For Arendt, the danger of "fabrication in all forms ["including the production of art"] is that it is utilitarian by its very nature" and thus "always involves means" and so promotes "the banausic mentality" (CC 215, 216, 219). Pragmatism, a philosophy with a more democratic vision, argues instead that if you value the ends, you must also value the means necessary to achieve those ends. Moreover, it reconstructs our concept of means to show how they may be integrated into the ends they serve, the way the means of a painting—its brushstrokes, paint, and so on—form part of the final work of painting.

Arendt's advocacy of a world of culture, art, and beauty that exists beyond the needs and purposes of human life may appeal to theorists who are weary of modern aesthetics' preoccupation with the human perspective on things. But pragmatism's affirmation of the life values of art, beauty, and entertainment need not be construed as confined exclusively to the human realm. Beauty of color, shape, movement, and song are part of the dance of life of the wider natural world that humans belong to and through which they are constituted. The energies and material that constitute aesthetic experience for the human subject belong to the wider environing world; aesthetic experience, properly speaking, is never located only in the head of the human subject but always exists in the wider context that frames the subject's interaction with the object of art or natural beauty. And, for pragmatism, the human subject itself is but a shifting, temporary construction from the materials and energies of the larger world of nature and history. Ironically, in advocating art (against entertainment) as a way of transcending the service of human life, Arendt is arguing from a perspective that she explicitly identifies as "humanism"—the glorification of the enduring manmade world of culture and its "cultura animi" (CC 225).

Still more paradoxically, though she claims to regard art and beauty as pure ends of delightful appearance with no functional reference to life, she actually ends up insisting that they perform perhaps the greatest service to life—its justification through immortalization. "The fleeting greatness of word and deed can endure in the world to the extent that beauty is bestowed upon it [through works of art]. . . . Without the beauty, that is, the radiant glory in which potential immortality is made manifest in the human world, all human life would be futile and no greatness could endure" (CC 218). Conversely, beauty, in her account, seems to need the public objecthood of human cultural creation as a medium in order to endure and achieve its immortality. If art serves life with immortalization, then entertainment is condemned because its meanings and pleasures are alleged to be more transient.

Pragmatism does not scorn the pleasures of art and entertainment because they are transitory in contrast to the imperishability of beauty claimed by Arendt. Regarding our entire universe as a realm of flux with no absolute permanence but only relative stabilities, pragmatism appreciates beauty and pleasure all the more because of its fragile, fleeting nature. By refusing to equate reality with permanence, it recognizes that short-lived loveliness or brief spasms of delight are no less real or cherished because they are momentary. Our pleasures of beauty, art, and entertainment are often more precious because they are fleeting. Philosophy's pleasures are also transient. If one such pleasure was reading this essay, I dare not try to prolong it.

Chapter Twelve

Art and Religion

I

Art emerged in ancient times from myth, magic, and religion, and it has long sustained its compelling power through its sacred aura. Like cultic objects of worship, artworks weave an entrancing spell over us. Though contrasted to ordinary real things, their vivid experiential power provides a heightened sense of the real and suggests deeper realities than those conveyed by common sense and science. While Hegel saw religion as superseding art in the evolution of Spirit toward higher forms that culminate in philosophical knowledge, subsequent artists of the nineteenth century instead saw art as superseding religion and even philosophy as the culmination of our human spiritual quest. Artistic minds as different as Matthew Arnold, Oscar Wilde, and Stéphane Mallarmé predicted that art would supplant traditional religion as the locus of the holy, of uplifting mystery and consoling meaning in our increasingly secular society dominated by what Wilde condemned as a dreary "worship of facts."[1] By expressing "the mysterious sense . . . of existence, [art] endows our sojourn with authenticity and constitutes the sole spiritual task," claims Mallarmé.[2] "More and more," writes Arnold, "mankind will discover that we have to turn to poetry to interpret life for us, to console us, to sustain us. Without poetry, our science will appear incomplete; and most of what now passes with us for religion and philosophy will be replaced by poetry."[3]

Such prophecies have largely been realized. In contemporary Western culture, artworks have become the closest thing we have to sacred texts, and art almost seems a form of religion with its prophetic breed of creative artists perennially purveying new gospels and its priestly class of interpretive critics who explain them to a devotional public. Despite wide recognition that art has an important commercial aspect, art sustains its cultural image as an essentially sanctified domain of higher spiritual values, beyond the realm of material life and praxis. Its adored relics (however profane they strive to be) are sacredly enshrined in temple-like museums that we dutifully visit for spiritual edification, just as religious devotees have long frequented churches, mosques, synagogues, and other shrines of worship.

In advocating a pragmatist aesthetics I have criticized this otherworldly religion of art because of the way it has been shaped by more than two centuries of modern philosophical ideology aimed at disempowering art by consigning it to an unreal, purposeless world of imagination. Such religion, I have argued, is the enemy of pragmatism's quest to integrate art and life, a quest exemplified both in the classical Western notion of the art of living and in some Asian artistic traditions, where art is less importantly the creation of objects than the process of refining the artist who creates and the audience who absorbs that creative expression.[4]

There is good reason, however, why this sacralization of art should remain so powerfully appealing despite the widespread recognition of art's mercantile dimensions and worldly concerns. The reason, I believe, is that art expresses very deep meanings and spiritual insights that religion and philosophy once most powerfully provided but that they now no longer convey in a convincing way to most of today's secular populations throughout the world. So, in this essay I wish to explore the idea that art provides a useful, even superior, substitute for religion, one that is free from the latter's many disadvantages and that should be vigorously championed as an alternative that could eventually free our transcultural world from the hostile divisiveness and backward-looking attitudes that religions have inspired and that could instead lead us toward greater understanding, peace, and harmony.

But a contrary yet equally interesting hypothesis likewise demands consideration: that art cannot be separated from religion, that rather than a real alternative, art is simply another mode or expression of religion. Or, to put it in a provocatively suggestive paraphrase, art is simply the continuation of religion by other means. If this hypothesis has merit—indeed, even if there is simply some deeply indissoluble link between art and religion—then we cannot simply look progressively past religion toward art. For our philosophy of art will be seen to express the metaphysics and ideologies generated by a religious worldview, which thus indirectly (if not also directly) shapes our aesthetic philosophy, even if we are unaware of this religious influence or deny real credence to the religion in question. To make this point more concretely I will later take up two examples that show how different metaphysics of religion engender different philosophies of aesthetic experience and the relationship of art to life.

II

Before focusing more narrowly on the spiritual paths and promise of religion and art, let me briefly consider philosophy's current contribution to spiritual life. Through its modern professionalization and consequent desire to be scientific, philosophy has largely foregone the pursuit of the fuzzy realm of wisdom and emotionally tinged spirituality. It prefers, at least in its dominant form, to maintain the status of objective, rigorous knowledge explored through a cool attitude of critical analysis, characterized by deadly "dryness" (as Iris Murdoch and others have so described it).[5] Though wisdom and spiritual feelings still find powerful expression in religion, its intimate connection with the supernatural and with dogmatic theological faith in truths about the world's creation that have been decisively discredited by modern science has made religion an unconvincing option for most intellectuals in the West. Moreover, the long and appallingly painful history of religious discrimination, intolerance, persecution, and even crusades of vicious warfare makes it hard for many minds to embrace religion as their source of spiritual edification and salvation.

This should remind us of a further problem with religion in an ever more tightly knit and explosively globalized world. Religion (whose Latin etymology, *religare*, highlights the role of gathering, tying, and binding together) has long been recognized by sociologists as providing the essential glue of social unity in traditional societies. But its fractious pluralities and sects have also generated enormous division and disunity, combined with fanatical zealotry and intolerance that threaten to blow the world apart instead of bringing it together. The so-called clash of civilizations that is today so ominously trumpeted is largely a euphemism for a clash rooted in different religious outlooks, roughly that of the Judaeo-Christian West and that of Islam, the last of the three great Abrahamic religions to emerge from the spiritually fertile Middle East. Even within the same religious civilization, region, and time, religion is just as likely to generate angry dissension as it is to ensure harmonious cohesion. I witnessed such internal religious wars as a student in Jerusalem, where I was frequently reviled and stoned by fanatical orthodox Jews because of my secular Jewish comportment. But that is nothing in comparison to the bloodshed suffered between Suni and Shia Muslims in Iraq. Finally, the distinctly dour and ascetically demanding dimensions of most religions, with their strict and restrictive commandments often accompanied by dire threats of severe (even eternal) punishments for disobedience, can hardly attract contemporary sensibilities that seem much more inclined to open-minded freedom in the pursuit of happiness, including the pursuit of sensory pleasures.

Art, in contrast, seems to be free of these disadvantages, thus promising a more fruitful and satisfying way for the expression of wisdom and spiritual meaning, replete with abundant sensory, emotional, and intellectual pleasures. It provides the joys of mystery and myth without committing our faith to dubious dogma and thus inducing the bitter aftertaste of shame that our scientific conscience is likely to experience upon attempts to swallow discredited otherworldly beliefs. As Arnold therefore argues, art is where our intellectually evolving human race

> will find an ever surer and surer stay. There is not a creed which is not shaken, not an accredited dogma which is not shown to be questionable, not a received tradition which does not threaten to dissolve. Our religion has materialized itself in the fact, in the supposed fact; it has attached its emotion to the fact, and now the fact is failing it. But for poetry the idea is everything. . . . Poetry attaches its emotion to the idea; the idea is the fact. The strongest part of our religion to-day is its unconscious poetry.[6]

Not only poets but philosophers have similarly advocated art's subsuming the role of religion. G. E. Moore, one of analytic philosophy's founding fathers and the philosophical inspiration of the Bloomsbury aesthetic circle, wrote in 1902 that "Religion [is] merely a subdivision of Art" since "every valuable purpose which religion serves is also served by Art," while "Art perhaps serves more" since "its range of good objects and emotions is wider."[7] The idea that art provides a broader and more convincing alternative to religion has been recently reaffirmed by outspoken secular philosophers such as Richard Rorty. In rejecting religion as a "conversation stopper," Rorty champions the "inspirational value of great works of literature," proclaiming "the hope for a religion of literature, in which works of the secular imagination replace Scripture as the principal source of inspiration and hope for each new generation." This artistic religion he calls an "atheist's religion." Pluralistically liberal, it makes no claim to coerce behavior in the public sphere but only to console us individuals "in our aloneness" by connecting us with something far greater and inspiring beyond us—the marvelous world of great art—while guiding our efforts toward realizing both private perfection and more loving kindness to our fellow humans.[8]

If Rorty's religion of art seems an overly private one, it is easy to find aesthetic thinkers who insist on art's essential public role of social unity, including Rorty's pragmatist hero (and mine), John Dewey. Describing art as "a remaking of the experience of the community in the direction of greater order and unity," Dewey is even ready to suggest "that if one could control the songs of a nation, one need not care who made its laws."[9] Art has long been celebrated for the unifying, harmonizing power of its communicative expression, which joins the most diverse audiences into a spellbound whole. Recall Friedrich Schiller's praise that art, through its pleasures of taste, "brings harmony in society, because it fosters harmony in the individual." "All other forms of perception divide man" by overly stressing either the sensuous or the rational, while aesthetic perception harmoniously combines them. "All other forms of communication divide society" by appealing to differences, while art's "aesthetic mode of communication unites society because it relates that which is common to all."[10] Xunzi already made the same argument two thousand years earlier in China with respect to music (there construed to include also dance and poetic song): "When music is performed . . . the blood humour becomes harmonious and in equilibrium. . . . The entire world is made tranquil and enjoys together beauty and goodness. . . . Thus music is the most perfect way to bring order to men . . . [because it] joins together what is common to all."[11] And are we not witnessing an international art world where national and cultural borders are continuously being crossed in friendly exchanges of creative artistic understanding rather than weapons of destruction?

Of course, we should also realize that the realm of art is not without its fractious divisions, fanaticisms, and intolerance. Besides the conflicts between proponents of elite and popular arts (that occasionally, as in the New York Astor Square riots, have even erupted into real bloodshed), there is often fierce rivalry and bitter critique between different artistic styles—the schisms of "isms." Such artistic contention, however, rarely generates physical violence or cultural harm. In fact, it often provides a positive competitive spur to creativity. A more damaging and comprehensive, but sometimes less visible, form of art's oppressive divisions is when the historically dominant concept of art disenfranchises the many forms of art that do not seem paradigmatic of that concept. From my Japanese colleagues I learned that this is what happened in the Meiji period, when the Western conception of art was so coercively self-imposed on Japanese culture that its traditional arts (such as tea ceremony and calligraphy) were declassed from the category of art—*geijutsu*—and demoted to mere cultural practice, or what is called *geidoh*: literally ways of culture.[12] Clearly, in this case a particular hegemonic concept of art has done very painful cultural damage, which is now, fortunately, being rectified. But just as clearly, the damages of artistic bigotry and enmity are infinitesimal when compared to the ravages wrought by religion.

There are many wonderful things about religion. Without its positive workings in the past, it is hard to believe that humankind would have developed the level of morality, rationality, love, community coherence, emotional richness, imaginative grandeur, and artistic creation that we have achieved. The argument for art replacing religion is that art sustains the valuable features of religion while minimizing or refining out the bad aspects. Dewey, for instance, who falls short of proposing art as a substitute for religion, nonetheless makes the argument that religion needs a process of purification through which its "ethical and ideal content" is separated from its unhealthy connection with belief in a "Supernatural Being" and with the often unsavory and outmoded ideologies, social practices, and ritual forms of worship that are simply the "irrelevant" accretion of "the conditions of social culture in which" the various traditional religions emerged. (For he recognizes that "there is no such thing as religion in the singular."[13]) Dewey therefore recommends that we distinguish and preserve what he calls "the religious," in contrast to religion in the concrete traditional sense. He defines the religious as an experience or attitude "having the force of bringing a better, deeper and enduring adjustment in life" that is "more outgoing, more ready and glad" than stoicism and "more active" than mere submission (*CF* 11–13). Moreover, in affirming that "any activity pursued in behalf of an ideal end against obstacles and in spite of threats of personal loss because of conviction of its general and enduring value is religious in quality" (*CF* 19), Dewey notes that the artist (along with other types of committed inquirers) displays such activity.

In making his case for the religious dimension as a commitment to the ideals and purposes of life, Dewey appeals to George Santayana's identification of the religious imagination with the artistic. "Religion and poetry," writes Santayana, "are identical in essence, and differ merely in the way they are attached to practical affairs. Poetry is called religion when it intervenes in life, and religion, when it merely supervenes upon life, is seen to be nothing but poetry."[14] The conclusion that Dewey wants to draw from this, however, is that poetic imagination, with its "moral function . . . for . . . the ideals and purposes of life" (*CF* 13), should not be a mere compartmentalized, supervenient expression of art for art's sake. Instead, it should be a formative force in making social and public life, as well as private experience, more beautiful and rewarding. In short, Dewey holds the pragmatist ideal that the highest art is the art of living with the goal of salvation in this world rather than the heaven of an afterlife.

III

So far, so good, we secular progressives would like to believe. But, in the questioning words of Shakespeare, "Hath not this rose a canker?" Is art really so free of religion and those contingent societal ideologies and institutional practices that turn the ideal *religious* into objectionable *religion*? Could art have emerged and flourished, and could it continue to survive, without the beliefs, practices, and institutions of the cultures that gave birth to it and continue to sustain it, however contingent, imperfect, and questionable those impure societal dimensions of culture are? It is hard to see how it could, and how art could find meaningful content without these cultural beliefs, values, and practices deemed to be contingent, gratuitous, and impure. But even if it could exist in this purified ideal state, could art then be what Dewey desires: a formative influence for aesthetically reconstructing the world in better ways? How could it, if its imaginative ideals were not solidly connected with the webs of beliefs, practices, and institutions that structure society and thus are the necessary means for introducing positive changes to it? Dewey seems strangely unpragmatic here in advocating ideal ends while regarding the concrete cultural means—our institutional prac-tices—as irrelevant.

If art is an emergent product of culture that cannot be meaningfully separated from it in the full-blown concrete sense of culture—including its superstitions, prejudices, and other ills—then one could make the fol-lowing argument for art being essentially inseparable from religion. Art is indissolubly linked to culture. But culture, construed in the broad anthro-pological sense, is indissolubly linked to religion. In that important sense (influentially elaborated by Franz Boas and a host of other anthropologists and ethnographers) culture is "the system of shared beliefs, values, customs, behaviors, and artifacts that the members of society use to cope with their world and with one another, and that are transmitted from generation to generation through learning."[15] In that sense, it seems that, historically, "no culture has appeared or developed except together with a religion"; and, as T. S. Eliot further remarks, "according to the point of view of the observer, the culture will appear to be the product of the religion, or the religion the product of the culture."[16] In more primitive societies, the different aspects of cultural or religious life are more intimately enmeshed so that they are hard to distinguish, and it is only through the process Max Weber describes as "rationalizing modernization" that what we now regard as the distinct cultural fields of science, politics, religion, and art came to be conceived abstractly as separate from each other. But even in the modern, secular West, their clear separation cannot hold, as the manifold mixings and tumultuous frictions between these fields so often demonstrates. Consider the issue of abortion or stem cell research, or that of the public funding (or simply display) of religiously controversial art.

Now, if art is inseparable from culture, and culture is inseparable from religion, then it seems likely that art is also indissolubly linked to religion in a significant way. Certainly there is an essential and intimate historical linkage. We would like to think that modern rationalization in the last two centuries has gradually severed the link. But history is not so easily undone in such short time; and perhaps our religious traditions, more than we think, remain vibrantly formative beneath the surface of the secular field of aesthetics and autonomous art. Consider for instance, our notions of artistic genius and creation, of art's lofty spiritual values, of its elevation from worldly interests and mere real things, and in our models (and terms) for interpreting art's mysteries. I cannot treat all these topics here but instead will focus on a very influential notion in recent aesthetics that has been repeatedly deployed by nonreligious philosophers of art but that seems hard to appreciate without taking seriously its religious meaning and aura. I refer to the concept of transfiguration.

Arthur Danto, the most influential of contemporary analytic aestheticians, makes transfiguration the keystone of his philosophy of art. Noting that an artwork may be an object visually identical with another quite ordinary thing that is not art, Danto argues that art requires the artist's interpretation of the object as art, and this interpretation must also be rendered possible by the state of art history and theory. Such interpretation is what transfigures ordinary objects (what Danto calls "mere real things") into works of art, which for Danto are things of an altogether different category and ontological status.[17] Even before his famous 1981 book *The Transfiguration of the Commonplace*, Danto deployed the idea of transfiguration to explain his crucial concept of the artworld, a concept that inspired the institutional theories of art.[18] His 1964 essay "The Artworld" defines that world as "stand[ing] to the real world . . . [as] the City of God stands to the Earthly City" (*AT* 582). This artworld is a world where objects are somehow transfigured into a higher, sacred, ontological realm, wholly different from the real things of this world from which they may be visually or sensorily indiscernible or, as in readymades, with which they may even be physically identical. Already in this essay Danto alludes to Andy Warhol's Brillo Boxes (his inspirational icon of miraculous artistic transfiguration) in terms of the Catholic mystery of transubstantiation, as symbolizing a whole world "of latent artworks waiting, like the bread and wine of reality, to be transfigured, through some dark mystery, into the indiscernible flesh and blood of the sacrament" (*AT* 580–81).

Though Danto describes his philosophy of art as inspired by Hegel, he distinguishes himself from Hegel in denying "that art has been superseded by philosophy" (*AB* 137). Indeed, in some ways he regards art as having taken over not only philosophy's role of theorizing about art but also philosophy's traditional concern with wisdom about life's deep questions; for he insists: "Philosophy is simply hopeless in dealing with the large human issues" (*AB* 137). Danto, moreover, clearly concurs with the dominant modern trend to see art as superseding religion by conveying (in his words) "the kind of meaning that religion was capable of providing": the highest spiritual truths and meanings, including the "supernatural meanings" of "metaphysics or theology."[19]

Whenever I pointed to Danto's very Catholic religious rhetoric, he always replied that he was a wholly secular person of Jewish descent, the son of a Jewish Freemason.[20] All the Catholic rhetoric of transfiguration in his theory, he insisted, does not reflect his personal religious beliefs but is merely a *façon de parler*, a manner of speaking. But does the religious dimension really disappear by calling it a mere manner of speaking? I don't think so. First, manners of speaking cannot be easily separated from manners of living: real matters of belief, practice, and fact. Otherwise, those ways of speaking lose their efficacy. If the religious tenor of transfiguration did not still somehow resonate with our spiritual sensibility, with our religious experience, faith, or imagination (however displaced and disguised it may be), then this manner of speaking would not be as captivating and influential as it has proven to be.

This brings up a second point. Why did a secular Jewish philosopher choose this particular way of speaking about art, and why has it been so successful and influential? The reason, I think, is that the religious other-worldliness of Christianity is deeply embedded in our Western traditions of art and philosophy of art. It therefore shapes the artistic thinking in these traditions, even for artists, critics, and philosophers who do not consciously ascribe to Christian beliefs and attitudes. We should not think that we secular or non-Christian theorists of the Western artworld are entirely free of our culture's religion in our theorizing; and in the globalized contemporary artworld shaped by the West, perhaps no one is completely free of it.

I am not claiming that art's transfigurative power is a narrowly Christian idea. If there is anything that the world's different cultures ascribe to art, it could be the transfigurative, transformative power of its creative expression and aesthetic experience. My claim is that if we wish to understand art's experience in terms of transfiguration, we should insist on recognizing that there are different underlying religious ontologies and ideologies of transfiguration. I discern at least two, which I elaborate in what follows. First, there is the dominant, familiarly Christian style of otherworldly elevation—based on a transcendental theology with an eternal, unchanging, immaterial God existing apart from the world he created (though miraculously embodying himself in his Son to save the human creatures of that world). Central to this theology is the corresponding notion of an immaterial, eternal human essence (the soul) that can be saved and elevated to God's otherworldli-ness. In such religion of the transcendental gap, spirituality (be it in art or elsewhere) means an elevated distance from the ordinary material world, an ascent to a radically other world, whether the artworld or heaven. Here transfiguration typically implies a radical shift of metaphysical status, from the realm of mere spatiotemporal entities to a different, spiritually transcen-dent existence; so works of art must be distinguished (in Danto's terms) from "mere real things."

In contrast, Zen Buddhist culture offers a religion of immanence with no transcendental, personal God existing outside the world of creation; no eternal, personal, immaterial soul existing apart from its embodied man-ifestations; and no sacred world (an artworld or heaven) existing beyond the world of experienced flux. The essential distinction between the sacred and the profane (or between art and nonart) no longer marks a rigid ontological divide between radically different worlds of things but rather a difference of how the same world of things is perceived, experienced, and lived—whether artistically, with an inspiring spirit of presence and an absorbing sense of profound significance or sanctity, or instead as merely insignificant, routine banalities. Transfiguration does not entail a change of ontological status through elevation to a higher metaphysical realm but is rather a transformation of perception, meaning, use, and attitude. Not a matter of vertical transposition to an elevated ethereal realm, it is rather a vividness and immediacy of being in this world, of feeling the full power and life of its presence and rhythms, of seeing its objects with a wondrous clarity and freshness of vision. Consider this description of the path to transfigured insight provided by the Chinese Zen master Qingyuan Weixin of the Tang Dynasty: "Before I had studied Zen for thirty years, I saw mountains as mountains and waters as waters. When I arrived at a more intimate knowledge, I came to the point where I saw that mountains are not mountains, and waters are not waters. But now that I have got the very substance I am at rest. For it's just that I see mountains once again as mountains, and waters once again as waters."[21]

IV

Let me now offer two concrete examples to illustrate these contrasting notions of artistic transfiguration. For the transcendental, classically Catholic notion, consider Raphael's famous painting *Transfiguration*,[22] which depicts the episode (related, with some minor variations, in the three gospels of Matthew, Mark, and Luke) in which Jesus—taking along Peter, James, and John—goes up "into a high mountain apart by themselves" (Mark 9:2). There Jesus is visually transfigured before their eyes and then approached in conversation by (the long-dead prophets) Moses and Elijah, whose appearance affirms Jesus's divine status as the Messiah. In coming down from the mountain, Jesus and his three disciples encounter the other disciples among a multitude in which a man cries out for Jesus's help to cure his son from possession by an evil spirit, which Jesus's disciples had not been able to exorcize. Raphael's rendition of this episode includes both elements of the story—the miraculous transfiguration on the mountain and the distraught crowd with the demonically possessed boy down below. The canvas is divided vertically into two distinct parts depicting these two storylines. The mountaintop transfiguration scene understandably occupies the upper part of the picture, while the lower part portrays the agitated crowd before Jesus's descent, with one red-robed figure (apparently a disciple) emphatically pointing up toward the mountain (and the picture's center), thus pictorially linking with a dramatic diagonal the upper and lower parts of the canvas and their narrative elements.

Most significantly, for my argument, is that in the upper transfiguration scene, the figure of Christ is not simply elevated by being on the mountaintop but actually hovers distinctly above it (and the prostrate accompanying disciples) in airborne levitation, flanked by but obviously higher than the two prophets who arrive to talk with him. His figure, moreover, is framed in a nimbus of bright light with just the hint of a golden aura around his head. The gospel of Matthew (17:2) indeed asserts that when Jesus "was transfigured," "his face did shine as the sun, and his raiment was white as the light." But none of the Gospel versions describes Christ's transfiguration as transcendental levitation above the mountain. Nonetheless, Raphael's picture clearly depicts this, probably to highlight Christ's heavenly, otherworldly essence and to suggest the essential otherworldliness of true spirituality, its indispensable transcendent movement beyond the world of ordinary real things.

Hegel deploys this painting to argue for art's transfigurative elevation and capacity to sensuously convey the highest spiritual truths, even when they depart from the visual truth, since no normal view could, in truth, simultaneously include both the picture's scenes. Yet Hegel writes, "Christ's visible Transfiguration is precisely his elevation above the earth, and his departure from the Disciples, and this must be made visible too as a separation and a departure."[23] If we go by the Gospel narratives, Raphael's painting of the transfigured Jesus in complete "elevation" and "separation" from the earth lacks not only visual truth but also scriptural truth. But it wonderfully conveys the alleged truth of Christian transcendentalism (just as Hegel's philosophical idealism does) while just as superbly implying its artistic analogue—that art's transfiguration is an "elevation and separation" into some higher otherworldliness.

Moreover, through the implied narrative of Jesus's success in curing by touch the demon-possessed boy after his disciples had failed to achieve this, the painting also conveys an artistic allegory about the divine transcendence of artistic genius. The hand of the great artist—someone like Raphael (whose very name in Hebrew means "God has healed")—is analogically linked to the divine healing hand of Jesus himself, the Son of God. This analogy has enormous implications for our culture's sharp divide between the heights of artistic genius and its lowly audiences, or between the high arts and the evil-possessed frenzy of the mass media arts of popular culture. But let us leave these issues of cultural politics aside so we can return to Hegel's claim that this painting is a masterpiece through its communication of the spiritual truth of Christianity, even if it lacks, through its unrealistically divided canvas, objective visual truth.

Arthur Danto, in *The Abuse of Beauty*, defends Hegel's view in using Raphael's *Transfiguration* (which Danto finds great but not beautiful) to argue that aesthetic visual qualities, including beauty, are never essential to artistic greatness. "Beauty is really as obvious as blue," a simple perceptual matter grasped immediately "through the senses," Danto claims, while art "belongs to thought" and therefore "requires discernment and critical intelligence" (*AB* 89, 92). He castigates a long tradition of theorists who think there is a kind of difficult beauty in art (or elsewhere) that is not a mere matter of immediate sensation but that requires the sort of "hard looking" that Roger Fry argued was necessary for seeing the beauty of Postimpressionist paintings that were, on first impression, deemed hideous by the public. Rejecting the very idea of "deferred beauty that rewards hard looking" as a confusion of beauty and artistic insight, Danto scoffs at the thought that such looking could ever give us "the kind of sensuous thrill that beauty in the aesthetic sense causes in us without the benefit of argument or analysis" (*AB* 92–93).

While agreeing with Danto that beauty is not always essential to artistic success, I think there does exist beauty that is difficult to perceive but that is revealed through a kind of disciplined hard looking. Consider an example that also illustrates the Zen and pragmatist notion of immanent transfiguration I sketched above. My example derives neither from the official art world nor from the realm of natural beauty. It instead involves a large rusty iron barrel whose surprisingly wondrous beauty suddenly revealed itself to me after some sustained contemplative efforts during my own initiation into the disciplines of Zen during the year I spent in Japan doing research in somaesthetics.

Set on a hill near the coastal village of Tadanoumi on Japan's beautiful Inland Sea, the Zen cloister Shorinkutzu where I lived and trained was directed by Roshi (Master) Inoue Kido. Roshi was liberal enough to take me on as a student (when he knew no English and my Japanese was very limited) and to recognize that the disposition of one's *kokoro* (the heart-and-mind) is infinitely more important than having one's legs tightly and enduringly entwined in a full lotus. Analogizing that rice plants could not be cut with a dull blade, he advised me to get up from my meditation cushion at the Zendo whenever I felt tired and go back to my sleeping hut for a nap to refresh and thus sharpen my mind. My powers of sustained concentration, he explained, would grow through enhanced mental acuity, not through merely stubborn efforts of willful endurance. However, in every-thing he thought essential to the practice of Zen, Roshi was an effectively strict purist. A humane disciplinarian, Roshi did not spare the rod on his students when he thought it would instruct them. (I avoided his instructive boxing of the ears only because my Japanese was too poor to formulate a stupid question, though I once was severely reprimanded for leaving three grains of rice in my bowl.)

Near one of the two paths connecting the Zendo and the trainees' sleeping quarters, I noticed a small clearing with an especially open and beautiful view of the sea, dotted with a few small islands of lush, soft, bushy green. In the clearing was a primitive stool, rudely constructed from a round section of log on whose short upright column (still adorned with bark) there rested a small rectangular wooden board to sit on and with no nails or adhesive other than gravity to fix it to the log. A couple of feet in front of the stool stood two old, rusty, cast-iron oil barrels (see fig. 1),[24]

Figure 1. The drum cans of Shorinkutzu-Dojo. *Source:* Photo by the author.

the kind I had often seen used as makeshift open-air stoves by homeless people in America's poor inner-city neighborhoods. Readers more familiar with artworld usage might recognize them as the kind of barrels that Christo and Jeanne Claude painted and massively piled on their sides in two notable installations—*Iron Curtain* (Paris, 1962), and *The Wall* (Oberhausen, Germany, 1999).[25] Sitting on the stool to look at the sea beyond the dojo, one's view was inescapably distracted by the two corroding brownish barrels. I wondered why this ugly pair was left in such a lovely spot, spoiling the sublime natural seascape with an industrial eyesore.

One day I got the courage to ask Roshi whether I would be permitted to practice meditation for a short while in that spot overlooking the sea, though I dared not ask him why the hideous barrels (which the Japanese call "drum cans") were allowed to pollute the aesthetic and natural purity of that perspective. Permission was readily granted, since Zen meditation can, in principle, be done anywhere, and Roshi felt I had progressed enough to practice outside the Zendo. I sat myself down on the stool and, having directed my gaze above the barrels, I fixed my contemplation on the beautiful sea while following Roshi's meditation instructions of focusing attention on my breathing and trying to clear my mind of all thoughts. After about twenty minutes of effective meditation, I lost my grip of concentration and decided to end the session. Turning my glance toward the closest of the two barrels, my perception grew more penetrating, and I found this object suddenly transfigured into a vision of breathtaking beauty, just as beautiful as the sea, indeed even more so. I felt I was really seeing that drum barrel for the first time, savoring the subtle sumptuousness of its coloring, the shades of orange, the tints of blue and green that highlighted its earthy browns. I thrilled to the richness of its irregular texture, its tissue of flaking and peeling crusts embellishing the hard iron shell—a symphony of soft and firm surfaces that suggested a delicious *feuilleté*.

Perhaps what seized and delighted me most of all was the beautiful fullness of its perceived presence. The rusty barrel had an immediate, robust, absolutely absorbing reality that made my vision of the sea pale in comparison. Rather than being transfigured into a transcendent world of immaterial spirituality, it transfiguratively radiated the gleam and spiritual energy with which the wondrous flow and flux of our immanent material world resonates and sparkles. Thus, I too felt transfigured, without feeling that either the barrels or I had changed ontological categories and levitated into transcendent ideality. Conversely, I realized that it was mainly the *idea* of the sea that I had been regarding as beautiful, not the sea itself, which I saw through a veil of familiar thoughts—its conventional romantic meanings and the wonderful personal associations it had for me, a Tel Aviv beach boy turned philosopher. The barrel, in contrast, was grasped as a beauty of the most concrete and captivating immediacy, but seeing that beauty required a sustained period of disciplined contemplation. Though the hard looking was initially not directed at the drum can, this alone was what enabled the perception of its beauty, and I could, on subsequent occasions, recover this vision of its beauty by foregoing the seascape and directing my absorbed contemplation at the barrels themselves.

The phenomenology of such hard looking, which I suspect is rather different from what Fry recommended for art, is complex. Part of the complexity relates to distinctively Zen paradoxes of perception and being: my hard looking could also be understood as hard nonlooking, since it was not motivated by a penetrative hermeneutic quest for the hidden true meaning of the object, just as Zen thinking is often described as nonthinking and the fullness of its enlightenment as an emptiness. There is also the question of whether such immanent transfigurations should be most closely identified with the particular object in focus (the barrel), or the experience of the perceiving subject, or the whole energized situation that shapes both object and subject and their encounter.

However we address these issues, one question must be faced forthwith: Were those transfigured drum barrels art? Though clearly not part of the institutional artworld, they were just as obviously part of an installation work of deliberate design aimed at providing experiences that could be described as meaningful, thought-provoking, and aesthetically evocative.[26] And the deliberative design of this installation suggests that it was obviously "about something" (a condition of meaning generally deemed necessary for art). But what, exactly, the barrels were about is a question that has many possible answers: the powers and possibilities of meditation, the surprising uses of industrial detritus, the contrast yet continuity of nature and artifact, the question of beauty (elusive and surprising versus easy and conventional), but also the philosophical meaning I eventually found in them—the immanent transfiguration of ordinary objects that could make them art without taking them out of the real world and into a compartmentalized, transcendent artworld whose objects have an entirely different metaphysical status. Such immanent transfiguration, whose meaning of enriched presence is to fuse art and life rather than suggest their essential contrast and discontinuity, is where Zen converges with pragmatist aesthetics.

But what, then, becomes of works like Raphael's *Transfiguration*? To recognize its religious meanings, must we insist exclusively on a transcendent metaphysics of art that separates art from real things and life? I do not see how this is any more necessary for understanding this work than zealously insisting that the Transfiguration episode with Jesus really happened and that its theological underpinnings are metaphysically true, thus excluding conflicting religious or scientific doctrines. I think I can appreciate the transcendent religious meanings of such works without sharing the relevant metaphysical and theological faith. But I suspect that a true believer could have a greater appreciation of the painting through such faith.

V

Must we choose irrevocably between these two forms of transfiguration and their respective religious ideologies of art?[27] One reason for resisting this choice is that these options do not seem to exhaust the forms or interpretations of art's transfigurative experience. I have not considered here the meaning of aesthetic transfiguration for the Confucian religious tradition, whose emphasis on aesthetic ritual and art over supernatural creeds have made it, for millennia, extremely attractive and influential for East Asian minds. It proved immensely more attractive than the religion of Mozi (an early rival of Confucius), whose more Christian doctrine of universal love came with the belief in a supreme supernatural deity (and lesser spirits and ghosts) but also with a bleak anti-aesthetic asceticism (that is dourly Protestant in character). Part of the genius of the early Confucians was to accept the growing force of the theological skepticism of their time by essentially eschewing supernatural religious metaphysics and confining their focus to the rescue and revitalization of the positive ideals and values embedded in traditional religious ritual and art. By expressing these ideals and values through more intellectually convincing interpretations that were focused on the aesthetic and ethical cultivation of both individual and society, Confucianism could thus offer an elaborately harmonious redemption of *this*-worldly life. Indeed, our own contemporary moment, with its growing skepticism in the supernatural and its pervasive aesthetic turn that tends to emphasize formal richness and complexity rather than Daoist or Zen simplicity, may make Confucianism the most appealing religion for the twenty-first century, at least for secular minds. I confess to be touched by its attractions, as I am touched by Zen and pragmatist meliorism.

Rather than selecting a favorite here, I close by briefly raising another option since my survey of art's religious traditions has been so sketchy and limited, neglecting the rich artistic traditions of other religious cultures such as Islam, Judaism, and the indigenous religions of Africa, America, and other regions. Might we not adopt a more pluralistic approach to the religious ontology of art and perhaps let the context of the artwork and its cultural tradition determine for us which approach is best for appreciating its transfigurative meaning and spiritual truth? Can we be pluralist syncretists in our "religions" of art, even if we lack such flexibility in our traditional theologies, metaphysics, and religiously shaped ethics? A pragmatist aesthetic pluralism would like to admit this possibility. If it were indeed possible, aesthetics could really be a wonderful bridge between cultures, even warring ones. But if aesthetics cannot be ultimately separated from a culture's under-lying religious attitudes, then it may not be feasible to realize this possibility in our imperfect world until we also work not only through but beyond aesthetics to transform our cultures and religious attitudes in the direction of deeper, more open-minded understanding of religious diversity. This does not mean a spineless, anything-goes tolerance of evident evil and flagrant falsehood. Nor should this involve the quest to abolish all real difference and deny the positive role of disharmony and dissent, without which we could never appreciate the agreeable harmonies of art.

IV

Somaesthetics

Chapter Thirteen

Soma and Media

The human body is the magazine of invention. . . . All the tools and engines on earth are only extensions of its limbs and senses.

—Emerson, "Works and Days"

I

One striking paradox of our new media age is its heightened concentration on the body. As advanced telecommunications render bodily presence unnecessary, while novel technologies of mediatic body construction and plastic cyborg-surgery challenge the traditional notion of the real body, our culture seems increasingly fixated on the soma, serving it with the adoring devotion once bestowed on other worshiped mysteries. In postmodern urban culture, gyms and fitness centers proliferate, largely replacing both church and museum as the preferred site of self-meliorative instruction where one is obliged to visit in one's leisure as a duty to oneself, even if it involves inconvenience and discomfort. Ever more money, time, and pain are being invested in cosmetics, dieting, and plastic surgery. Despite mediatic dematerialization, bodies seem to matter more.

The media's advertisement of good-looking bodies has partly fueled this interest, but only in part. Much somatic interest, as I elsewhere explain,[1] is not at all directed at representational beauty but instead at the quality of immediate experience: the endorphin-enhanced glow of high-level cardiovascular functioning; the slow savoring awareness of improved, deeper breathing; the tingling thrill of feeling into new parts of one's spine. Pursuit of such heightened bodily experience is typically portrayed and celebrated as the very antithesis of "couch-potato" media consumption, as an antidote to what it sees as media-induced passivity.

Such revalidation of the active, transformative body is something very different from the vision of the body held by media advocates: the body as dull and inert—a sluggish antithesis to the media's electric flexibility. Yet the opposition of body and media remains. This contrasting vision of the media—not as a passive, pacifying mirror but as an active creator, generating new realities and possessing apparently limitless range and power—finds its most extreme and futuristic expression in William Gibson's vision of cyberspace, a fiction that nonetheless has been inspiring real research links between scientists working in artificial intelligence, telecommunications, and virtual reality. In contrast to cyberspace's dynamic freedom and protean mobility that defy traditional spatiotemporal constraints, the body is opposed as a lifeless, inert prison. "The body was meat," writes Gibson, "the prison of [one's] own flesh."[2]

That both critiques and theodicies of the media portray the body as its antipode renders this opposition an unremarkable commonplace. It nonetheless strikes me as strange, indeed uncanny. For the body was always the primordial *paradigm* of the media—by constituting the most basic medium of human life. In fact, for much of ancient and non-Western culture, the body also constituted an essential site of philosophy, conceived as a critical, self-fashioning life-practice, an art of living. In *Practicing Philosophy*, I tried to revive and reconstruct this notion of embodied philosophy by introducing a field called *somaesthetics*, with its key notion of the *soma*, the living, sentient, purposive body. This chapter explains the structure of this field and explores how it can be useful in philosophy and cultural studies. Since the problematic relationship between soma and media commands considerable attention, it provides a good way to present somaesthetics here.

II

Somaesthetics is devoted to the critical, ameliorative study of the experience and use of one's body as a locus of sensory-aesthetic appreciation (*aisthesis*) and creative self-fashioning. It is therefore devoted to the knowledge, discourses, practices, and bodily disciplines that structure such somatic care or can improve it. Though modern Western philosophy has largely slighted the body, if we put aside this prejudice and simply recall philosophy's central aims of knowledge, self-knowledge, right action, and quest for the good life, then the crucial philosophical value of somaesthetics becomes clear in several ways.

1. Since knowledge is largely based on sensory perception whose reliability often proves questionable, philosophy has always been concerned with the critique of the senses, exposing their limits and avoiding their misguidance by subjecting them to discursive reason. Philosophy's work here (at least in Western modernity) has been confined to the sort of second-order discursive analysis or critique of sensory propositional judgements that constitutes standard epistemology. The complementary route offered by somaesthetics is instead to correct the actual functional performance of our senses by an improved direction of one's body, as the senses belong to and are conditioned by the soma. Since Socrates, philosophy has often recognized that physical ill health (through resulting organ malfunctioning or distracting stress and fatigue) was a major source of error. But therapies such as the Alexander Technique, Feldenkrais Method, and Reichian bio-energetics (like older Asian practices of hatha yoga and Zen meditation) go further by claiming to improve the acuity, health, and control of our mind and senses by cultivating heightened attention and mastery of their somatic functioning, while also freeing us from bodily habits and defects that tend to impair cognitive performance.

2. If self-knowledge is a central aim of philosophy, then knowledge of one's bodily dimension must not be ignored. Somaesthetics, whose concern is not simply with the body's external form or representation but with its lived experience, works toward improved awareness of our feelings, thus providing greater insight into both our passing moods and lasting attitudes. It can therefore reveal and improve somatic related issues that normally go undetected even though they impair our well-being and per-formance. Consider two examples. We rarely notice our breathing, but its rhythm and depth provide rapid, reliable evidence of our emotional state. Consciousness of breathing can therefore make us aware that we are angry or anxious when we might otherwise remain unaware of these feelings and thus vulnerable to their misdirection. Similarly, a chronic contraction of certain muscles that not only constrains movement but results in tension and pain may nonetheless go unnoticed because it has become habitual. As unnoticed this chronic contraction cannot be relieved, nor can its resultant disability and discomfort. Yet once such somatic functioning is brought to clear attention, there is the possibility of modifying it and avoiding its unpleasant consequences.

3. A third central aim of philosophy is right action, for which we need not only knowledge and self-knowledge but also effective will. As embodied creatures, we can act only through the body, hence our power of volition—the ability to act as we will to act—depends on somatic efficacy. By exploring and refining our bodily experience, we can gain a practical grasp of the actual workings of effective volition—a better mastery of the will's concrete application in behavior. Knowing and desiring the right action will not avail if we cannot will our bodies to perform it; and our surprising inability to perform the simplest bodily tasks is matched only by our astounding blindness to this inability, these failures resulting from inadequate somaesthetic awareness. Just think of the struggling golfer who tries to keep his head down and his eyes on the ball and who is completely convinced that he is doing so, even though he fails miserably. His conscious will is unsuccessful because deeply ingrained somatic habits override it, and he does not even notice this failure because his habitual sense perception is so inadequate and distorted that it feels as if the action intended is indeed performed as willed. In too much of our action we are like the golfer whose will is strong yet impotent, since lacking the somatic sensibility to make it effective. This argument, advanced by body therapists outside the standard discourse of philosophy (such as F. M. Alexander and Moshe Feldenkrais), was long ago asserted by Diogenes the Cynic in advocating rigorous body training as "that whereby, with constant exercise, perceptions are formed such as secure freedom of movement for virtuous deeds."[3]

4. If philosophy is concerned with the pursuit of happiness and better living, then somaesthetics' concern with the body as the locus and medium of our pleasures clearly deserves more philosophical attention. Even the joys and stimulations of pure thought are embodied, and thus can be intensified or more acutely savored through improved somatic awareness and discipline. Somatic theorists such as Willhelm Reich, F. M. Alexander, and Moshe Feldenkrais have shown reciprocal influences between bodily experience and character development. Somatic malfunctioning can be both a consequence and a reinforcing cause of personality problems, which themselves may be remedied only through body work. Here somatic health, training, and know-how are presented as effective means for promoting mental well-being and ethical self-mastery. Similar claims are made by yogis and even by body builders such as Arnold Schwarzenegger.[4] The soma plays a crucial role in aesthetic pleasure and expression; we can neither create art nor appreciate it without bodily means. We use our hands to paint and sculpt, our vocal cords to sing, our limbs to dance, and our eyes and ears

to appreciate an opera. Moreover, since all affect is grounded in the body, the soma is essential for appreciating the qualitative feelings expressed in art and for enjoying the emotions of aesthetic experience, whether aroused by art or nature. Improving our somatic aptitudes and sensibilities can help us improve our aesthetic capacities.

5. Seeing that the body is a docile, malleable site for inscribing social power means recognizing the value of somaesthetics for political philosophy.[5] It offers a way of understanding how complex hierarchies of power can be widely exercised and reproduced without any need to make them explicit in laws or have them enforced; entire ideologies of domination can thus be covertly materialized and preserved by encoding them in somatic norms that, as bodily habits, get typically taken for granted and so escape critical consciousness. Take, for example, the sociocultural norm that women should speak softly, eat dainty foods, sit with their knees close together, keep the head and eyes down while walking, and assume the passive role or lower position in copulation. However, just as repressive power relations are encoded in our bodies, so they can be challenged by alternative somatic practices. Michel Foucault joins Wilhelm Reich and other body therapists in advocating this message, though the recommended somatic methods vary greatly.

6. Beyond these essential epistemological, ethical, aesthetic, and sociopolitical issues, the soma can play a key role in ontology. As Maurice Merleau-Ponty explains the body's ontological centrality as the focal point from which we and our world are reciprocally projected, so analytic philosophy examines the body as a criterion for personal identity and as an ontological ground (through the brain and central nervous system) for explaining mental states.[6] In pragmatist somaesthetics, the soma—conceived as the living, sentient, purposive body, in short as embodied subjectivity—aims to overcome the troubling ontological dualism of body and mind, physicality and subjectivity, by being an entity that ontologically embraces both these dimensions, seeing them as different aspects or features of a single existent that embraces such difference rather than being a mere physical body connected to an ontologically different mind. The porous transactional nature of the soma, the ways it absorbs and is shaped by its physical and social environment to which it reciprocally contributes its energies and helps reshape, opens a fruitful direction for understanding our fundamentally interactive being in the world.

Although contemporary theory pays increasingly more attention to the body, it tends to lack two important features. The first is a structuring overview or architectonic to integrate its very different, seemingly incommensurable discourses into a more productively systematic field, some comprehensive framework that could fruitfully link the discourse of biopolitics with therapies of bioenergetics, or perhaps even connect analytic philosophy's doctrines of psychosomatic supervenience with bodybuilding principles of supersets. The second thing lacking in *philosophical* discourse on the body is a clear pragmatic orientation, something that the individual can directly translate into a discipline of improved somatic practice. The field of somaesthetics tries to remedy both these lacks.

III

Somaesthetics has three fundamental branches, all of which are present in exemplary somatic philosophers such as John Dewey and Michel Foucault. The first, *analytic somaesthetics*, describes the nature of our bodily perceptions and practices and their function in our knowledge and construction of reality. This theoretical branch involves ontological and epistemological issues of embodiment but also includes the sort of sociopolitical inquiries that Foucault made central: how the body is both shaped by power and employed as an instrument to maintain it, how bodily norms of health and beauty and even the most basic categories of sex and gender are constructions sustained by and serving social forces. Foucault's approach to these somatic issues was typically genealogical, portraying the historical emergence of various doctrines, norms, and disciplines pertaining to the body. This approach can be extended by a comparative form of analytic somaesthetics that contrasts the body views and practices of two or more synchronic cultures. But there is also place for analytic somaesthetics of a more general approach, like the kind one finds, for example, in typical philosophical theorizing of the mind-body relationship in analytic philosophy or in the phenomenology of Merleau-Ponty.

A second branch, *pragmatic somaesthetics*, is concerned with methods of somatic improvement and their comparative critique, along with critique of the values implied in these melioristic methods. Since the viability of any proposed method will depend on certain facts about the body (whether ontological, physiological, or social), this pragmatic branch always presupposes the analytic. But it transcends mere analysis, not simply by evaluating the facts that analysis describes but also by proposing various methods to improve certain facts by remaking the body. Over the course of history, a vast variety of disciplines have been recommended to improve our experience and use of the body: diverse diets, forms of dress, gymnastic training, dance and martial arts, cosmetics, body piercing or scarification, yoga, massage, aerobics, bodybuilding, S/M, and disciplines of psychosomatic well-being such as the Alexander Technique, the Feldenkrais Method, and bioenergetics. These diverse methodologies of practice can be roughly classified into *representational* and *experiential* forms: representational somaesthetics emphasizes the body's external appearance while experiential disciplines focus not on how the body looks from the outside but on the aesthetic quality of its felt experience. Such experiential methods aim to make us feel better, in both senses of this ambiguous phrase: they aim to make the quality of experience richer and more satisfying but also to render our awareness of somatic experience more acute and perceptive. Cosmetic practices (from makeup to plastic surgery) exemplify the representational side of somaesthetics, while practices like Zen meditation or Feldenkrais Method are paradigmatic of the experiential.

The experiential/representational distinction is helpful for showing that somaesthetics cannot be globally condemned as superficial on the grounds that it is confined to surface appearances. But this distinction should not be taken as a rigidly exclusive dichotomy, since there is an inevitable complementarity of representation and experience, of outer and inner. As advertising constantly reminds us, how we look influences how we feel, but also vice versa. Practices like dieting or bodybuilding that are initially pursued for representational ends often produce feelings that are then sought for their own sake. The dieter thus becomes an anorexic craving the inner feel of hunger and hunger-mastery; the bodybuilder turns into an addict of the experiential surge of "the pump." On the other hand, somatic methods aimed at inner experience sometimes employ representational means as cues to achieve the body posture necessary for inducing the desired experience, whether by consulting one's image in a mirror, by focusing one's gaze on a body part (like the tip of the nose or the navel), or simply by visualizing a body form in one's imagination. Conversely, representational practices like bodybuilding utilize improved awareness of experiential clues to serve its ends of external form, using one's qualitative feelings to distinguish, for example, the kind of pain that builds muscle from the pain that indicates injury, or to distinguish the proper full range of muscle extension versus a dangerous overextension.

The distinction between the experiential and representational forms of pragmatic somaesthetics is also not exhaustive; a third category of *performative* somaesthetics could be introduced to group methodologies that focus primarily on building skill, strength, or health in such fields as sports, athletics, martial arts, or exercise regimes. But to the extent that such performance-oriented practices aim primarily at external exhibition of one's performative appearance or at one's inner feeling of power, they might be assimilated into the representational or experiential categories. Sport is useful for clarifying the representational, experiential, and performative dimensions of somaesthetics. Consider for example a tennis stroke. Viewers can appreciate it for how it looks, such as the player's graceful, coordinated alignment and movement of feet, legs, hips, torso, arms, and head along with the smooth trajectory of the swing. This is its visual representational dimension. But the tennis player herself can appreciate the gracefulness of her stroke from her felt proprioceptive experience of her soma, without looking at the stroke's external representation. The swing can simply feel gracefully smooth and harmonious from inside the movement. This is the experiential dimension of somaesthetics. Finally, the swing can deliver the ball to a place on the court and in a manner in which it will win a point for the player, even if the stroke looks clumsy and feels awkward. Here we have the performative dimension of somaesthetics. Strokes that look good and feel good will be performatively deficient if the ball goes out of the court or into the net.

Whatever ways we classify them, the methodologies of pragmatic somaesthetics need to be distinguished from their actual practice. This third branch I call *practical* somaesthetics. Here it is not a matter of producing texts about the body, not even those offering pragmatic programs of somatic care. Instead, this practical branch is about physically engaging in such care, not by pushing words but by moving limbs, that is, in reflective, disciplined, demanding corporeal practice aimed at somatic self-improvement (whether representational, experiential, or performative). This dimension not of saying but doing is the most neglected by academic body philosophers, whose commitment to the *logos* of discourse typically ends in textualizing the body. About practical somaesthetics, the less said the better, *if* this means the more done. Unfortunately, however, it usually means that actual body-work simply gets left altogether out of philosophical practice and its quest for self-knowledge and self-care. Since, in philosophy, what goes without saying typically goes without doing, the concrete activity of bodywork *must* be named as the crucial practical dimension of somaesthetics, conceived as a comprehensive philosophical discipline concerned with embodied self-care.

Is such a discipline possible? Aren't embodied selves just too distinctively different for philosophy to offer any explicit general theory with concrete recommendations of somatic techniques? As I argue in *Practicing Philosophy*, since philosophy as an art of living must be contextualized to be effective, and since every self is in some sense the unique, unrepeatable product of countless contingent factors (physiological, societal, historical, and the more personal circumstances of family and private experience), each individual needs to fashion her own somaesthetic practice to suit her specific life conditions. But, on the other hand, don't our embodied selves share significant commonalities both of biological makeup and societal conditioning (at least within a given cultural tradition, historical period, age group, social class, and gender identity) that would allow some interesting generalizations about the values and risks of different somatic methods? What could philosophy or social science be without such generalization?

IV

Bracketing for now these metaphilosophical questions, I return to the vexed issue of the body/media relationship, beginning with an all-too-hasty genealogical analysis of how the body seems to be escaping its former, diminished media identity as *means* to become a worshiped *end*. I suggest that part of the explanation is that our modern technological revolutions have so powerfully transformed our notions of medium and reality that our body—formerly declassed as merely a medium of, or mere means to, the real (hence subordinate, derivative, distortive)—now gets elevated (as our core medium) to the status of constructor and locus of the real. Hence it becomes a real value or end in itself. Once reality is seen as a construction, the media that construct it can no longer be disdained. Further, since the soma is more basic, familiar, and organic than the newer electronic media, the soma comes to seem so immediate as to occlude its old mediatic image. Nonetheless, the somatic constructor of reality is itself also continuously constructed through other varieties of media and mediations (including reconstructive surgery). So even if the media revolution emancipates the soma in recognizing its constructing powers and its openness to reconstruction, it also presents the further task of discriminating what, with respect to the body, should be reconstructed and how the newer digital media serve and sabotage our desired constructions (questions for pragmatic somaesthetics). That is the thrust of my discussion here, which is caught, like all of us, between conceptual history and futuristic speculation.

We may begin historically by recalling the body's forgotten role as media paradigm, a role that reflects but goes beyond the image of instrumentality through which the somatic terms "organism" and "organ" emerged from the Greek word for tool—*organon*. But we should first ask: What, fundamentally, is a medium or means of communication? As its etymology (*meson, medius, Mittel, moyen*) makes evident, a medium is something that stands in the middle, typically between two other things or terms, between which it mediates. Being in the middle, a medium has two aspects. An interface with two faces, it both connects the mediated terms and separates them by standing between them. This double aspect is also present in the instrumental sense of medium as means to an end. Though it is a way to the end, it stands *in* the way, a distance to be traveled between purpose and its fulfilment.

Plato's seminal account of the body as medium insists on the negative, separative aspect, though the positive, constructive one is always resurfacing, *malgré lui*. His classic attack on the body (in the *Phaedo*) reads like the *ur*-formula of contemporary media critique. The body is such a miserably poor means to the truth that it actually constitutes an obstacle. First, it provides "innumerable distractions," "filling us with loves and desires and fears and all sorts of fancies and a great deal of nonsense, with the result that we literally never get a chance to think at all about anything." Second, if we finally find a quiet time to think, it will suddenly "intrude once more into our investigations, interrupting, disturbing, distracting, and preventing us from getting a glimpse of the truth." Third, it distorts our vision of the real so that when we take its reports for truth about the world, we are deceived. Only by keeping ourselves "uncontaminated by its follies," can we hope to get real knowledge.[7]

Plato could be denouncing the time-wasting nonsense of TV entertainment; the disruptive intrusion of incessant of phone calls, emails, and text messages; and the tendentious untruth of media reporting. But his target is what he sees as the primal mother of all evil media—the body. This single body, however, is already portrayed as a multimedia conglomerate (of different sensory modalities and technologies, e.g., eyes, ears, feeling limbs, etc.), and such plurality and divisiblity of parts provide all the more reason for Plato to degrade the body by contrast to the indivisible soul that nobly seeks the truth despite its confinement in the body's distortive prison. However, given the conceptual doubleness of media as both obstruction and connection, the soul seeks truth not only despite the body but inevitably through it. Not only the soul's jailer, the body (Plato insists) is also its servant. If the imperfections of bodily senses distract us from the divine Forms, their imperfect perceptions are what remind us in the first place that such perfect Forms should exist and be sought.[8] If this means that the soul must be purified from bodily contamination, the only medium for such purification is the body itself, through the *askesis* of its stringent control. Indeed, Plato's very word for purification here is the somatically evocative notion of catharsis. Purity of soul is not so much an immediate given as a task to be realized through disciplined bodily means. Indeed, Socrates's most convincing argument for the soul's immortal privilege over the body is not his abstract doctrines and polemics, but rather his embodied example of calm readiness to face somatic death. If the body proves such a necessary means, it cannot be scornfully neglected without harming the desired ends it serves. Hence Plato later insists (in *Timaeus*, 88a) that we should care for the body, even protecting it from an overly dominant, excitable soul, which "wears the body out."

Christianity exploits the same mediatic doubleness of the soma. Though condemned as an obstacle to the soul's purity, the bodily medium still provided a prime instrument of salvation through purification—by serving as an ascetic altar of self-sacrifice. Clearly symbolized in the corporeal incarnation, temptation, and suffering passion of Christ, this ascetic usefulness of the body is even recognized by theologians who most fervently condemned the body's sensuality and ardently urged its transcendence. Thus, Origen, who not only advocated virginal chastity but had himself castrated, still claimed "the body was necessary for the slow healing of the soul" and could provide a site of ascetic worship through which the material soma is transformed into what Origen called a "temple of God." Vividly portraying the baneful body as purificatory medium, he wrote: "You have coals of fire, you will sit upon them, and they will be of help to you."[9] This fundamental doubleness, where the very obstruction of the medium is part of its enabling, suggests two conclusions. First, in analyzing any form of media we should expect both obstructive and facilitating dimensions, so our critique should thus consider both constraining and emancipatory effects. Second, if the bodily medium is necessary not only for achieving but also for even conceiving such presumedly absolute realities as "the pure soul" (whose meaning as end depends on its contrast to the body as means), then we can suspect that our reality is always constructed through some form of media. Hence we should be suspicious of any claims to absolute immediacy. This point becomes important in assessing contemporary claims for the body as locus of immediacy.

Underlying Plato's specific attacks on the body as a medium for truth is a more basic dissatisfaction with two of its metaphysical limitations. First, because the body is always confined to a particular spatiotemporal location, perception through it is always only from a particular perspective or point of view. For Plato (as later for Descartes) such limitation of perspective is insufficient for truly scientific knowledge, which must provide an absolute, God's-eye vision of the real. Second, the individual body is subject not only to limited location but also to considerable instability, change, and corruption. So if reality is taken to be permanent, unchanging, and independent of perspective, then, in Plato's view, it can be properly grasped only by an intelligence that is similarly perspectiveless and incorruptibly permanent. The mutable body, then, could only distort the vision of the immutably real. However, by the late nineteenth century, this metaphysical vision of an unchanging reality had been abandoned, partly through Darwin's influence but also through the industrial revolution and the great changes wrought by its new means of production and communication: steam engines, railroads, telegraph and telephone. Both change and perspective could thus be positively revalued, along with the constructive role of material media, including their original somatic paradigm.

We see this most clearly in Nietzsche, where reality is identified as an interpretive construction and the body is privileged as the primary, basic constructor. In paragraph 492 of *The Will to Power* Nietzsche advocates the body as "the starting point" because it provides not only one's basic, spatiotemporal perspective toward the world but also one's basic drives toward pleasure, power, and life enhancement, which underlie our desire for knowledge. Inverting Plato, Nietzsche argues that the body, as the source of all value, should be master rather than servant. The soul is instead the distracting, pernicious illusion whose shadowy life depends on the body, which the soul imprisons and persecutes. "All virtues [are] physiological conditions," moral judgements being but "symptoms . . . of physiological prosperity or failure." "Our most sacred convictions, the unchanging elements in our supreme values, are judgements of our muscles."[10] The soul neither is nor should be the master of bodily activity, since consciousness is but its supervenient product, blind to most somatic behavior and most often a thorn to the rest (*WP* 674, 676). Recalling but reversing Plato's mediatic image, Nietzsche declares that consciousness "is only a means of communication" with no real agency of its own (*WP* 524, 526). Indeed, it is the body rather than the soul that generates the notion of subjecthood and agency by spatially awakening "the distinction between a deed and a doer" (*WP* 547). The body should therefore be cherished not only for its life-enhancing pleasures but "as our most personal possession, our most certain being, in short our ego" (*WP* 659).

In this, if in nothing else, Nietzsche speaks for today's individual, whose surrounding world is mediatically reconstructed and deconstructed at ever increasing speed. While Plato could dismiss the body as too ephemeral to be real and valuable, today the body seems more stable, durable, and real than most of our world of experience, and more familiar and easier to grasp and guide. The media's unmanageable overload of unintegrated information is a strongly decentering force, turning consciousness into a flux of swirling, disconnected ephemeral elements. Walter Benjamin complained of this already in the 1930s, long before computers, cell phones, and the Internet.[11] The body can now present itself in contrast as an organizing center, where things are brought together and organically conserved. The muscle memory of bodily habit provides an organic enduring presence that outlasts the fragmentary moments of media bytes and cannot be erased as easily as a data file or an SMS chat. So buffeted by the intrusive new technologies, while stressed and baffled by the many changing language games that socially define us and our thoughts, we are tempted to seek the body as a means of escape to a calming silent realm of identity and personal autonomy. Influential body therapists such as Feldenkrais, Alexander Lowen, Stanley Keleman, and Thomas Hanna advocate heightened body awareness and gratification of our "private organic life" as a way of coming to know oneself more closely and immediately so as to resist the dominant "trend to uniformity within our society."[12] The soma thus emerges as who we most deeply and immediately are; its foundational, privileged status forms part of the implicit common sense of today's secular society, which spends fortunes on the soma's care and adornment, even if most philosophers remain resistant to this trend.

Nietzsche was more dialectical in his approach. For all his privileging of the body as constructive force, directive value, and basic ground, he avoids erecting it into an entirely unconstructed and immediate foundation. Though grasped as the single, unified thing with which one most closely identifies, the body is in fact a construction from a vast multiplicity of different elements and "life-processes"; its image of unity is but a " 'whole' constructed by the eye" (*WP* 547, 674, 676). But as Merleau-Ponty and Jacques Lacan have emphasized, the eyes do not suffice to provide this whole.[13] For without a mirror or other means of reflection, our eyes can neither see themselves nor the entire head in which they are fixed. The representational perception of our somatic integrity is not an immediate given but a specular media product, requiring even more media than our own body parts provide. Here we have the germ of the media's intrinsic control over our external body image, a control that must itself be monitored for techniques and messages that misguide or oppress our sense of bodily self. This is a crucial task for media culture critique.

Recognition of the problematic mediacy of body representations has led body-centered thinkers to locate the body's foundation and immediacy not in its external form but in its lived experience, its inner sense of itself. William James and John Dewey therefore insist on the importance of immediate bodily feeling,[14] while Merleau-Ponty has the same goal in celebrating the lived "phenomenal body" as more real and basic than the objective body constructed through science and its representations. Providing our original, permanent, yet always changing perspective on the world, this lived body is claimed as a "primordial presence" that we immediately grasp and directly move without any representation, "without having to make use of [our] 'symbolic' or 'objectifying' function." It is from the center of "this immediately given invariant" of inner bodily sense perspective that our identity and world are constructed.[15]

However, as Merleau-Ponty also insists, this foundational presence and world-maker is itself reciprocally conditioned by the world that it structures, since that world (as the horizon or "other" outside the body) provides the necessary intentional target into which the lived body can project itself so as to realize its perspectival world-organizing function.[16] The world's construction of the experiencing body is more than an abstract argument based on the Hegelian logic of complementarity, where anything is defined by what it is not. Marx's historical materialist insights about the senses and consciousness have been deployed and refined by thinkers such as Benjamin, Foucault, Theodor Adorno, and Pierre Bourdieu to show how the concrete quality of immediate somatic experience can be socially conditioned and transformed.[17] The notion of immediate experience can still maintain a useful meaning—as experience whose sense or value is directly (and often nondiscursively) grasped rather than subsequently inferred. But such immediacy cannot claim an absolute pristine character because it relies on prior constructions, on habits of response formed through the influence of historical and social conditions already in place.

V

If the body is always somehow constructed, the important question becomes what values should guide its construction and what role should be played here by the media, which function as extensions of our original bodily medium. I turn now from conceptual history to present proposals. First, we must encourage two features of today's media scene: its diversity of forms and its recent trend toward increased interactivity. Every mediatic form or genre—radio, television, video, film, newspapers, books, email, blogs, podcasts, et cetera—has its advantages and limitations; each encourages certain perceptions, experiences, or constructions while not serving or even hindering others. We must not let our ardent enthusiasm for the newer media convince us that the old ones can be abandoned as simply *aufgehoben*. Television did not make the radio obsolete, nor will the Internet replace the telephone. Even the book, whose imminent death is often declared by culture theorists, continues to flourish not only in its digital versions but also in its old hardcopy form; and so it should. The firm, compact tangibility, the look, feel and smell of its pages, presents a special axis or horizon of experience. It is not only the Braille reader who can get something from a tangible text that one cannot get in an e-book, podcast, or video.

In short, reducing our choice of media to those that are newest or most technologically advanced, or even to those that engage the most sensory modalities, will result in an impoverishment of our experience. Paradoxically, such reducing of diversity will also render our experience less coherent, because the coherence of our experience is not simply a synchronic function of the quantity and consistency of media sources; it is also a diachronic, dialogical function of our familiarity with those media through entrenched habits of use. Media pluralism and the open flow of information between the different media modes are just as central for democracy as are political pluralism, freedom of expression, and the effective circulation of information and critique. Such pluralism and interfacing of informational horizons are also crucial to the successful quest for knowledge, a point that pragmatism deploys in making a cognitive justification of democracy.[18]

These democratic and cognitive concerns underscore the importance of interactivity in the media, so that communication is not bifurcated into a small group of producers and a mass of passive consumers who have no influence on the media products they consume. Though our new interactive media show uncontestable progress and promise, we need to register three qualifications. First, the products of mass media consumption have long been interactive in the sense that the audience often creatively interprets and constructs the message rather than simply and passively receiving the interpretation favored by the message producer. Second, the range of interaction in the new forms of interactive media still remains significantly constrained, including the constraint that the most dominant and pervasive digital media and platforms are largely controlled by a small number of powerful individuals or corporations. Third, encouragement of new interactive media should not come at the expense of abandoning older forms, including the interactive engagement of our original medium—the soma—in its full material presence, dynamic experience, and interaction with other somas that are similarly present, dynamically engaged, and somaesthetically sensitive.[19]

Besides encouraging media pluralism and interactivity, something must be done to discourage the media's tendency to establish oppressive norms of external bodily form through advertising that systematically suggests that pleasure, success, and happiness belong only to the young, thin, and beautiful of certain races. Anorexia is one documented by-product of this pressure. Apart from the moral and social problem of causing pain and stigmatizing people whose bodies look different, there is also a potential aesthetic problem: a tedious homogeneity of standardized looks, achieved through digital editing, if not through surgery, cosmetics, or body sculpting exercises. Media advocates are quick to argue that these problems are easily avoided through the Internet, where one's external bodily form can be excluded from the communication situation, and even one's gender identity can be withheld. But studies of the Internet, virtual reality, and the sociology of their production suggest that even when we seem freest to dispense with old body identities, we seem intent on reproducing them, replete with the social hierarchies encoded in race and gender markings that bodies manifest.[20]

If censorship of somatic advertising is undemocratic and impractical, while the traditional condemnatory style of body-culture critique seems hopelessly ineffective (as essentially retrograde, negative nagging), somaesthetics could be helpful in reducing our unhappy bondage to norms of external beauty by highlighting and cultivating somatic beauty and pleasure in its experiential forms. People could be encouraged to transfer their focus of concern from the external shape and attractiveness of the body to an improved qualitative feeling of its lived experience and functioning. Since we are speaking here of an individual's felt improvement, there is no fixed external standard, no stereotypical representation, of what good or improved somatic feeling must be. Yet one can still talk of real improvement and even of directions of improvement that are shared rather than narrowly subjective. While everyone may have a somewhat different rhythm and depth of breathing or a different way of walking, certain ways breathing or walking that may be habitual for a given person and thus seem initially easier or best, can nonetheless be shown, through therapy and improved habit, to be less rewarding than others that initially require more effort because they are nonhabitual.

Experiential somaesthetics comprises a wide range of disciplines and ideologies, from the very ancient to the New Age: from Asian practices of hatha yoga, *taijiquan*, and Zen meditation to Western therapies like Alexander Technique and Feldenkrais Method. This somatic domain may strike us as disturbingly nebulous and alien, but part of the reason for this is its gross neglect by modern philosophy with its logocentrism and neglect of the nonlinguistic. Even somatic philosophers such as Merleau-Ponty seem content with theoretically proving the lived body's primacy in perception but do not seem much concerned with concrete proposals for its improvement. Nietzsche's advocacy of "an ever-greater spiritualization and multiplication of the senses" (*WP* 820) remains too vague and short on detail, while the concentration by Foucault, Georges Bataille, and Giles Deleuze on radical, sensationalistic "limit-experiences" of the body seems far too narrow and problematic for practice.[21]

Though experiential somaesthetics is not a well-articulated domain, it concerns an essential, inescapable dimension of life, and therefore deserves greater attention. We may substitute computerized holograms or screen images for our external forms, we may even develop machines to punch our keyboards for us and read our screens. But we cannot get away from the experienced body, with its feelings and stimulations, its pleasures, pains, and emotions. In the highest flights of mediatic technology, it is always present. Virtual reality is experienced through our eyes, brain, glands, and nervous system. Even in the mediatic fantasy of Gibson's *Neuromancer*, cyberspace is savored and suffered sensuously through the body; the cyber-cowboy Henry Case emerges physically drained from his escapades in the Matrix. How else could it be? For all affect is somatically grounded. As William James argued, "A purely disembodied human emotion is a nonentity." If we try to abstract from any strong emotion "all the feelings of its bodily symptoms, we find we have nothing left behind."[22]

Cognitive scientists and evolutionists agree that there is good reason for conscious affect to be grounded in the body, since its primordial function was to help the embodied organism survive. The vividness of conscious pleasures and pains usefully directs the organism to what will promote the survival of the species. Moreover, on a more general level, pleasurable feeling has "the most central of biological functions—of insisting that life is worthwhile, which after all, is the final guarantee of its continuance."[23] Finally, affect is the basis of empathy, which can ground communal living and progressive social action far more firmly and satisfyingly than can mere rational self-interest. If experiential somaesthetics provides techniques for the development, refinement, and regulation of affect, it also has a social potential that should not be ignored. Bodily rigidities and blockages are often both the product and a reinforcing support of social intolerance and political repression.

We should therefore reject the intellectualist dogma that condemns the pursuit of somatic improvement as a selfish escape into private narcissism. Disciplines of body care provide instead a promising path toward a better public by creating individuals who are healthier and more flexibly open, perceptive, and effective through heightened somatic sensibility and mastery. We tend to forget, moreover, how much public harm results from the somatic misuse of ourselves that leads to unnecessary fatigue, pain, injury, accident, and the abuses of addiction.

Chapter Fourteen

Thinking through the Body,
Educating for the Humanities

I

What are the humanities and how should they be cultivated? With respect to this crucial question, opinions differ as to how widely the humanities should be construed and pursued. Initially connoting the study of Greek and Roman classics, the concept now more generally covers arts and letters, history, and philosophy.[1] But does it also include the social sciences, which are often distinguished from the humanities and grouped as a separate academic division with greater pretensions to scientific status? And should our pursuit of humanistic study be concentrated on the traditional methods and topics of high culture that give the humanities an authoritative aura of established nobility, or should it extend to new and funkier forms of interdisciplinary research such as popular culture or race and gender studies?

Despite such questions and controversy, it is clear (even from etymology) that the meaning of the humanities essentially relates to our human condition and our efforts to perfect our humanity and its expression. But what, then, does it mean to be human? I cannot pretend here to answer such a difficult question. I will, however, argue that because the body is an essential and valuable dimension of our humanity, it should be recognized as a crucial topic of humanistic study and experiential learning. Although the truth of this thesis should be obvious, it goes sharply against the grain of our traditional understanding of the humanities. One striking example of such antisomatic bias is the very term that German speakers use to designate the humanities—*Geisteswissenschaften*—whose literal English translation would be "mental (or spiritual) sciences," in contrast to the natural sciences—*Naturwissenschaften*—which treat physical life (with which, of course, the body is clearly linked). Hence, given the pervasive physical/ mental opposition, the body is essentially omitted or marginalized in our conception of humanistic studies.[2]

We humanist intellectuals generally take the body for granted because we are so passionately interested in the life of the mind and the creative arts that express our human spirit. But the body is not only an essential dimension of our humanity; it is also the basic instrument of all human performance, our tool of tools, a necessity for all our perception, action, and even thought. Just as skilled builders need expert knowledge of their tools, so we need better somatic knowledge to improve our understanding and performance in the arts and human sciences, and to advance our mastery in the highest art of all—that of perfecting our humanity and living better lives. We need to think more carefully through the body in order to cultivate ourselves and edify our students, because true humanity is not a mere genetic given but an educational achievement in which body, mind, and culture must be thoroughly integrated. To pursue this project of somatic inquiry, I introduced the interdisciplinary field of somaesthetics, whose disciplinary connections extend beyond the humanities to the biological, cognitive, technological, and health sciences, which I see as valuable allies for humanistic research.[3]

Somaesthetics concerns the body as a locus of sensory-aesthetic appreciation (aesthesis) and creative self-fashioning. As an ameliorative discipline of both theory and practice, it aims to enrich not only our abstract, discursive knowledge of the body but also our lived somatic experience and performance; it seeks to enhance the understanding, efficacy, and beauty of our movements and improve the environments to which our movements contribute and from which they draw their energies and significance. Somaesthetics therefore involves a wide range of knowledge forms and disciplines that structure such somatic care or can improve it. Recognizing that body, mind, and culture are deeply codependent, somaesthetics comprises an interdisciplinary research program to integrate their study. Mental life relies on somatic experience and cannot be wholly separated from bodily processes, even if it cannot be wholly reduced to them. We think and feel with our bodies, especially with the body parts that constitute the brain and nervous system. Our bodies are likewise affected by mental life, as when certain thoughts bring a blush to the cheek and change our heart rate and breathing rhythms. The body-mind connection is so pervasively intimate that it seems misleading to speak of body and mind as two different, independent entities. The term "body-mind" would more aptly express their essential union, which still leaves room for pragmatically distinguishing between mental and physical aspects of behavior and for the project of increasing their experiential unity.[4]

But whether we speak of body-mind or body and mind, we are dealing with what is fundamentally shaped by culture. For culture gives us the languages, values, social institutions, and artistic media through which we think and act and also express ourselves aesthetically, just as it gives us the forms of diet, exercise, and somatic styling that shape not only our bodily appearance and behavior but also the ways we experience our body—whether as a holy vessel or a burden of sinful flesh; a pampered personal possession for private pleasure or a vehicle of labor to serve the social good. Conversely, culture—its institutions and humanistic achievements—cannot thrive or even survive without the animating power of embodied thought and action. And one measure of a culture's quality of life and humanity is the level of body-mind harmony it promotes and displays.

For continued progress to be made in somaesthetics, resistance to body-focused learning and somatic training in the humanities must be overcome. This essay seeks to challenge this resistance by exposing its roots. I will argue the paradoxical thesis that the body has been rejected in the humanities precisely because it so powerfully expresses the fundamental ambiguity of being human, and because of its all-pervasive, indispensable instrumentality in our lives. In striving for a nobler, less vulnerable, and thus more one-sided vision of the human, our tradition of humanistic research implicitly shuns the body—just as our humanistic focus on valuable intellectual and moral goals tends to obscure or marginalize the study of the very somatic means necessary for achieving those goals and other worthy ends of action.

II

The living body—a sensing, sentient *soma* rather than a mere mechanical corpse—embodies the fundamental ambiguity of human being in several ways. First, it expresses our double status as object and subject—as something in the world and as a sensibility that experiences, feels, and acts in the world. When using my index finger to touch a bump on my knee, my bodily intentionality or subjectivity is directed to feeling another body part as an object of exploration. I both *am* body and *have* a body. In much of my experience, my body is simply the transparent source of perception or action, not an object of awareness. It is that *from which* and *through which* I perceive or manipulate the objects of the world on which I am focused, but I do not grasp it as an explicit, external object of consciousness, even if it is sometimes obscurely felt as a background condition of perception. But often I perceive my body as something that I have rather than am: something I must drag out of bed to do what I wish to do; something I must command to perform what I will but that often fails in performance; something that includes heavy limbs, rolls of fat, a sometimes aching back, and a too often unshaven, tired-looking face, all of which I recognize as mine but do not identify as who I really am.

The body further expresses the ambiguity of human existence as both shared species being and individual difference. Philosophers have emphasized rationality and language as the distinguishing essence of humankind; but human embodiment seems at least as universal and essential a condition of the human species. Try to imagine a human being, and you cannot help but call up the image of the human bodily form. If we imagine creatures displaying human language and behavior but having a very different kind of body, we would think of them not as humans but as monsters, mermaids, robots, aliens, angels, or persons whose humanity has been somewhat robbed or diminished, perhaps by some inhuman spell, as in fables such as "Beauty and the Beast."[5] But though our bodies unite us as humans, they also divide us (through their physical structure, functional practice, and sociocultural interpretation) into different genders, races, ethnicities, classes, and further into the particular individuals that we are. We may all use legs to walk or hands to grasp, but each person has a different gait and fingerprint. Our experience and behavior are far less genetically hardwired than in other animals: A bird of the same species will sing much the same in Boston and Beijing, whereas human vocalization patterns vary quite widely because they depend on learning from the experienced environment. There are anatomical reasons for this greater role of individual experience. The pyramidal tracts—which connect the cerebral cortex to the spinal cord and are essential for all voluntary movement (including vocalization)—are not fully formed and fixed at birth but continue to develop during infancy through the movement a baby is made to perform.[6] This means the precise makeup of an individual's nervous system (her preferred repertoire of neural pathways) is partly a product of her individual experience and cultural conditioning. The body thus shows that human nature is always more than merely natural.

The commonality and difference of our bodies are deeply laden with social meaning. We appeal to our shared somatic form, experience, needs,

and suffering when charitably reaching out to people of very different ethnicities and cultures. But the body (through its skin and hair color, facial
features, and even its gestural behavior), conversely, is the prime site for
emphasizing our differences and for uncharitable profiling. Most ethnic and
racial hostility is the product not of rational thought but of deep prejudices
that are somatically marked in terms of vague uncomfortable feelings aroused
by alien bodies, feelings that are experienced implicitly and thus engrained
beneath the level of explicit consciousness. Such prejudices and feelings
therefore resist correction by mere discursive arguments for tolerance, which
can be accepted on the rational level without changing the visceral grip
of the prejudice. We often deny we even have such prejudices because we
do not realize that we feel them, and the first step to controlling them or
eventually expunging them is to develop the somatic awareness to recognize
them in ourselves. To cultivate such skills of enhanced awareness is a central
task of somaesthetics.[7]

The body exemplifies our multiform ambivalent human condition
between power and frailty, worthiness and shame, dignity and brutishness,
knowledge and ignorance. We invoke the notion of humanity to urge a person
toward moral excellence and rationality that transcend mere animality, but
we also use the predicate "human" to describe and excuse our flaws, failures,
and lapses into base or even bestial behavior: they are human weaknesses,
limits linked to the frailties of the flesh we share with common beasts. Yet
despite its animal nature, the body serves as a symbol of human dignity,
expressed in the irrepressible desire to depict the body in art's beauteous
forms and to portray even the gods in human shape.[8] Respect for the
body's dignity forms part of our basic respect for personhood and human
rights; it is implicit in the right to life and in our tacit sense of respecting
a certain physical distance from each other to allow some free space for the
body—a basic *Lebensraum* or kinesphere. But even in death is the body
respected; most cultures dispatch the corpse with some dignifying ritual of
burial or cremation.

Moralists often inveigh against the body as the enemy of righteous-
ness, as when Saint Paul declares, "Nothing good dwells in me, that is, in
my flesh" (Romans 7:18). Although frailty of flesh often undermines our
moral aspirations, we should realize that all our ethical concepts and norms
(and even the very notion of humanity that underwrites them) depend on
social forms of life involving the ways we experience our bodies and the
ways that others treat them. As Wittgenstein remarked in a strangely brutal
passage of his *Notebooks*:

> Mutilate completely a man, cut off his arms & legs, nose & ears,
> & then see what remains of his self-respect and his dignity, and
> to what point his concepts of these things are still the same. We
> don't suspect at all, how these concepts depend on the habitual,
> normal state of our bodies. What would happen to them if we
> were led by a leash attached to a ring through our tongues?
> How much humanity still remains in him then?[9]

In a world where bodies were always mutilated, starved, and abused, our
familiar concepts of duty, virtue, charity, and respect for others could get
no purchase and make no sense. Moreover, bodily abilities set the limits of
what we can expect from ourselves and others, thus determining the range
of our ethical obligations and aspirations. If paralyzed, we have no duty to
leap to the rescue of a drowning child. Virtue cannot require constant labor
with no rest or nourishment because these needs are physical necessities.

Besides grounding our social norms and moral values, the body is the
essential medium or tool through which they are transmitted, inscribed,
and preserved in society. Ethical codes are mere abstractions until they are
given life through incorporation into bodily dispositions and action. Any
properly realized ethical virtue depends not only on some bodily act (speech
acts included) but also on having the right somatic and facial expression,
indicative of having the right feelings. A stiffly grudging, angry-faced offering
cannot be a true act of charity or respect, which is why Confucius insisted
on the proper demeanor as essential to virtue.[10]

Moreover, by being inscribed in our bodies, social norms and ethical
values can sustain their power without any need to make them explicit and
enforced by laws; they are implicitly observed and enforced through our
bodily habits, including habits of feeling (which have bodily roots). Confucius therefore insists that exemplary virtue is somatically formed through
"the rhythms of ritual propriety and music," and wields its harmonizing
power not by laws, threats, and punishments but by inspiring emulation
and love.[11] Michel Foucault and Pierre Bourdieu, in contrast, highlight
the oppressive aspects of social embodiment, how ideologies of domination are secretly sustained by encrypting them in somatic habits that are
commonly taken for granted and so escape critical consciousness. Women
in many cultures are socially habituated into norms of conduct that both
embody and reinforce gender oppression. Domination of this subtle sort is
especially hard to challenge, because our bodies have so deeply absorbed it
that they themselves revolt against the challenge—as when a young secretary

involuntarily blushes, trembles, flinches, or even cries when trying to raise a voice of protest toward someone she has been somatically trained to respect as her superior. Any successful challenge of oppression should thus involve somaesthetic diagnosis of the bodily habits and feelings that express that domination so that they, along with the oppressive social conditions that generate them, can be overcome.

Our ethical life is grounded in the body in a still more basic way. Ethics implies choice, which in turn implies freedom to choose and to act on that choice. We cannot act without somatic means, even if these means are reduced (through the wonders of technology) to pressing a button or blinking an eye to implement our choice of action. The soma may even be the prime source of our very ideas of agency and freedom. What could be a better, more fundamental paradigm of voluntary or willed action than the way we move our bodies to do what we will—raise a hand, turn the head?[12] What could provide a clearer, more immediate sense of freedom than the freedom to move our bodies, not merely in locomotion but in opening our eyes and mouth or regulating our breathing? Life implies some sort of animating movement, and the freedom to move is perhaps the root of all our more abstract notions of freedoms. On the other hand, true to its essential ambiguity, the body also clearly symbolizes our unfreedom: the bodily constraints on our action; the corporeal bulk, needs, and failures that weigh us down and limit our performance; the relentless degeneration of aging and death.

If we turn from ethics and action to epistemology, the body remains emblematic of human ambiguity. As both an indispensable source of perception and an insurmountable limit to it, the soma epitomizes the human condition of knowledge and ignorance. Because, as a body, I am a thing among things in the world in which I am present, that world of things is also present and comprehensible to me. Because the body is thoroughly affected by the world's objects and energies, it incorporates their regularities and thus can grasp them in a direct, practical way without needing to engage in reflective thought. Moreover, to see the world, we must see it from some point of view: a position that determines our horizon and directional planes of observation, that sets the meaning of left and right, up and down, forward and backward, inside and outside, and that eventually shapes the metaphorical extensions of these notions in our conceptual thought. The soma supplies that primordial point of view through its location both in the spatiotemporal field and in the field of social interaction. As William James remarks, "The body is the storm centre, the origin of co-ordinates, the constant place of stress in [our] experience-train. Everything circles round it, and is felt from its point of view." "The world experienced," he elaborates, "comes at all times with our body as its centre, centre of vision, centre of action, centre of interest."[13]

But every point of view has its limitations, and so must that provided by the body, whose sensory teleceptors all have limits of sensory range and focus. Our eyes are fixed forward in the head, so that we cannot see behind it or even see our own face without the aid of reflecting devices; nor can we simultaneously focus our gaze forward and backward, left and right, up and down. Philosophy is famous for radically critiquing the body and its senses as instruments of knowledge. Ever since the Socrates of Plato's *Phaedo* defined philosophy's aim as separating the knowing mind from its deceptive bodily prison, the somatic senses and desires have been repeatedly condemned for both misleading our judgment and distracting our attention from the pursuit of truth. But according to Xenophon (another of his close disciples), Socrates affirmed a much more body-friendly view, recognizing that somatic cultivation was essential because the body was the primordial, indispensable tool for all human achievement. "The body," Socrates declared, "is valuable for all human activities, and in all its uses it is very important that it should be as fit as possible. Even in the act of thinking, which is supposed to require least assistance from the body, everyone knows that serious mistakes often happen through physical ill-health."[14]

The basic somaesthetic logic here (also affirmed by other Greek thinkers) is that rather than rejecting the body because of its sensory deceptions, we should try to correct the functional performance of the senses by cultivating improved somatic awareness and self-use, which can also improve our virtue by giving us greater perceptual sensitivity and powers of action.[15] The advocacy of somatic training for wisdom and virtue is even more striking in Asian philosophical traditions, where self-cultivation includes a distinctive bodily dimension developed through ritual and artistic practice (both conceived in highly embodied terms) and through specifically somatic training (such as disciplines of breathing, yoga, Zen meditation, and martial arts) that aim to instill better body-mind harmony, proper demeanor, and superior skill for appropriate action.[16] As Mencius insists, care of the body is the basic task without which we cannot successfully perform all our other tasks and duties: "Though the body's functions are the endowment of nature [or heaven, 天 *tian*], it is only the Sage who can properly manipulate them."[17]

If the body captures the ambiguous human condition of subject and object, power and vulnerability, dignity and indignity, freedom and constraint, commonality and difference, knowledge and ignorance, why does modern humanistic philosophy tend to take the positive sides of this ambiguity for granted and negatively marginalize the body by emphasizing its weaknesses? Part of the reason is our profound reluctance to accept our human limitations of mortality and frailty that the body so clearly symbolizes. Though the field of humanities was first introduced in contrast to theological studies devoted to divinity,[18] humanist thinkers do not seem content to be human; they secretly want to transcend mortality, weakness, and error and to live like gods. Because bodily life does not allow this, they focus on the mind.

Transcendence, as the urge to reach beyond oneself, may be basic to human existence and is certainly central to pragmatist meliorism, but it need not be interpreted in supernatural terms. Our very being is a flux of becoming something else, which can be construed and developed constructively in moral terms of self-improvement. Like other aspects of our humanity, transcendence has a distinctive bodily expression in the soma's basic urge for locomotion; in its reaching out to the world for nutrition, reproduction, and a field of action; in its natural normativity of developmental growth and self-transformations of its physiological systems. Essentially top-heavy when erect, the living body finds it easier to sustain dynamic equilibrium through movement than to stay in place.[19] Even at rest, however, the soma is not a motionless thing but a complex field of multiple movement, a surge of life, a projection of energy that Henri Bergson described as *élan vital*.

III

The body's instrumental function is etymologically indicated in words such as "organism" and "organ" that derive from the Greek word "*organon*," meaning "tool." So when humanists defend the body and advocate its cultivation, they usually do so in terms of its instrumentality, its necessary role in sustaining life and its service to higher functions of humanity identified with the soul. Rousseau, for instance, insists that "the body must be vigorous in order to obey the soul," because "a good servant ought to be robust. . . . The weaker the body, the more it commands," thus "a frail body weakens the soul." Strengthening the body helps develop the mind, which it nourishes and informs through its senses: Thus, "it is only with a surplus of strength beyond what [man] needs to preserve himself that there develops in him the speculative faculty fit to employ this excess of strength for other uses. . . . To learn to think, therefore, it is necessary to exercise our limbs, our senses, our organs, which are the instruments of our intelligence."[20] "The human body," Emerson later reaffirms, is the source of all invention: "All the tools and engines on earth are only extensions of its limbs and senses."[21]

To be recognized as humanity's primal and indispensable tool should constitute an unequivocal argument for humanistic cultivation of the body. But unfortunately, in humanistic culture, the very notion of instrumentality retains strong connotations of inferiority, as noble ends are contrasted to the mechanical means that serve them. This negative nuance can be seen in Rousseau's image of the body as servant to the soul, a familiar analogy from ancient Greek philosophy and traditional Christian theology that continues into modern times. Moreover, the analogy of instrumental servant to higher functions is often coupled with "gendering" the body in a way that underscores its inferior serving status while also reinforcing and naturalizing the second-class status of the gender with which it is associated—woman. Thus even Montaigne—a sincere lover of women and fervent advocate of embodiment—lapses into this devaluing figure in his very effort to affirm the body, urging that we "order the soul . . . not to scorn and abandon the body . . . but to rally to the body, embrace it, cherish it, assist it, control it, advise it, set it right and bring it back when it goes astray; in short, to marry it and be a husband to it, so that their actions may appear not different and contrary, but harmonious and uniform."[22]

Here we face the second of the two paradoxical reasons why somatic studies are demoted in humanistic education. Its indispensable instrumentality ironically relegates it to the devalued realm of service (associated with servants and women and the mere mechanics of material means), while the humanities are instead identified with the pursuit of the highest and purest of spiritual ends—venerated forms of knowledge concerning classics, philosophy, literature, and the arts. Why, then, (goes the argument) should we humanists busy ourselves with studying the body (as the *means*) when we can concentrate directly on enjoying the *ends*, on studiously appreciating our spiritual and artistic achievements? One answer, inspired by the pragmatist philosophy that shapes somaesthetics, is that if we truly care about the ends, we must care about the means necessary to realize those ends. The body deserves humanistic study to improve its use in the various artistic and scholarly pursuits it underlies and serves. Musicians, actors, dancers, and other artists can perform better and longer, with less attendant pain and fatigue, when they learn the proper somatic comportment for their arts: how to handle their instruments and themselves so as to avoid unwanted, unnecessary muscle contractions that result from unreflective habits of effort, detract from efficiency and ease of movement, and ultimately generate pain and disability. A famous case in point concerns the somatic theorist-therapist F. M. Alexander, who first developed his acclaimed technique to address his own problems of hoarseness and loss of voice in theatrical acting that were generated by faulty positioning of his head and neck. Such learning of intelligent somatic self-use is not a matter of blind drill in mechanical techniques but requires a careful cultivation of somatic awareness.

Philosophers and other humanities scholars can likewise improve their functioning as thinkers by improving their awareness and regulation of their somatic instrument of thought. Ludwig Wittgenstein frequently insists on the crucial importance of slowness for good philosophical thinking. Philosophers often err in rashly jumping to wrong conclusions by hastily misinterpreting the surface structure of language. To unravel and avoid such errors, philosophy needs painstaking linguistic analysis that requires slow, patient labor and thus demands a sort of practiced, disciplined slowness and calm. Hence Wittgenstein's appreciation of tranquil slowness, urging, "The salutation of philosophers to each other should be: 'Take your time!'" and advocating an "ideal [of] a certain coolness," a state of tranquility where "conflict is dissipated" and one achieves "peace in one's thoughts." Wittgenstein's own manner of reading and writing aims at attaining this calming slowness. "I really want my copious punctuation marks to slow down the speed of reading. Because I should like to be read slowly. (As I myself read.)"[23] But a more basic, versatile, and time-proven method for attaining the tranquility needed for slow, sustained thinking is focused awareness and regulation of our breathing. Because breathing has a profound effect on our entire nervous system, by slowing or calming our breathing, we can bring greater tranquility to our minds. In the same way, by noticing and then relaxing certain muscle contractions that are not only unnecessary but distractive to thinking (because of the discomfort or fatigue they create), we can strengthen the focus of our mental concentration and build its patient endurance for more sustained philosophical meditations. We can then afford to take our time.

Philosophers, however, often argue that thinking of our bodily means will harmfully distract attention from our ends and thus is more likely to cause problems. Despite the general thrust of his pragmatist and body-respecting philosophy, William James insists that bodily actions are more certain and successful when we focus on "the end alone" and avoid "consciousness of the [bodily] means." Given the parsimonious economy of consciousness, we should concentrate its limited attention on the most important features of action—namely our goals—and leave the bodily means to our established unreflective habits of somatic use: "We walk a beam the better the less we think of the position of our feet upon it. We pitch or catch, we shoot or chop the better the less" we focus on our own bodily parts and feelings, and the more exclusively on our targets: "Keep your *eye* on the place aimed at, and your hand will fetch it; think of your hand, and you will very likely miss your aim."[24]

Immanuel Kant further warns that somatic introspection "takes the mind's activity away from considering other things and is harmful to the head": "The inner sensibility that one generates through one's reflections is harmful. . . . This inner view and self-feeling weakens the body and diverts it from animal functions."[25] In short, somatic reflection harms both body and mind, and the best way to treat one's body is to ignore as much as possible the sensations of how it feels, while using it actively in work and exercise. As James put the point in his *Talks to Teachers*, we should focus on "what we do . . . and not care too much for what we feel."[26] Astutely recognizing that "action and feeling go together,"[27] James urged (in both public lectures and private advice) that we should just control our feelings by focusing on the actions with which they are linked. To conquer depression, we should "go through the *outward movements*"[28] that express cheerfulness, willfully making our body "act and speak as if cheerfulness were already there."[29] "Smooth the brow, brighten the eye, contract the dorsal rather than the ventral aspect of the frame, and speak in a major key."[30] "My 'dying words,'" he exhorted (more than thirty years before his actual death), "are, 'outward acts, not feelings!'"[31]

The Kantian-Jamesian rejection of somatic introspection is, I think, misguided (and largely a product of their avowed fears of hypochondria[32]). But their arguments do rest on a significant truth. In most of our usual activities, attention is and needs to be primarily directed not to our inner feelings but to the objects of our environment in relation to which we must act and react in order to survive and flourish. Thus, for excellent evolutionary reasons, nature positioned our eyes to be looking out rather than in. The error of Kant and James is in confusing ordinary primacy with exclusive importance. Though attention should be directed mostly outward, it is nevertheless often very useful to examine oneself and one's sensations. Consciousness of breathing can inform us that we are anxious or angry when we might otherwise remain unaware of these emotions and thus more vulnerable to their misdirection. Proprioceptive awareness of one's muscle tension can tell us when our body language is expressing a timidity or aggression that we wish not to display, just as it can help us avoid unwanted, parasitic muscular contractions that constrain movement, exacerbate tension, and eventually cause pain. In fact, discomfort or even pain itself—a somatic consciousness that informs us of injury and prompts a search for remedy—provides clear evidence of the value of attention to one's somatic states and sensations. Care of the self is improved when keener somatic awareness advises us of problems and remedies before the onset of pain's damage.[33]

Although James rightly affirms that it is generally more efficient to focus on the end and trust the spontaneous action of established habits to perform the bodily means, there are many times when those habits are too faulty to be blindly trusted and thus require somatic attention for their correction. For example, a batter will normally hit the ball better if she is concentrating on the ball, not on the stance of her feet, the posture of her head and torso, or the grip of her hands on the bat. But a poor or slumping batter may learn (often from a coach) that her stance, posture, and grip tend to put her off balance or inhibit movement in the ribcage and spine in a way that disturbs her swing and impairs her vision of the ball. Here conscious attention must, for a time, be directed to the somatic feelings of the problematic postures so that these postures can be proprioceptively identified and thus avoided while new, more productive habits of posture (and their attendant feelings) are developed and attended to. Without such proprioceptive attention, the batter will spontaneously relapse to (and thus reinforce) the original, problematic postural habits without even being aware of this.

Once an improved habit of swinging is established, the somatic means and feelings of swinging should no longer claim our primary attention, as the ultimate end remains hitting the ball. However, achieving that end requires treating the means as a temporary end and focus, just as hitting the ball—itself only a means to get on base or score a run or win the game—is treated as a temporary end in order to achieve those further ends. Direct seeking of ends without careful attention to the needed means will only bring frustration. Consider the batter who wills herself with all her might to hit the ball with distance yet fails because her eagerness to attain the end prevents her from concentrating on the required bodily means, such as simply maintaining the proper head posture needed to keep her eye on the ball. Likewise, scholars whose creative productivity is constrained by recurrent headaches and writing pains resulting from bad bodily habits of self-use at their workstations cannot remedy or overcome these problems by mere willpower; the bodily habits and their attendant consciousness need to be examined before they can be properly transformed. We must know what we actually do in order to correct it reliably, into doing what we want.

Although wise to advocate the value of somatic actions for influencing our feelings, James fails to recognize the corresponding importance of somatic feelings for guiding our actions. We cannot properly know how to smooth the brow if we cannot feel that our brow is furrowed or know what it feels like to have one's brow smooth. Similarly, since most of us have been habituated to faulty posture, the ability to hold ourselves straight in a way that avoids excessive rigidity requires a process of learning that involves sensitive attention to our proprioceptive feelings. James's unfeeling insistence on vigorous dorsal contraction and stiff upright posture ("bottle up your feelings . . . and hold yourself straight," he exhorted[34]) is thus a sure prescription for the kind of back pain he indeed suffered throughout his life, just as it is surely an expression of his puritan ethics more than a product of careful clinical research. If "action and feeling go together," as James remarked, they *both* warrant careful consideration for optimal functioning, just as both ends and means require our attention. Though knives are most clearly means for cutting rather than ends of sharpening, we sometimes need to focus on improving their sharpness and other aspects of their use in order to improve their effectiveness. Such means-respecting logic underlies the project of somaesthetics as a meliorative study of the use of our bodily instrument in perception, cognition, action, aesthetic expression, and ethical self-fashioning that together constitute humanistic research, artistic creation, and the global art of perfecting our humanity through better living.

IV

The question of how to improve an instrument's use helps introduce the three major branches of somaesthetics whose structure I elaborate elsewhere in more detail.[35] First, a tool is better deployed when we have a better understanding of its operational structure, established modes of use, and the relational contexts that shape them. *Analytic somaesthetics*—the most distinctively theoretical and descriptive branch of the project—is devoted to such research: explaining the nature of somatic perceptions and comportment and their function in our knowledge and action. Besides traditional topics in philosophy concerning the mind-body issue and somatic aspects of consciousness and action, analytic somaesthetics is concerned with physiological factors that relate to somatic self-use. How, for example, greater flexibility in the spine and ribcage can increase one's range of vision by enabling greater rotation of the head while, on the other hand, more intelligent use of the eyes can conversely (through their occipital muscles) improve the head's rotation and eventually the spine's.

This does not mean somaesthetics should be assimilated into physiology and expelled from the humanities; it simply indicates that humanities research should be properly informed by the best scientific knowledge relevant to its studies. Renaissance art and art theory owe much of their success to their study of anatomy, mathematics, and the optics of perspective. Philosophers' traditional disdain for the body may be largely a product of their ignorance of physiology (as Nietzsche suggested), coupled with their pride in privileging only the knowledge that they do master.[36] Analytic somaesthetics is likewise concerned with what the social sciences have to say about the structuring social contexts of somatic experience. This includes genealogical, sociological, and cultural analyses that show how the body is both shaped by social power and employed as an instrument to maintain it; how bodily ideals and norms of health, skill, and beauty and even our categories of gender are constructed to reflect and sustain social forces.

Second, use of a tool can be improved by studying the range of already proposed methods for its most successful and efficient use. Such critical and comparative study of somatic methods constitutes what I call *pragmatic somaesthetics*. Although presupposing certain facts about the body, it goes beyond the facts of analytic somaesthetics through its normative, evaluative, melioristic character—its aim of improving somatic experience and performance. An extensive range of pragmatic methods have been designed to achieve this improvement: various forms of diet and exercise; modes of grooming and decoration; meditative, martial, and erotic arts; and modern psychosomatic disciplines such as the Alexander Technique and the Feldenkrais Method.

We can distinguish between holistic or more atomistic methods. While the latter focus on individual body parts or surfaces (styling the hair, painting the nails, shortening the nose through surgery), the former techniques (such as Hatha yoga, *taijiquan*, and the Feldenkrais Method) comprise systems of somatic postures and movements to develop the harmonious functioning and energy of the person as an integrated whole. Penetrating beneath skin surfaces and muscle fiber to realign our bones and better organize the neural pathways through which we move, feel, and think, these practices insist that improved somatic harmony is both a contributory instrument and a beneficial by-product of heightened mental awareness and psychic balance. Such disciplines refuse to divide body from mind in seeking to improve the entire person. Somatic practices can also be classified in terms of being directed primarily at the individual practitioner herself or instead primarily at others. A massage therapist or a surgeon works on others; but in doing *taijiquan* or bodybuilding, one is working more on oneself. The distinction between self-directed and other-directed somatic practices cannot be rigidly exclusive, for many practices are both. Applying cosmetic makeup is frequently done to oneself and to others; erotic arts display a simultaneous interest in both one's own experiential pleasures and one's partner's by maneuvering the bodies of both self and other. Moreover, just as self-directed disciplines (like dieting or bodybuilding) often seem motivated by a desire to please others, so other-directed practices like massage may have their own self-oriented pleasures.

Despite these complexities (which stem in part from the interdependence of self and other), the distinction between self-directed and other-directed body disciplines is useful for resisting the common presumption that to focus on the body implies a retreat from the social. My experience as a Feldenkrais practitioner has taught me the importance of caring for one's own somatic state in order to pay proper attention to one's client. In giving a Feldenkrais lesson of Functional Integration, I need to be aware of my own body positioning and breathing, the tension in my hands and other body parts, and the quality of contact my feet have with the floor in order to be in the best condition to assess the client's body tension, muscle tonus, and ease of movement and to move him in the most effective way.[37] I need to make myself somatically very comfortable in order not to be distracted by my own body tensions so I can better perceive my client's somatic state and communicate to him haptically the right messages. Otherwise, when I touch him, I will be passing on to him my feelings of somatic tension and unease. Because we often fail to realize when and why we are in a state of slight somatic discomfort, part of the Feldenkrais training is devoted to teaching how to discern such states and distinguish their causes.

Somatic disciplines can further be classified by whether their major orientation is toward external appearance or inner experience. Representational somaesthetics (such as cosmetics) is concerned more with the body's surface forms, while experiential disciplines (such as yoga) aim more at making us feel better in both senses of that ambiguous phrase: to make the quality of our somatic experience more satisfying and more acutely perceptive. The distinction between representational and experiential somaesthetics is one of dominant tendency rather than rigid dichotomy. Most somatic practices have both representational and experiential dimensions (and rewards) because there is a genuine connection of representation and experience, of outer and inner, as the soma is at once corporeal body and embodied subjectivity. Given its ontological oneness, it is understandable that how we feel influences how we look and vice versa. In my essay "Soma and Media" (reprinted here as chapter 13), I discuss how representational and experiential ends can mingle and interchange, as can representational and experiential means. Besides the representational and experiential orientations, another form of pragmatic somaesthetics—*performative somaesthetics*—may be distinguished for disciplines that focus primarily on performance. Here sports and the performing arts are paradigmatic, and we can take a tennis example to illustrate the difference between experiential, representational, and performative dimensions of somaesthetics. A stroke may feel good (experientially) without looking graceful or good (representationally) and without having success (performatively) in getting the ball over the net and inside the proper lines. In the same way the stroke can look good without being successful or feeling good, just as it can successfully win a point without either looking or feeling good.

Finally, a third way to improve our use of a tool is actual practice with it, as we learn to do by doing. Thus, besides the analytic and pragmatic branches of somaesthetics, we also need a branch I call *practical somaesthetics*, which involves actually engaging in programs of disciplined, reflective, corporeal practice aimed at somatic self-improvement (whether representational, experiential, or performative). This dimension of not just reading and writing about somatic disciplines but systematically performing them is sadly neglected in contemporary philosophy, though it has often been crucial to the philosophical life in both ancient and non-Western cultures.[38]

V

In arguing for the humanistic study and cultivation of the body as our primordial, indispensable instrument, we should not forget that the body—as purposeful subjectivity—is also the user of the tool it is. Moreover, we should question the body's presumed status as mere means in contrast to higher ends. This disparaging categorization rests on an implicit means-ends dichotomy that needs to be challenged. The means or instrumentalities used to achieve something are not necessarily outside the ends they serve; they can be an essential part of them. Paint, canvas, representational figures, and the artist's skillful brush strokes are among the means for producing a painting, but they (unlike other enabling causes, such as the floor on which the artist stands) are also part of the end product or art object, just as they are part of the further end of our aesthetic experience in viewing the painting. In the same way, the dancer's body belongs as much to the ends as to the means of the dance work. As William Butler Yeats poetically put it (in "Among School Children"), "O body swayed to music, O brightening glance, / How can we know the dancer from the dance?" More generally, our appreciation of art's sensuous beauties has an important somatic dimension, not simply because they are grasped through our bodily senses (including the sense of proprioception that traditional aesthetics has ignored) but, in addition, because art's emotional values, like all emotion, must be experienced somatically to be experienced at all.

Beyond the realm of art, somatic experience belongs to higher ends, not merely menial means. Athletic exercise may be a means to health, but we also enjoy such exercise in itself, as part of what health actually signifies—the ability to enjoy strenuous movement. And bodily health itself is enjoyed not just as a means to enable laboring for other ends; it is enjoyed intrinsically as an end in its own right. Happiness and pleasure are often prized as highest ends, but somatic experience clearly forms part of them. What are the joys of love without desiring and fulfilled emotions that are always experienced bodily, no matter how pure or spiritual one's love is claimed to be? How can we appreciate even the pleasures of thought without recognizing their somatic dimensions—the pulsing of energy, flutters of excitement, and rush of blood that accompany our impassioned flights of contemplation? Knowledge, moreover, is sturdier when incorporated into the muscle memory of skilled habit and deeply embodied experience.[39] As human thought would not make sense without the embodiment that situates the sensing, thinking subject in the world and thereby gives her thought both perspective and direction, so wisdom and virtue would be empty without the diverse, full-bodied experience on which they draw and through which they manifest themselves in exemplary embodied speech, deeds, and radiating presence.

We thus conclude with another double feature of the living body. Not only instrumentally valuable for perfecting our humanity, the soma is also part of this valued end. In educating and cultivating the sensibility of somaesthetic awareness to improve our thinking through the body, we not only enhance the material means of human culture but also our capacities as subjects to enjoy it.[40]

Chapter Fifteen

Muscle Memory and the
Somaesthetic Pathologies of Everyday Life

I. Muscle Memory as Implicit Memory

"Muscle memory" is a term commonly used in everyday discourse for the sort of embodied implicit memory that unconsciously helps us to perform various motor tasks we have somehow learned through habituation, either through explicit, intentional training or simply as the result of informal, unintentional, or even unconscious learning from repeated prior experience. In scientific terminology, such memory is often designated as "procedural memory" or "motor memory" because it enables us to perform various motor procedures or skills in an automatic or spontaneous fashion, without conscious deliberation of how the procedure should be followed and without any explicit calculation of how one identifies and achieves the various steps involved in the procedure and how one proceeds from step to step. Paradigmatic of such muscle-memory motor skills of performance are walking, swimming, riding a bicycle, tying one's shoes, playing the piano, driving a car, or typing on a keyboard. To be precise, these motor skills should be described as sensorimotor, because they involve coordinating sensory perception with the movement of action. Moreover, because these skills apparently rely on schemata or patterns deeply embedded in an individual's central nervous system, the core engine of memory in so-called muscle memory is not simply the body's muscles but instead also involves the brain's neural networks.

The term "muscle memory" is nonetheless deeply entrenched, perhaps because it serves some key rhetorical functions. Muscle suggests body in contrast to mind, as muscular effort is frequently contrasted to mental effort, or as muscle men are typically opposed to men of thought. Because of this common brain/brawn opposition, muscle memory conveys a sense of mindless memory.[1] Such memory is mindless, however, only if we identify mind with mindfulness in the sense of explicit, critically focused consciousness or deliberate, reflective awareness. Procedural or performative tasks of implicit motor memory often require and exhibit significant mental skills and intelligence, as, for example, when a good pianist plays with spontaneity yet also with aesthetically sensitive mindfulness. In demonstrating that intelligent mind extends beyond clear consciousness, muscle memory also makes manifest the mind's embodied nature and the body's crucial role in memory and cognition.

The idea that our normal somatic skills of performative muscle memory are intelligently deployed without explicit thought or deliberation has played an important part in the cognitive rehabilitation of body and habit in contemporary philosophy, a project we can trace back to pragmatists such as William James and John Dewey and to phenomenologists such as Maurice Merleau-Ponty. In celebrating the body's effectively purposive yet unthinking spontaneous performance in perception, speech, art, and other forms of action, these philosophers recognize that such intelligent spontaneity is not mere uneducated reflex but rather the acquired product of somatically sedimented habit, which often goes by the name of "muscle memory." Because the somatic self is essentially expressed through this purposive intelligence while the term "body" is too often identified with mere physicality, I use the term "soma" to designate the living, sentient, purposive, perceptive body that forms the locus of the transdisciplinary project of somaesthetics.

The performative procedural skills of muscle memory comprise only one of the different kinds of implicit memory that are deeply grounded in the soma. Although the habits and skills of such memory are typically very welcome and useful, we also develop bad habits of muscle memory, many of which go unnoticed not only because of their implicit character but also because their detrimental effects are usually not so extreme as to call our conscious attention to them. Such habits of muscle memory (though undetected and seemingly benign) impair our somaesthetic perception and our consequent experience and performance. Their remedy requires a disruption of implicit memory so that it can be improved through reconstruction. After exploring the soma's role in diverse modes of implicit memory, this chapter analyzes a cluster of everyday problems that arise from such memory, and then suggests how such problems can be treated through methods of heightened body consciousness that render the implicit more explicit.[2]

II. Six Forms of Muscle Memory

1. Perhaps the most basic implicit memory is that of oneself, the implicit sense of continuing personal identity. When I awake in the morning, even before I open my eyes, I have the implicit memory (as an implicit feeling) of being the same person that went to sleep the night before. I do not need to recall explicitly that I am the same person, nor do I even explicitly recognize or thematize the feeling of sameness; but this implicit feeling of being the same person abides with me and provides a narrative ground or core for my sense of self and for my perception of the world. This implicit body memory or feeling of continuity was recognized by William James, who construed it as the foundational factor not only for personal identity but also for the unity of consciousness and thus essentially for the coherence of a person's thinking.

This implicit feeling of being the same self as one was before (even if only a split second before), James argues, is essentially a bodily feeling and so can count as muscle memory. As he puts it in *The Principles of Psychology*, our thoughts are united as being ours because "as we think we feel our bodily selves as the seat of the thinking. If the thinking be *our* thinking, it must be suffused through all its parts with that peculiar warmth and intimacy" involving the implicit felt memory of being the same body, "the feeling of the same old body always there," even though the body is, strictly speaking, always changing.[3] This implicit memory of feeling the same body, James insists, helps "form a *liaison* between all the things of which we become successively aware" (*PP* 235) and thus serves to organize and unify the complexity of experience through its relation to "the objective nucleus of every man's experience, his own body," which he feels implicitly as "a continuous percept."[4]

2. If one basic mode of implicit memory is the self-memory of being the same person, of remembering implicitly who one is,[5] a second crucial mode is remembering *where* one is; and very often this memory includes implicitly recalling how one gets from where one is to where one wants to go. We have all had experiences of walking a familiar route, say from one's office to the bookshop a few blocks away, and suddenly realizing one has arrived at one's destination without ever having thought about or explicitly

remembered the path taken. Similarly, when we arrive at the bookshop, we implicitly remember its familiar feel and layout without consciously recalling it to memory. These implicit memories of location are, of course, deeply grounded in the soma, which essentially determines one's location and sense of place, one's perspective on the world and one's coordinates of direction in it.

We know the world largely because we inhabit it through our soma. Because, as a body, I am also a thing among things in the world, that world of things is also present and comprehensible to me. Because the soma as subjectivity is affected by the world's objects and energies, it incorporates and implicitly remembers their regularities, thus recalling features of spaces and places without needing to engage in explicit recollection or reflection. To see any place (or any object), we must see it from some point of view, a position that determines our horizon and directional planes of observation, that sets the meaning of left and right, up and down, forward and backward, inside and out. One's body, of course, supplies this primordial point, the center or origin of coordinates, by being what locates us in space and gives that lived space its directionality. Moreover, it also gives us our sense of the volume of space, since this sense relies on our experience of moving through space, an experience and ability that depends on the body's powers of locomotion.

As a holistic sensorimotor subjectivity, the soma is essential to spatial memory in yet another way. Unlike some other perceptual dimensions, our sense of space does not directly depend on a specific sensory organ but is instead essentially the product of multisensory representations that build up a spatial map through a learning process, either implicit or explicit. In the implicit learning process, where the forming of a spatial map does not involve special attention or explicit conscious effort, it is through the soma's unreflective perceptions of space that a space is learned and remembered. Not only can we remember spaces we have inhabited and how to negotiate our ways through them through implicit memory without consciously reflecting on representations of those spaces in explicit thought, but we can also first come to know and learn to remember a space through implicit means, without consciously making an effort to remember, without engaging our explicit, voluntary attention to learn the space. Experimental studies have confirmed what we know from ordinary experience: that while explicit, focused attention facilitates the forming and stabilizing of a spatial map, such maps can be formed and stabilized (though not as powerfully) through the sort of unreflective ambient attention that an animal has just by moving through or inhabiting space.[6]

The soma's potent role in understanding and remembering space is highlighted and heightened by its asymmetries. The body's front is different from its back, its top is different from its bottom; and these asymmetries are reflected in differential capacities of memory. Studies show that it is harder to retrieve spatial memory of left and right (dimensions that are symmetrical in the body) than the asymmetrical dimensions of front/back and top/bottom. For the upright observer, the head/foot axis is the easiest for recalling spatial information, because it is also "correlated with the only asymmetric axis of the world, the axis created by gravity." But when reclining, observers remember information fastest on the front/back axis, which roughly correlates with the axis of what can be seen versus not seen.[7]

We sometimes distinguish place from mere space by characterizing the former as a particular landmark with value or meaning (a home, school, stadium, mall, or parking lot). Place in this sense helps define the more abstract concept of space as a general area through which movement is possible (and where places represent distinct points where one might pause in that movement). Similarly, we can distinguish memory of space from memory of place, the latter being easier and very useful for the former. For example, we implicitly remember to turn right at a certain point because we implicitly remember the corner café as the place where we need to turn right. The body plays a central role in such memory through its remembered feel of certain places (the smell of the coffee, the need to navigate one's path around the outdoor tables, etc.).

Certain places leave such strong somatic imprints of feeling that the feeling is involuntarily evoked whenever we enter them. My life as Philosophy Department chair at Temple University was so pressured that each time I entered my office there, even during vacation, I shivered with memories of hectic work and stress so that it was impossible for me to relax or think about anything but my administrative duties, even when I was in principle free to do so. My muscle memory of that place was automatically triggered, shortening my breath and tensing my posture, though it also provided implicit recall of where all the necessary tools could be found to perform my job. And while we're considering my office, it's worth mentioning another sort of memory (implicit or explicit) that could be grouped with memory of space and place—situational memory.

My chairman's office was a place of repeated situation types, for example, interviewing a job candidate or meeting individually with junior faculty members to discuss their progress toward promotion and tenure. Implicit somatic memory of such situations allowed me with smooth spontaneity (i.e., without the awkward hesitancy of deliberative thought) to offer the appropriate greeting and comfortable chair to my interlocutor, to assume the appropriate posture, tone, and demeanor that such situations call for, where one must be kind and encouraging but at the same time represent the impersonal authority and responsibility of one's executive position. There are countless situations in which the soma enacts such implicit situational memory. Sports provide excellent examples; experienced athletes spontaneously recognize (through implicit somatic memory) those situations in which they should pass the ball and to whom and at what speed and trajectory they should pass it.

3. A third form of implicit memory with deep bodily grounding might be described as interpersonal or more broadly as intersomatic—so as to include nonhuman companions such as animals. We develop ways of being with and reacting to certain other bodies, and these modes of relationship are incorporated into our muscle memory as habitual attitudes or schemata of action that are spontaneously recalled and repeated in the presence of those other bodies, with the appropriate contextual variations. Did you ever notice that although you have shared with your spouse or longtime lover countless beds in countless bedrooms, you always seem to lie together in the same orientation, on the same side? You do not have to think about which side of the bed you should take; and if, for some reason, you find yourself lying next to your lover on the nonhabitual side, it will probably feel odd or perhaps even awkward. Similarly, when walking hand in hand or with their arms around each other, couples spontaneously take up their habitual positioning. These habitual postures are assumed without thinking about them, and they establish a feeling of comfortable familiarity that typically escapes explicit recognition but nonetheless pervasively influences one's experience. The same sort of intersomatic attunement is developed between horse and rider or between a person and her pets.

Because emotions are grounded in the body, our implicit somatic memories have an affective dimension. We carry these implicit intercorporeal memories and corresponding somatic attitudes into our encounters with new people, which is why we often have an immediate, visceral feeling of comfort or discomfort when we meet someone new who is implicitly perceived as suggesting positive or negative memories. We develop such intersomatic patterns of interactions already from infancy, as Daniel Stern has shown in his extensive studies of infant interpersonal relations, and these early schemata of interaction powerfully integrate motor, cognitive, and affective dimensions.[8] By means of such somatic patterns and attunements we learn to understand and navigate our immediate interpersonal world (through embodied patterns of implicit relational knowing) even before mastering linguistic expression. Although such intersomatic memories are first developed with respect to one's parents (in most cases, especially to one's mother) and other significant others, they become generalized yet also modified by later experience; and they are unreflectively woven into a complex embodied structure of habits—of affective, cognitive, social, postural, and motor dispositions that are intimately intertwined and that essentially constitute one's personality.

Such implicit affective intersomatic memories, I have argued, can help explain why ethnic and racial prejudices prove extremely resistant to rational arguments of tolerance. Because such prejudices are grounded in implicit visceral feelings and muscle memory of discomfort of which we are not fully conscious, we may not even be aware of them and of the prejudice they generate, although others will note it in our behavior. Parents can unwittingly instill such feelings in their children without saying a word and without any dramatic display of prejudice but simply by subtle postural and facial expressions of discomfort that the sensitive child absorbs and responds to.[9]

4. Our interpersonal relations take place within a larger social setting. But if interpersonal implicit memory in some way already implies the social, we can also distinguish a more distinctively social form of implicit memory, in terms of inhabiting, recalling, or replaying distinctive social roles. These roles very often involve a distinctive form of embodiment. One example I remember from military service in Israel is that of the drill sergeant major at our unit's headquarters. Though typical Israeli military posture is rather relaxed, reflecting a general somatic (and more general military) ideology that advocates the supple, fluid, and flexible, our drill sergeant major had instead learned to incorporate the rigidly erect posture and very stiff, mechanical movements that define the more traditional conventions of military drill and thus of his special social role. Even when he was not performing his official duties, we could always easily recognize him on the base by his stiff posture and gait, even if we could only view him from the back and at a great distance.

Other roles have their characteristic embodiment. A policeman, a judge, and a doctor all possess different forms of authority in their roles, and they display distinctively different forms of embodying those forms of authority. Success in their roles requires incorporating the right bodily attitudes and comportment, whose mastery involves implicit muscle memory in spontaneously performing them.[10] Moreover, we deploy implicit memory in transitioning from one role to another. When the female police officer comes home to assume the role of a tenderly loving mother to her infant son, she does not need to explicitly remind herself to generate the different somatic dispositions and feelings appropriate to her maternal role. Muscle memory instructs her how to transition without her needing to remind herself explicitly what it means to be a mother. Just thinking of her baby while she is driving home may initiate the proper somatic changes, even before she actually sees him and removes her uniform so her badge won't scratch his tender flesh.

5. Putting on and taking off clothes are typical examples of the most obvious type of muscle memory: performative or procedural memory. Normally we do not have to think about how to dress or undress ourselves. We typically do not notice which sock or shoe we put on first, which arm or leg is first inserted into a sleeve or trouser, which button is first buttoned, and whether in buttoning we use the index or pointer finger with the thumb. On many occasions, one decides to get ready for bed, and suddenly finds oneself in pajamas without remembering the various stages of undressing and then dressing for bed. Other skills of experienced mastery in performing sequential tasks range from the most common functions of walking, running, tying one's shoes, or eating with utensils to more complicated skills like swimming, dancing the tango, riding a bicycle, touch typing, driving a car, shooting a turn-around jump shot, or playing a piano sonata. These tasks include distinctively cognitive ones such as speaking, reading, and writing. We perform such skills with such effortless unthinking spontaneity that we can understand why philosophers such as Merleau-Ponty describe such somatic performance in terms of "marvels," "miracles," and "magic."[11]

This sort of muscle memory is certainly most efficient by allowing us to direct our always limited resources of explicit consciousness to other places that need it. We can thus concentrate our attention on the ideas we are writing rather than thinking of the location of the letters on the keyboard which we want to type. I can look down the basketball court to see if a teammate is open near the basket rather than having to think about how I handle the ball to dribble and then pass it to him. By freeing our consciousness to engage other things, muscle memory extends our range of attention and perception, and thus enhances our freedom of action. With many complex motor skills, moreover, it is often claimed (by philosophers, psychologists, and movement experts) that if we tried to perform them by explicitly recalling and deciding our movements at each step, we would awkwardly stumble. As the great choreographer George Balanchine would tell his dancers, "Don't think, dear; just do."[12]

6. The last kind of implicit muscle memory I note here is an unhappy one of unfreedom—traumatic memory. Pain is implicitly remembered in the body and projected through it into future attitudes, as proverbs such

as "Once bitten, twice shy" suggest. Many forms of education involve painful disciplines of training, an approach that may have helped prompt Nietzsche's overstatement that only what does not cease to cause pain remains in memory.[13] In productive forms of disciplinary education, if pain is deployed it is carefully controlled and framed in relationship to positive meaning and value. Traumatic memory, in contrast, is characterized by its inability to connect positively to meaning and value. Because of trauma's intense shock and pain, the victim cannot properly integrate it into a clear, conscious, meaningful memory, since the experience overwhelms one's normal sense of self, rupturing the narrative continuity that gives meaning and stability to experience, including remembered experience. Instead, as the explicit narrative memory of trauma is significantly blurred or even lost in many of its details, so the traumatic memory thrives in implicit behavioral form—in terms of somatic complaints such as flashbacks (that repeatedly relive the trauma); physical symptoms such as sweating or a racing heartbeat; frightening dreams; behavioral reactions of avoiding things that might recall the traumatic experience; being easily startled, tense, or edgy; or being contrastingly emotionally numb. Such traumatic memory forms the crux of what is diagnosed as posttraumatic stress disorder (PTSD). Because traumatic memory withdraws from explicit consciousness while implicitly working through the body to preserve, reinforce, and spread its painful effects, it is very difficult to treat and overcome its devastations. Therapy thus often involves making the implicit memory more explicit in some way so that it can be more clearly identified and treated.[14]

If traumatic memory is one form of implicit somatic memory whose implicitness is not entirely advantageous, I shall now consider how the other forms of implicit or muscle memory also can prove problematic, albeit in a generally milder way. When I first spoke of such problems (in a paper in French), I called them *petites pathologies*,[15] but here I wish to explore them under the category of somaesthetic pathologies of everyday life, alluding to Freud's book on the *Psychopathologies of Everyday Life*, which also deals with problems far less severe than trauma, such as slips of the tongue or other minor lapses.

III. Somaesthetic Pathologies of Muscle Memory and Their Treatment

There is not space here to treat all the different ways that insufficient somaesthetic awareness (i.e., inadequate perception of our somatic comportment and feelings) leads to minor everyday problems of dysfunction, error, discomfort, pain, or decline from proper efficiency. They include unnecessary self-induced accidents such as biting one's tongue when eating, tripping over one's own feet, choking by swallowing food or drink down the wrong "pipe," hurting one's back or knee by lifting or turning in the wrong position, and straining one's lower back by not noticing the discomfort experienced in having sat too long at one's workstation. Then there are everyday somaesthetic pathologies involving a variety of malfunctions in sports-related skills—such as failing to hit a ball properly (in tennis, golf, or baseball) because one is unaware that one's eyes, hands, and other body parts are not in the right position for making proper contact. We also find similar motor malfunctions in work-related activities, such as mistakenly clicking on the mouse when not really ready to send one's message or similar errors arising from not being sufficiently aware of one's handling of the computer keyboard or one's cell phone touch screen. Other common somaesthetic problems include not being able to sleep because one is not aware that one's breathing is too short and one's body too tensely held to induce a condition of repose that can induce sleep.

The various somaesthetic pathologies of everyday life could be grouped in different ways, but rather than proposing a general taxonomy here, I will discuss some examples drawn from the five positive forms of implicit memory noted earlier, while suggesting how these pathologies may be remedied through heightened somaesthetic awareness. Organizing the discussion in terms of these different modes of muscle memory should give greater clarity and unity to this chapter, though I can imagine there may be better ways of classifying the wide variety of everyday somaesthetic pathologies or even the few we shall presently consider.

1. In affirming an implicit abiding memory of self that provides our sense of personal identity and continuity of consciousness, James insists that it is essentially somatic, a muscle memory of feeling oneself as the same person. Even in our moments of pure thinking, "we feel the whole cubic mass of our body all the while, [and] it gives us an unceasing sense of personal existence" (*PP* 316). If James describes "the past and present selves" as unified by "a uniform feeling of 'warmth,' of bodily existence . . . that pervades them all . . . and . . . gives them a *generic* unity," he insists that "this generic unity coexists with generic differences just as real as the unity" (*PP* 318).

James's language here is not entirely clear, but I think he is not (and should not be) asserting that there is one single, isolatable, constant, and unchanging somatic "me" feeling that accompanies all my other bodily feelings and that defines my sense of unity. Rather, one's sense of being the same person is an emergent, holistic feeling of sameness based on a whole network of feelings of "warmth and intimacy" (*PP* 235) between the generic pattern of one's present somatic feelings and that of one's remembered counterparts. One's actual body feelings will always change with changing conditions, though the generic pattern can remain stable while also expressing significant differences. Not all somatic feelings, according to James, have the same weight in determining one's sense of self. In *The Principles of Psychology*, he identifies the crucial somatic feelings of the core self (the innermost self of active consciousness which he calls the "nuclear self" or "the Self of selves") with various "muscular adjustments"—"for the most part taking place within the head" or "between the head and throat" (*PP* 287, 288). By this he means to include adjustments of the cephalic sense organs associated with thinking, such as pressure and orientation of the eyeballs, as well as muscular contractions of the brow, jaw, and glottis. It is understandable to highlight feelings in the head and neck area, which not only houses the brain; the organs of vision, hearing, and taste; and the vestibular system of the inner ear (that provides stability of posture and gaze) but also the first two cervical vertebra (the atlas and axis) whose articulations and attached ligaments and muscles are what enable us to raise, lower, and rotate the head, thus affording greater scope for the head's sensory organs.

James later particularly emphasizes the bodily feelings of breathing as what gives felt unity to one's "stream of thinking," locating those feelings of breath too narrowly in the nose and throat.[16] Without insisting that feelings in the head and neck area are what defines our inner self-feeling, we can recognize that those feelings could be very important to one's sense of self, so that even when we do not explicitly notice these feelings they form a familiar perceptible background to our more explicit objects of consciousness and foci of attention. Such feelings can become so habitual and pervasively familiar that they form part of one's implicit sense of self. This can happen even if these particular feelings in the head and neck are neither necessary (i.e., alternative feelings are equally possible) nor beneficial.

Many individuals suffer from a somaesthetic pathology that exemplifies this situation. They have a condition of chronic excessive tension in the neck, caused by habitual reactions of muscular contraction to repeated situations of stress. Because this condition of excessive tension is habitual, it also becomes familiar as a background feeling. The affected individuals typically do not even know that they have this problem because the excessive tension feels familiar (and in that sense normal) to them; indeed, it forms part of their core feeling of who they are, even if such tension results eventually in the noticeable discomfort of headaches, neck aches, and backaches. We can recognize such people by the way they always have their shoulders quite tensed and elevated closer to the upper neck and ears than one's shoulders should normally be in a proper, adequately relaxed posture. The pressure of the raised shoulders involves muscular tensions that in turn put excessive pressure on the muscles of the neck and the cervical vertebrae; we thus could describe this pathology as the chronically pinched neck. Besides the pain and damage to the cervical spine that this chronic contraction can eventually cause, such posture hinders the efficiency of our action, since its tensed posture inhibits movement in the neck, shoulders, and ribcage. Nonetheless, through its habituated incorporation into a familiar bodily feeling, the pinched-neck posture feels normal to those who suffer from this somaesthetic pathology, which is thus a pathology of perception (aesthesis) as well as of posture.

Clinical experience has taught me that when such a person is asked to relax his shoulders to ease his neck, he will happily assent to the request but essentially fail to comply, though he thinks he is complying (very often by making a sort of shrug that just raises the shoulders further before letting them subside to their habitual raised position). Not only does he not realize that his elevated shoulders and neck are excessively tensed (because they feel normal to him), but he also does not know how to lower or relax them because he no longer knows what that relaxed posture feels like. When, after some hands-on work with him, I induce a relaxation in his neck and shoulders, he reports that it feels a bit strange to him, that he feels somehow lazy or soft and not quite himself. He confuses the release from chronic hypertension with a loss of the familiar sense of his forceful dynamic self that has become habitually linked to his chronic feelings of excessive muscular contractions. This change of posture may thus not be psychologically comfortable for him, even though it is physiologically more comfortable and can be behaviorally more advantageous.

A patient's identity may be so intimately linked to her handicap or problem that even when she complains about the problem, she may at a deeper level resist efforts to rid herself of it. (I knew a talented, beautiful, and wealthy Parisian academic who, for many years, complained to me about being miserable because of the man she lived with. But whenever I suggested she leave him, she replied that this problematic relationship had become a cornerstone of her identity and her psychological coping structure, supplying her with an excuse for being unhappy and for not writing all the books she thought she should write. Without this problem, she argued, she would have no adequate excuse for her failures and would thus be even more miserable and full of self-loathing.) With respect to the somaesthetic pathology of the pinched neck, if the chronic feeling of tension is felt as an important part of the person's sense of self, then he must take the trouble of revising his familiar sense of self so that a more relaxed muscular tonus is not confused with torpor and can instead be associated with his resilient dynamism. For many individuals, to take the time and effort to make this transition may not seem worth the sacrifice, especially since the advantages of the new posture and sense of self are neither very clear nor guaranteed in advance, while the problems they currently suffer from their pinched-neck pathology seem manageably minor and familiar. That is one reason why this somaesthetic pathology remains so prevalent.

2. Muscle memory guides us in spatial orientation but it can also misguide us. One space-related somaesthetic pathology of everyday life is orientational bias. Did you ever notice that whenever you go to a movie or lecture without assigned seats you tend to sit on one side (left or right) of the room rather than the other? Did you ever notice that when you are standing or sitting your range of vision is greater on one side than the other? The reason is that one's body frequently has an orientational bias; many people feel more comfortable turning toward one side rather than another, and this bias is also reflected in posture, as a tendency (when standing or sitting) to have one's body or head not perfectly straight but slightly turned toward one direction. Perhaps you sit on the right side of the movie theater because your left eye is stronger and thus sitting on the right puts the left eye more toward the center especially when tilting your gaze leftward (which sitting on the right enables you more comfortably to do). Or perhaps your right-side seating habit is because you implicitly feel (for a variety of possible reasons relating to your somatic history) more comfortable with your body slightly turned or shifted toward your left.

There is nothing wrong with this sort of postural bias in itself, but if we fail to recognize it and compensate for its effects, it can lead to problems. For instance, a teacher or lecturer who has a left orientational bias will often unintentionally turn his side or even back to those people in the audience who are seated to his right, without even knowing that he is excluding them from eye contact. If he is aware of this bias, he can correct or compensate for it by readjusting his posture so that he is facing more of his audience (either by centering his orientation or by stepping further back to minimize the effects of the bias). A much more dangerous result of such orientational bias is reduced ability to notice oncoming traffic from the side somewhat blinded by the bias; experience indeed shows that many individuals tend to suffer accidents significantly more on one side than another. If orientational bias seems a likely cause for such accidents, then improved awareness of such bias through heightened somaesthetic perception is a likely remedy.

As orientational bias concerns issues of how we *situate* ourselves in space, so there are everyday somaesthetic pathologies of navigating our trajectories through space. Too many times my muscle memory directs my walking and driving through habitual paths toward familiar locations that are, however, not the ones I meant to choose, so I am forced to backtrack and consciously remind myself of the right destination and path. Muscle memory likewise induces everyday somaesthetic pathologies of inhabiting place, one of which was already introduced in discussing my implicit "chairman's office" memory. It was pathological to be suddenly thrust into a state of breathless tension (and without even explicitly recognizing it) just by entering that place, even if I had nothing more urgent to do there that day than chat with an old friend who found it the most convenient place to meet. After somatic training improved my somaesthetic awareness, I was able to identify my pathological reaction but also treat it by explicitly applying various strategies of breathing and muscle relaxation.

3. In my discussion of implicit interpersonal muscle memory, I argued that racial and ethnic prejudice—an all-too-common everyday pathology—has roots in visceral feelings and that its incorporation in implicit memory makes it very difficult for the person with the prejudice to properly recognize it, let alone extinguish it by a mere conscious judgment that such prejudice is unreasonable. Sharpening a person's awareness of her bodily feelings so that she can recognize the mild discomfort that certain races, ethnicities, or other groups provoke in her can help her to identify the prejudice and its roots, so that she may try to contain it or even overcome it, if she wishes to, perhaps by trying to reeducate her somatic feelings. As we know from acquired tastes, visceral reactions or dispositions can be to some extent refined or transformed through sensory reeducation. Of course, if the person with prejudice has no such meliorative desire for reform, then heightening the awareness of visceral discomfort and its relation to the prejudice may not result in efforts to control or eliminate the prejudice. Indeed, heightened awareness might even strengthen the feelings of discomfort, and in that way reinforce the prejudice in rendering it more conscious. Knowledge, including self-knowledge, is not always beneficial; it depends on how it is

used. One could argue, however, that knowing one is prejudiced is at least a cognitive improvement on not knowing it, even if positive ethical results of such knowledge are not forthcoming.

Muscle memory can generate another minor pathology of interpersonal interaction. Some persons have characteristic postures that others find disturbing, even if the disturbing feelings remain rather mild and implicit. For example, some individuals have a way of engaging their interlocutors in conversation by coming very close to them and then tilting or leaning toward them with a rather tensely contracted soma. The motivation for this posture is typically friendly, but it often conveys a disturbingly aggressive stance to the interlocutor, who feels somehow threatened by this intrusion in her personal space, especially if the overly proximate body leaning toward her is considerably larger than her own. Her implicit reaction is to withdraw both posturally and psychologically from the friendly speaker with the aggressive stance, which tends to evoke in him a further implicit adjustment of looming still closer, perhaps with the feeling that his interlocutor is not a friendly person, even though she may indeed harbor friendly inclinations to him, at least initially, before this unfortunate dance of approach and withdrawal that results from his somaesthetic insensitivity to posture.

Such interpersonal problems are magnified when culturally different senses of appropriate distance come into play. Recall the joke about the international conference cocktail party where one can identify the Finns by the fact that they're the ones gradually withdrawing toward the walls of the room, retreating while conversing with the Brazilians, who are recognized by their constant forward-pressing, hands-on approach in the same conversations. Consulting intercultural guidebooks about the appropriate posture to adopt in various cultures will not solve the problem, if one remains insufficiently aware of the posture one is actually assuming, as well as the postural reaction of the soma with whom one is interacting. Somaesthetic awareness is necessary for both, and while many individuals spontaneously display such awareness, many others require an effort of conscious attention to cultivate and deploy this awareness.

4. Muscle memory's incorporation of social roles can create its own somaesthetic pathologies of everyday life. Take the drill sergeant from my days as an officer in Israeli military intelligence. So fully had he absorbed his professional persona—with his body always held rigidly erect in hyperextension and his habitual stiff, jerky gait and sharp, mechanical hand movements—that he seemed incapable of shedding this attitude. We laughingly imagined how he returned home to make love to his wife in the same

barking cadence, mechanical gestures, and jerky rhythms that defined his military somatic behavior, without his even realizing that he was behaving like a drill sergeant rather than a lover and thus missing out on love's more tender and fluid communicative pleasures. Although we never followed him home to see (or ask his wife) whether he indeed suffered from this somaesthetic pathology, I did indeed witness during my years in Israel a different form of incorporated role fixation that was implicit, unintentional, and unnoticed by the role player.

My then father-in-law, a Tel Aviv judge who dearly loved his family, did not realize that he daily brought his courtroom *habitus* back to the dinner table, augustly bellowing orders to family members as if they were bailiffs or accused criminals. He did not realize that his tone and body language were inappropriate, until his daughter and wife called them to his attention, and he apologized with genuine embarrassment. Fortunately, after his postprandial siesta, he awoke largely freed from his courtroom soma that had earlier been primed by a stressful morning in court. Because it often takes time, distraction, and relaxing substances to free oneself from a deeply embodied and labor-intensified social role and prepare a differently embodied persona, I understand why bars have been so important on evening commuter trains and on the pedestrian's and motorist's way home from work.

5. Implicit performative or procedural memory is indispensable for getting us efficiently through countless everyday activities. By enabling us to perform so many familiar tasks with no explicit attention, it allows us to direct our limited resources of attentive consciousness to more difficult problems. As noted earlier, a writer can focus on how to express his philosophical ideas instead of how to position his hands and flex and move his fingers to perform the necessary actions for pressing the right keys to generate the letters of the words he wishes to compose. A violinist can likewise concentrate on the expressive qualities she wants to produce rather than on the way she is gripping her instrument and positioning or moving her shoulders, torso, and arms when performing. In the same way, a DJ can concentrate on the songs or tracks he is sampling rather than on the posture of his ribcage and hips when he is spinning those records. In these and similar cases, their muscle memory performs the necessary sequential acts of muscular contraction, positioning, and movement without explicit consciousness.

Unfortunately, however, as I learned from clinical practice, the habits of muscle memory formed to perform such spontaneous body adjustments often do so in ways that are not somatically advantageous and lead to unnecessary fatigue, pain, or injury. The writer develops carpal tunnel syndrome from holding his wrists too rigidly; the violinist suffers pain in the back, neck, and arms because she holds her shoulders and ribcage too tight, thus forcing her bow strokes to be more effortful. The DJ (who happened to be a graduate student at the New School for Social Research) fell victim to a very sore elbow, because his habit of freezing his hips and ribcage in mental concentration (a habit quite common in academic readers who daily spend many hours in focused seated study) put extra pressure on the elbow joint in its effort of spinning the records. But when he learned how to relax the hips and torso so they could rotate with the record-spinning arm, his elbow problem disappeared.

Let me conclude by noting some pathologies relating to a much more basic activity typically governed by performative muscle memory: eating. For all its natural or instinctive aspects, eating is a sequential activity that we learn how to perform through both implicit and explicit forms of learning. We learn the sequence of cutting and chewing a large slice of meat before we try to swallow it, or the sequence of first lifting and then tilting the cup to one's mouth to drink our water rather than lowering the mouth and extending the tongue to lap it up. We develop distinctive habits in the way we eat, and these go beyond the obvious examples of formal table manners and the handling of various eating utensils (knives, forks, spoons, chopsticks, cups, glasses, bowls, pitchers, saltshakers, etc.). There are different habits of how one deploys one's lips and tongue, and what part of the mouth one uses in chewing; how fast, how long, and how vigorously one chews; how fast, how often, and how hard one swallows; how often one pauses during eating in order to drink, to speak to one's dining companion, or to reflect on the food's taste, aroma, or texture or on one's diverse feelings in eating, including the feeling of becoming satiated. The performative muscle memory of eating is very deeply entrenched because it is a procedural skill we use daily. The result is that we typically eat without thinking explicitly about it.

This is surely convenient because attention instead can be wholly absorbed on something more interesting or useful, such as listening to the news or reviewing one's notes for an ensuing lecture. But such muscle-memory automatism of eating can prove problematic if one's dining habits are faulty, and they can be flawed in a variety of everyday ways. For example, there are people with habits of ugly, sloppy, or excessively noisy ways of eating that pose somaesthetic problems for dining companions who are forced to witness them. Besides the visual or auditory displeasure they experience, observing such unaesthetic eating styles may rob these fellow diners of their own appetite and enjoyment of food. Other somaesthetic pathologies resulting from habits of muscle memory can affect the problematic eater himself. One touted feature of habit is that its muscle memory increases speed of performance because no time is taken (or needed) to deliberate in action. So relying purely on muscle memory without attentive deliberation about how we eat enables us to eat more quickly. But those who habitually eat too quickly often suffer from poor digestion and a variety of related somatic discomforts (whose portrayal and medicinal remedies fill countless hours of television advertising). Many who suffer in this way know that part of their problem is eating too fast, but one reason they continue to eat too fast is that they do not notice how fast they are eating because muscle memory sets the rhythm and style of their eating. They thus pay no attention to how they perform this sequential, temporal activity; and without such attention they cannot monitor it so as to slow it down. Recent studies show, moreover, that eating fast also promotes obesity; and, once again, if we are unaware of our speed of eating, we cannot know how to slow it down to avoid its negative consequences.[17]

Another somaesthetic pathology of inattentive habit contributes to overeating. When food or drink is consumed rapidly and inattentively, we are less able to appreciate its taste. As our eating enjoyment is diminished by this inability to properly savor our food, so we tend to compensate by eating more. Unsatisfied by the flavors and textures of what we've already eaten (because they have gone largely unnoticed through our habitual hurried or inattentive eating), our quest for the satisfaction which we know *should* come from food drives us to continue eating in the hope that such satisfaction *will* eventually come. This unfulfilled hope often keeps us eating even after we've already had our fill. Such frustrations of satisfaction through inattentive eating habits that rely entirely on the swift efficiency of muscle memory may be one cause for the common pathology of overeating in America and other fast-food, rapid consumption societies. In any case, its failure of gustatory and hedonic appreciation constitutes in itself a regrettable somaesthetic pathology of everyday life.

These are not the only somaesthetic pathologies that contribute to the overeating and consequent obesity from which so many suffer in contemporary consumerist culture. Driven to consume through persistent and ever-increasing stimulation that continuously strains and blunts our discriminatory sensitivities (in ways described by the Weber-Fechner law), many people are unable to perceive that they have eaten enough until they have considerably overeaten. They have lost the somaesthetic discrimination of the proprioceptive feelings of having their hunger satiated or being comfortably full. They can discriminate only the stronger, discomforting overstimulation of feeling "stuffed," so they identify that unpleasant feeling with having reached satiety or eating satisfaction, and they thus continue to eat until they feel such discomfort. We thus have a vicious cycle of eating more but enjoying it less, because one is not properly aware of when to stop eating, and such awareness is a matter of somaesthetic discrimination.

These arguments regarding eating and obesity have a particular relevance to the ramified project of somaesthetics, an interdisciplinary field of theory and practice broadly defined as the critical study and meliorative cultivation of the soma as a site of sensory appreciation (aesthesis), performative action, and creative self-fashioning. As creative self-fashioning suggests the aesthetic stylizing of the soma as an external object of attractive representations, so the focus on aesthesis concerns the soma's perceptual acuity and inner experience, where cultivation of improved aesthesis means "feeling better" both in the sense of enjoying better feelings but also in the sense of perceiving what we experience more accurately and clearly. It is sometimes useful to emphasize the distinction between the perceptual or inner dimension of somaesthetics and the dimension of external body representation that so dominates our culture's concerns with embodiment.[18] But if deficient somaesthetic perception of our eating can be causally linked to problems in maintaining one's external somaesthetic form, then there exists an important connection between somaesthetics' perceptual and representational dimensions. It is common to say that how we feel affects how we look; happiness can give us a winning smile, while depression, the pains of illness, or fatigue can make us look unattractively dull and diminished. Our brief, closing arguments for deploying somacsthetic perception to overcome obesity from eating habits of inattentive muscle memory provides, however, a new meaning to this familiar saying.

Chapter Sixteen

Somaesthetics and Politics

I

Briefly defined as the critical study and meliorative cultivation of the experience and use of the body a site of sensory appreciation (*aesthesis*), effective action, and creative self-fashioning, somaesthetics emerged from two main philosophical roots. First, it built on pragmatist aesthetics, which emphasizes the active, sentient, purposive body (or soma) as the necessary energetic ground and skilled medium for our capacities of artistic creation and aesthetic appreciation. Second, somaesthetics drew on the ancient idea of philosophy as a critical, disciplined, meliorative art of living. As the soma is the essential medium of life, crucial to our perception, feeling, thought, and action, the classical philosophical quest for self-knowledge and self-improvement should clearly involve somatic self-cultivation, and ancient philosophy (both Western and Asian) frequently made it central.[1]

   Modern philosophy, with its focus on theoretical issues and general claims rather than on the personal practice of the art of living, neglects somatic cultivation; its ideology tends to view concern for the body as merely a personal, private concern and thus a retreat from the social and the political. Marxist theorist Frederic Jameson claims that care for the body concerns only "my individual relationship with my own body . . . and not that very different relationship between myself or my body and other people."[2] The presumption is that somatic attention is inherently private and fiercely individualistic, that a person's body is somehow essentially disconnected and hidden from social perception in the way that Descartes thought that the nature of one's own body is somehow hidden from mental perception while thought is wholly transparent to the mind. However, as *Pragmatist Aesthetics* long ago maintained, "Not only is the body shaped by the social, it contributes to the social. We can share our bodies and bodily pleasures as much as we share our minds, and they can be as public as our thoughts."[3] In fact, our bodies are often more visible and transparent than our thoughts. It is easier to lie in words than to lie in body language.

Fortunately, other social thinkers, such as Simone de Beauvoir, Michel Foucault, Pierre Bourdieu, and the many feminist and gender theorists inspired by their work, have increasingly urged that seemingly private body matters have a significant social dimension, being both shaped by social factors (including class and gender markings) and contributing to the preservation of the society that shapes our somatic subjectivities. Somaesthetics joins these voices but also adopts another argument linking the personal and the political. This is the ancient Confucian argument for the crucial importance of personal action in the political. The idea is that all good government requires good self-government, and that political action can usefully start with that dimension.

Here is the argument's original and still classic statement in Confucius's *The Great Learning*, referring to the exemplary governing leaders of the past: "Their persons/bodies [身 *shen*] being cultivated, their families were regulated. Their families being regulated, their states were rightly governed. Their states being rightly governed, the whole kingdom was made tranquil and happy."[4] As the Chinese word *shen* 身 is the character both for the human body and the human person, so the notion of a person's self-cultivation (*xiushen* 修身) clearly includes somatic cultivation. The same idea that the macrorealm of political governance is fundamentally based on the microrealm of self-governance is also suggested (albeit more on the conceptual level) in Plato's *Republic*, where Socrates argues that the way to understand the right order of justice in the state is by first determining the right governing order of the individual's soul.

Highlighting the political importance of individual agents' efforts is often considered and critiqued by social theorists as the product of our individualistic neoliberal ideology. But we can hardly call Confucianism (or Platonism) an individualistic, liberal political philosophy that celebrates the self over the social. Confucianism insists rather that the individual self is essentially socially constructed. The particular self is defined by the various social relations that shape it. One is the son of M and F, the student of X, the classmate of Y, the teacher of Z, the father of A and B, the husband of W, and so on. For Confucianism, these social roles structure one's self-cultivation and shape the general orientation of one's self-realization. Self-cultivation is always socially situated, and somatic self-cultivation is significantly shaped by one's social roles and duties. Consider, for example, an argument that Mencius brings for somatic self-care and self-cultivation. Recognizing the primacy of one's duty to one's parents, Mencius maintains that satisfying that duty requires fulfilling a prior trust to one's own body or self. "I have heard of those who, having kept their bodies inviolate, could serve their parents, but not of those who failing to do so, still served their parents. Whichever duty I fail to perform, it must not be my duty to my parents, for that is the duty from which all others spring. Whichever trust I fail to fulfill, it must not be that of keeping my body inviolate, for that is the trust from which others arise."[5] In other words, duties to the somatic self are logically implicated in our duties to others, just as our relations to others essentially define the self.

These reciprocal implications suggest an important pragmatist insight and strategy: that conventional oppositions are often mere polar points connected by a complex continuity of relations. Just as we do with nature and culture (or body and mind, or art and life), we can, of course, distinguish the self from society, but we should not erect this into a rigid dichotomy, because these concepts define and shape each other. As pragmatism is an American philosophy and thus associated with American traditions of individualism, it is important to highlight its emphasis on the essentially social character of thought and conduct. C. S. Peirce fiercely argued against Descartes's epistemological method of basing the criterion of truth on the clearness and distinctness of ideas in the critical consciousness of the individual's mind. He insisted instead that truth and knowledge essentially depended on intersubjective, collaborative inquiry and communication. Community is an indispensable medium for the pursuit of better beliefs, fruitful knowledge, and even for the basic achievement of meaning through language and the arts. Social life provides the framework for the transmission and sustenance of culture without which our cognitive, technological, and cultural achievements could not be preserved and advanced. Besides providing for a sharing and critique of alternative viewpoints through which the individual can correct her beliefs, society provides the very contrasts an individual needs to understand herself. Through others, we learn not only a common language to express shared ideas and values and to express our differences from others, but also our ability to develop new ways of thinking and speaking originally for ourselves.

Echoing Peirce's affirmation of the social's essential cognitive role, John Dewey also made the social an ethico-political ideal. Because the self, even in its individual self-realization, is a product of social life, the kind of self that is shaped by rich social engagement and concern for others "will be a fuller and broader self than one which is cultivated in isolation from or in opposition" to them. Yet conversely, Dewey argues that society also benefits from individual free expression. As he puts it, if the individual is robbed of her particular individuality, "the whole social body is deprived of the potential resources that should be at its service."[6] Even William James, the most individualistic of the classical pragmatists, insists that the self is essentially formed by society, arguing that persons are "bundles of habits" and that our habits are socially shaped and that their social shaping helps keep society going in ways that maintain social order, thus discouraging political upheaval:[7]

> Habit is thus the enormous fly-wheel of society, its most precious conservative agent. It alone is what keeps us all within the bounds of ordinance, and saves the children of fortune from the envious uprisings of the poor. It alone prevents the hardest and most repulsive walks of life from being deserted by those brought up to tread therein. It keeps the fisherman and the deck-hand at sea through the winter; it holds the miner in his darkness, and nails the countryman to his log-cabin and his lonely farm through all the months of snow; it protects us from invasion by the natives of the desert and the frozen zone. It dooms us all to fight out the battle of life upon the lines of our nurture or our early choice, and to make the best of a pursuit that disagrees, because there is no other for which we are fitted, and it is too late to begin again. It keeps different social strata from mixing. . . . It is well for the world that in most of us, by the age of thirty, the character has set like plaster, and will never soften again.[8]

This does not mean James despaired of social change. He simply recognized that the mere formulation of new laws or new institutions does not entail that people's actual behavior will change, while likewise realizing how difficult it is for people to change their habits. James, the psychologist-cum-moralist, therefore explored the best ways to form good habits and reform bad ones, formulating them in some pithy maxims that he recommended to his readers. A key element in practical somaesthetics is the critical analysis and transformation of problematic habits through the discipline of reflective awareness and conscious control.

For pragmatism and somaesthetics, it is a grave mistake to think that one must choose exclusively between self-cultivation and social action. There is no reason why a person cannot do both, alternating one's focus between efforts of self-improvement and endeavors of social reform. Sometimes one can even simultaneously do both. In preparing and giving a speech at a political meeting one is both cultivating one's writing and oratory abilities as well as engaging in meaningful social action. Oratory abilities are performative somaesthetic skills; and if one prefers a more explicitly physical example of effort, think of participating in a 10K race to raise money for some worthy social or political cause.

More generally, developing one's somatic capacities can increase one's strength, confidence, poise, and efficacy to engage in social action. I make this argument in *Body Consciousness* to counter Simone de Beauvoir's fear that somaesthetic attention is dangerous for women because it distracts them from political engagement and focuses their consciousness on private, personal matters, despite her own recognition that building bodily strength and acquiring more somatic knowledge and mastery can make women more confident and less vulnerable to exploitative manipulation by men.[9] I do not advocate somaesthetic cultivation as a substitute for broader social action and political engagement but rather as a means of strengthening our somatic capacities (which include our capacities for courage, endurance, empathetic social perception, and nurturing care) so that we are better equipped to engage in social and political struggles.

II

Pragmatist philosophy highlights the importance of practice, and somaesthetics defines itself as a field of practice and theory, where two of its major branches—pragmatic and practical somaesthetics—are primarily oriented toward practice. But besides the general points made above, what practical political applications could somaesthetics have through its highlighting of somatic consciousness and care?

The recent COVID-19 pandemic provides convincing evidence for the political relevance of personal and interpersonal somatic care. The most repeated instructions for slowing the spread of the virus insist on three key points: social distancing, more frequent and more thorough washing of hands, and the wearing of face masks that cover the mouth and nose. All these demands involve suddenly changing our deeply entrenched bodily habits;

and this in turn calls for greater somaesthetic awareness and self-knowledge to ensure better somatic self-control. Enhanced body consciousness enables much better monitoring of one's distance from others and more successful restraining of our naturally felt impulses to shake hands or embrace those dear to us, as we (through habit) automatically tend to do. Better body awareness enables more mindfulness of proper handwashing, and it can help us learn to be more somatically comfortable wearing face masks and to talk and breath more effectively through them. In the West, where mask wearing for health reasons is far less common than in East Asia, we needed to transform our aesthetic perception concerning the mask-wearing faces of others, so as not to judge mask wearers as weird or menacing in some way. Certainly, at the outset of the crisis, such feelings of aesthetic unease or psychological discomfort in seeing masked faces created an unpleasant atmosphere that troubled personal interaction in public places.

Somaesthetics can explain and treat many of our irrational political enmities. I have argued that the fanatical kind of hatred that some people have for certain foreign races, cultures, classes, and nations displays a deep visceral quality, an enmity reflecting profound concerns about the integrity and purity of the familiar body in a given culture or social class.[10] Bodies unfamiliar in their appearance or conduct often elicit subtle feelings of somatic discomfort (typically beneath the level of explicit consciousness), simply through being different, as their difference is instinctively felt as a challenge to the comfortable, familiar norm. The irrationality of homophobia and the hatred toward trans individuals have similar origins (even if it also draws on traditional religious views of gender): discomforting feelings resulting from bodily appearance or conduct that defies the norm. In racial and ethnic prejudices such discomfort is unconsciously translated into hostility toward the people whose mere existence challenges a culture's familiar body image and threatens its corruption through racial or ethnic mixing that can alter the body in both external appearance and behavior. Rational arguments for multicultural tolerance and racial harmony, though intellectually convincing, fail to eradicate the prejudicial attitude and behavior, because the enmity is acquired not by rational thought but through discomforting somatic feelings whose unpleasant qualities are often only distractedly or implicitly felt and thus escape rational, critical consciousness.

Wittgenstein, for example, explains the rabid anti-Semitism of highly rational European countries in terms of a somatic metaphor and a corresponding somaesthetic feeling. The Jews are felt as a diseased tumor in Europe. "'Look on this tumor as a perfectly normal part of your body!'

Can one do that, to order? Do I have the power to decide at will to have, or not to have, an ideal conception of my body?" he asks, then continues:

> Within the history of the peoples of Europe . . . the Jews . . . are experienced as a sort of disease, and anomaly, and no one wants to put a disease on the same level as normal life. . . . We may say: people can only regard this tumor as a natural part of the body if their whole feeling for the body changes (if the whole national feeling for the body changes). Otherwise the best they can do is *put up with* it. You can expect an individual man to display this sort of tolerance, or else to disregard such things; but you cannot expect this of a nation, because it is precisely not disregarding such things that make it a nation. I.e., there is a contradiction in expecting someone *both* to retain his former aesthetic feeling for his body [*aesthetische Gefuhl für seinen Körper*] and *also* to make the tumor welcome.[11]

It may indeed seem contradictory to expect a person to welcome a tumor while retaining his former aesthetic feeling for the body. But this does not mean that the tumor (or the foreign population) must be exterminated. An alternative would be to modify that person's aesthetic feeling for the body and further modifying the citizens' feelings for their nation's body politic. Here, somaesthetics' discipline of body consciousness can provide a pragmatic remedy. If racial and ethnic enmity resists resolution through logical means of verbal persuasion because it has a visceral basis of discomforting unfamiliarity, then as long as we do not consciously attend to these deep visceral feelings, we can overcome neither them nor the enmity they generate and foster. Improved body consciousness can help us identify these disturbing somatic sensations so that we can better control, neutralize, or overcome them. Moreover, it can help us transform them through somaesthetic training because they are already the product of learning. Such feelings of discomfort from foreign bodies are almost entirely the result of implicit learning and habit rather than innate instinct; as such they are malleable to efforts of reformation. This is a commonplace of gastronomy, athletics, and somatic therapies; but modern philosophical ethics and political theory have not given it enough attention. Somaesthetics is helping to initiate a change here, suggesting how sensitizing, consciousness-raising somatic training can deal with issues of racism, sexism, homophobia, and violence.[12] Such somaesthetic consciousness-raising, it has been argued, should not be limited to the awareness of momentary bodily feelings but can include the aesthetics of compelling somatic-oriented genealogical narrative.[13]

Every situation has its enveloping atmosphere that has a somatically felt dimension. In every face-to-face political meeting there is an underlying, nondiscursive, somatic communication that pervades and shapes the meeting's general atmosphere and the momentary energies, attitudes, and feelings of the participants. It is therefore important for political agents to somaesthetically sense that unarticulated atmosphere and to regulate their bodily conduct and gestural expression accordingly to improve the atmosphere in the desired direction. Negotiations often go much more smoothly and successfully in situations where the atmosphere is friendly, pleasurable, and relaxed, such as in contexts of dining together, where trust comes to be shared through shared pleasure.[14] The power of political mass protests or rallies also depends on how bodies create atmospheres by their somaesthetic presence and conduct. Though digital social media have crucial political uses, online participation is no substitute for the somatic mass created by free individuals who demonstrate their commitment through their physical presence and energetically heightened somaesthetic expression.

III

Wittgenstein's analogizing of the Jews to a tumor on the body of nations in Europe recalls the deeply entrenched notion of the *body politic* as a metaphor for the corporate identity of the nation state (and we should note how the word "corporate" likewise suggests embodiment). The metaphor (which also exists in French as *corps politique*) is typically extended to view the governing ruler as the *head* of state, an image concretely rendered in the famous cover of Thomas Hobbes's *Leviathan* showing a body formed of a multitude of citizens on top of which rests the head of a king.[15] The body politic metaphor is likewise extended to regard political dysfunction, disorder, corruption, and conflict in terms of somatic problems such as physical weakness, disease, or disability. Wittgenstein's tumor metaphor is an example of this tradition. Sometimes the body politic metaphor is also read back the other way in terms of classifying various body parts in terms of their more "aristocratic" status or governing function.[16]

The centrality of this body metaphor suggests another way that somaesthetics might be useful for political thinking. Analogizing the nation state to the body obviously carries the risks of excusing intolerance for the sake of policing purity on the model of old-fashioned eugenics, but a more accurate and scientific view of the human body reveals that it cannot thrive in self-sufficient somatic purity. Most of the cells in the human body are not human at all. Foreign bacterial cells in our bodies outnumber our human cells ten to one and provide vital help with basic physiological processes such as digestion, growth, and self-defense. The body can be likened to a complex ecosystem made up of various subsystems containing trillions of bacteria and other microorganisms inhabiting our skin, genital areas, mouth, and especially intestines.

This image of the body as a system of systems is useful for providing an answer to a dilemma of political critique that has become prominent since postmodernism. The critical attitude has long been thought to require critical distance, and such distance is presumed to require a perspective from outside the object being criticized. Yet in our postmodern globalized world, there seems to be no truly external, autonomous vantage point outside of and detached from the globalized world of politics. Somaesthetics helps challenge the presumption that such critical distance is always necessary by showing how we can critically examine aspects of our somatic experience without going outside our bodies to some putative detached, disembodied mind. We use a finger to probe a small bump on our face; we use our tongue to discover and remove the traces of food on our upper lip or on our teeth. We discriminate or assess our pain within the painful experience, not only after it has passed and we are, in that sense, beyond or outside it. Beyond these ordinary practices of somatic consciousness, a variety of meditative disciplines are structured on heightening the soma's conscious critical self-examination. Moreover, even beneath the level of explicit conscious awareness, the soma critically monitors and corrects itself unreflectively through entrenched motor schemas.

In short, somatic self-examination provides a model of immanent critique where one's critical perspective does not require being entirely outside the situation critically examined but merely requires a reflective perspective on it that is not wholly absorbed in the immediacy of what is experienced. Such a perspective is better described (through Helmuth Plessner's terms) as having a positionality that is "excentric" (or decentered) rather than external.[17] Such excentric perspectives can be achieved by efforts of disciplined willful attention, but they also often arise spontaneously through experiences of *somatic dissonance* where unreflective coordination is disrupted, thus stimulating a decentered, reflective critical attention to what is going on. Critical somatic consciousness involves some aspects of the soma's complex array of systems examining other aspects of that complexity. In the same way we can explain how individuals pervasively shaped by sociopolitical forces can develop critical sociopolitical consciousness through internal tensions or coordination breakdowns between diverse ideals embedded in the nation's social traditions and actual political practices. Like the individual human body, the political body of a society presents a comprehensive, cohesive, relatively stable system that integrates smaller systems that cohere but that also can function somewhat independently. The diverse functioning of its different parts or subsystems sometimes fails to integrate harmoniously, and this experienced dissonance can stimulate critical consciousness, an awareness that something is wrong. Some of that political dissonance can be experienced in distinctly somatic terms.

IV

A good example of this somatic reaction can be found in the experience of oppressive colonization that Franz Fanon described so powerfully in *The Wretched of the Earth*. Fanon's analysis also exemplifies how even extremely astute thinkers who recognize the somatic dimension of political experience nonetheless fail to explore it far enough to articulate a way of thoughtfully using this dimension to advance their political ends.[18] Fanon repeatedly characterizes the suffering of the colonized "native" subject in terms of perpetual muscle tension that comes from colonialism's repressing of the native's freedom and movement and from the native's self-repression in conforming to colonial dictates and stifling his anger and desire to strike out against the colonizing oppressors.

"The native's muscles are always tensed," writes Fanon, because he "is a being hemmed in; apartheid is simply one form of the division into compartments of the colonial world. The first thing which the native learns is to stay in his place, and not to go beyond certain limits. This is why the dreams of the native are always of muscular prowess; his dreams are of action and of aggression . . . he finds he is in a state of permanent tension" (*WE* 52). This intensified "tonicity of muscles the whole time" disturbs the thought processes and behavior of the colonized subjects, resulting in a variety of psychosomatic ailments that Fanon (as a trained psychiatrist) outlines at the end of the book. This chronic somatic reaction affects even the intellectual native's thinking and listening powers so that whenever

"Western values are mentioned they produce in the native a sort of stiffening or muscular lockjaw" (*WE* 43).

Rather than having the somaesthetic skills to create a calmer somatic state for carefully reflecting on their problems and possible solutions, the natives' heightened tension desperately seeks relief through some sort of explosive bodily experience whether in the outbursts of bloody violence or the ecstasy of frenzied dance. As Fanon describes it,

> The native's muscular tension finds outlet regularly in blood-thirsty explosions—in tribal warfare, in feuds between sects, and in quarrels between individuals. . . . Tribal feuds only serve to perpetuate old grudges buried deep in the memory. By throwing himself with all his force into the vendetta, the native tries to persuade himself that colonialism does not exist, that everything is going on as before, that history continues. Here on the level of communal organizations we clearly discern the well-known behavior patterns of avoidance. It is as if plunging into a frater-nal bloodbath allowed them to ignore the obstacle, and to put off till later the choice, nevertheless inevitable, which opens up the question of armed resistance to colonialism. Thus collective autodestruction in a very concrete form is one of the ways in which the native's muscular tension is set free. All these patterns of conduct are those of the death reflex when faced with danger, a suicidal behavior which proves to the settler (whose existence and domination is by them all the more justified) that these men are not reasonable human beings. (*WE* 54)

Besides its expression in such pernicious "fratricidal combats," the pent-up muscular tension of the native finds relief in "the emotional outlets of dance and possession by spirits" (*WE* 58). But these do not promote the rational search for promising political solutions to the natives' plight. The oppressed natives must develop and deploy a more acute and rational consciousness in order to achieve a better understanding of their political situation and possibilities so that they can unite and channel their energies of violence in a more productive way. Fanon's text suggests a sort of mind-body dualism in which the natives' consciousness lags behind their bodily power and their sense of "the strength of their own muscles," so that their actions are too often governed by "biological decision" (*WE* 127, 130).

Fanon therefore regards with suspicion any focus on sports as a tool of confidence building and national pride: "The youth of Africa ought not to be sent to sports stadiums but into the fields and into the schools," so they can learn the productive values of agricultural and intellectual work. "The African politician should not be preoccupied with turning out sportsmen, but with turning out fully conscious men, who play games as well" (*WE* 196).

Although Fanon's views are extremely insightful, somaesthetics would suggest a small corrective here. Sport is wrongly contrasted to being fully conscious, since success in sport surely requires a conscious knowledge of various rules, strategies, and tactics that govern the playing of games while also developing important rational skills of discipline and order that are needed for the regimes of training and competition. Sport also involves the rational and volitional skills of properly channeling one's energy and regulating one's emotions. More generally, a somaesthetic approach would not oppose soma and consciousness, since all our perception and thought (as well as all action) is done through the soma, the basic instrument, medium, or site of consciousness. A somaesthetic approach to the troubled somatic consciousness of colonized subjects would involve developing their reflective, critical awareness of their muscular tensions so that such tensions could be released in a controlled and measured way when they threaten to hamper important thought and action processes, but also, conversely, so that they could be intensified and channeled in a conscious, controlled way for more effective use when their explosive energy is needed in violent political struggles. Developing critical mastery over one's muscular tensions and other somatic habits does not mean turning oneself into a purely docile subject with no powerful emotions. We need strong, energizing affect as well as rationality for good political solutions; solidarity, for example, so important for political action (including political resistance) is not simply enhanced by strong bonds of feeling but is largely constituted by them.

Solidarity expresses the ideal of fraternal harmony, which in turn recalls the Chinese political notion of governing the state harmoniously by drawing on more basic ideas of personal and family harmony. In Confucian thought, the aesthetic value of harmony and grace is essential both to successful self-government and broader social government. One governs better through the aesthetics of harmony and attraction than through rigid rules, harsh commandments, and cruel punishments. The Confucian *Analects* underline this point: "The exemplary person (*junzi*) attracts friends through refinement (*wen*), and thereby promotes virtuous conduct (*ren*)."[19]

Admirable persons of authority spread virtue by attracting others to emulate their virtuous acts to become similarly attractive and admirable. Virtue thus includes an essential aesthetic dimension, and with a distinctively somaesthetic aspect. Appearances are essential for expressing the proper feelings of virtue—hence the Confucian emphasis that virtuous conduct must include "the proper countenance" or "demeanor," and that deeply embodied aesthetic practices such as ritual and music (including the recitation of the poetry) are crucial for cultivating this proper demeanor of virtue. Another ancient Chinese text likewise insists on the aesthetic value of harmonious unity for a good political state, where the state's unity ultimately derives from the attractive harmony of virtue radiating from its noblest citizens and ultimately from its king: "Where sageness, wisdom, ritual, and music are born is the harmonious combination. . . . Being unified you are musical. If there is music there is virtue[,] and a state and its families can arise. King Wen's appearance was like this."[20]

The ancient Chinese idea that somaesthetic attractiveness is important for leadership might seem quaintly outmoded and foreign to Western political thinking. But is it really? Think of how much money and effort is spent on choosing political candidates partly for their physical attractiveness and personability, and then how much more is further spent on finding ways to make them even more attractive to the voting public. It is foolish for philosophy to dismiss these considerations as trivial when their pragmatic effects are so significantly real. It is also wrong to condemn attractiveness as irrelevant to good leadership, even if it is certainly not sufficient for being an effective leader. We surely should condemn the worship of superficial, stereotypical beauty as a criterion for choosing political leaders, but that does not mean that an attractive style is not beneficial to good governing. Attractiveness (including the attractiveness of somatic style) is more than a matter of visual appearance, of having an appealing face and figure; it includes habits of action and styles of attractive conduct that in turn imply behavior that embodies admirable virtues. There is a substantial overlap of ethics and ethics that our compartmentalizing modernist logic often obscures but that the Greek notion of *kalon-kai-agathon* (the beautiful and good) and the ancient Confucian notion of the five virtues as "five beauties" usefully highlight.[21] We speak morally of things being "right," "just," "fair," "fitting," or "appropriate," but all of these terms have clear aesthetic connotations.

"Harmony" is another word with tonalities that extend from aesthetics to ethics to politics. It is an important value for pragmatist aesthetics and somaesthetics, but it should not be erected as a supremely overriding value.

Some harmonies may be experienced as forced and unhappily stifling, as something that suppresses or neutralizes difference and dissent. (Contemporary Chinese Internet slang indeed uses the expression "to be harmonized" in order to indicate being neutralized or forced into conformity.) Sometimes a dose of dissonance usefully adds a tonic note of freedom, openness, and change that is both aesthetically and politically positive and promising. One reason my 1992 book *Pragmatist Aesthetics* took "knowledge rap" as its exemplar for an embodied, progressive, and politically engaged popular art was rap's astute recovery of the positive aesthetic and political values of dissonance—reflected both in its aggressive musical style deploying various techniques of fragmentation and in its defiant political attitude. This choice of rap also helped distance my pragmatist theory from Dewey's inspiring aesthetic whose celebration of unity seemed too one-sided and not sufficiently nuanced and contemporary. His praise of art as "a remaking of the experience of the community in the direction of greater order and unity" and his celebration of "the power of music in particular to merge different individualities in a common surrender, loyalty, and inspiration" could easily suggest the aesthetic designs of the fascist state.[22] Our aesthetic appreciation of social and political harmonies should always be alert to hear discordant voices that are being muffled or excluded from expression.

From our study of Fanon, we have argued that the somaesthetic dissonance, discomfort, or disharmony expressed in muscle tension could be useful if it were channeled toward political resistance to oppression rather than wasted on "fratricidal combat." Such discomforting tension and feelings of disharmony can be better directed and deployed when we have a more perspicuous and critically reflective awareness of them. Pragmatic somaesthetic disciplines of body consciousness can provide us that superior awareness and control (where control does not mean simply suppression). To promote such aims of heightening somatic awareness in my practical somaesthetic workshops, I make a point of introducing feelings of disharmony, usually by disrupting—in a safely gentle way, for a brief period, and in a protected environment—our normal sense of bilateral equilibrium. Introducing such disharmonies is cognitively useful for developing a person's perceptual discriminations of differences in one's body feelings and a clearer recognition of one's normal feelings of equilibrium. In making us appreciatively aware of the lost harmony of equilibrium, it stimulates the cognitively creative challenge to regain that equilibrium or find a new, perhaps better, harmonious balance.

In addition, a more penetrating awareness of somatic dissonance and harmony in oneself can easily translate into more careful and caring appreciation of these feelings in others, because we humans, as essentially social creatures, have fundamental capacities for empathy. Perceptive somaesthetic self-awareness is always an awareness that goes beyond the self. We can never feel the body alone, we always feel it with its environment (physical or social). If you close your eyes to focus on feeling only your body itself, you will also feel the seat, bed, floor, or sandy beach on which you are resting. Through similar dialectics of self and other, the cultivation of somaesthetic awareness (by helping us to identify our own oppressive attitudes and habits) can transform our subjective sensibilities and socially relevant actions, which then can better engage the somatic subjectivities of other agents and consequently translate into broader social and political reform.

As Herbert Marcuse remarks, it is a superficial "vulgar Marxism" that rejects the powers "of the individual consciousness and subconscious" for political liberation, failing to see that "the need for radical change must be rooted in the subjectivity of individuals themselves, in their intelligence and their passions, their drives and their goals."[23] What we most need, he claims, is to develop a new sensibility that is far more appreciative of the pleasure principle and oriented toward freedom:

> Before being able to build and live in a truly free society among equals, man must free himself from his own repressed and distorted humanity, and this liberation begins where we experience most directly and most immediately our world, namely, with our senses, with our sensibility. This is the concrete link between aesthetics and the practice of social change—the need not only for a new consciousness, not only for a new theory, but for a new sensibility, for new ways and modes of perception in man himself.[24]

Because my pragmatism emphasized aesthetic pleasures and their emancipatory powers both for the individual and society, its politics was described as suggesting "a *con-sensualist* society rather than a merely consensual one," a society whose democratic ideal is to afford more egalitarian access to "pleasurable activities."[25]

Some philosophers have therefore connected my aesthetics with the liberational politics of Marcuse, especially after my extensive study of eroticism.[26] One key difference, however, is that Marcuse locates aesthetics' emancipatory potential narrowly in high culture's fine art with its aesthetic form and fictionality that serve "the critical, negating function" of protesting current social reality (*AD* 7), whereas *Pragmatist Aesthetics* also celebrates popular art genres such as "knowledge rap" for their emancipatory role in personal subjectivity and sociocultural praxis. In contrast, Marcuse rejects the very idea of a politically engaged popular art as "spurious art," because it tries to violate what he regards as "the essential tension between art and praxis," the fact that "art cannot translate its vision into reality" because its critical power rests precisely in its distance from reality (*AD* 36,57; JL 164). A second key difference is that my project of transforming our sensibilities and modes of perception to promote social change includes the crucial role of somaesthetics for providing positive practical means of transforming our sensibilities—our senses, feelings, desires, attitudes, and habits—by working directly on their essential somatic site and medium. In contrast, Marcuse's liberational program is limited to working indirectly through art's fictional forms and critical negations of the real rather than on real bodies with their powers of perception and performance.[27]

Somaesthetics therefore offers a more robust and multifaceted way of enlisting the sensory dimension to promote both personal emancipation and broader social reform. The idea that the transfiguring liberation of the individual's senses and sensibility is key to sociopolitical transformation goes back to the early Karl Marx. Lamenting that private property has diminished the rich potential of our senses by subjugating them all to "the sense of having," he claimed, "The transcendence of private property is therefore the complete *emancipation* of all human senses and attributes; but it is this emancipation precisely because these senses and attributes have become, subjectively and objectively, *human*" and social.[28] For Marx, what makes our experience and conduct human and social is not that they are done in the company of others but that they have "lost their *egotistical* nature" by expressing and promoting "the richness of subjective *human* sensibility" and aiming to produce human beings "as profoundly endowed with all the senses" (*PPC* 109). For Marx, as for somaesthetics, one's cultivated sensory consciousness is not merely perceptive but also critical and reflective, and in this sense theoretical. He speaks of socialism providing us with a sensuous "positive self-consciousness" whose "senses have therefore become directly in their practice *theoreticians*" (*PPC* 107, 113).

Somaesthetics echoes Marx in rejecting the presumed dichotomy between individual and social existence. "What is to be avoided above all is the re-establishing [fixating, *fixieren*] of 'Society' as an abstraction *vis-à-vis* the individual. The individual *is the social being*" (*PPC* 105). "Social activity" therefore is not "only in the form of some *directly* communal activity." Marx claims: "My *own* existence *is* social activity, and therefore that which I make of myself, I make of myself for society and with the consciousness of myself as a social being" (*PPC* 105). Somaesthetic working on oneself is not intrinsically egotistical but rather the product of socially shaped desires and is most properly directed by melioristic social aims. Somaesthetics further follows Marx (but also pragmatism) in affirming the primacy of practice. Philosophical problems (including abstract ones such as reconciling the oppositions of "subjectivity and objectivity, spirituality and materiality, activity and suffering") find their real solution not through pure theory but through changes of practice that theory can suggest but not accomplish in itself. For Marx, as for somaesthetics, "the resolution of the *theoretical* antitheses is *only* possible *in a practical* way. . . . Their resolution is therefore by no means merely a problem of knowledge, but a *real* problem of life, which *philosophy* could not solve precisely because it conceived this problem as *merely* a theoretical one" (*PPC* 109).

In explaining that an individual's practical work of improving her somatic consciousness and enriching her sensibility should not be considered a private, selfish pursuit but instead constitutes an essential tool for social liberation, Marx is one of the great thinkers who anticipated somaesthetics and led me to describe it as a new *name* for some old ways of thinking. However, he never focused his attention on specific techniques of critically reflective somatic practice for cultivating our critical sensory capacities and reeducating our sensibilities in the ways that somaesthetics endeavors to do and continues to promote. I therefore hope that somaesthetics still has something more to offer, for personal and political life, than merely its name.

Notes

Preface

1. Richard Shusterman, "What Pragmatism Means to Me: Ten Principles," *Revue Française d'Études Américaines* 124 (2010): 59–65; "Thought in the Strenuous Mood: Pragmatism as a Philosophy of Feeling," *New Literary History* 43, no. 3 (2012): 433–54; "Affective Cognition: From Pragmatism to Somaesthetics," *Intellectica* 60, no. 2 (2013): 49–68, and chap. 4 here; *Act and Affect: Paths of Pragmatism* (in Chinese), ed. and trans. Gao Yanping (Shanghai: The Commercial Press, 2018): 《情感与行动: 实用主义之道》, 商务印书馆 2018年8月.

2. Richard Shusterman, *The Adventures of the Man in Gold / Les Aventures de l'homme en or*, trans. Thomas Mondemé (Paris: Hermann Editions, 2016), with images from Yann Toma. For philosophical interpretations of this work, see the six chapters about it in Jerold J. Abrams, ed., *Shusterman's Somaesthetics: From Hip Hop Philosophy to Politics and Performance Art* (Boston: Brill, 2022), 125–240; and the published discussions collected on my chair's website at Florida Atlantic University, Dorothy F. Schmidt College of Arts and Letters, "The Adventures of the Main in Gold," https://www.fau.edu/artsandletters/humanitieschair/books/man-in-gold/man-in-gold-reviews/.

Introduction

1. "Regarding Oneself and Seeing Double," in *The Philosophical I: Personal Reflections on Life in Philosophy*, ed. George Yancy (New York: Rowman and Littlefield, 2002), 5–6.

2. Richard Shusterman, *Pragmatist Aesthetics: Living Beauty, Rethinking Art* (Oxford: Blackwell, 1992), 6.

3. In *Practicing Philosophy: Pragmatism and the Philosophical Life* (London: Routledge, 1997), 177.

4. Shusterman provides a provocative sketch of his ontological position in "What Pragmatism Means to Me: Ten Principles," *Revue Française d'Études Américaines*

124 (2010): 59–65. He goes into greater depth on the ontology of the soma in *Body Consciousness: A Philosophy of Mindfulness and Somaesthetics* (Cambridge: Cambridge University Press, 2008); "Soma and Psyche," *Journal of Speculative Philosophy* 24, no. 3 (2010): 205–23; and "Somaesthetics in Context," *Kinesiology Review* 9, no. 3 (2020): 245–53.

Chapter One

1. In an earlier version of this chapter I was tempted, by alliteration, to describe this position as "hermeneutic holism" (see "Beneath Interpretation, Against Hermeneutic Holism," *Monist* 73 [1990]: 181–204). Though the term "hermeneutic universalism" is longer and more plodding, it has the advantage of more clearly distinguishing the position I attack from another position that the term "hermeneutic holism" might suggest. This second view maintains that the meaning of a word or statement, or the justification of a knowledge claim, is not an affair of simple atomistic reference to foundational objects or atomistic correspondence to privileged representations but instead always depends on a larger context of words, statements, beliefs, and a whole background of social practice, and one that is not immune to change. The nonfoundationalist pragmatism I advocate is not at all opposed to this second sense of interpretive holism; what I challenge is the idea that interpretation constitutes the whole of understanding and meaningful experience. Since several readers found the term "hermeneutic holism" confusingly ambiguous with respect to these issues, it is here replaced "hermeneutic universalism" or occasionally "universal hermeneutics."

2. Friedrich Nietzsche, *The Will to Power* (New York: Vintage Press, 1968), para. 481.

3. See Alexander Nehamas, *Nietzsche: Life as Literature* (Cambridge, Mass.: Harvard University Press, 1985; hereafter cited as *N*. In challenging my own view of aesthetic experience, Nehamas, however, makes very strong demands on what can count as an interpretation of art. See his article "Richard Shusterman on Pleasure and Aesthetic Experience," *Journal of Aesthetics and Art Criticism* 56 (1998): 49–51; and my response in the same issue, "Interpretation, Pleasure, and Value in Aesthetic Experience," 51–53.

4. Stanley Fish, *Is There a Text in This Class?: The Authority of Interpretive Communities* (Cambridge, Mass.: Harvard University Press, 1980), 350, 352.

5. Stanley Fish, "Working on the Chain Gang: Interpretation in the Law and in Literary Criticism," *Critical Inquiry* 9 (1982): 204.

6. Hans-Georg Gadamer, *Truth and Method* (New York: Crossroad, 1982), 350; hereafter cited as *TM*.

7. Susan Sontag, "Against Interpretation," in *Against Interpretation and Other Essays* (New York: Dell, 1966); hereafter cited as AI.

8. Arthur Danto, *The Philosophical Disenfanchisement of Art* (New York: Columbia University Press, 1986), 45.

9. See Nietzsche, *Will to Power*, paras. 556, 557, 559, 560. I examine Nietzsche's alternative account of objects (viz., as interpreted unities) in "Nietzsche and Nehamas on Organic Unity," *Southern Journal of Philosophy* 26 (1988): 379–92.

10. I discuss the intellectual demands and social preconditions of formalist appreciation in "Of the Scandal of Taste: Social Privilege as Nature in the Aesthetic Theories of Hume and Kant," in *Eighteenth-Century Aesthetics and the Reconstruction of Art*, ed. Paul Mattick, 96–119 (Cambridge: Cambridge University Press, 1993). Pierre Bourdieu's empirical treatment of this topic of form, intellect, and social class with respect to aesthetic appreciation in his *Distinction: A Social Critique of the Judgement of Taste* (Cambridge, Mass.: Harvard University Press, 1984) is very illuminating. However, I reject his radical conclusion that the presence and appreciation of form cannot be found in popular art. See my discussion in "Form and Funk: The Aesthetic Challenge of Popular Art," in *Pragmatist Aesthetics: Living Beauty, Rethinking Art* (Oxford: Blackwell, 1992), chap. 7.

11. T. S. Eliot, "Hamlet," in *Selected Essays* (London: Faber, 1976), 142, and his introduction to G. W. Knight, *The Wheel of Fire* (London: Methuen, 1962), xix. For a detailed account of the arguments motivating Eliot's hermeneutic turn with a critical analysis of his mature theory of interpretation, see my *T. S. Eliot and the Philosophy of Criticism* (New York: Columbia University Press, 1988),107–55.

12. I have elsewhere suggested that in pragmatic terms we can have complete (albeit perspectival) understanding and that only in pragmatic, contextual terms is the idea of complete understanding at all intelligible. The idea of completeness always presupposes a particular and limited context or purpose of fulfillment, so the foundationalist idea of completeness in and for itself, without aspects or horizons or purpose, is simply a meaningless notion, not a regrettably unreachable ideal. For more on this, see my *T. S. Eliot and the Philosophy of Criticism,* 126–28. A radical break with foundationalism would also allow us to regard things themselves (in the nonfoundational sense of objects we experience) as perspectival. The keyboard I press is (and is not simply interpreted as) a writing tool, though I can also treat it as a paperweight or a book prop. For more detailed discussion of the problematic (but still functional) distinction between description and interpretation in literary criticism, see *Pragmatist Aesthetics*, chap. 4.

13. John Dewey, *Experience and Nature* (La Salle, Ill.: Open Court, 1929), 21–24.

14. See Dewey's remark that "primary non-reflectional experience . . . has its own organization of a direct, non-logical character" in John Dewey, *Essays in Experimental Logic* (Chicago: University of Chicago Press, 1916), 6.

15. Of course, the hermeneutic universalists would contest such a view of standard usage and insist that even unconscious actions and immediate perceptions must be interpretive, and that they may be so described without gross violation

of diction. My point is that the universalists give no compelling reason to extend the use of interpretation this way, and that in recommending linguistic revision or the denial of a useful distinction, the burden of proof lies heavily with them. The appeal of their case rests on the view that uninterpreted understanding is impossible because it must be conceived foundationally.

16. Ludwig Wittgenstein, *Philosophical Investigations* (Oxford: Blackwell, 1968), 212. Wittgenstein quickly goes on to specify the sort of thinking we do in interpretation: "When we interpret we form hypotheses, which may prove false" (p. 212).

17. Donald Davidson, "Radical Interpretation" and "The Very Idea of a Conceptual Scheme," in *Inquiries into Truth and Interpretation* (Oxford: Oxford University Press, 1984), 125, 185.

18. Hans-Georg Gadamer, "On the Scope and Function of Hermeneutical Reflection," in *Philosophical Hermeneutics* (Berkeley: University of California Press, 1989), 19, 32. Gadamer, however, does not always seem perfectly consistent on this last matter. At one point in *Truth and Method* he speaks of an "understanding of language" that "is not yet of itself a real understanding and does not include an interpretive process but it is an accomplishment of life. For you understand a language by living in it" (346). Could Gadamer here be acknowledging, albeit in a rather odd and contorted manner, my point that interpretation does not go all the way down but always relies on some more primitive linguistic understanding?

19. See, for example, Ludwig Wittgenstein, *Zettel* (Oxford: Blackwell, 1967), para. 419, and *Philosophical Investigations,* paras. 4–6, 9, 86.

20. See Dewey, *Essays in Experimental Logic,* 4, 6, 9.

21. Moreover, there is good evidence that many linguistic structures (including some of our more abstract logical principles) seem to be shaped by more basic preconceptual and prelinguistic patterns of bodily experience. See Mark Johnson, *The Body in the Mind* (Chicago: University of Chicago Press, 1987).

22. But such uninterpreted experiences and understandings, can, of course, also be found in our professional activities, as underlying more deliberative, reflective thought.

23. See John Lyons, *Semantics,* vol. 1 (Cambridge: Cambridge University Press, 1977), 33–50.

24. Martin Heidegger, *Being and Time* (New York: Harper and Row, 1962), 194.

25. Wittgenstein, *Philosophical Investigations,* paras. 198, 201.

26. The same can be said for another problematic distinction that much contemporary philosophy seems bent on confusing and then denying—the conventional versus the natural. Convention is always more superficial than the natural which grounds it; but what we regard in one context as conventional in contrast to its more natural background can itself be regarded as natural in relation to something still more superficial or artificial. For more detailed argument of this thesis, see Richard Shusterman, "Convention: Variations on a Theme," *Philosophical Investigations* 9 (1986): 36–55.

27. This is one reason why my rehabilitation of uninterpreted understanding should not be seen as a resurrection of what Sellars called "the myth of the given." See Wilfred Sellars, "Empiricism and the Philosophy of Mind," in *Science, Perception and Reality* (New York: Routledge & Kegan Paul, 1963), 127–63; and Richard Rorty's supportive elaboration in *Philosophy and the Mirror of Nature* (Princeton: Princeton University Press, 1979), 182–92. I agree with Sellars and Rorty that any understanding which functions as epistemological grounding for another understanding must always exist within "the logical space of reasons" and hence be conceptual. But I maintain, first, that such conceptual understandings can still be immediately (though not apodictically) given; they need not be interpretations. Second, I would hold that nonconceptual, nondiscursive experiences (though they be beneath the logical space of reasons) may nonetheless be meaningful and constitute a form of understanding. Finally, though I agree with Sellars and Rorty that such experiences cannot provide epistemological grounding or justification for further understanding unless they get conceptualized, they can still provide the practical ground and orienting background for such understanding.

In other words, I am urging recognition of a category of embodied, experienced practice that grounds and guides intelligent activity but that is neither at the discursive and epistemological level of the logical space of reasons nor simply reducible to the physical conditions and causes described by natural science. Nor should this category be seen as *epistemologically* grounding the categories of reasons and physical causes. Sellars and Rorty are surely right not to confuse logical reasons with physical causes, but their regarding the two as constituting an exhaustive dichotomy seems an unnecessary limitation on understanding human experience and an unfortunate vestige of Cartesianism, with its rigid and exhaustive dualism of mind and body, thought and physical extension. These points are developed in greater detail in my *Practicing Philosophy: Pragmatism and the Philosophical Life* (New York: Routledge, 1997), chap. 6; cf. chapter 2 of this volume.

28. Wittgenstein, *Zettel*, para. 234. The imagery of this remark makes me hazard the suggestion that we are today so preoccupied with interpretation largely because we so rarely feel comfortably at home in the often-conflicting worlds of our understanding, that our age is an age of interpretation because it is one of alienation and fragmentation. We need not mourn this nostalgically as the loss of unity and certainty but can rather recognize it as the price of our greater freedom and pluralistic possibilities.

29. See Stanley Fish, "No Bias, No Merit: The Case Against Blind Submission," *PMLA* 103 (1988): 739; "Working on the Chain Gang," 211; "Profession Despise Thyself: Fear and Self Loathing in Literary Studies," *Critical Inquiry* 10, no. 2 (1983): 349–64; and "Change," *South Atlantic Quarterly* 86, no. 4 (1987): 423–44.

30. In glossing Heidegger's notions of "circumspection" and the "ready-to-hand," Hubert Dreyfus aptly describes this smoothly coordinated understanding as "everyday skillful coping" or "absorbed coping." See Dreyfus, *Being-in-the-World: A*

Commentary on Being and Time, Division I (Cambridge, Mass.: MIT Press, 1991), chap. 4. The idea is also central to Dewey's concept of unreflective intelligent behavior versus conscious inquiry. See, for example, John Dewey, "The Practical Character of Reality" and "The Unit of Behavior," in *Philosophy and Civilization* (New York: Capricorn, 1963), 36–55, 233–48.

31. It might seem that artistic interpretation, i.e., interpretive performance, would constitute a refutation of this claim, since Rubinstein's interpretation of Beethoven's *Moonlight Sonata* is not a linguistic text. One need not meet this objection by arguing that "interpretation" is here used in a different, derivative sense. For again we have the translation of one articulated text (the score) into another articulated form (the actual musical performance), and the criterion for having an artistic interpretation is expressing it in such an articulated performance or in explicit instructions for one.

32. Ludwig Wittgenstein, *Tractatus Logico-Philosophicus* (London: Routledge & Kegan Paul, 1961), 6.522 (I depart from the translation of David Pears and Brian McGuinness by more simply rendering *zeigt* as "show" rather than "make manifest" and translating *das Mystiche* as "the mystical" rather than "what is mystical"). I examine Wittgenstein's relation to the nonlinguistic and the somatic in *Practicing Philosophy*, chap. 1.

Chapter Two

1. See Richard Rorty, "Dewey Between Hegel and Darwin," in *Modernist Impulses in the Human Sciences, 1870–1930*, ed. Dorothy Ross (Baltimore: Johns Hopkins University Press, 1994), 60, henceforth referred to as DHD; and also "Dewey's Metaphysics" in *Consequences of Pragmatism* (Minneapolis: University of Minnesota Press, 1982), henceforth cited as DM. Dewey's second thoughts about the efficacy of the term "experience" are forcefully expressed in a letter to Arthur Bentley, when he considered the idea of changing the title and content of a new edition of *Experience and Nature*, by substituting the term "culture" for "experience." In the end, however, Dewey refused to renounce the notion of experience—as the unfinished revisions for the new edition make clear: "We need a cautionary and directive word, like experience, to remind us that the world which is lived, suffered and enjoyed, as well as logically thought of, has the last word in all human inquiries and surmises." See *John Dewey and Arthur Bentley, A Philosophical Correspondence, 1932–1951* (New Brunswick: Rutgers University Press, 1964), 643; and "Appendix 2" (1951) to John Dewey, *Experience and Nature* (1925, rev. ed. 1929) (Carbondale: Southern Illinois University Press, 1981), 372, henceforth cited as *EN*.

2. Rorty underlines this point in his *Objectivity, Relativism, and Truth* (Cambridge: Cambridge University Press, 1991), 16–17.

3. Dewey writes of such immediate experiences that we "*have* them, but . . . do not know [we] have them" (*EN* 198). Moreover, in the following paragraph

Dewey goes on to deny the empiricist idea of immediate nondiscursive knowledge: "The notion that sensory affections discriminate themselves, apart from discourse, as being colors and sounds, etc., and thus ipso facto constitute certain elementary modes of knowledge, even though it be only knowledge of their own existence, is inherently so absurd that it would never have occurred to any one to entertain it, were it not for certain preconceptions about mind and knowledge" (*EN* 199).

4. Ludwig Wittgenstein, *Philosophical Investigations*, 3rd ed. (Oxford: Black-well, 1968), part 1: paras. 190, 197, 217, 485, 654; part 2: pp. 208, 226.

5. John Dewey, "Qualitative Thought," repr. in *Philosophy and Civilization* (New York: G. P. Putnam's Sons, 1931), 93–116, cited as Q; and *Logic: The Theory of Inquiry* (1938) (Carbondale: Southern Illinois University Press, 1986), cited as *L*.

6. "Confusion and incoherence are always marks of lack of control by a single pervasive quality. . . . The underlying unity of qualitativeness regulates pertinence or relevancy and force of every distinction and relation; it guides selection and rejection and the manner of utilization of all explicit terms. . . . For the latter are *its* distinctions and relations" (Q 98–99).

7. Dewey later adds: "Were not the sequence [of inquiry] determined by an inclusive situation, whose qualitative nature pervades and holds together each successive step, activity would be a meaningless hop-skip-jump affair" (*L* 126).

8. Such unity is largely prospective, an impulse or aim of coordinated action. See John Dewey, *Human Nature and Conduct* (1922) (Carbondale: Southern Illinois University Press, 1983), chaps. 2 and 4, cited as *HNC*.

9. For Dewey, "habits are abilities" that provide the initial, prereflective structure for "all the perceiving, recognizing, imagining, recalling, judging" we perform, while the "selective-restriction" that determines more specific situational subjects or elements is "made for a definite purpose" (*HNC* 47,121,124; *L* 131).

10. John Dewey and James H. Tufts, *Ethics* (1932) (Carbondale: Southern Illinois University Press, 1985), 185.

11. This point, of course, has been emphasized by Merleau-Ponty. His account of the lived body as the experiential unifying ground of perception has many similarities to Dewey's use of the unifying ground of felt quality; and it could be vulnerable to similar criticisms. There is no space to pursue this here, nor to pursue what I think is a more important criticism: Merleau-Ponty's lack of attention to the project of how to *improve* this experience rather than simply describe it as it is and show its philosophical importance. This suggests a basic difference between phenomenology and pragmatism as I conceive it. For a detailed critique of this issue in Merleau-Ponty, see my *Body Consciousness: A Philosophy of Mindfulness and Somaesthetics* (Cambridge: Cambridge University Press, 2008), chap. 2.

12. Rejecting dualism to embrace an emergent naturalism, Dewey and I share the view that all experience, even abstract thinking, is body-dependent, just as our bodily functioning is often influenced by thought. Body and mind are functional distinctions of an organic whole Dewey called "body-mind" (*EN* 191). My ensuing emphasis on the *soma* should not therefore be taken as implying a new

inverted dualism. Nor is the notion of nondiscursive quality limited to the somatic disciplines I later cite. Nondiscursive quality plays a wide-ranging role in everyone's everyday understanding and praxis. Though insisting that everyday experience is not an intrinsically inferior realm, pragmatism still advocates that it can be improved through intelligent means. Somatic disciplines claim to provide such means and therefore warrant pragmatist consideration.

13. Robert Westbrook's landmark biography mentions Alexander only once in a footnote; and even there he is mentioned not in terms of his own work or relationship to Dewey but only as an "occasion" for a polemical exchange between Dewey and Randolph Bourne. See Robert Westbrook, *John Dewey and American Democracy* (Ithaca: Cornell University Press, 1991), 221n26. Alan Ryan gives Alexander a rather dismissive short paragraph in his *John Dewey and the High Tide of American Liberalism* (New York: Norton, 1995), 187–88. This neglect is sadly the norm in Dewey studies. But there is a longer discussion of Alexander's influence on Dewey in Steven Rockefeller, *John Dewey: Religious Faith and Democratic Humanism* (New York: Columbia University Press, 1991), 333–44. For a deeper account of Dewey's relations with Alexander and of the scientific evidence for Alexander's theories, see F. P. Jones, *Body Awareness in Action: A Study of the Alexander Technique* (New York: Schocken, 1979). For a philosophical analysis of the Alexander Technique, see chapter 8 ("The Somatic Turn") in my *Performing Live* (Ithaca: Cornell University Press, 2000), and chapter 6 ("Redeeming Somatic Reflection") in *Body Consciousness*.

14. John Dewey, introduction to *Constructive Conscious Control of the Individual*, by F. Matthias Alexander (New York: Dutton, 1923), reprinted in John Dewey, *The Middle Works of John Dewey*, vol. 15 (Carbondale: Southern Illinois University Press, 1983), 313.

15. John Dewey, "Reply to Reviewer" (1918), in *The Middle Works of John Dewey*, vol. 11 (Carbondale: Southern Illinois University Press, 1982), 354, cited as RR. Dewey is replying to Randolph Bourne's review of F. Matthias Alexander, *Man's Supreme Inheritance* (New York: Dutton, 1918), cited as *MSI*. The same volume also contains Dewey's "Introductory Word" to Alexander's book, cited as IMSI. Dewey also wrote an "Introduction" to a third book by Alexander, *The Use of the Self* (New York: Dutton, 1932), reprinted in Dewey, *The Later Works of John Dewey*, vol. 6 (Carbondale: Southern Illinois University Press, 1985), 315–20, in which Dewey describes his long experience as a pupil of Alexander.

16. This is reflected in the title of Alexander's book *Constructive Conscious Control of the Individual*. Dewey also advocates Alexander's idea of "conscious control" in *Experience and Nature* (*EN* 225).

17. The question of what exactly qualifies as "conscious" is a complex problem that I should raise but cannot answer here. In describing certain habits or experiences as unconscious, I mean here simply that they are not thematized objects of consciousness or objects of reflection. I am not implying that we are unconscious when they

occur, nor that they are not in some way mentally processed or grasped. John Searle, for example, argues that such unthematized events or objects in sentient experience are conscious, though they are not objects of attention. He thinks that "we need to distinguish the conscious/unconscious distinction from the center of attention/ periphery distinction." See John Searle, *The Rediscovery of the Mind* (Cambridge, Mass.: MIT Press, 1992), 138. Certainly, we need to distinguish different levels of attention, if we do not distinguish different levels or degrees of consciousness. But the point I am making about the unappreciated somatic background can be made just as easily in terms of the "unattended" as the "unconscious." I explain four levels of consciousness in *Body Consciousness*, 54–56.

18. Rorty's argument against using the concept of "experience" for ontological and epistemological matters of continuity is as follows: "The problem with this way of obtaining continuity between us and the brutes is that it seems to shove the philosophically embarrassing discontinuity back down to the gap between, say viruses and amoeba. . . . Only by giving something like experience to protein molecules, and perhaps eventually to quarks—only a full-fledged panpsychism—will span this gap. But when we invoke panpsychism to bridge the gap between experience and nature, we begin to feel something has gone wrong. For notions like 'experience,' 'consciousness,' and 'thought' were originally invoked to *contrast* something which varied independently of nature with nature itself. The philosophically interesting sense—the only sense relevant to epistemology—of experience . . . [applies] to a realm which might well be 'out of touch' with nature because it might vary when nature remained the same, and remain the same when nature varied" (DHD 58–59).

I doubt that our notions of experience, consciousness, and thought were first invoked for philosophical purposes of epistemological contrast with nature rather than for more practical functions of interacting with it. I also question Rorty's narrow identification of "the philosophically interesting sense" of "experience" with its traditional epistemological use of contrast to reality. There are other interesting senses to which Dewey's philosophy of experience is, in fact, directed (e.g., aesthetic and ethical). For an account of Dewey's aesthetic use of the concept of experience, see Richard Shusterman, *Pragmatist Aesthetics* (Oxford: Blackwell, 1992), 25–33, 46–59.

19. The quote is taken from *Collected Papers of Charles Sanders Peirce*, vol. 5 (Cambridge, Mass.: Harvard University Press, 1934), para. 314.

20. In *Dialectic of Enlightenment* (New York: Continuum, 1986, 234), Horkheimer and Adorno savage the idea of "remaking the body into a noble object," and Susan Bordo's *Unbearable Weight: Feminism, Western Culture, and the Body* (Berkeley: University of California Press, 1993) provides useful critiques of today's ideals and ideologies of somatic plasticity. Her work is heavily shaped by Foucault, as is Judith Butler's influential work on the body, which emphasizes the body's plasticity but concentrates on gender and the body's discursive nature. See *Gender Trouble: Feminism and the Subversion of Identity* (New York: Routledge, 1990), and *Bodies that Matter: On the Discursive Limits of "Sex"* (New York: Routledge, 1993).

Foucault's somatic philosophy is richly complex and ambivalent. Though critical of society's use of "biopower" to normalize and subjugate the subject, he also urged the emancipatory potential of powerful somatic experiences to break through society's repressive discursive regimes. For a detailed study of the relationship between Foucault's embodied philosophy and pragmatist somaesthetics, see *Foucault's Aesthetics of Existence and Shusterman's Somaesthetics: Ethics, Politics, and the Art of Living*, ed. Valentina Antoniol and Stefano Marino (London: Bloomsbury, 2024).

21. Richard Rorty, *Philosophy and the Mirror of Nature* (Princeton: Princeton University Press, 1980), 183, cited as *PMN*.

22. See Richard Rorty, *Contingency, Irony, and Solidarity* (Cambridge: Cambridge University Press, 1989), cited as *CIS*, where Rorty argues that the privileged use of language is not to represent or justify something already there, but to cause something different, "to make something that never had been dreamed of before" (*CIS* 13).

23. Wilfred Sellars, *Science, Perception, and Reality* (London: Routledge & Kegan Paul, 1963), 60; Hans-Georg Gadamer, *Philosophical Hermeneutics* (Berkeley: University of California Press, 1976), 19; Rorty, *CIS* 88; Jacques Derrida, *Of Grammatology* (Baltimore: Johns Hopkins University Press, 1976), 158. I provide a more detailed critique of these textualists in "Beneath Interpretation," chap. 1 of this volume.

24. See Richard Rorty, "Introduction: Pragmatism and Philosophy," in *Consequences of Pragmatism*, xix. The other citation in this paragraph is from another chapter of that book, "Nineteenth Century Idealism and Twentieth Century Textualism," 140.

25. Despite its dominant trend to deprecate the body, Christianity included thinkers and sects who saw the body—despite its material inferiority and even because of it—as a central tool to achieve greater spirituality, notably through somatic asceticism. Jesus, after all, needed incarnation to go through the passion of crucifixion. Origen, in the third century, urges this ascetic route to making the body into a "temple to the Lord" with the following metaphorical injunction: "You have coals of fire, you will sit upon them, and they will be of help to you." For more on this topic, see Peter Brown, *The Body and Society: Men, Women, and Sexual Renunciation in Early Christianity* (New York: Columbia University Press, 1988), citations from 165, 175.

26. This tradition can be traced from Democritus, Epicurus, and Lucretius to Hobbes, La Mettrie, Marx, and into our own century. Despite the influence of these thinkers, they obviously do not constitute the core of academic philosophy. Hobbes and Marx are, of course, more central, but this is mainly because of their influential political philosophy, not their materialist metaphysics.

27. Rorty opposes what he calls my "somatic aesthetics" for its commitment to philosophical concern for the nondiscursive. See Richard Rorty, "Response to

Richard Shusterman," in *Richard Rorty: Critical Dialogues*, ed. M. Festenstein and S. Thompson (Cambridge: Polity Press, 2001), 153–57.

28. Daniel Stern, *The Interpersonal World of the Infant* (New York: Basic Books, 1985).

29. I take up this project by studying the techniques and ideologies of three popular body practices (Alexander Technique, Feldenkrais Method, and bioenergetics) and examining our culture's growing concern with somatic techniques of self-transformation. See chapter 8 of *Performing Live*, "The Somatic Turn: Care of the Body in Contemporary Culture."

30. See Henry David Thoreau, *Walden*, chap. 1 ("Economy"), in *The Portable Thoreau* (New York: Viking, 1964), 270; and R. W. Emerson, "Experience," in *Essays* (London: Everyman, 1942), 236. Thoreau insists that man's "mind descend into his body to redeem it" (469).

31. See Michel Foucault, *The Courage of Truth* (New York: Palgrave Macmillan 2011), 265.

32. For my critical analysis of Foucault's somatic philosophy with its focus on limit-experiences, see *Body Consciousness*, chap. 1; "Somaesthetics and the Philosophical Life," in *Foucault's Aesthetics of Existence and Shusterman's Somaesthetics*, 121–43; and "Foucault and Somaesthetics," *Foucault Studies* 36 (2024): 142–69, https://doi.org/10.22439/fs.i36.7233

Chapter Three

1. This emphasis on unity as a foundation or criterion of aesthetic value is evident in G. E. Moore, Harold Osborne, I. A. Richards, Monroe Beardsley, and the New Criticism but is equally central to Dewey's aesthetics, which speaks of the work of art as an "organism" so "unified" that its "different elements and specific qualities . . . blend and fuse in a way which physical things cannot emulate" in *Art as Experience* (Carbondale: Southern Illinois University Press, 1987), 196. For its presence in see G. E. Moore, see his *Principia Ethica* (Cambridge: Cambridge University Press, 1959), 27–30, 189–208, cited as *PE*. Harold Osborne treats organic unity as the defining characteristic of beauty and works of art—"A work of art is an organic whole of interlocking organic wholes"—in *The Theory of Beauty* (London: Routledge & Kegan Paul, 1952), 203. I. A. Richards defines the aesthetic experience with which he identifies the work of art in terms of its distinctive unity and completeness in *Principles of Literary Criticism* (London: Routledge & Kegan Paul, 1976), 142–43, 184–87. Beardsley's organicism is evident in his definition of the aesthetic experience as a complete and coherently unified experience and in his insistence on unity as one of the three objective canons of aesthetic criticism; see his *Aesthetics: Problems in Philosophy of Criticism* (New York: Harcourt, Brace,

1958), 462–63, 527–30. Cleanth Brooks in "The Heresy of Paraphrase" provides an example of New Criticism's commitment to the idea of a richly complex unity of parts, all of which help constitute the poem as a well-wrought whole. For Brooks this essential unity that informs the good poem is a matter of "imaginative" rather than strictly "logical coherences," "of balancing and harmonizing connotations, attitudes, and messages . . . [which] unite the like with the unlike" in a polyphonic "achieved harmony"; see his *The Well Wrought Urn* (New York: Harcourt, Brace, 1947), 195, 202.

2. See Michel Foucault, *The Archaeology of Knowledge* (New York: Harper and Row, 1976), 4–38; and Pierre Macherey, *A Theory of Literary Production* (London: Routledge & Kegan Paul, 1970), 78–79.

3. Jacques Derrida, "Structure, Sign, and Play in the Discourse of the Human Sciences," in *The Structuralist Controversy*, ed. R. Macksey and E. Donato, 247–72 (Baltimore: Johns Hopkins University Press, 1972), 260.

4. Aristotle's *Poetics* 7–8. I use the translation of S. H. Butcher in his *Aristotle's Theory of Poetry and Fine Art* (London: Macmillan, 1911), 31, 35. Plato adumbrates this idea of organic unity in his *Phaedrus*, where he says that "every discourse ought to be a living creature, having a body of its own and a head and feet; there should be a middle, beginning and end, adapted to each other and to the whole"; *The Dialogues of Plato*, ed. Benjamin Jowett, vol. 3 (Oxford: Clarendon Press, 1953), 172–73.

5. See Paul de Man, "Form and Intent in the American New Criticism," in *Blindness and Insight*, 2nd ed., 20–35 (Minneapolis: University of Minnesota Press, 1983), 28. Christopher Norris follows de Man's critique of New Criticism's "formalist" organicism in *Deconstruction: Theory and Practice* (London: Methuen, 1982), 103–5. Jonathan Culler's attack on the aesthetic idea of organic unity is expounded in his *On Deconstruction: Theory and Criticism after Structuralism* (Ithaca: Cornell University Press, 1982), cited as *OD*, and receives detailed attention later in this chapter.

6. Heraclitus clearly advocates a unity embracing difference and conflict when he states, "Opposition unites. From what draws apart results the most beautiful harmony. All things take place by strife" (fragment 46); in Milton Nahm, *Selections from Early Greek Philosophy* (New York: Crofts, 1934), 91. Samuel Taylor Coleridge, who introduced the term "organic unity" into English criticism, spoke of its expression in the imagination of poetic genius as a "unity that . . . reveals itself in the balance or reconciliation of opposite or discordant qualities; of sameness with difference," in his *Biographia Literaria* (London: Dent, 1965), 174. Most strikingly, Martin Heidegger—an avowed influence on de Man—describes artistic unity as a conflictual striving between "world" and "earth," where "the unity of the work comes about in the fighting of the battle"; see his "The Origin of the Work of Art," in *Poetry, Language, Thought* (New York: Harper and Row, 1971), 49–50.

7. Both these works were first published the same month of October 1903, so the conflicting valencies and applications of organic unity must have been very clear in Moore's mind. Page references to "The Refutation of Idealism," cited as RI, are to its reprinting in Moore's *Philosophical Studies* (London: Routledge & Kegan Paul, 1922), 1–30. I explore other points of deep opposition and surprising convergence between deconstruction and analytic aesthetics, in Richard Shusterman, "Analytic Aesthetics, Literary Theory, and Deconstruction," *Monist* 69 (1986): 22–38; and "Deconstruction and Analysis: Confrontation and Convergence," *British Journal of Aesthetics* 26 (1986): 311–27.

8. This argument, however, was enough for Moore's teacher John M. E. McTaggart to maintain that all wholes are organic wholes and, from this, to conclude that the universe must ultimately be one necessary monistic whole, all of whose so-called different, independent parts are actually, intrinsically, internally related. See John M. E. McTaggart, *The Nature of Existence* (Cambridge: Cambridge University Press, 1921), chap. 20.

9. See James Benziger, "Organic Unity: Leibniz to Coleridge," *PMLA* 66 (1951): 24–48.

10. Ferdinand de Saussure, *Course in General Linguistics* (London: Peter Owen, 1960), 120. Deconstructionists would insist, however, that one of Derrida's aims is precisely to undermine the whole Saussurian project of explaining language as a closed and totalizable differential system. Derrida might also dispute my talk of the "concept of *différance*," since he repeatedly insists that it is "neither a word nor a concept." See Jacques Derrida, "Différance," in *Speech and Phenomena and Other Essays on Husserl's Theory of Signs* (Evanston: Northwestern University Press, 1973), 29–60; and his *Positions* (London: Athlone, 1981), 39–40, hereafter cited as *Pos*. With respect to this second point, I would reply with Rorty that authorial fiat cannot immunize an expression against concepthood, that all that it takes for an expression to be a concept is "a place in a language-game," and that *différance* clearly has such a place in the language game(s) of deconstruction; see Richard Rorty, "Deconstruction and Circumvention," *Critical Inquiry* 11 (1984): 18. As to the first point, it is not clear that the strategy of *différance* can be fully decisive against analytic philosophy and aesthetic unity without an appeal to some sort of totalizing move regarding objects as differential relations.

11. See Derrida, "Différance," 141, and *Pos* 58.

12. G. W. F. Hegel, *Hegel's Logic*, trans. William Wallace (Oxford: Oxford University Press, 1975), 191.

13. See Friedrich Nietzsche, *The Will to Power* (New York: Vintage Press, 1968), paras. 559, 584, 635. Nietzsche's organicistic dissolution of things into differential relations within a whole is shown to underlie his doctrines of the will to power and the eternal recurrence, in Alexander Nehamas, *Nietzsche: Life as Literature* (Cambridge, Mass: Harvard University Press, 1985). For a Nietzschean critique of

Moore's and my analytic account of organic unity, see Thomas Leddy, "Moore and Shusterman on Organic Wholes," *Journal of Aesthetics and Art Criticism* 49 (1991): 63–73. For clarification of my pragmatist position on this issue, see Richard Shusterman, "Pragmatism and Perspectivism on Organic Wholes," *Journal of Aesthetics and Art Criticism* 50 (1992): 56–58.

14. Jacques Derrida, "The Parergon," *October* 9 (1979): 26.

15. See Andrew Harrison, "Works of Art and Other Cultural Objects," *Proceedings of the Aristotelian Society* 68 (1967–68): 125; and Nelson Goodman, *Languages of Art* (Oxford: Oxford University Press, 1969), 115–21. Their theorizing reflects the discourse and practice of traditional criticism, which characteristically seeks to determine not simply what is in the work but what is its central and most formative dimension—in Helen Gardner's words "a work's centre, the source of its life in all its parts"; see her *The Business of Criticism* (Oxford: Oxford University Press, 1970), 230.

16. I have elsewhere argued that in many literary works, particularly in poetry, the visual features of the written or printed text are aesthetically very relevant and sometimes essential. The dogma that poetry is only sound and sense but never sight is largely the product of an ancient philosophical bias for the phonocentric and the mental as nonphysical, coupled with a misguided metaphysical superstition that sees the oral as somehow less physical than the written. On this issue, see Richard Shusterman, "The Anomalous Nature of Literature," *British Journal of Aesthetics* 18 (1978): 317–29; "Aesthetic Blindness to Textual Visuality," *Journal of Aesthetics and Art Criticism* 41 (1982): 87–96; and "Ingarden, Inscription, and Literary Ontology," *Journal of the British Society for Phenomenology* 18 (1987): 103–19.

17. Paul de Man, foreword to Carol Jacobs, *The Dissimulating Harmony* (Baltimore, MD: Johns Hopkins University Press, 1978), ix–x.

18. See Richard Shusterman, "Convention: Variations on a Theme," *Philosophical Investigations* 9 (1986): 36–55. The common confusion of the conventional with the superficial is nourished by the conflation of two different senses of "arbitrary": contingent or not ontologically necessary versus capricious, haphazard, unreasoned, and easily reversible.

19. See Hans-Georg Gadamer, *Truth and Method* (New York: Crossroad, 1982), 261; and John Dewey, *Logic: The Theory of Inquiry* (Carbondale: Southern Illinois University Press, 1986), chap. 6.

20. De Man, "Form and Intent," 31–32.

21. Jacques Derrida, "Interpreting Signatures (Nietzsche/Heidegger): Two Questions," *Philosophy and Literature* 10 (1986): 256–57.

22. A distinction can be made between being an individual (i.e., a one) and being a distinctively unified individual (i.e., a unified one), between having mere "unicity" and having unity in a stronger sense.

23. To make the Hegelian-Nietzschean point, I am using "interpretation" in its widest philosophical sense as any perspectival understanding or construal of things. I believe, however, that not all such perspectival understanding should be

regarded as interpretation, for reasons that I set out in "Beneath Interpretation," chapter 1 in this volume.

24. William James, *Pragmatism and Other Essays* (New York: Simon and Schuster, 1963), 76.

25. The analyst might also object that without foundational essences to constitute identity there could be no shared and stable objects of reference, hence no effective discourse. Pragmatism's response to this has already been suggested: the shared normative regularities necessary for effective individuating reference and speech need not be based on any unchanging ontological referent outside a culture's social practices and can admit of some change or divergence without necessarily incurring a breakdown of communication. The shared referents of our language could be traditionally shared and pragmatically constituted "unities" or "individuals" rather than foundational substances.

26. Jacques Derrida, "Limited Inc.," *Glyph* 2 (1977): 236.

27. These roots are also clearly recognized by analytic philosophy's sympathetic historians. See, for example, J. O. Urmson, *Philosophical Analysis: Its Development Between the Two World Wars* (Oxford: Oxford University Press, 1969), 45–47.

28. Hegel, *Hegel's Logic*, 191; Nietzsche, *Will to Power*, paras. 584, 634, 635.

29. Derrida, "Interpreting Signatures," 258–61. Derrida's specific target is Heidegger's interpretation of Nietzsche, one that recognizes and emphasizes this totalization. My more detailed critique of Nietzsche's notion of organic unity is in "Nietzsche and Nehamas on Organic Unity," *Southern Journal of Philosophy* 26 (1988): 379–92.

30. See W. V. Quine, *From a Logical Point of View* (New York: Harper and Row, 1963), 4, 16–19, 46.

31. William James, *Collected Essays and Reviews* (New York: Longmans, 1920), 18; and James, *Pragmatism*, 36, 98.

32. James, *Pragmatism*, 72.

33. James, *Pragmatism*, 71. John Dewey makes the same pragmatist point of mediation: "The need . . . is to find a viable alternative to an atomism which logically involves a denial of connections and to an absolutistic block monism which, in behalf of the reality of relations, leaves no place for the discrete, for plurality, and for individuals." See John Dewey, "Experience, Knowledge, and Value," in *The Philosophy of John Dewey*, ed. Paul A. Schilpp (LaSalle: Open Court, 1989), 544. For both James and Dewey, the insistence on ontological individuality and pluralism has a distinct ethical-political motivation.

34. Richard Rorty, *Contingency, Irony, and Solidarity* (Cambridge: Cambridge University Press, 1989), 26.

Chapter Four

1. Noam Chomsky, "A Review of B. F. Skinner's Verbal Behavior," *Language* 35 (1959): 26–58.

2. William James, *Pragmatism: A New Name for Some Old Ways of Thinking,* in *Pragmatism and Other Writings* (New York: Penguin, 2000), 25, cited as *P.*

3. See C. S. Peirce, *Collective Papers of Charles Sanders Peirce* (Cambridge, Mass.: Harvard University Press, 1931–58), vol. 5, para. 402 (5.402), cited as *CP.*

4. William James, "Philosophical Conceptions and Practical Results," *University Chronicle, University of California* 1, no. 4 (1898): 292. This sentence is repeated with minor variations in *P* 27.

5. Maurice Merleau-Ponty, "In Praise of Philosophy," in his *In Praise of Philosophy and Other Essays,* trans. John Wild, James Edie, and James O'Neill (Evanston: Northwestern University Press, 1970), 58–59.

6. John Dewey and James H. Tufts, *Ethics,* 2nd ed. (Carbondale: Southern Illinois University Press, 1985), 189, cited as *E.*

7. William James, *The Principles of Psychology* (Cambridge, Mass.: Harvard University Press, 1983), 1140, cited as *PP.* James, *The Varieties of Religious Experience: A Study in Human Nature* (New York: Penguin, 1985), 264. James, "The Moral Philosopher and the Moral Life," *P* 260–62.

8. William James, "On a Certain Blindness in Human Beings," *P* 267.

9. John Dewey, *Reconstruction in Philosophy* (New York: Henry Holt, 1920), 103–4.

10. John Dewey, "Affective Thought," in *The Later Works of John Dewey,* vol. 2 (Carbondale: Southern Illinois University Press, 1988), 106.

11. Jonathan Edwards, *A Treatise Concerning Religious Affections* (1746), in *The Works of Jonathan Edwards,* vol. 2, ed. John E. Smith (New Haven: Yale University Press, 1959), cited as *E.*

12. James, *Varieties of Religious Experience,* 20.

13. For a detailed discussion of this issue, see C. J. Beedie, P. C. Terry, and A. M. Lane, "Distinctions Between Emotion and Mood," *Cognition and Emotion* 19, no. 6 (2005): 847–78.

14. On these points, see Antonio Damasio, *The Feeling of What Happens: Body and Emotion in the Making of Consciousness* (New York: Harcourt, 1999), 286, 341–42n; Paul Ekman, "Moods, Emotions, and Traits," in *The Nature of Emotion,* ed. P. Ekman and R. J. Davidson (Oxford: Oxford University Press, 1994), 56–58; R. J. Davidson, "On Emotion, Mood, and Related Affective Constructs," in *The Nature of Emotion,* 51–55; John Searle, *The Rediscovery of the Mind* (Cambridge, Mass: MIT Press, 1992), 140.

15. The English word "mood" is ambiguous partly because it derives both from the Germanic emotional term "*Mut*" and from the Latin term "*modus*" that designates mode, method, or way. The notion of grammatical mood (imperative, indicative, interrogative, etc.) comes from this latter root and suggests a matter of style, manner, or genre of utterance rather than the idea of affect (although we might connect some grammatical moods with affect, e.g., the imperative mood with impatience). Similarly, the traditional classification of categorical syllogisms

by mood that Peirce extensively uses has no essential connection with mood in the affective sense that is my concern here.

16. John Dewey, *Art as Experience* (Carbondale: Southern Illinois University Press, 1987), 73, cited as *AE*.

17. John Dewey, *Reconstruction in Philosophy* (Carbondale: Southern Illinois University Press, 1982), 82–83.

18. James, "On a Certain Blindness," *P* 268.

19. William James, "The Sentiment of Rationality," in *Collected Essays and Reviews* (London: Longmans, Green, 1920), 84, 99.

20. Antonio Damasio, *Descartes' Error: Emotion, Reason, and the Human Brain* (New York: Avon, 1995), 94–96, cited as *DE*.

21. The first logical need James also calls "the aesthetic Principle of Ease." It expresses the harmonic order underlying the complex variety that is characteristic of beauty, and he identifies this aesthetic ease with the logical principle of parsimony: "Our pleasure at finding that a chaos of facts is at bottom the expression of a single underlying fact is like the relief of the musician at resolving a confused mass of sound into melodic or harmonic order." James, "The Sentiment of Rationality," in *Collected Essays and Reviews*, 89.

22. John Dewey, "Philosophy and Civilization," *The Later Works of John Dewey*, vol. 3 (Carbondale: Southern Illinois University Press, 1988), 5.

23. Although Peirce is far less outspoken about the cognitive role of the aesthetic, he does maintain that aesthetics should not only be classed with logic and ethics among the normative sciences but can in some sense be seen as the highest (or most foundational or ultimately subsuming) of them all. This is because "the logically good is simply a particular species of the morally good" and "the morally good appears as a particular species of the esthetically good" (*CP* 5.130). For more on the importance of the aesthetic in Peirce, see "The Aesthetic Imperative: From Normative Science and Self-Control to Somaesthetics," in Cornelis de Waal, ed., *The Oxford Handbook of Charles S. Peirce* (Oxford: Oxford University Press, 2024), 111–28.

24. See F. M. Alexander, *Man's Supreme Inheritance* (New York: Dutton, 1918), 22, and Dewey's "Introduction," xvii.

25. Much of this training seems to have been devoted to feelings relating to pain, so that Peirce could anticipate and deal with his frequent, debilitating attacks of trigeminal neuralgia whose intense pain rendered him incapable of serious work or even normal daily functioning. Besides this training in pain, Peirce cultivated himself in the pleasurable somaesthetic skills of a sommelier. For more on these matters, see my "Somaesthetics and C. S. Peirce," *Journal of Speculative Philosophy* 23 (2009): 8–27. For a more extensive discussion of Dewey and James on somatic training and introspection, see *Body Consciousness*, chaps. 5 and 6. For more details on James's claims for the aesthetic dimension of cognition, see my paper "The Pragmatist Aesthetics of William James," *British Journal of Aesthetics* 51 (2011): 347–61.

26. David Chalmers, "How Can We Construct a Science of Consciousness?" in *The Cognitive Neurosciences III*, ed. Michael Gazzaniga (Cambridge, Mass.: MIT Press, 2004); Francisco J. Varela et al., *The Embodied Mind* (Cambridge, Mass.: MIT, 1991); and Morten Oevergaard et al., "An Integration of First-Person Methodologies in Cognitive Science," *Journal of Consciousness Studies* 15 (2008): 100–120.

27. See, for example, Kristina Höök, *Designing with the Body: Somaesthetic Interaction Design* (Cambridge, Mass.: MIT Press, 2018).

Chapter Five

1. Ludwig Wittgenstein, *Tractatus Logico-Philosophicus* (London: Routledge & Kegan Paul, 1963). The English translation in this dual-language edition, "Ethics and aesthetics are one and the same," makes the assertion of identity much stronger than in the German original, which says only "Ethik und Ästhetik sind Eins." I cite from the *Tractatus* as *T* with proposition number.

2. Ludwig Wittgenstein, *Notebooks, 1914–1916,* 2nd edn (Chicago: University of Chicago Press, 1979), cited as *N*.

3. See *T* 6.45 and Wittgenstein's "Lecture on Ethics," written sometime between 1929 and 1930 and posthumously published in the *Philosophical Review* 74 (1965): 3–12. In this lecture and in *N* 86, Wittgenstein refers to the mystical through the notion of the wonderful or miraculous (*das Wunder*).

4. See Jean-François Lyotard, *The Postmodern Condition* (Minneapolis: University of Minnesota Press, 1984), 10, 40–41.

5. The classic case for the logical differences between ethics and aesthetics is found in Stuart Hampshire, "Logic and Appreciation," repr. in *Aesthetics and Language*, ed. W. Elton (Oxford: Blackwell, 1954), 161–69.

6. I discuss this and other aspects of Wittgenstein's later aesthetic theory in "Wittgenstein and Critical Reasoning," *Philosophy and Phenomenological Research* 47 (1986): 91–110.

7. For Plato and generally for the Greeks, the ideas of the good and the beautiful were not so clearly differentiated. This can be seen from the fact that they were frequently referred to collectively in the composite term *kalon-kai-agathon* ("beautiful and good") and that *kalos,* the specific term for the beautiful, was frequently used like *agathos* to denote moral goodness. Once the Greek ethical world governed by the goal of *eudaemonia* gave way to ethics dominated by the ideas of divine commandment and duty or obligation, it was much easier to separate the ethical from the aesthetic and even to regard them as conflicting principles. The famous postclassical connections made between aesthetics and ethics express a salient awareness of their perceived divide. Kant saw beauty as a symbol of morality; Schiller saw aesthetic education as a means to morality; and Kierkegaard saw an aesthetic attitude to life as an inferior alternative to the ethical life. Postmodernism's ethics

of taste is perhaps distinctive only in its attempt at really merging the two spheres in defiant awareness of a long tradition of philosophical bifurcation (which would distinguish it from the Greek overlap), so that the aesthetic is neither a symbol of, means to, or surrogate for an ethic, but rather the constitutive substance of one.

8. See Richard Rorty, "Freud and Moral Reflection," in *Pragmatism's Freud: The Moral Disposition of Psychoanalysis*, ed. J. H. Smith and W. Kerrigan (Baltimore: John Hopkins University Press, 1989), 1–27, cited as R, quotations here from 10–11; and *Contingency, Irony, and Solidarity* (Cambridge: Cambridge University Press, 1989), cited as *CIS*, xiv, 29.

9. Richard Rorty, "Freud, Morality, and Hermeneutics," *New Literary History* 12 (1980): 180.

10. Bernard Williams, *Ethics and the Limits of Philosophy* (London: Fontana, 1985), 29, cited as *ELP*.

11. See T. S. Eliot, "Tradition and the Individual Talent," in *Selected Essays* (London: Faber, 1976), 16.

12. See Lyotard, *Postmodern Condition*, 27–41.

13. Richard Wollheim, *The Thread of Life* (Cambridge, Mass.: Harvard University Press, 1984), 215–16, cited as *TL*. Wollheim does not use the term "ethics" here; but he makes the same essential distinction as Williams by speaking of "morality broadly conceived," which includes nonobligational values, versus "morality narrowly conceived," which is dominated by obligation and founded on introjection (e.g., *TL* 221). Neither Wollheim nor Williams should be seen as a postmodern philosopher, even if they do challenge modernity's dominant ethic of morality governed by obligational reason. Although their critique no doubt reflects postmodern experience, their philosophical style and general objectivist outlook remain traditionally modern. Rorty, by contrast, identified himself as a postmodern philosopher, though he later distanced himself from the label. I provide a more detailed account of postmodernism in "Aesthetics and Postmodernism," in *The Oxford Handbook of Aesthetics*, ed. J. Levinson (Oxford: Oxford University Press, 2003), 771–82.

14. Viewing ethics as a creative art might suggest that the ethical agent has the same kind of freedom and power in life that the artist has in her art. This is certainly not the case for most members of society, notwithstanding the fact that even the poor have some options for stylization of life. For this reason, social (as well as aesthetic) reform is needed to make the ethical ideal of living life as art a more accessible and shared option.

15. Alisdair MacIntyre, *After Virtue* (London: Duckworth, 1982), 191.

16. See G. E. Moore, *Principia Ethica* (Cambridge: Cambridge University Press, 1959), 188–89, cited as *PE*.

17. Oscar Wilde, *The Works of Oscar Wilde* (New York: Dutton, 1954), 934. Wilde's advocacy of the aesthetic life seems to combine aspects of all the three genres I distinguished. He variously urges (1) a life of the pleasures of aesthetic consumption (with the inspired momentary states of stasis and inactivity they afford); (2) the need

for one's life to form an aesthetically pleasing whole; and (3) something approaching the Rortian-Faustian aesthetic life when he recommends that such unity be found in constant change. Indeed, Wilde already expounded Rorty's postmodern model of the ironist in the 1890s when he stated that the ideal aesthete "will realize himself in many forms, and by a thousand different ways, and will ever be curious of new sensations and fresh points of view. Through constant change, and through constant change alone, he will find his true unity" (p. 987). Walter Pater also anticipated Rorty's Faustian aesthetic life in advocating a "quickened, multiplied consciousness," a thirst for the intense excitement of novelty, and a pragmatic experiential view of knowledge, not as providing any permanent truth (which is unattainable) but simply as "ideas," "points of view," or "instruments of criticism" (in Rorty's terms, "vocabularies") for enriching our experience and quickening its appreciation; see W. Pater, *The Renaissance* (London: Macmillan, 1917), vii–xv, 233–39.

18. Michel Foucault, "On the Genealogy of Ethics: An Overview of Work in Progress," in *The Foucault Reader*, ed. Paul Rabinow (New York: Pantheon, 1984), 341, 343. For elaboration of this idea, see Foucault, *The History of Sexuality* (New York: Random House, 1985, 1986), vols. 2 and 3.

19. Foucault, *The Care of the Self* (*History of Sexuality*, vol. 3), 40, 65–66.

20. See Alexander Nehamas, *Nietzsche: Life as Literature* (Cambridge, Mass.: Harvard University Press, 1985), who writes: "The unity of the self, which therefore also constitutes its identity, is not something given but something achieved, not a beginning but a goal" (p. 182).

21. One might argue more generally that our culture's preoccupation with visibly standing out as a firmly determinate individual results from a male-dominated identification of the self with the phallus. Female sexuality, which lacks this protrusive visuality and singularity of the phallus but is rather constituted of overlapping, multiple folds, can suggest another model of self and society. See Luce Iriguray, *This Sex Which Is Not One* (Ithaca: Cornell University Press, 1985), 23–33.

22. Such pluralism is, in fact, more in tune with his advocacy of "an increasing willingness to live with plurality" and "an increasing sense of the radical diversity of private purposes." But Rorty too narrowly identifies this diversity with the ambitiously original self-creations of strong poets and ironists, "the radically poetic character of individual lives" (*CIS* 67). A more consistent pragmatic pluralism would recognize in the diversity of private purposes also the desire to be accepted as just one of the gang, a desire for similarity and belonging, free from the quest for radical distinction and individual originality.

23. See Pierre Bourdieu, "The Market of Symbolic Goods," *Poetics* 14 (1985): 13–44; and "The Production of Belief" in *Media, Culture, and Society: A Critical Reader*, ed. Richard Collins et al. (London: Sage, 1986), 131–63.

24. See Wolfgang F. Haug, *Critique of Commodity Aesthetics: Appearance, Sexuality, and Advertising in Capitalist Society* (Minneapolis: University of Minnesota Press, 1986).

25. Fredric Jameson, *The Ideologies of Theory*, vol. 2 (Minneapolis: University of Minnesota Press, 1988), 70.

26. William James, *Pragmatism and Other Essays* (New York: Simon and Schuster, 1963).

Chapter Six

1. This maxim is Μηδέν άγαν ("nothing too much"). The third of the maxims was Εγγύα, πάρα δ'άτή ("Give a pledge, and trouble is at hand"). See E. G. Wilkins, *The Delphic Maxims in Literature* (Chicago: University of Chicago Press, 1929), 1–10.

2. Daniel Graham, ed., *The Texts of Early Greek Philosophy* (Cambridge: Cambridge University Press, 2010), 147, 149.

3. Aeschylus, *Prometheus Bound*, trans. Arthur S. Way (London: Macmillan, 1907), 19.

4. See John Cooper, ed. *Plato: Complete Works* (Indianapolis: Hackett, 1997), 22; references to Plato in this chapter use translations from this source, indicated by Stephanus numbers rather than the book's page numbers.

5. Cicero, *Letters to Quintus*, trans. D. R. Shackleton Bailey (Cambridge, Mass.: Harvard University Press, 2002), 187. Plutarch likewise affirms that self-examination and self-knowledge should involve knowing one's positive gifts, but also one's special proclivities; hence, to obey the Delphic maxim one must "use oneself for that one thing for which Nature has fitted one" rather than "dragging oneself to the emulation of . . . another." See Plutarch, "Tranquility of Mind," in *Plutarch's Moralia*, vol. 6, trans. W. C. Helmbold (Cambridge, Mass.: Harvard University Press, 1939), 209.

6. Cicero, *De re publica, De legibus*, trans. Clinton Walker Keyes (Cambridge, Mass.: Harvard University Press, 1928), 59, 365.

7. Plotinus, *The Enneads*, IV.vii.10; V.iii.4, using the translation from Pierre Hadot, *Philosophy as a Way of Life* (Oxford: Blackwell, 1995), 100; and Wilkins, *Delphic Maxims in Literature*, 66.

8. Proclus, "Commentary on Plato's *Alcibiades I*," in *The Golden Chain: An Anthology of Pythagorean and Platonic Philosophy*, ed. Algis Uždavinys (Bloomington: World Wisdom, 2004), 202.

9. Cited from Catherine and Algar Labouchere Thorold, "A Treatise of Discretion," in *Dialogue of St. Catherine of Siena* (New York: Cosimo Classics, 2007), 62.

10. Juan d'Avila, *Epistolario Espiritual*, vol. 12 (Madrid: Espasa-Calpe, 1962), 153.

11. Michel de Montaigne, *The Complete Essays of Montaigne*, trans. Donald Frame (Stanford: Stanford University Press, 1958), 821; cited as *M*.

12. For an analysis of Montaigne's influential views on the importance of entertainment, see my "Entertainment: A Question for Aesthetics," *British Journal of Aesthetics* 43 (2003): 289–307; chapter 11 of this volume.

13. Blaise Pascal, *Pensées* (London: Penguin, 1966), 67–68.

14. René Descartes, "Description of the Human Body and All of Its Functions" and "The Passions of the Soul," in *The Philosophical Writings of Descartes*, trans J. Cottingham, R. Stoothoff, and D. Murdoch, vol. 1 (Cambridge: Cambridge University Press, 1985), 314, 348.

15. Immanuel Kant, *The Metaphysics of Morals*, trans. M. J. Gregor (Cambridge: Cambridge University Press, 1996), 191.

16. Immanuel Kant, *The Conflict of the Faculties*, trans. M. J. Gregor (Lincoln: University of Nebraska, 1992), 187, 189.

17. Immanuel Kant, *Reflexionen zur Kritische Philosophie*, ed. Benno Erdmann (Stuttgart: Frommann-Holzboog, 1992), 68.

18. G. W. F. Hegel, *Hegel's Philosophy of Mind*, trans. William Wallace (Oxford: Clarendon, 1894), 1, 377.

19. G. W. F. Hegel, *Lectures on the History of Philosophy: Medieval and Modern Philosophy*, trans. E. S. Haldane (Lincoln: University of Nebraska, 1995), 7.

20. Edward Young, *Night Thoughts* (London: C. Whittingham for T. Heptinstall, 1798), 75, 180, 235.

21. Samuel T. Coleridge, *Aids to Reflection* (New York: Stanford and Swords, 1854), xlvii.

22. Samuel T. Coleridge, *Biographia Literaria* (London: J. M. Dent & Sons, 1956), 154.

23. Coleridge, *Aids to Reflection*, xlvii.

24. Alexander Pope, *An Essay on Man* (London: Cheapside, 1811), 61. John Ruskin, "Wisdom and Folly in Science II," in *The Eagle's Nest: Ten Lectures on the Relation of Natural Science to Art, given before the University of Oxford in Lent Term, 1872* (London: Smith, Elder, 1872), 30.

25. Leo Tolstoy, *Confession*, trans. David Patterson (New York: Norton, 1983), 30, 71, 72, 75.

26. Soren Kierkegaard, *The Sickness unto Death* in *Fear and Trembling and The Sickness unto Death*, trans. W. Lowrie (New York: Anchor, 1954), 163, 175.

27. Julia Kristeva, *Black Sun: Depression and Melancholia*, trans. L. Roudiez (New York: Columbia University Press, 1989), 5.

28. Johann Wolfgang Goethe, *Maxims and Reflections*, trans. Elisabeth Stopp (London: Penguin, 1988), 88; "Sprüche: Aus Makariens Archiv," in *Goethes Werke*, vol. 6 (Frankfurt: Insel Verlag, 1966), 479.

29. Johann Wolfgang Goethe, "Allgemeine Naturwissenschaft," in *Goethes Werke*, vol. 13 (Hamburg: Christian Wegner Verlag, 1955), 38.

30. Johann Wolfgang Goethe, *Gespräche mit Eckermann* (Leipzig: Insel Verlag, 1921), 490. I use the English translation from *Conversations of Goethe with Eckermann and Soret*, vol. 2, trans. John Oxenford (London: Smith, Elder, 1850), 180.

31. William James, *The Principles of Psychology* (Cambridge, Mass.: Harvard University Press, 1983), 1107.

32. Johann Wolfgang Goethe, "Sprichtwörtlich," in *Goethes Werke*, ed. Eduard Scheidemantel, vol. 1 (Berlin: Deutsches Verlagshaus Bong, 1891), 366.

33. Thomas Carlyle, *Sartor Resartus* (London: Chapman and Hall, 1831), 114.

34. Thomas Carlyle, *Past and Present*, 2nd ed. (London: Chapman and Hall, 1845), 264.

35. Friedrich Nietzsche, "Schopenhauer als Erzieher," in *Sämtliche Werke*, vol. 1, ed. G. Colli and M. Montinari (Berlin: de Gruyter, 1999), 340 (my translation); cf. the English translation "Schopenhauer as Educator," in *Nietzsche: Untimely Meditations*, trans. R. J. Hollingdale (Cambridge: Cambridge University Press, 1983), 129.

36. Friedrich Nietzsche, "Über Wahrheit und Lüge im aussermoralischen Sinne," in *Sämtliche Werke*, vol. 1, 877 (my translation).

37. Friedrich Nietzsche, *Human, All Too Human*, trans. R. J. Hollingdale (Cambridge: Cambridge University Press, 1996), 294.

38. Friedrich Nietzsche, *Ecce Homo*, trans. R. J. Hollingdale (London: Penguin, 1992), 35.

39. See William James, *The Principles of Psychology*, 1140; and *Talks to Teachers on Psychology and to Students on Some of Life's Ideals* (New York: Dover, 1962), 143.

40. Ray Monk, *Ludwig Wittgenstein: The Duty of Genius* (London: Penguin, 1990), 111–12; and Ludwig Wittgenstein, *Culture and Value*, trans. Peter Winch (Oxford: Basil Blackwell, 1980), 27.

41. Michel Foucault, "Technologies of the Self," in *Technologies of the Self*, ed. Luther H. Martin, Huck Gutman, and Patrick Hutton (Amherst: University of Massachusetts Press, 1988), 9.

42. See Wittgenstein, *Culture and Value*, 57; and Foucault, "Technologies of the Self," 16–49.

43. On Wittgenstein's preoccupation with suicide and his great admiration for Otto Weininger, who theatrically killed himself in the home where Beethoven died, see Monk, *Ludwig Wittgenstein*, 19–25, 185–86. For Foucault's preoccupation with suicide, see James Miller, *The Passion of Michel Foucault* (New York: Simon and Schuster, 1993), 54–55; and for his subordination of self-knowledge to self-cultivation or self-care, see Foucault, "Technologies of the Self," 16–49.

44. On the "philosophical hypochondria" of "introspective studies," see James's letter to brother Henry of August 24, 1872, in *The Correspondence of William James*, vol. 1 (Charlottesville: University Press of Virginia, 1992), 167.

45. William James, "The Gospel of Relaxation," in *Talks to Teachers*, 108–9.

46. James, "Gospel of Relaxation," 109.

47. William Styron, *Darkness Visible: A Memoir of Madness* (New York: Random House, 1990), 35–36. Styron also notes the suicide of Primo Levi, while further suggesting that the apparently accidental deaths of Randall Jarrell and Albert Camus also bore a distinct suicidal flavor (pp. 22–23, 30–32). We should recall that Camus, in defining suicide as the "one truly serious philosophical problem," also cautions, "Beginning to think is beginning to be undermined." See Albert Camus,

"The Myth of Sisyphus," in *The Myth of Sisyphus and Other Essays*, trans. Justin O'Brien (New York: Random House, 1955), 3–4.

48. Paul Verhaeghen, Jutta Joormann, and Rodney Kahn, "Why We Sing the Blues: The Relation Between Self-Reflective Rumination, Mood, and Creativity," *Emotion* 5 (2005): 226–32. See also Susan Nolen-Hoeksema, "Responses to Depression and Their Effects on the Duration of Depressive Episodes," *Journal of Abnormal Psychology* 100 (1991): 569–52; and Susan Nolen-Hoeksema and Jannay Morrow, "Effects of Rumination and Distraction on Naturally Occurring Depressed Mood," *Cognition & Emotion* 7 (1993): 561–70.

49. James, *The Principles of Psychology*, 109.

50. Rush Rhees, ed., *Recollections of Wittgenstein* (Oxford: Blackwell, 1984), 174. See also Wittgenstein, *Culture and Value*, 49: "A man will never be great if he misjudges himself."

51. Nietzsche, "Schopenhauer as Educator," 127, 129, 143, 144.

52. Nietzsche, *The Gay Science*, trans. Walter Kaufmann (New York: Vintage, 1974), 232.

53. Wittgenstein, *Culture and Value*, 18, 49.

54. Kant, *The Conflict of the Faculties*, 187, 189; and see Styron, *Darkness Visible*, 44.

55. Kant, *Reflexionen zur Kritische Philosophie*, 68 (my translation).

56. Susan Nolen-Hoksema, Judith Larson, and Carla Grayson, "Explaining the Gender Difference in Depressive Symptoms," *Journal of Personality and Social Psychology* 77 (1999): 1061–72.

57. Paul Trapnell and Jennifer Campbell, "Private Self-Consciousness and the Five-Factor Model of Personality: Distinguishing Rumination from Reflection," *Journal of Personality and Social Psychology* 76 (1999): 284–304.

58. See, for example, Jon Kabat-Zinn et al., "Effectiveness of a Meditation-Based Stress Reduction Program in the Treatment of Anxiety Disorders," *American Journal of Psychiatry* 149 (1992): 936–43; and Jon Kabat-Zinn et al, "The Relationship of Cognitive and Somatic Components of Anxiety to Patient Preference for Alternative Relaxation Techniques," *Mind/Body Medicine* 2 (1997): 101–9. The meditative disciplines used were yoga, body scan, and seated meditation.

59. See Richard J. Davidson et al., "Alterations in Brain and Immune Function Produced by Mindfulness Meditation," *Psychosomatic Medicine* 65 (2003): 564–70; and Richard J. Davidson, "Well-Being and Affective Style: Neural Substrates and Biobehavioural Correlates," *Philosophical Transactions of the Royal Society Series B* 359 (2004): 1395–411.

60. Friedrich Nietzsche, *The Will to Power*, trans. Walter Kaufmann and R. J. Hollingdale (New York: Random House, 1967), 132, 133, 271, 347, 348.

61. Friedrich Nietzsche, "Thus Spoke Zarathustra," in *The Portable Nietzsche*, trans. Walter Kaufmann (New York: Penguin, 1976), 145, 146–47.

62. Dewey avowed he "had to control the direction" of his introspection, in a letter to Scudder Klyce cited in Steven Rockefeller, *John Dewey: Religious Faith*

and Democratic Humanism (New York: Columbia University Press, 1991), 318. This suggests the useful distinction between disciplined somatic reflection for self-knowledge and uncontrolled ruminations about one's condition and life. For Dewey's praise and application of the Alexander Technique, see Richard Shusterman, *Body Consciousness: A Philosophy of Mindfulness and Somaesthetics* (Cambridge: Cambridge University Press, 2008), chap. 6.

63. John Dewey, *The Middle Works of John Dewey*, vol. 11, ed. Jo Ann Boydston (Carbondale: Southern Illinois University Press, 1982), 351.

64. See Walpoa Rahula, *What the Buddha Taught*, 2nd ed. (New York: Grove Press, 1974), 111.

65. Selfish self-absorption remains a real risk in the quest for self-knowledge. "Many good words get spoiled when the word self is prefixed to them: Words like pity, sacrifice, control, love," Dewey remarks, without continuing the list to include knowledge. But he does explain the reason for the poison in the prefix: "The word self infects them with a fixed introversion and isolation." His worry about self-control is that, if taken too far, it will repress beneficial "growth that comes when the self is generously released." John Dewey, *Human Nature and Conduct* (Carbondale: Southern Illinois University Press, 1983), 96–97.

Chapter Seven

1. For a trenchant critique of globalization from the European perspective, see Pierre Bourdieu, *Acts of Resistance: Against the Tyranny of the Market* (New York: New Press, 1999). I review this work in "France's Philosophe Impolitique," *The Nation*, May 3, 1999, https://www.thenation.com/article/archive/frances-philosophe-impolitique/.

2. See Jürgen Habermas, "Struggles for Recognition in the Democratic Constitutional State," in *Multiculturalism: Examining the Politics of Recognition*, ed. Amy Gutmann (Princeton: Princeton University Press, 1994), 144–46. As the result of a much-debated citizenship law enacted May 1999, starting from January 1, 2000, German citizenship can be granted to people born in Germany whose parents were not considered German in terms of cultural ancestry and blood links. However, at least one of the parents must have already been legally resident in Germany for eight years and possess the proper long-term residence certificates. The eight-year requirement was reduced to five years in June 2024.

3. On this point, see historian David Hollinger, *Postethnic America: Beyond Multiculturalism* (New York: Basic Books, 1995).

4. Charles Taylor, "The Politics of Recognition," in *Multiculturalism: Examining the Politics of Recognition*, ed. Amy Gutmann (Princeton: Princeton University Press, 1994), 25–74, hereafter abbreviated as *PR*, cited on *PR* 30.

5. The phrase is that of Will Kymlicka, *Liberalism, Community, and Culture* (Oxford: Oxford University Press, 1991).

6. Like artists, philosophers are often thought to need a critical distance from a culture's common ways of thought in order to express themselves authentically. We see this not only in defiant iconoclasts like Nietzsche but even in someone such as Ludwig Wittgenstein, who was deeply appreciative of the commonalities of language and culture: "The philosopher is not a citizen of any community of ideas. That is what makes him a philosopher." Ludwig Wittgenstein, *Zettel* (Oxford: Blackwell, 1967), para. 455.

7. Until the mid-1970s, South Asian Indians were classified in the United States as Caucasian. They then successfully petitioned to be reclassified as a minority and are now categorized (e.g., in the 2000 census) as Asian Indians. However, in de facto affirmative action practice and in other multicultural contexts, their Asian-American status is still often neglected.

8. For more details on this dialectic of exclusion, see my essay "Ghetto Music" in the Philly rap fanzine *JOR Quarterly* (Winter 1992): 11–12, 18; accessible on my FAU website at https://www.fau.edu/artsandletters/humanitieschair/ghetto-music.pdf.

9. Richard Rorty, *Contingency, Irony, and Solidarity* (Cambridge: Cambridge University Press, 1989), 192.

10. Another part of the problem is the failure to recognize how porous and interpenetrating different cultures often are.

11. Though I concentrate on understanding the culturally other as a crucial means for understanding and enriching oneself, it could also be argued that some knowledge of oneself is necessary for a good understanding of the other. We need to know something of our own beliefs and point of view in order to appreciate the other more accurately and better assess both her similarity to and difference from ourselves. We understand anything in terms of a field, and the self is as much the background field of the other as the other is that of the self.

12. I discuss the genealogy of this logic, its deployment by Nietzsche and deconstruction, and its link to the central concept of organic unity in *Pragmatist Aesthetics* (Oxford: Blackwell, 1992) chap. 3; and chapter 3 of this volume.

13. H-G. Gadamer, *Truth and Method* (New York: Crossroad, 1982), 266.

14. This phrase, which forms the subtitle of Nietzsche's book *Ecce Homo*, is discussed more fully in Richard Shusterman, "Genius and the Paradox of Self-Styling," in *Performing Live: Aesthetic Alternatives for the Ends of Art* (Ithaca: Cornell University Press, 2000), 201–17.

15. See Stephen Spender's "Remembering Eliot," in *T. S. Eliot: The Man and His Work*, ed. Allen Tate (New York: Delacorte Press, 1966), 55–56.

16. The quotations here are from T. S. Eliot, *Essays Ancient and Modern* (London: Faber, 1936), 102–3; and "Poetry and Propaganda," *Bookman* 70 (1930): 602. For my analysis of Eliot's views on reading and culture, see Richard Shusterman, *T. S. Eliot and the Philosophy of Criticism* (New York: Columbia University Press, 1988), and "Eliot and Adorno on the Critique of Culture," in *Surface and Depth: Dialectics of Criticism and Culture* (Ithaca: Cornell University Press, 2002), chap. 8.

17. Diogenes Laertius, *Lives of Eminent Philosophers*, vol. 1 (Cambridge, Mass.: Harvard University Press, 1931), 445.

18. For a detailed discussion of these issues in county music, see "Affect and Authenticity in Country Musicals," in *Performing Live*, chap. 4.

19. I treat these issues of Jewish identity in "Next Year in Jerusalem?," in Richard Shusterman, *Practicing Philosophy* (London: Routledge, 1997), chap. 7.

20. See, for example, Richard Shusterman, "The Urban Aesthetics of Absence: Pragmatist Reflections in Berlin," *New Literary History* 28 (1997), 739–55.

Chapter Eight

1. The texts of Putnam used here are cited with the following abbreviations: Hilary Putnam, *The Many Faces of Realism* (LaSalle: Open Court, 1987), as *MFR*; *Realism with a Human Face*, ed. James Conant (Cambridge, Mass.: Harvard University Press, 1990), as *RHF*; *Renewing Philosophy* (Cambridge, Mass.: Harvard University Press, 1992), as *RP*; and *Words and Life*, ed. James Conant (Cambridge, Mass.: Harvard University Press, 1994), as *WL*. The texts of Cavell here cited (with abbreviations) are: Stanley Cavell, *In Quest of the Ordinary: Lines of Skepticism and Romanticism* (Chicago: Chicago University Press, 1988), as *QO*; *Conditions Handsome and Unhandsome: The Constitution of Emersonian Perfectionism* (Chicago: Chicago University Press, 1990), as *CH*; *A Pitch of Philosophy: Autobiographical Exercises* (Cambridge, Mass.: Harvard University Press, 1994), as *AP*; and *Philosophical Passages: Wittgenstein, Emerson, Austin, Derrida* (Oxford: Blackwell, 1995), as *PP*. The quotations in this paragraph are from *QO* 10, 12; *RP* 200; and *MFR* 50.

2. This chapter quotes from the following works by John Dewey, with the following abbreviations: *Art as Experience* (Carbondale: Southern Illinois University Press, 1987), as *AE*; *Experience and Nature* (Carbondale: Southern Illinois University Press, 1981), as *EN*; *Liberalism and Social Action* (Carbondale: Southern Illinois University Press, 1987), as *LSA*; *The Public and Its Problems* (Carbondale: Southern Illinois University Press, 1988), as *PIP*. John Dewey and James H. Tufts, *Ethics*, 2nd ed. (Carbondale: Southern Illinois University Press, 1989), as *E*.

3. Putnam's account of this demand and of "the absolute conception of the world" is based on the work of Bernard Williams, which he criticizes in "Bernard Williams and the Absolute Conception of the World," *RP* 80–107.

4. I doubt whether Dewey would have used the term "epistemological" to characterize the argument for democracy that Putnam finds in his work, since epistemology had for Dewey rather narrow and negative connotations. He probably would have preferred the term "logical" in the general sense he gave it as ordered, rational inquiry.

5. Part of Putnam's aim in invoking the notion of "right" is to criticize Dewey's ethics for ignoring it by simply reducing the idea of right and duty to questions of

good consequences. "Like all consequentialist views," Putnam argues, "Dewey's has trouble doing justice to considerations of right" as opposed to questions of good (*RP* 190). But Putnam's complaint of consequentialism is problematic. First, it seems valid only for Dewey's earlier ethical theory. By 1930 (in his "Three Independent Factors in Morals"), and with the publication of the second edition of his and Tufts's *Ethics* in 1932, Dewey insisted that right and obligation (as well as virtue) were independent factors in morals, irreducible to consequentialist considerations of good. See John Dewey, "Three Independent Factors in Morals," in John Dewey, *The Later Works,* ed. Jo Ann Boydston, vol. 5 (Carbondale: Southern Illinois University Press, 1984), 279–88. Putnam may not have noticed this, because he cites (in *RP* 189) from the first edition of *Ethics.* Moreover, Putnam himself ultimately formulates the personal ethical question in terms of good rather than right: "Whether it is good that I, Hilary Putnam, do that thing," (*RP* 194).

6. In other writings, Putnam also links James's will to believe with existentialism and notes James's own allusion to Kierkegaard, "the Danish thinker," when advocating the individual's right to believe in cases "that cannot . . . be decided on intellectual grounds," "the right of the existentialist to believe ahead of the evidence." The difference Putnam draws here between pragmatism and existentialism is that only the former can see one's leap of faith as fallible and "subject to revision." See Putnam's "William James's Ideas," (*RHF* 227, 229).

7. See Michel Foucault, "What Is Enlightenment?," in *The Foucault Reader,* ed. Paul Rabinow (New York: Vintage, 1984), 32–50.

8. I discuss Rorty's creative misprisions of Deweyan democratic theory and ethics of self-realization in Richard Shusterman, *Practicing Philosophy: Pragmatism and the Philosophical Life* (New York: Routledge, 1997), chaps. 2 and 4.

9. We never enjoy, however, the radical freedom existentialists claim, because our behavior, desires, and beliefs have always been partly prestructured by habits that are shaped (though not mechanically determined) by our social conditions, training, and past experience. By turning to existentialism in order to maintain individual freedom against social determination, Putnam courts an unhappy opposition between individual and society that risks forgetting that this freedom is largely an emergent product of social structures rather than an autonomous, oppositional force.

10. Cavell would regard such a view as a form of moralism morally inferior to perfectionism, "the form of moralism that fixates on the presence of ideals in one's culture and promotes to distract one from the presence of otherwise intolerable injustice." The other form of moralism "is the enforcement of morality, or a moral code, by immoral means." "It is," Cavell adds, "to John Dewey's eternal credit to have combated, unrelentingly, both forms of moralism" (*CH* 13).

11. John Rawls, *A Theory of Justice* (Oxford: Oxford University Press, 1973), 325.

12. In this conversation, perfectionism "is the idea of the cultivation of a new mode of being, of being human, where the idea is not that this comes later

than justice but that it is essential in pursuing the justice of sharing one another's fate without reducing that fate, as it were, to mitigation" (*CH* 25).

13. Ralph Waldo Emerson, *The Journals and Miscellaneous Notebooks of Ralph Emerson*, ed. William H. Gilman et al., vol. 15 (Cambridge, Mass.: Harvard University Press, 1960–82), 462.

14. Dewey in contrast suggests a historicist outlook for understanding and assessing the good life. Although he criticizes Epicureanism for concentrating on the individual rather than the social, he recognizes that self-absorption may be the best option when social conditions are too unfavorable for a robustly social realization of self (*E* 202).

15. Such ad hominem arguments that appeal to the attraction of a life can cut both ways, involving the judger as well as the judged. In other words, my judgment of whether Cavell's philosophical life of perfectionism has enough democratic (or other) attraction will be a comment not only on his life, but on my own aesthetic taste and the life it reflects.

16. At one point Cavell speaks of the self's need to exemplify its intelligibility not only "when words are called for" but also "when there are no words" (*CH* xxvii). But this vague idea is never developed, and, as the above citations indicate, he tends to identify the philosophical life essentially with textual activity.

17. See my case for philosophical intervention in the praxis of cultural and university politics in *Practicing Philosophy*, chap. 2.

18. Stanley Cavell, *Little Did I Know: Excerpts from Memory* (Stanford: Stanford University Press, 2010).

19. See Pierre Hadot, "Spiritual Exercises," in his *Philosophy as a Way of Life*, ed. Arnold Davidson (Oxford: Blackwell, 1995), 81–125. Davidson himself suggests the connection between this idea and Cavell's view of philosophical writing, 40n91.

20. Alexander Nehamas, *Nietzsche: Life as Literature* (Cambridge: Mass.: Harvard University Press, 1985), 233–34.

21. Friedrich Nietzsche, "Schopenhauer as Educator," in *Untimely Meditations*, trans. R. Hollingdale (Cambridge: Cambridge University Press, 1983), 187.

22. Henry David Thoreau, *Walden*, in *The Portable Thoreau*, ed. Carl Bode (New York: Viking, 1969), 270, cited as *W*.

23. Putnam and Cavell, of course, recognize our embodied condition. As Putman critiques mind-body dualism (e.g., *WL* 3–61), so Cavell praises Austin's account of excuses for turning attention to "something philosophy would love to ignore—to the fact that human life is constrained to the life of the human body, to what Emerson calls the giant I always take with me. The law of the body is the law." But in treating embodiment as governed by unmodifiable law beyond our control and thus constituting the realm for excuses, Cavell effectively excludes the body from his perfectionist project. In contrast to bodily efforts, "the saying of words is not excusable" and marks the realm of responsibility. Hence it is in language that Cavell urges perfectionist striving, assuming "the unending responsibility

of responsiveness, of answerability, to make [oneself] intelligible." Similar demands (even if likewise not fully achievable) might be toward somatic improvement, and it is hard to see how Cavell would wish to separate words and voice from the body from which they issue and in which they resonate. Quotations here are from Cavell's *PP* 53, 63, 65; see also *AP* 87, 125.

24. This includes critique of the deeply entrenched oppression of conventional binary gender norms. For my somaesthetic discussion of this issue, see "Self-Transformation as Trans-formation: Rilke on Gender in the Art of Living," *Journal of Somaesthetics* 9, no. 1 (2023): 46–57.

Chapter Nine

1. One reason for my interest in this concept is its important role in my pragmatist aesthetics. See Richard Shusterman, *Pragmatist Aesthetics* (Oxford: Blackwell, 1992), especially chap. 2.

2. See Arthur Danto, *The Philosophical Disenfranchisement of Art* (New York: Columbia University Press, 1986), 13; henceforth cited as *PD*. I shall also be using the following abbreviations in citing other works of Danto, Beardsley, Dewey, and Goodman: Arthur Danto, *The Transfiguration of the Commonplace* (Cambridge, Mass.: Harvard University Press, 1981), *TC*; Monroe C. Beardsley, *Aesthetics: Problems in the Philosophy of Criticism* (New York: Harcourt Brace, 1958), *A*, and Beardsley, *The Aesthetic Point of View* (Ithaca, N.Y.: Cornell University Press, 1982), *APV*; John Dewey, *Art as Experience* (Carbondale: Southern Illinois University Press, 1987), *AE*; Nelson Goodman, *Languages of Art* (Oxford: Oxford University Press, 1968), *LA*, and Goodman, *Ways of Worldmaking* (Indianapolis, Ind.: Hackett, 1978), *WW*, and Goodman, *Of Mind and Other Matters* (Cambridge, Mass.: Harvard University Press, 1984), *OMM*.

3. See, for example, the account by the renowned Polish historian of aesthetics, Władysław Tatarkiewicz, in his *A History of Six Ideas* (The Hague: Nijhoff, 1980), 310–38.

4. See David Hume, "Of the Standard of Taste," in *Essays Moral, Political, and Literary* (Oxford: Oxford University Press, 1963), 234; and Immanuel Kant, *The Critique of Judgement* (Oxford: Oxford University Press, 1957), 41–42.

5. See George Dickie, "Beardsley's Phantom Aesthetic Experience," *Journal of Philosophy* 62 (1965): 129–36. Eddy Zemach also argues that there is no such thing as the aesthetic experience in his (Hebrew) book, *Aesthetics* (Tel Aviv, Israel: Tel Aviv University Press, 1976), 42–53.

6. Theodor Adorno, *Aesthetic Theory* (London: Routledge, 1984), 474, 476; henceforth *AT*.

7. Though he advocates *Erfahrung* over *Erlebnis*, Benjamin is critical of the neo-Kantian and positivist notion of *Erfahrung* as being too narrowly rationalistic and thin. My compressed account of Benjamin is based on his essays "The

Storyteller," "On Some Motifs in Baudelaire," and "The Work of Art in the Age of Mechanical Reproduction." All are found in Walter Benjamin, *Illuminations* (New York: Schocken, 1968).

8. Challenging the idea that art is something for detached, immediate "appreciation and enjoyment," Heidegger insists that "art is by nature . . . a distinctive way in which truth comes into being, that is, becomes historical." It therefore cannot be separated from the world of its truth-disclosure simply for the narrow goal of experienced pleasure. In this sense, Heidegger warns, "perhaps experience is the element in which art dies." Martin Heidegger, "The Origin of the Work of Art," in *Poetry, Language, Thought* (New York: Harper & Row, 1975), 78,79.

9. Hans-Georg Gadamer, *Truth and Method* (New York: Crossroad, 1982), 86–87; henceforth *TM*.

10. In highlighting the cognitive dimension of aesthetic experience, Gadamer writes, "What one experiences in a work of art and what one is directed towards is rather how true it is, i.e., to what extent one knows and recognizes something and oneself." The joy of aesthetic experience "is the joy of knowledge" (*TM* 101, 102).

11. See Pierre Bourdieu, "The Historical Genesis of a Pure Aesthetic," in *Analytic Aesthetics*, ed. Richard Shusterman (Oxford: Blackwell, 1989), 148, 150.

12. For more detailed argument of this point, see chapter 1, "Beneath Interpretation," in this volume.

13. Dewey thus sees aesthetic experience as central not only to art but to the philosophy of experience in general. "To esthetic experience," he therefore claims, "the philosopher must go to understand what experience is" (*AE* 11).

14. Although this seems obvious, there is an argument that denies it, asserting that our appreciation of natural beauty is entirely dependent on and constrained by our modern concept of fine art, as indeed is all our aesthetic experience. For a critique of this argument and a fuller discussion of Dewey's views, see *Pragmatist Aesthetics*, chaps. 1 and 2.

15. As Dewey later adds, "The experience is marked by a greater inclusiveness of all psychological factors than occurs in ordinary experiences, not by reduction of them to a single response" (*AE* 259).

16. Even if we could effect this reclassification, Dewey's definition of art as aesthetic experience would remain problematic. For this experience is itself never clearly defined but instead asserted to be ultimately indefinable because of its essential immediacy; "it can," he says, "only be felt, that is, immediately experienced" (*AE* 196). For more detailed critique of Dewey's definition of art as experience, see *Pragmatist Aesthetics*, chaps.1 and 2.

17. Beardsley's precise list of defining characteristics of aesthetic experience changes slightly over the years, but almost all his accounts insist on the features I mention. Apart from his book *Aesthetics*, his most detailed treatments of aesthetic experience can be found in "Aesthetic Experience Regained" and "Aesthetic Experience," both reprinted in *APV* 77–92, 285–97.

18. See Dickie's "Beardsley's Phantom Aesthetic Experience," and his *Art and the Aesthetic: An Institutional Analysis* (Ithaca, N.Y.: Cornell University Press, 1974).

19. Beardsley himself cites Maslow's psychological research into peak experiences (*APV* 85). See A. H. Maslow, *Toward a Psychology of Being* (Princeton, N.J.: Princeton University Press, 1962). Use of the notion of experience and its characterization in terms of coherence and intensity is also found in more contemporary experimental psychology. For one example, see the influential work of Daniel Stern, *The Interpersonal World of the Infant* (New York: Basic Books, 1985).

20. For a vigorous defense of the centrality of consciousness, see John Searle, *The Rediscovery of the Mind* (Cambridge, Mass.: MIT Press, 1992). I defend the notion of immediate experience against charges that it entails commitment to foundationalism's myth of the given in *Practicing Philosophy* (London: Routledge, 1997) and chapter 2 of this volume; and I explore the central and multifaceted role of somatic consciousness in *Body Consciousness: A Philosophy of Mindfulness and Somaesthetics* (Cambridge: Cambridge University Press, 2008).

21. See Joel Kupperman, "Art and Aesthetic Experience," *British Journal of Aesthetics* 15 (1975): 29–39, and Beardsley's response in *APV* 296. Dewey, however, failed to consider the aesthetic dimension of sexual experience and, like other leading pragmatists, shied away from the topic of sex. I discuss this unfortunate lacuna in the pragmatist tradition in "Pragmatism and Sex: An Unfulfilled Connection," *Transactions of the Charles S. Peirce Society: A Quarterly Journal in American Philosophy* 57, no. 1 (2021): 1–31. I try to remedy this omission in *Ars Erotica: Sex and Somaesthetics in the Classical Arts of Love* (Cambridge: Cambridge University Press, 2021).

22. There is also the problem that aesthetic experience is too elusive, ineffable, subjectively variable, and immeasurable in magnitude to provide sufficient grounds for justifying particular evaluative verdicts. Thus, when it came to actual critical practice, Beardsley recognized that we have to demonstrate the unity, complexity, and intensity of the actual work, not of its experience. However, he held that demonstration of the former could allow inference of capacity for the latter, and it was the latter (i.e., experience) that constituted actual aesthetic value.

23. Since these characteristics make no reference to phenomenological consciousness, Goodman's concept of aesthetic experience can be characterized as semantic rather than phenomenological. Like Dewey and Beardsley, Goodman insists on the dynamic nature of aesthetic experience, but he does not emphasize, as they do, the passive aspect in which one surrenders oneself to the work. This idea may be too suggestive of subjectivity and affect for Goodman. But the etymology of "experience" suggests the peril of undergoing something, and it is perhaps not too fanciful to note that some notion of submission is even hinted at by the "under" in the word "understanding."

24. T. S. Eliot, "The Frontiers of Poetry," in *Of Poetry and Poets* (London: Faber, 1957), 115. For Eliot this means "enjoying it to the right degree and in the right way, relative to other poems," and he adds that "this implies one *shouldn't*

enjoy bad poems—unless their badness is of a sort that appeals to our sense of humour." For more details on Eliot's theory of literary understanding, see Richard Shusterman, *T. S. Eliot and the Philosophy of Criticism* (New York: Columbia University Press, 1988), chaps. 5 and 6.

25. A growing number of sociobiologists further maintain that the gratifications of aesthetic experience not only explain art's emergence and staying power but also help account for the survival of humanity itself. Such experiences, says the Oxford anatomist J. Z. Young, "have the most central of biological functions—of insisting that life be worthwhile, which, after all, is the final guarantee of its continuance." J. Z. Young, *An Introduction to the Study of Man* (Oxford: Oxford University Press, 1971), 38.

26. The idea that aesthetic experience fails miserably at formally defining art's extension but nonetheless is essential for understanding art's point and value is developed in more detail in my *Pragmatist Aesthetics*, chaps. 1 and 2. I emphasize there (and the point bears repeating) that art's valuable uses extend far beyond the creation of aesthetic experience.

27. See "Painting by Numbers: The Search for a People's Art," in *The Nation* (March 14, 1994): 334–48, particularly questions 68 and 70, which relate to art's coherence and ability to "make us happy."

28. These values include not only heightened, positive affect but also an enhanced appreciation of the nonconceptual and the sensual. Another possible value of aesthetic experience comes from its making us aware, through its power to transport us, of the benefits that can be derived by opening or submitting oneself to things typically seen as mere objects of our domination and use. This holds, of course, as much for the experience of nature as well as art, and it suggests the transformational role of experience in which, as Dewey insisted, we are subjects as well as agents, undergoing as well as acting. Heidegger makes a similar point: "To undergo an experience of something . . . means that this something befalls us, strikes us, comes over us, overwhelms and transforms us." Martin Heidegger, *On the Way to Language* (New York: Harper & Row, 1971), 57.

29. Fredric Jameson, *Postmodernism, or the Cultural Logic of Late Capitalism* (Durham, N.C.: Duke University Press, 1991), 10–16.

30. See the film *Blade Runner* (1982), based on Philip K. Dick's novel *Do Androids Dream of Electric Sheep?* (New York: Ballantine: New York, 1968).

31. Ludwig Wittgenstein, *Philosophical Investigations* (Oxford: Blackwell, 1956), para. 127.

32. For a provocative critique of the arguments of this chapter, and particularly of my concern for pleasure, see Alexander Nehamas, "Richard Shusterman on Pleasure and Aesthetic Experience," *Journal of Aesthetics and Art Criticism* 56 (1998): 49–51; and Wolfgang Welsch, "Rettung durch Halbierung? Zu Richard Shustermans Rehabilitierung asthetischer Erfahrung," *Deutsche Zeitschrift für Philosophie* 47 (1999): 111–26. I reply to their critique in "Interpretation, Pleasure, and

Value in Aesthetic Experience," *Journal of Aesthetics and Art Criticism* 56 (1998): 51–53; and "Provokation und Erinnerung," *Deutsche Zeitschrift for Philosophie* 47 (1999): 127–37.

Chapter Ten

1. See Henry James, preface to "The Altar of the Dead," in *The Art of the Novel* (New York: Scribner's, 1934), 265. In this same preface, the variation "Dramatise it, dramatise it" is also thrice invoked (249, 251, 260).

2. These quotes from Henry James are taken from the introductory essays of Leon Edel, in his edition of *The Complete Plays of Henry James* (New York: Oxford University Press, 1990), 10, 62, 64.

3. Friedrich Nietzsche, "Richard Wagner in Bayreuth," in *Unzeitgemäßen Betrachtungen*, IV, in *Friedrich Nietzsche: Sämtliche Werke*, ed. G. Colli and M. Montinari (Berlin: De Gruyter, 1999), vol. 1, 472; cf. trans. R. J. Hollingdale as *Untimely Meditations* (Cambridge: Cambridge University Press, 1994), sec. 8, 227.

4. T. S. Eliot, *The Use of Poetry and the Use of Criticism* (London: Faber, 1964), 152–53. See also his "Poetry and Drama," in *On Poetry and Poets* (London: Faber, 1957), 72–88.

5. *Complete Plays of Henry James*, 34–35.

6. Morris Weitz's famous critique of the possibility of "true and real definitions" of art gave the term "real definition" its centrality in aesthetic debate and led aestheticians to use the terms more or less interchangeably. See his "The Role of Theory in Aesthetics," *Journal of Aesthetics and Art Criticism* 15 (1956): 35.

7. Robert Stecker, *Artworks: Definition, Meaning, Value* (University Park: Pennsylvania State University Press, 1997), 14.

8. The goal of defining the concept of art once and for all by a single set of necessary and sufficient conditions that neatly and informatively divide all actual and possible objects into those that are art and those that are not art seems problematic to me for many reasons: (1) the multiple meanings and uses of the term "art"; (2) art's open, creative nature; (3) its essentially valued, hence essentially contested, character; (4) the changing conceptions of art over history; and (5) the very different and changing ways that art is deeply connected yet also distinguished from other practices in the different societies in which it is situated. But I also question the explanatory power and the conservative, narrowing effect of such extension-coverage definitions, which I call "wrapper theories of art." For more details on these points, see my *Pragmatist Aesthetics: Living Beauty, Rethinking Art* (Oxford: Blackwell, 1992), chap. 2.

9. Weitz, "Role of Theory in Aesthetics," 35.

10. I am, of course, aware that the terms "naturalism" and "historicism" have many different meanings in aesthetic theory, some of which are much more specific than the general meanings they bear in this chapter.

11. See Aristotle, *Poetics*, 1448b, in *The Basic Works of Aristotle*, ed. Richard McKeon (New York: Random House, 1968), 1457–58: "It is clear that the general origin of poetry was due to two causes, each of them part of human nature. . . . Imitation, then being natural to us—as also the sense of harmony and rhythm, the metres being obviously species of rhythm—it was through their original aptitude, and by a series of improvements for the most part gradual on their first efforts, that they created poetry out of their improvisations."

12. Friedrich Nietzsche, *Die Geburt der Tragodie*, in *Friedrich Nietzsche, Sätmtliche Werke*, vol. 1, 12, 28, 35, 61, hereafter cited as *DG*; cf. trans. Francis Golffing as *The Birth of Tragedy*, in *The Birth of Tragedy and the Genealogy of Morals* (New York: Doubleday, 1956), 4, 22, 29, 55, hereafter cited as *BT*. I give page references to both editions but sometimes use my own translation.

13. See John Dewey, *Experience and Nature* (Carbondale: Southern Illinois University Press, 1981), 269; and especially *Art as Experience* (Carbondale: Southern Illinois University Press, 1987), hereafter cited as *AE*.

14. Ralph Waldo Emerson, "Nature," in *Ralph Waldo Emerson*, ed. Richard Poirier (New York: Oxford University Press, 1990), 12. Further quotes from Emerson in this chapter are taken from other texts in this collection of his essays and poems, hereafter cited as *RWE*.

15. See, for instance, the work of Paul O. Kristeller, "The Modern System of the Arts: A Study in the History of Aesthetics," which is very frequently cited by analytic aestheticians, in *Journal of the History of Ideas* 12 (1951): 496–527, and 13 (1952): 17–46.

16. See Pierre Bourdieu, "The Genesis of the Pure Aesthetic," in *Analytic Aesthetics*, ed. Richard Shusterman (Oxford: Blackwell, 1989), 148–49.

17. Another reason to resist choosing simply one of these dualist alternatives relates to a general principle of pragmatic pluralism that I call "the inclusive disjunctive stance." The familiar logical disjunction "either p or q" is here understood pluralistically to include either one or both alternatives (as it does in standard propositional logic and in the common occasions of everyday life where one can choose more than one thing, e.g., either wine or water or both). This is in contrast to the exclusive sense of "either/or" where one alternative strictly excludes the other, as indeed it sometimes does in life as well as in logic. With pragmatism's inclusive stance, we should presume that alternative theories or values can somehow be reconciled until we are given good reasons why they are mutually exclusive. That seems the best way to keep the path of inquiry open and to maximize our goods.

18. This chapter emphasizes certain German terms and gives page references to original German texts because it is based on the opening keynote address I had to give in German at the Frankfurt Opera on March 22, 2000, for a conference titled "Ästhetik der Inszinierung." My talk was titled "Kunst als Dramatisierung" and was published in *Ästhetik der Inszenierung*, ed. J. Fürchtl and J. Zimmermann (Frankfurt: Suhrkamp, 2002), 126–43.

19. Friedrich Nietzsche, *Ecce Homo,* in *Friedrich Nietzsche: Sämtliche Werke,* vol. 6, 288–89, 326; or in R. J. Hollingdale's English translation, *Ecce Homo* (London: Penguin, 1992), 30.

20. *Chambers 21st Century Dictionary* (Cambridge: Chambers, 1996). This second sense of dramatize is very similar to the dominant contemporary meaning of the French verb *"dramatiser"* as emphasizing or exaggerating the importance, gravity, or drama of an event.

21. This Hebrew stem clearly seems related to the Greek stem for "dwelling," from which *"skene"* and "scene" are derived.

22. Aristotle, *Poetics*, chap. 7, 1450b.

23. William James, *The Principles of Psychology* (Cambridge, Mass.: Harvard University Press, 1983), 924.

24. The quotes are from Shakespeare's *As You Like It*, act 2, scene 7, 139, and *Macbeth* act 5, scene 5, 23.

25. J. L. Austin, *Sense and Sensibilia* (Oxford: Oxford University Press, 1964), 70.

Chapter Eleven

1. See Richard Shusterman, *Pragmatist Aesthetics: Living Beauty, Rethinking Art* (Oxford: Blackwell, 1992), and *Performing Live: Aesthetic Alternatives for the Ends of Art* (Ithaca: Cornell University Press, 2000).

2. See *The Oxford English Dictionary*, 2nd ed., vol. 10, entry for "popular," 125.

3. I prefer the term "popular" because "mass" suggests an undifferentiated and typically inhuman aggregate, while the audiences of the popular arts are in fact often quite differentiated, even if they to some extent overlap. For an art to be popular it does not require a mass or mainstream audience of the most common tastes. It is enough for it to have what I call a "multitudinous" audience. In this way, genres like punk rock or rap music can be popular arts even when they oppose the taste and values of mainstream society.

4. See Lawrence W. Levine, *Highbrow/Lowbrow: The Emergence of Cultural Hierarchy in America* (Cambridge, Mass.: Harvard University Press, 1988).

5. The Latin word for entertainment, *"oblectatio,"* which has the primary sense of an alluring diversion or distraction, also has connotations of the childish, since it is derived from the verb *"lacto,"* which means both to allure and to take milk from the breast. The mother's breast provides the child with entertainment both in the sense of sustenance and in the sense of pleasurable comforting distraction from unpleasant feelings or anxieties. The mother's breast is probably one's first entertainment in both these vital senses. Could philosophy's haughty devaluation of entertainment be partly an unconscious rejection of man's childish dependence on mothers and on women more generally?

6. Aristotle, *Poetics*, 1451b, trans. Ingram Bywater (Oxford: Clarendon Press, 1909), 27.

7. I generally adopt the translations of Donald Frame, *The Complete Works of Montaigne* (Stanford: Stanford University Press, 1957), cited parenthetically as *M*.

8. See "Entertainment" in the *Oxford English Dictionary*, vol. 3 (Oxford: Clarendon Press, 1933), 214.

9. See "divertissement" in *Encyclopédie ou dictionnaire raisonné des arts et des métiers, mis en ordre et publié par Diderot & quant à la partie mathématique par d'Alembert: Nouvelle impression en facsimile de la première édition de 1751–1780*, vol. 4 (Stuttgart: Friedrich Frommann Verlag, 1966), 1069; cf. online at https://artflsrv04.uchicago.edu/philologic4.7/encyclopedie0922/navigate/4/5285; and Denis Diderot, "D'Alembert's Dream: Conclusion of the Conversation," in *Diderot: Selected Writings*, ed. John Kemp (New York: International Publishers, 1943), 119.

10. Immanuel Kant, *Kritik der Urteilskraft* (Hamburg: Felix Meiner, 1974), 50, 84; cf. in English, *The Critique of Judgement*, trans. J. C. Meredith (Oxford: Oxford University Press, 1952), 53, 88.

11. Friedrich Schiller, *On the Aesthetic Education of Man*, bilingual ed. (Oxford: Clarendon Press, 1982), letter 15, 107: "Der Mensch spielt nur, wo er in voller Bedeutung des Worts Mensch ist, und er ist nur da ganz Mensch, wo er spielt."

12. G. W. F. Hegel, *Ästhetik*, vol. 1 (Berlin: Aufbau Verlag, 1984), 18–19; I generally adopt the English translation in *Introductory Lectures on Aesthetics*, trans. Bernard Bosanquet (London: Penguin, 1993), 9.

13. Friedrich Nietzsche, "Schopenhauer als Erzieher" (§6) and "Richard Wagner in Bayreuth" (§§4, 5, 8), in *Unzeitgemäßen Betrachtungen*, in *Sämtliche Werke* (Stuttgart: Alfred Kröner, 1976), 266–67, 322–24, 335. For the English translations, see R. J. Hollingdale, trans., *Untimely Meditations* (Cambridge: Cambridge University Press, 1988), 172–73, 210–11, 218, 229, although here as elsewhere I sometimes use my own translation.

14. Friedrich Nietzsche, *Ecce Homo* (§3), in *Sämtliche Werke* (Stuttgart: Alfred Körner, 1978), 320–21. Later in section 8, he suggests that recreation involves "an instinct of self-preservation" (329); cf. the English translation by Walter Kaufmann, *On the Genealogy of Morals and Ecce Homo* (New York: Vintage, 1969), 242, 252.

15. For an early but very lucid critical analysis of the Weber-Fechner theory, see William James, *The Principles of Psychology* (1890) (Cambridge, Mass.: Harvard University Press, 1983), 503–18.

16. Martin Heidegger, "The Origin of the Work of Art," in *Poetry, Language, Thought* (New York: Harper, 1975), 68, 71; Hans-Georg Gadamer, *Truth and Method* (New York: Crossroads, 1982), 58–90; Gadamer, however, is much more tolerant than Adorno toward popular music, regarding it as "legitimate." But he views this legitimacy not in terms of pleasure but merely in terms of its "capacity to establish [wide] communication" and to provide material for criticism in our "thirst for knowledge." Gadamer also positively connects art to the notion of festival, which

he understands in rather transcendental and often explicitly "theological" terms. See Hans-Georg Gadamer, *The Relevance of the Beautiful and Other Essays* (Cambridge: Cambridge University Press, 1986), 39, 51.

17. Theodor Adorno and Max Horkheimer, *Dialectic of Enlightenment* (New York: Continuum, 1986), 121; Theodor Adorno, *Aesthetic Theory* (London: Routledge, 1984), 18–21.

18. See T. S. Eliot, preface to *The Sacred Wood* (London: Methuen, 1968), viii–ix; and "The Frontiers of Poetry," in *Of Poetry and Poets* (London: Faber, 1957), 115. The subsequent quote from Eliot is from his *The Use of Poetry and the Use of Criticism* (London: Faber, 1964), 154.

19. The complexity of the so-called popular audience is a point likewise made by two of the twentieth century's strongest theoretical defenders of popular art, Antonio Gramsci and Mikhail Bakhtin. They also recognize that the entertainment function does not deprive popular culture of important aesthetic, cognitive, and political functions. Both theorists define the popular essentially in terms of its opposition to official culture, not in terms of its origin in a particular demographic group identified as "the people," because, as Gramsci notes, "the people themselves are not a homogeneous cultural collectivity." See Gramsci, *Selections from Cultural Writings* (Cambridge, Mass.: Harvard University Press, 1991), 195. In stressing that the popular aesthetic of carnival festivity embraces all strata of society and works to enhance their communication by a momentary erasure of official hierarchies, Bakhtin highlights the role of play and entertainment. In a variation of the dialectical argument for the productive power of distraction, Bakhtin suggests that carnival entertainment has recuperative power in letting us momentarily forget the constraints of official roles and established truths, thus helping us to open our hearts and minds to Utopian ideals and new possibilities. Because this recuperative Utopian function can serve all strata of the population, the appeal of popular entertainment is not narrowly linked to one particular social class.

20. See, for example, criticisms made by Rainer Rochlitz, "Esthétiques Hédonistes," *Critique* 540 (1992): 353–73; Alexander Nehamas, "Richard Shusterman on Pleasure and Aesthetic Experience," *Journal of Aesthetics and Art Criticism* 56 (1998): 49–51; Wolfgang Welsch, "Rettung durch Halbierung: Zu Richard Shustermans Rehabilitierung ästhetischer Erfahrung," *Deutsche Zeitschrift für Philosophie* 47 (1999): 111–26; and Kathleen Higgins, "Living and Feeling at Home: Shusterman's *Performing Live*," *Journal of Aesthetic Education* 36 (2002): 84–92.

21. In underlining the power and significance of these exalted pleasures, it is wrong to dismiss the value of lighter ones. Merriment can offer a welcome relief from the strains of ecstasy but also provides a useful contrast to highlight sublimity. Besides these uses of diversion, lighter pleasures have their own intrinsic charms. The purpose in learning the diversity of pleasures is not to select only the highest and reject the rest but to profit best from enjoying them all, at least all that we can happily manage.

22. Benedict de Spinoza, *The Ethics*, in *Works of Spinoza* (New York: Dover, 1955), 174. Aristotle, *Nicomachean Ethics*, 1175a, in *The Basic Works of Aristotle* (New York: Random House, 1968), 1100.

23. P. J. Chaudhury, "The Theory of Rasa," *Journal of Aesthetics and Art Criticism* 24 (1965): 145, 146. The great Indian thinker Abhinovagupta, writing in the tenth century, describes the pleasure of *rasa* as "like the relish of the ultimate reality" (148).

24. This early Japanese meaning of *goraku* is found in the Japanese literary classics *Konjakumonogatari* (twelfth century) and *Taiheiki* (fourteenth century). The *kanji* (or character) that forms the word suggests a person's head tilted back with the mouth wide open in joyful laughter (and perhaps also some other pleasure). I thank Professor Satoshi Higuchi for instructing me about the etymology of *goraku*, based on information from the comprehensive Japanese dictionary *Nihon Kogugo Daijiten*, vol. 8 (Tokyo: Shogakukan, 1974), 433. Confucianism advocates aesthetic pleasures for cultivating harmony and good order not only in the individual but also in society as a whole. That is why music and ritual are key pillars of Confucian ethics.

25. Dewey claims "art is the most effective mode of communication that exists" in *Art as Experience* (Carbondale: Southern Illinois University Press, 1987), 291.

26. Hannah Arendt, "The Crisis of Culture," in *Between Past and Future* (New York: Viking, 1961), 197–226. Quotations in these two sentences are from 205–6; other page references to this article (cited as CC) are given parenthetically in the text.

Chapter Twelve

1. Oscar Wilde, "The Decay of Lying," in *The Complete Works of Oscar Wilde* (New York: Barnes and Noble, 1994), 973.

2. Stephan Mallarmé, *Message Poétique du Symbolisme*, vol. 2 (Paris: Nizet, 1947), 321.

3. Matthew Arnold, "The Study of Poetry," in *The Portable Matthew Arnold*, ed. Lionel Trilling (New York: Viking, 1949), 300.

4. I elaborate these points in *Practicing Philosophy: Pragmatism and the Philosophical Life* (London: Routledge, 1997) and in *Philosophy and the Art of Writing* (London: Routledge, 2022), whose last chapter is devoted to self-cultivation through art in the Chinese literati tradition.

5. See Iris Murdoch, "Against Dryness" (1961), reprinted in *Existentialists and Mystics* (London: Chatto and Windus, 1997). Richard Rorty confirms this description of analytic philosophy's desire to be "dryly scientific" in his "The Inspirational Value of Great Works of Literature," in *Achieving Our Country* (Cambridge, Mass.: Harvard University Press, 1998), 129. Arthur Danto similarly describes contemporary philosophy (in the dominant analytic school he represents and favors) as professionally "cool" and remote from issues of wisdom; see his *The Abuse of Beauty* (Chicago: Open Court, 2003), xix, cited as *AB*; see also *AB* 20–21, 137.

6. Arnold, "Study of Poetry," 299.

7. G. E. Moore, "Art, Morals, and Religion," an unpublished paper of 1902 cited in Tom Regan's biographical study of Moore, titled *Bloomsbury's Prophet* (Philadelphia: Temple University Press, 1986).

8. Richard Rorty, "Religion as Conversation Stopper," in *Philosophy and Social Hope* (New York: Penguin, 1999), 118–24; *Achieving Our Country*, 125, 132, 136.

9. John Dewey, *Art as Experience* (Carbondale: Southern Illinois University Press, 1986), 87, 338; *Freedom and Culture*, in *Later Works*, vol. 13 (Carbondale: Southern Illinois University Press, 1991), 70.

10. Friedrich Schiller, *Letters on the Aesthetic Education of Man*, trans. E. M. Wilkinson and L. A. Willoughby (Oxford: Oxford University Press, 1983), 215.

11. Xunzi, "Discourse on Music," trans. John Knoblock, in *Xunzi*, vol. 3 (Stanford: Stanford University Press, 1980), 84.

12. See Aoki Takao, "Futatsu no Gei no Michi [Two Species of Art]: Geidoh and Geijutsu," *Nihon no Bigaku [Aesthetics of Japan]* 27 (1998): 114–27.

13. John Dewey, *A Common Faith* (Carbondale: Southern Illinois University Press, 1986), 6–8, cited as *CF*.

14. Santayana's remarks come from his *Interpretations of Poetry and Religion* (New York: Scribner, 1927). Dewey cites them in *CF* 13.

15. Daniel G. Bates and Fred Plog, *Cultural Anthropology* (New York: McGraw-Hill, 1990), 7.

16. T. S. Eliot, *Notes on the Definition of Culture* (London: Faber, 1965), 15.

17. See Arthur Danto, *The Transfiguration of the Commonplace* (Cambridge, Mass.: Harvard University Press, 1981), cited as *TC*, whose first chapter is titled "Works of Art and Mere Real Things."

18. Arthur Danto, "The Artworld," *Journal of Philosophy* 61 (1964): 571–84, cited as *AT*.

19. Arthur Danto, *After the End of Art* (Princeton: Princeton University Press, 1997), 188; and *The Madonna of the Future* (New York: Farrar, Strauss, and Giroux, 2000), 338.

20. See, for example, our discussion of the artworld, hosted by the Tate Britain, "Contested Territories: Arthur Danto, Thierry de Duve and Richard Shusterman," available at https://www.tate.org.uk/audio/contested-territories-arthur-danto-thierry-de-duve-and-richard-shusterman.

21. Alan Watts, *The Way of Zen* (New York: Pantheon Books, 1951), 126. It is interesting that Danto himself deploys this quotation in both "The Artworld" and *The Transfiguration of the Commonplace*.

22. Images of this work are available on the internet.

23. G. W. F. Hegel, *Aesthetics: Lectures on Fine Art*, trans. T. M. Knox (Oxford: Clarendon Press, 1998), 860.

24. See http://www.fau.edu/humanitieschair/images/barrels.jpg for a color image.

25. These images are available online, through the artists' website, at http://christojeanneclaude.net/fe.shtml and http://christojeanneclaude.net/gaso.shtml.

26. I should mention that some prominent artworld artists are similarly appreciative of the beauties of rust, deploying COR-TEN steel in their sculptures and installations because of its tendency to become rust-clad and thus potentially enhance their works' aesthetic effect through rust's subtle tones and textures. One striking example is Richard Serra's marvelous *Torqued Ellipses*.

27. A similar contrast might be discerned between different aesthetic interpretations of the notion of *aura* in different cultures that are shaped by different religious metaphysics. Walter Benjamin, for example, a secular Jew steeped in European culture (albeit much more engaged than Danto with his Jewish heritage), defines the aura in terms of "distance," "uniqueness and permanence." These features are, of course, connected with the idea of a transcendentally elevated sphere that is thus distant from ordinary reality and is permanent because impervious (through its divine nature) to change. Connection with the distantly elevated divinity of monotheism makes the notion of aura (in artistic authenticity as well as in the case of true divinity) also a matter of uniqueness, even in the mysterious unity of the divine trinity of the Christian godhead or the plural instances of authentic prints or sculptures that come from the same single block or cast. See Walter Benjamin, "The Work of Art in the Age of Mechanical Reproduction," in *Illuminations* (New York: Schocken, 1968), 222–23. In contrast, the aura of Zen aesthetic experiences highlights impermanence and the proximity of the everyday and the common; hence, reproducibility here need not destroy the aura.

Chapter Thirteen

1. See Richard Shusterman, "Somaesthetics: A Disciplinary Proposal," *Journal of Aesthetics and Art Criticism* 57, no. 3 (1999), 299–313; and "The Somatic Turn: Care of the Body in Contemporary Culture," in *Performing Live* (Ithaca: Cornell University Press, 2000), chap. 8.

2. William Gibson, *Neuromancer* (New York: Ace, 1984), 6.

3. Diogenes Laertius, *Lives of the Eminent Philosophers*, vol. 2 (Cambridge, Mass.: Harvard University Press, 1931), 71.

4. Arnold Schwarzenegger, *Encyclopedia of Modern Bodybuilding* (New York: Simon and Schuster, 1987), 201–15.

5. See Wilhelm Reich, *The Function of the Orgasm* (New York: Noonday, 1973); Michel Foucault, *Discipline and Punish* (New York: Vintage, 1979); and Pierre Bourdieu, *The Logic of Practice* (Stanford: Stanford University Press, 1990), chap. 4.

6. See Owen Flanagan, *The Science of the Mind*, 2nd ed. (Cambridge, Mass.: MIT Press, 1984); and Bernard Williams, *Problems of the Self* (Cambridge: Cambridge University Press, 1973).

7. See Plato's *Phaedo*, 65c–67a. I here use the translation of H. Tredenick, in *The Last Days of Socrates* (London: Penguin, 1969), 111–13.

8. Plato later asserts in the *Timaeus* (47b) that philosophy itself developed from the sense of sight. See *Plato: Complete Works*, ed. John Cooper (Indianapolis: Hackett, 1997), 1250.

9. Cited in Peter Brown, *The Body and Society: Men, Women, and Sexual Renunciation in Early Christianity* (New York: Columbia University Press, 1988), 164–65.

10. Friedrich Nietzsche, *The Will to Power* (New York: Vintage, 1968), paras. 255, 258, 314; cited as *WP*.

11. Walter Benjamin, *Illuminations*, ed. by Hannah Arendt (New York: Schocken, 1968).

12. Moshe Feldenkrais, *Awareness Through Movement* (New York: Harper Collins, 1977), 6–7. For more details on the theories and practice of these somatic theorists, see "The Somatic Turn" in *Performing Live*, chap. 8.

13. See Jacques Lacan, "The Mirror Stage as Formative of the Function of the I as Revealed in Psychoanalytic Experience," in *Écrits: A Selection*, trans. Alan Sheridan (London: Tavistock, 1977); and Maurice Merleau-Ponty, *The Phenomenology of Perception*, trans. Colin Smith (London: Routledge, 1962).

14. See William James, *The Principles of Psychology* (Cambridge, Mass.: Harvard University Press, 1983), 378; and John Dewey, *Experience and Nature* (Carbondale: Southern Illinois University Press, 1988), 227–32. For detailed analysis of their somatic philosophies, see Richard Shusterman, *Body Consciousness: A Philosophy of Mindfulness and Somaesthetics* (Cambridge: Cambridge University Press, 2008), chaps. 5 and 6.

15. Merleau-Ponty, *Phenomenology of Perception*, 92, 94, 140–41. For a pragmatist critique of Merleau-Ponty's views on the universal invariance of our somatic perspective (that does not properly accommodate differences of age, society, and gender), see *Body Consciousness*, chap. 2.

16. Merleau-Ponty writes that "the body is our general medium for having a world" and "our means of communication with it," but the world itself is "the horizon latent in all our experience and itself ever-present and anterior to every determining thought" (*Phenomenology of Perception*, 92, 146).

17. See K. Marx and F. Engels, *The German Ideology*, in *Karl Marx: Selected Writings*, ed. David McLellan (Oxford: Oxford University Press, 1977); Michel Foucault, *Discipline and Punish* (New York: Pantheon, 1978); Pierre Bourdieu, *Distinction: A Social Critique of the Judgement of Taste* (Cambridge, Mass.: Harvard University Press, 1984), and *Logic of Practice*.

18. See Shusterman, *Practicing Philosophy: Pragmatism and the Philosophical Life* (New York: Routledge, 1997), chap. 3; and chap. 8 of this volume.

19. The original version of this essay was written before the year 2000, thus prior to the adoption of somaesthetics by researchers in the field of human-computer

interaction design. Among the many applications of somaesthetics to HCI, the most substantial is by Kristina Höök, particularly her *Designing with the Body: Somaesthetic Interaction Design* (Cambridge, Mass.: MIT Press, 2018).

20. See, for instance, Ann Balsamo, "Will the Real Body Please Stand Up? Boundary Stories about Virtual Cultures," in *Cyberspace: First Steps,* ed. Michael Benedikt (Cambridge, Mass.: MIT Press, 1991): "Bodies in cyberspace are also constituted by descriptive codes that 'embody' expectations of appearance. Many of the engineers currently debating the form and nature of cyberspace are the young Turks of computer engineering, men in their late teens and twenties, and they are preoccupied with the things with which postpubescent men have always been preoccupied. This rather steamy group will generate the codes and descriptors by which bodies in cyberspace are represented"(103–4).

21. For more detailed arguments on these points, see Richard Shusterman, *Body Consciousness*, chap. 1; and "Somaesthetics and the Art of Living," in *Foucault's Aesthetics of Existence and Shusterman's Somaesthetics*, ed. Valentina Antoniol and Stefano Marino (London: Bloomsbury, 2024), 121–43.

22. James, *Principles of Psychology*, 1067–68.

23. J. Z. Young, *An Introduction to the Study of Man* (Oxford: Oxford University Press, 1971), 38.

Chapter Fourteen

1. *Webster's Third New International Dictionary* (Springfield, Mass.: Merriam, 1961), 1101, defines the humanities as "the branch of learning regarded as having primarily a cultural character and usually including languages, literature, history, mathematics, and philosophy." *The Random House College Dictionary* (New York: Random House, 1984), 645, defines it as "a. the study of classical Latin and Greek language and literature. b. literature, philosophy, art, etc. as distinguished from the sciences."

2. There is considerably more interest in the body in social sciences, especially sociology. The humanist neglect of the body is reflected even in basic arts education, where distinctively body-centered arts such as dance get far less attention in the curriculum. On this point, see Liora Bressler, "Dancing the Curriculum: Exploring the Body and Movement in Elementary Schools," in *Knowing Bodies, Moving Minds*, ed. Liora Bressler (Dordrecht: Kluwer, 2004), 127–51.

3. Though I first introduced the idea of somaesthetics in *Vor der Interpretation* (Vienna: Passagen Verlag, 1996) and *Practicing Philosophy* (London and New York: Routledge, 1997), I only later articulated its structure and genealogy in Richard Shusterman, "Somaesthetics: A Disciplinary Proposal," *Journal of Aesthetics and Art Criticism* 57 (1999): 299–313. It is further elaborated in my *Performing Live* (Ithaca: Cornell University Press, 2000), *Body Consciousness* (Cambridge: Cambridge University

Press, 2008), and *Thinking through the Body* (Cambridge: Cambridge University Press, 2012). For a critical overview of somaesthetics from multiple authors, see *Shusterman's Somaesthetics: From Hip Hop Philosophy to Politics and Performance Art*, ed. Jerold Abrams (Leiden: Brill, 2022). For an insightful article relating my work in somaesthetics to pragmatism and perfectionism in terms of both epistemological and ethical-political themes, see Matthias Girel, "Perfectionism in Practice: Shusterman's Place in Recent Pragmatism," *Contemporary Pragmatism* 12, no. 1 (2015): 156–79. See also Nicola Ramazzotto, "Shusterman's Somaesthetics as Meta-aesthetics," *Studi di estetica* 52, no. 1 (2024): 161–82. Bibliographies of writings on somaesthetics by myself and other authors can be found at my website at Florida Atlantic University, Dorothy F. Schmidt College of Arts and Letters, Humanities Chair, https://www.fau.edu/artsandletters/humanitieschair/articles/.

4. John Dewey employs the term "body-mind" in *Experience and Nature* (Carbondale: Southern Illinois University Press, 1988), 191; he later uses the term "mind-body" to designate "a unified wholeness" in his essay "Body and Mind" in John Dewey, *The Later Works*, vol. 3 (Carbondale: Southern Illinois University Press, 1988), 27. I prefer to use the notion of soma to indicate this unified wholeness because it avoids linguistically reinforcing the dualism of body and mind.

5. Of course, given the sloppy, haphazard abundance of nature, there are occasional human mutants, but such exceptions only confirm the bodily norm, which can be understood as an evolving form rather than a fixed, sacred, ontological essence.

6. Evidence for this includes the so-called sign of Babinski or plantar response—the toes in infants dorsiflex and fan with stroking of the sole, similar to the response of adults with damage to the motor cortex.

7. I elaborate this argument more fully in *Body Consciousness*, chap. 4.

8. Although proscribing graven images, the ancient Hebrew bible affirmed that humans were molded in God's image, suggesting our bodies have a divine source and paradigm. If the question of God's own body remains problematically mysterious in the Old Testament, then the New Testament's human incarnation of God in Christ, though adding further mystery, nonetheless reconfirms the human form as worthy of divine inhabiting. Hegel and others have admired Greek sculpture for capturing the way the harmonious proportions of the human body express the dignity of our rational spirit.

9. Ludwig Wittgenstein, *Denkebewegung: Tagebücher 1930–1932, 1936–1937*, ed. Ilse Somavilla (Innsbruck: Haymon, 1997), 139–40.

10. Roger Ames and Henry Rosemont Jr., trans., *The Analects of Confucius* (New York: Ballantine, 1998), books 2:8 and 8:4.

11. *The Analects*, book 16:5; see also books 4:1, 4:17, and 12:24. For more detailed discussion of Confucian somaesthetics, see my "Pragmatism and East-Asian Thought," in *The Range of Pragmatism and the Limits of Philosophy*, ed. Richard Shusterman (Oxford: Blackwell, 2004), 13–42.

12. Even willing that fails to issue in performing the willed action will still involve—especially if it is effortful willing—bodily means and be expressed in patterns of muscular contraction. For more detailed argument on the bodily nature of will, see *Body Consciousness*, chaps. 5 and 6.

13. See William James, "The Experience of Activity," in *Essays in Radical Empiricism* (Cambridge, Mass.: Harvard University Press, 1976), 86.

14. See Diogenes Laertius, *Lives of Eminent Philosophers*, trans. R. D. Hicks, vol. 1 (Cambridge, Mass.: Harvard University Press, 1991), 153, 163; Xenophon, *Conversations of Socrates*, trans. Hugh Tredennick and Robin Waterfield (London: Penguin, 1990), 172.

15. Aristippus, founder of the Cyrenaic school, insisted "that bodily training contributes to the acquisition of virtue," since fit bodies provide sharper perceptions and more discipline and versatility for adapting oneself in thought, attitude, and action. Zeno, founder of Stoicism, likewise urged regular bodily exercise, claiming that "proper care of health and one's organs of sense" are "unconditional duties." Cynicism's founder, Diogenes of Sinope, was even more outspoken in advocating bodily training as essential for the knowledge and discipline needed for wisdom and the good life. He also experimented with a striking range of body practices to test and toughen himself: extending from eating raw food and walking barefoot in the snow to masturbating in public and living in a tub. Of Diogenes the Cynic, it is said: "He would adduce indisputable evidence to show how easily from gymnastic training we arrive at virtue." Even the pre-Socratic Cleobulus, a sage "distinguished for strength and beauty," "advised men to practise bodily exercise" in their pursuit of wisdom. The citations in this paragraph come from Diogenes Laertius, *Lives of Eminent Philosophers*, vol. 1, 91, 95, 153, 221; and vol. 2, 71, 73, 215.

16. See, for example, Xunzi's emphasis on embodiment in "On Self-Cultivation," "Discourse on Ritual Principles," and "Discourse on Music," in *Xunzi*, trans. John Knoblock (Stanford: Stanford University Press, 1988), respectively vol. 1, 143–58; and vol. 3, 48–73; 74–87; the *Zhuangzi* and *Guanzi* on breathing, respectively in "The Great and Venerable Teacher," in *Chuang-Tzu*, trans. Burton Watson (New York: Columbia University Press, 1968), 77–92; and "Nei Yeh," in *Kuan-Tzu*, trans. W. A. Rickett, vol. 1 (Hong Kong: Hong Kong University Press, 1965), 151–68; and D. T. Suzuki on swordsmanship in his *Zen and Japanese Culture* (Princeton: Princeton University Press, 1973), chaps. 5 and 6. The contemporary Japanese philosopher Yuasa Yasuo insists that the concept of "personal cultivation" or *shugyo* (which is presupposed in Eastern thought as "the philosophical foundation") has an essential bodily component, since "true knowledge cannot be obtained simply by means of theoretical thinking" but only "through 'bodily recognition or realization' (*tainin* or *taitoku*)." See Yuasa Yasuo, *The Body: Towards an Eastern Mind-Body Theory*, trans. S. Nagatomo and T. P. Kasulis (Albany: State University of New York Press, 1987), 25.

17. *Mencius: A New Translation*, trans. W. A. C. H. Dobson (Toronto: Toronto University Press, 1969), 144. Mencius further claims: "Whichever trust I fail to fulfil, it must not be that of keeping my body inviolate, for that is the trust from which all others arise," 138.

18. See *The Oxford English Dictionary*, 2nd ed., vol. 7 (Oxford: Oxford University Press, 1989), 476.

19. Most of our body weight (head, shoulders, torso) is on top, while our legs and feet are much lighter. This anatomical structure contrasts with the stability of a pyramid and mechanically encourages us to move forward horizontally in reaction to gravitational pressure that tends to pull us earthward and bring us down.

20. Jean-Jacques Rousseau, *Emile* (New York: Basic Books, 1979), 54, 118, 125.

21. Ralph Waldo Emerson, "Works and Days," in *Society and Solitude, Works of Ralph Waldo Emerson*, vol. 2 (Boston: Houghton, Osgood Company, 1880), 129.

22. See Michel de Montaigne, *The Complete Essays of Montaigne*, trans. Donald Frame (Stanford: Stanford University Press, 1965), 484–85. Montaigne condemned as "inhuman" any philosophy "that would make us disdainful enemies of the cultivation of the body" (849).

23. Ludwig Wittgenstein, *Culture and Value* (Oxford: Blackwell, 1980), 2, 9, 43, 68, 80. I sometimes use my own translation from the German original.

24. William James, *The Principles of Psychology* (Cambridge, Mass.: Harvard University Press, 1983), 1128.

25. Immanuel Kant, *Reflexionen zur Kritische Philosophie*, ed. Benno Erdmann (Stuttgart: Frommann-Holzboog, 1992), 68–69. Kant later critically remarks that "man is usually full of sensations when he is empty of thought," 117.

26. William James, *Talks to Teachers on Psychology and to Students on Some of Life's Ideals* (New York: Dover, 1962), 99.

27. James, *Talks to Teachers*, 100.

28. James, *Principles of Psychology*, 1077.

29. James, *Talks to Teachers*, 118.

30. James, *Principles of Psychology*, 1078.

31. William James, *The Correspondence of William James*, vol. 4, ed. Ignas K. Skrupskelis and Elizabeth M. Berkeley (Charlottesville: University Press of Virginia, 1995), 586.

32. Noting his "disposition to hypochondria," Kant felt that heightened attention to inner somatic sensations resulted in "morbid feelings" of anxiety. See Imanuel Kant, *The Contest of the Faculties*, trans. Mary J. Gregor (Lincoln: University of Nebraska Press, 1992), 187–89. On James's hypochondria, see Ralph Barton Perry, *The Thought and Character of William James* (Nashville: Vanderbilt University Press, 1996), who also cites James's mother's complaints of his excessive expression of "every unfavorable symptom" (361). On the "philosophical hypochondria" of "introspective studies," see James's letter to brother Henry of August 24, 1872, in *The*

Correspondence of William James, vol. 1, ed. Ignas K. Skrupskelis and Elizabeth M. Berkeley (Charlottesville: University Press of Virginia, 1992), 167. James repeatedly confessed, in private correspondence, to being "an abominable neurasthenic." See, for example, his letters to F. H. Bradley and George H. Howison in *The Correspondence of William James*, vol. 8, ed. Ignas K. Skrupskelis and Elizabeth M. Berkeley (Charlottesville: University Press of Virginia, 2000), 52, 57.

33. In advocating the cultivation of somatic awareness, I am far from suggesting that our bodily feelings are infallible guides to practice and self-care. On the contrary, I recognize that the average individual's somatic self-perception is often quite inaccurate (not noticing, for instance, excessive and harmful chronic muscular contractions). This is precisely why somatic awareness needs to be cultivated in order to make it more accurate and discriminating, and why such cultivation typically requires the aid of a teacher. I also do not want to suggest that our somatic self-awareness could ever be complete in a way that we become totally transparent to ourselves. For the limits and difficulties of somatic introspection, see *Body Consciousness*, chaps. 2, 5, and 6.

34. James, *The Correspondence of William James*, vol. 9, ed. Ignas K. Skrupskelis and Elizabeth M. Berkeley (Charlottesville: University Press of Virginia, 2001), 14.

35. See, for example, Shusterman, *Performing Live*, chap. 7; and chap. 13 of this volume.

36. See Friedrich Nietzsche, *The Will to Power*, trans. Walter Kaufmann and R. J. Hollingdale (New York: Vintage, 1968), 220.

37. The Feldenkrais Method deploys an educational rather than therapeutic-pathological model. Clients are regarded as students rather than patients, and we speak of our work as giving lessons rather than therapy sessions. I analyze the Feldenkrais Method in *Performing Live*, chap. 8. Functional Integration is only one of the two central modes of the method, the other being Awareness Through Movement. The latter is best described in Feldenkrais's introductory text *Awareness Through Movement* (New York: Harper and Row, 1972). A very detailed but difficult account of Functional Integration is provided in Yochanan Rywerant, *The Feldenkrais Method: Teaching by Handling* (New York: Harper and Row, 1983).

38. See Richard Shusterman, *Practicing Philosophy* (New York: Routledge, 1997), 1–64.

39. Hence, Montaigne wisely urged that "we must not [merely] attach learning to the mind, we must incorporate it; we must not sprinkle, but dye"; Montaigne, *Complete Essays*, 103.

40. Heightened awareness enables us to increase our pleasures by making them more consciously savored and deepening them with the pleasures of reflection. As Montaigne writes, "I enjoy [life] twice as much as others, for the measure of enjoyment depends on the greater or lesser attention that we lend it"; Montaigne, *Complete Essays*, 853.

Chapter Fifteen

1. Here I should note that another meaning of muscle memory refers to the phenomenon that when a person suspends a sustained weightlifting program for a period of time and then resumes it, his earlier trained muscles are able to return to their previous levels of size and strength more quickly and easily than was necessary to reach those levels originally, as if the muscles recalled their prior levels.

2. My account of these methods relies on my professional practice as a somatic educator and therapist in the Feldenkrais Method, from which I have also been able to study some of the somaesthetic pathologies I discuss in this chapter.

3. William James, *The Principles of Psychology* (Cambridge, Mass.: Harvard University Press, 1983), 235; hereafter *PP*.

4. William James, *Essays in Radical Empiricism* (Cambridge, Mass.: Harvard University Press, 1976), 33; hereafter *RE*.

5. Such implicit memory of knowing who one is in terms of knowing one is the same person now as in the past does not, as implicit memory, require that one remembers who one is in terms of an explicit descriptive identity of being a certain person with a particular name, age, gender, and profession. The formulation of such descriptive terms involves, of course, explicit thought, but on the basis of one's implicit memory of self, one could normally recall these descriptions if one were asked.

6. Erik R. Kandel, *In Search of Memory* (New York: Norton, 2006), 312–13.

7. Barbara Tversky, "Remembering Spaces," in *The Oxford Handbook of Memory*, ed. Endel Tulving and Fergus Craik (New York: Oxford University Press, 2000), 371.

8. Daniel Stern, *The Interpersonal World of the Infant* (New York: Basic Books, 1985), chaps. 6–7.

9. Richard Shusterman, *Body Consciousness: A Philosophy of Mindfulness and Somaesthetics* (Cambridge: Cambridge University Press, 2008), chap. 4.

10. In these roles, the distinctive uniforms that are worn on one's body serve as cues or tools to help individuals incorporate the proper somatic dispositions and comportment.

11. See Maurice Merleau-Ponty, *Phenomenology of Perception*, trans. Colin Smith (London: Routledge, 1962), 94, and *Signs*, trans. R. C. McCleary (Evanston: Northwestern University Press, 1970), 66. For more discussion of this point, see my *Body Consciousness*, 59–61.

12. This frequently quoted saying of Balanchine can be found, for example, in Deborah Jowitt, *Time and the Dancing Image* (Berkeley: University of California Press, 1989), 273. Some renowned masters of dance do not share this view, notably the most influential expert of Nō theater and dance, Zeami Motokiyo. I explore his theories in refuting the claim that explicit attention to one's action is always detrimental to effective performance after the performed actions have been learned

and habituated into muscle memory. See Richard Shusterman, "Body Consciousness and Performance: Somaesthetics East and West," in *Thinking Through the Body* (Cambridge: Cambridge University Press, 2012), chap. 9.

13. "A thing must be burnt in so that it stays in the memory: only something that continues to hurt stays in the memory." Friedrich Nietzsche, *On the Genealogy of Morality*, ed. Keith Ansell-Pearson (Cambridge: Cambridge University Press, 2007), 38.

14. For more on this topic, see B. A. van der Kolk, J. Hopper, and J. Osterman, "Exploring the Nature of Traumatic Memory: Combining Clinical Knowledge with Laboratory Methods," in *Trauma and Cognitive Science: A Meeting of Minds, Science, and Human Experience*, ed. J. Freyd and A. DePrince (Philadelphia: Haworth Press, 2001), 9–31.

15. Richard Shusterman, "Le corps en acte et en conscience," in *Philosophie du corps*, ed. Bernard Andrieu (Paris: Vrin, 2010), 349–72.

16. My consciousness or "stream of thinking," James argues, relying on his own introspection, "is only a careless name for what, when scrutinized, reveals itself to consist chiefly of the stream of my breathing. The 'I think' which Kant said must be able to accompany all my objects, is the 'I breathe' which actually does accompany them." James concludes that "breath, which was ever the original of 'spirit,' breath moving outwards, between the glottis and the nostrils, is, I am persuaded, the essence out of which philosophers have constructed the entity known to them as consciousness" (*RE* 19). James surprisingly ignores both the feelings of inhalation and the fact that one very often feels one's breathing not only in the head and neck but also down into one's thoracic area, where the movement of the lungs interacts with movements in the chest or ribcage; and that same thoracic area provides the familiar background feelings of one's beating heart.

17. There are studies that link fast eating with obese adults and adolescents; and experimental studies also show that "increase in the speed of eating in normal weight volunteers caused overeating . . . replicating the pattern of eating in a group of obese patients." One study showed that the use of a Mandometer (a machine that tells eaters while they are eating that they are consuming food more rapidly than their eating therapist designates) led to loss of weight. See S. Shechner and J. Ronin, *Obese Humans and Rats* (New York: Wiley, 1974), 6–9; M. Zandian, I. Ioakimidis, C. Bergh, and P. Södersten, "Decelerated and Linear Eaters: Effect of Eating Rate on Food Intake and Satiety," *Physiological Behavior* 96 (2009): 270–75; I. Ioakimidis, M. Zandian, C. Bergh, and P. Södersten, "A Method for the Control of Eating Rate: A Potential Intervention in Eating Disorders," *Behavioral Research Methods* 41 (2009): 755–60; and A. Ford, C. Bergh, P. Södersten, M. A. Sabin et al., "Treatment of Childhood Obesity by Retraining Eating Behaviour: Randomized Controlled Trial," *British Medical Journal* 340b (2010): 5388. In that article, the authors note that earlier efforts to reduce obesity through therapy lifestyle interventions were more effective in younger children than in adolescents. There may be

many reasons for this, but one reason might be that the eating habits of adolescents are more deeply entrenched, hence more resistant to change.

18. Our culture's fascination with advertised ideals of bodily beauty and pleasures (along with our unavoidable failures to achieve them) might encourage the mistaken presumption that somaesthetics is focused on the quest to possess perfectly beautiful bodies and to enjoy those of others. This misreading of somaesthetics disregards its focus on the soma as embodied subjectivity, as a perceiving, intentional, locus or subject of consciousness, whose powers of sensory perception can be heightened through cultivation and reflection. Through such enhanced perceptual powers, we can improve our self-use (including the stylizing of our external somatic form) by overcoming problematic habits of muscle memory, including overeating. In contrast to German phenomenology's sharp ontological distinction between *Körper* and *Leib* (body as physical object and body as experiential subject), somaesthetics understands and treats the soma as one entity encompassing both material and subjective dimensions. For more detailed discussion of these ontological matters, see Richard Shusterman, "Soma and Psyche," *Journal of Speculative Philosophy* 24, no. 3 (2010): 205–23, and "Somaesthetics in Context," *Kinesiology Review* 9, no. 3 (2020): 245–53.

Chapter Sixteen

1. For an explanation of these roots of somaesthetics, see Richard Shusterman, *Thinking Through the Body: Essays in Somaesthetics* (Cambridge: Cambridge University Press, 2012), 1–8.

2. Fredric Jameson, "Pleasure: A Political Issue," in *The Ideologies of Theory*, vol. 2 (Minneapolis: University of Minnesota Press, 1988), 70

3. Richard Shusterman, *Pragmatist Aesthetics: Living Beauty, Rethinking* Art (Oxford: Blackwell, 1992), 260.

4. James Legge, trans., *Confucian Analects, The Great Learning, and The Doctrine of the Mean* (Oxford: Clarendon Press, 1893), 266.

5. W. A. C. H. Dobson, trans., *Mencius: A New Translation* (Toronto: University of Toronto Press, 1969), 138, para. 4A20.

6. John Dewey and James H. Tufts, *Ethics*, 2nd ed. (Carbondale: Southern Illinois University Press, 1985), 302; and John Dewey, "Democracy and Educational Administration," in *The Later Works of John Dewey*, vol. 11, ed. Jo Ann Boydston (Carbondale: Southern Illinois University Press, 1981), 219.

7. William James, *The Principles of Psychology* (Cambridge, Mass.: Harvard University Press, 1983), 130

8. James, *Principles of Psychology*, 125.

9. Richard Shusterman, *Body Consciousness* (Cambridge: Cambridge University, Press, 2008), chap. 3.

10. Shusterman, *Body Consciousness*, chap. 4.

11. Ludwig Wittgenstein, *Culture and Value*, trans. Peter Winch (Oxford: Blackwell, 1980), 20–21.

12. See David Granger, "Somaesthetics and Racism: Toward an Embodied Pedagogy of Difference," *Journal of Aesthetic Education* 44, no. 3 (2010): 69–81; Andrew Fitz-Gibbon, "Somaesthetics: Body Consciousness and Nonviolence," *Social Philosophy Today* 23 (2012): 85–89; my discussions of these matters in *Body Consciousness* and *Thinking Through the Body*, and most recently the articles in *Somapower: Somaesthetics Reads Politics*, ed. Leszek Koczanowicz (Leiden: Brill, 2024).

13. Marjorie Jolles, "Between Embodied Subjects and Objects: Narrative Somaesthetics," *Hypatia* 27 (2012): 301–18.

14. This is suggested from narratives of some of the more successful Middle East political negotiations, and we can also find experimental evidence in a recent study on business negotiations, Lakshmi Balachandra, "Should You Eat While You Negotiate?," *Harvard Business Review*, January 29, 2013, https://hbr.org/2013/01/should-you-eat-while-you-negot.

15. The English indeed distinguished between the king's two bodies: that of his mortal flesh and another of a more abstract and divine character.

16. Friedrich Nietzsche, *The Will to Power*, trans. Walter Kauffman and R. J. Hollingdale (New York: Random House, 1968), para. 660.

17. Helmuth Plessner, *Laughing and Crying: A Study of the Limits of Human Behavior*, trans. J. S. Churchill and Marjorie Grene (Evanston: Northwestern University Press, 1970), 36.

18. Frantz Fanon, *The Wretched of the Earth*, trans. Constance Farrington (New York: Grove Press, 1963); hereafter abbreviated as *WE*.

19. Roger T. Ames and Henry Rosemont, trans., *The Analects of Confucius: A Philosophical Translation* (New York: Ballantine, 1998), 160. For the following points, see also 71, 78, 89, 92, 121, and 163.

20. I cite from the ancient "Five Aspects of Conduct" as translated in K. W. Holloway, *Guodian: The Newly Discovered Seeds of Chinese Religious and Political Philosophy* (Oxford: Oxford University Press, 2009), 136.

21. In the *Analects* (20.2) Confucius speaks of the five virtues (*wu mei* 五美), which could also be translated as "the five beauties," as 美 (*mei*) is the Chinese character for "beauty." The term is translated as "the Five Lovely Things" as contrasted with "the Four Ugly Things" in Arthur Waley, trans., *The Analects of Confucius* (New York: Vintage, 1938), 232, while the same contrast is rendered as "the five virtues" and "the four vices" in the Ames and Rosemont's translation, 228.

22. John Dewey, *Art as Experience* (Carbondale: Southern Illinois University Press, 1987), 87, 338. For criticism of Dewey's one-sided emphasis on unity (including its political dangers), see Richard Shusterman, "Pragmatism and East-Asian Thought," in *The Range of Pragmatism and the Limits of Philosophy*, ed. Richard Shusterman (Oxford: Blackwell, 2004), 13–42. Dewey later condemned the totalitarianism of

Nazi Germany and Stalinist Russia (and their repressive use of culture) in his 1939 book *Freedom and Culture*, in *The Later Works of John Dewey*, vol. 13, ed. Jo Ann Boydston (Carbondale: Southern Illinois University Press, 1988), 69–72.

23. Herbert Marcuse, *The Aesthetic Dimension: Toward a Critique of Marxist Aesthetics* (Boston: Beacon Press, 1978), 3–4, hereafter cited as *AD*.

24. Herbert Marcuse, "The Jerusalem Lectures," in *Art and Liberation: Collected Papers of Herbert Marcuse*, ed. Douglas Kellner (London: Routledge, 2007), 152, hereafter JL.

25. Antonia Soulez, "Practice, Theory, Pleasure and the Forms of Resistance: Shusterman's *Pragmatist Aesthetics*," *Journal of Speculative Philosophy* 16, no. 1 (2002): 3.

26. See Leszek Koczanowicz, "Toward a Democratic Utopia of Everydayness: Microphysics of Emancipation and Somapower," *History of European Ideas* 46 (2020): 1122–33; "Beauty between Repression and Coercion: A Few Thoughts on Richard Shusterman's *Ars Erotica: Sex and Somaesthetics in the Classical Arts of Love*," *Foucault Studies* 31 (2021): 36–43; and Stefano Marino, "Sexuality and/as Art, Power, and Reconciliation: Preface to Symposium on Richard Shusterman's *Ars Erotica: Sex and Somaesthetics in the Classical Arts of Love*," *Foucault Studies* 31 (2021): 1–13.

27. I elaborate these points in Richard Shusterman, "Art, Eros, and Liberation: Aesthetic Education between Pragmatism and Critical Theory," *Journal of Aesthetic Education* 58, no. 1 (2024): 1–24.

28. Karl Marx, *Economic and Philosophic Manuscripts of 1844 and the Communist Manifesto* (with Frederick Engels), trans. Martin Milligan (Amherst: Prometheus Books, 1988), 106, hereafter *PPC*.

Books by Richard Shusterman

The Object of Literary Criticism. Amsterdam: Rodopi, 1984.

- *L' Objet de la critique littéraire.* Paris: Questions Théoriques, 2009.

T. S. Eliot and the Philosophy of Criticism. London: Duckworth / and New York: Columbia University Press, 1988.

Analytic Aesthetics. Oxford: Blackwell, 1989. Editor.

The Interpretive Turn: Philosophy, Science, Culture. Ithaca: Cornell University Press, 1991. Edited with James Bohman and David Hiley.

Pragmatist Aesthetics: Living Beauty, Rethinking Art. Oxford: Blackwell, 1992; 2nd edition with new introduction and additional chapter, New York: Rowman and Littlefield, 2000.

- *L'art à l'état vif: La pensée pragmatiste et l'esthétique populaire.* Trans. Christine Noille. Paris: Minuit, 1992; 2nd pocketbook edition with a new introduction and appendix, Paris: L'éclat, 2018.

- *Kunst Leben: Die Ästhetik des Pragmatismus.* Trans. Barbara Reiter. Frankfurt: Fischer, 1994.

- *Taide, elämä ja estetiika: Pragmatistinen filosofia ja estetiika.* Trans. Vesa Mujunen. Helsinki: Gaudeamus, 1997.

- *Vivendo a Arte: O Pensamento Pragmatistist e a Estética Popular.* Trans. Gisela Domschke. São Paulo: Editora 34, 1998.

- *Estetyka pragmatyczna: Żywe piękno i refleksja nad sztuka.* Trans. Adam Chmielewski and Leszek Koczanowicz. Wroclaw: University of Wroclaw Press, 1998; 2nd edition with additional chapter, Krakow: Aureus, 2015.

- ポピュラー芸術の美学: プラグマティズムの立場から. Trans. Fuminori Akiba. Tokyo: Keiso Shobo, 1999. (Title in English would be *Aesthetics of Popular Art: From the Perspective of Pragmatism.*)

- 프라그마티즘 미학: 살아 있는 아름다움, 다시 생각해 보는 예술. Trans. Jinyup Kim and Gwangmyeong Kim, 2002; 2nd edition, Seoul: Book Korea Publishers, 2009.

- 《实用主义美学: 生活之美, 艺术之思》. Trans. Peng Feng. Beijing: The Commercial Press, 2002; 2nd Chinese edition, Beijing: The Commercial Press, 2016.

- *Estética Pragmatista: Viviendo la belleza, repensando el arte.* Trans. Fernando González del Campo Román. Barçelona: Idea Books, 2002.

- *Estetika Pragmatizmu: Krása a umenie života.* Trans. (Slovak) Emil Visnovsky and Zdenka Kalnická. Bratislava: Kalligram, 2003.

- *Pragmatista Esztétika: A szépség megélése és a művészet újragondolása.* Trans. (Hungarian) József Kollár. Bratislava: Kalligram, 2003.

- *Estetica Pragmatistă: Arta În Stare Vie.* Trans. (Romanian) Ana-Maria Pascal. Iaşi: Institutul European, 2004.

- *Estetica Pragmatista.* Trans. Teresa Di Folco and Giovanni Matteucci. Palermo: Aesthetica Edizione, 2010.

- *Прагматическая эстетика: Живая красота, переосмысление искусства.* Trans. Marina Kukartseva, N. Sokolova, and V. Volkov. Moscow: Kanon+ Publishers, 2012.

Sous l'interprétation. Trans. Jean-Pierre Cometti. Paris: Éditions de l'éclat, 1994.

- *Vor der Interpretation: Sprache und Erfahrung in Hermeneutik, Dekonstruktion und Pragmatismus.* Trans. Barbara Reiter. Vienna: Passagen Verlag, 1996.

Practicing Philosophy: Pragmatism and the Philosophical Life. New York: Routledge, 1997.

- *Philosophie als Lebenspraxis.* Trans. Heidi Salaverria. Berlin: Akademie Verlag, 2001.

- *Vivre la philosophie.* Trans. Charles Fournier and Jean-Pierre Cometti. Paris: Klincksiek, 2001.

- 《哲学实践》. Trans. Peng Feng. Beijing: Peking University Press, 2002.

- *Praktyka Filozofii, Filozofia Praktyki.* Trans. Alina Mitek. Krakow: Universitas, 2005.

- プラグマティズムと哲学の実践. Trans. Higuchi Satoshi, Aoki Takao, and Maruyama Yasushi. Yokohama: Seori Shobo, 2012.

La modernité en questions. Paris: Cerf, 1998. Edited with Françoise Gaillard and Jacques Poulain.

Interpretation, Relativism, and the Metaphysics of Culture. New York: Humanity Books, 1999. Edited with Michael Krausz.

Bourdieu: A Critical Reader. Oxford: Blackwell, 1999. Editor.

La fin de l'expérience esthétique. Trans. Jean-Pierre Cometti. Pau: Presse Universitaire de Pau, 1999.

Performing Live: Aesthetic Alternatives for the Ends of Art. Ithaca: Cornell University Press, 2000.

- *Leibliche Erfahrung in Kunst und Lebensstil.* Trans. Robin Celikates. Berlin: Akademie Verlag, 2005.

- 《生活即审美: 审美经验和生活艺术》. Trans. Peng Feng. Beijing: Peking University Press, 2007.

- 삶의 미학:예술의 종언 이후 미학적 대안. Trans. Jinyup Kim and Jeongseon Huh. Seoul: Ehak Publishing, 2012.

- *Le style à l'état vif: Somaesthétique, Art Populaire, and Art de Vivre.* Trans. Thomas Mondémé. Paris: Questions Théoriques, 2015.

Surface and Depth: Dialectics of Criticism and Culture. Ithaca: Cornell University Press, 2002.

- 《表面与深度: 批评与文化的辩证法》. Trans. Li Luning. Beijing: Peking University Press, 2014.

The Range of Pragmatism and the Limits of Philosophy. Oxford: Blackwell, 2004. Editor.

O sztuce i życiu: Od poetyki hip-hopu do filozofii somatycznej. Trans. Wojciech Małecki. Wroclaw: Alta 2, 2007.

Aesthetic Experience. New York: Routledge, 2008. Edited with Adele Tomlin.

- تجربه ی زیبا شناختی Trans. Shahriar Vaghfipour. Tehran: Eejaz Publishing, 2017.

Body Consciousness: A Philosophy of Mindfulness and Somaesthetics. Cambridge: Cambridge University Press, 2008.

- *Conscience du corps: Pour une soma-esthétique.* Trans. Nicolas Vieillescazes. Paris: l'éclat, 2007; 2nd edition, Paris: l'éclat, 2008.

- *Świadomość Ciała: Dociekania z Zakresu Somaestetyki.* Trans. Wojciech Małecki and S. Stankiewicz. Krakow: Universitas, 2010; 2nd edition, Krakow: Universitas, 2016.

- 몸의 미학: 신체미학—솜에스테틱스. Trans. Hyijin Lee. Seoul: Book Korea, 2010; 2nd edition, Seoul: Book Korea, 2014.

- 《身体意识与身体美学》. Trans. Cheng Xiangzhan. Beijing: The Commercial Press, 2011; 2nd edition, Beijing: The Commercial Press, 2014.

- *Consciência Corporal.* Trans. Pedro Sette-Câmara. São Paulo: É Realizacoes, 2012.

- *Körper-Bewusstsein: Für eine Philosophie der Somästhetik.* Trans. Heidi Salaverria. Hamburg: Felix Meiner, 2012.

- *Conscienza del corpo: La filosofia come arte di vivere e la somae-stetica.* Trans. Salvatore Tedesco and Valeria Costanza D'Agata. Milano: Christian Marinotti Edizione, 2013.

Soma-esthétique et architecture: Une alternative critique. Geneva: Haute Ecole d'Art et Design, 2010.

Thinking through the Body: Essays in Somaesthetics. Cambridge: Cambridge University Press, 2012.

- *A Gondolkodó Test: Szómaesztétikai esszék*. Trans. Sándor Kremer et al. Szeged: Jate Press, 2015.

- *Myślenie ciała: Eseje z zakresu somaestetyki*. Trans. Patrycja Poniatowska. Warsaw: Le Monde diplomatique, 2016.

- 《通过身体来思考: 身体美学文集》. Trans. Zhang Baogui. Beijing: Peking University, 2020.

Stili di vita: Qualche istruzione per l'uso. Milan: Mimesis Edizioni, 2012. Coauthored with Roberta Dreon and Daniele Goldoni.

Aesthetic Transactions: Pragmatist Philosophy through Art and Life. Paris: Galerie Michel Journiac / L'éclat, 2012.

스타일의 미학. (*Aesthetics of Style*). Trans./ed. Hyijin Lee. Seoul: Book Korea, 2013.

Chemins de l'art: Transfigurations, du pragmatisme au zen. With afterword by Arthur Danto. Trans. Raphaël Cuir. Paris: Al Dante, 2013.

Szómaesztétika és az élet művészete. Trans. Sándor Kremer. Szeged: Jate Press, 2014.

The Adventures of the Man in Gold / Les Aventures de l'homme en or. Trans. Thomas Mondemé and with images from Yann Toma. Paris: Hermann Editions, 2016; 2nd pocket edition with added essays but without images, Paris: Hermann, 2020.

- 《金衣人历险记—徘徊在艺术与生活之间的哲学故事》 Trans. Lu Yang. Hefei: Anhui Publishing, 2020.

Aesthetic Experience and Somaesthetics. Leiden: Brill, 2018. Editor.

《情感与行动: 实用主义之道》, 商务印书馆 2018年8月 (*Act and Affect: Paths of Pragmatism*) Trans./ed. by Gao Yanping. Shanghai: The Commercial Press, 2018. (Based on Shusterman's May 2017 "Summit Lectures" at Fudan University, Shanghai.)

身体感性と文化の哲学: 人間・運動・世界制作 (*Philosophy of Somaesthetics and Culture: Human Being, Movement, Worldmaking*). Tokyo: Keiso Shobo, 2019, coauthored with Higuchi Satoshi and Gunter Gebauer, trans. Higuchi Satoshi.

Bodies in the Streets: The Somaesthetics of City Life. Leiden: Brill, 2019. Editor.

Ars Erotica: Sex and Somaesthetics in the Classical Arts of Love. Cambridge: Cambridge University Press, 2021.

Philosophy and the Art of Writing. New York: Routledge, 2022.

Doświadczenie estetyczne I potęga owładnięcia. Trans. Sebastian Stankiewicz. Krakow: ASP, 2023.

Esperienza Estetica e Arti Popolari: Prospettive Somaestetiche Sulla Teoria e la Practica. Trans. Teresa Gallo and Stefano Marino. Milan: Mimesis, 2023.

Somaesthetics and Design Culture. Leiden: Brill, 2023. Edited with Bálint Veres.

Somaestetica, Architettura, e Città. Trans. Aurosa Alison. Bologna: Bologna University Press, 2024.

Books about Richard Shusterman

Wojciech Małecki. *Embodying Pragmatism: Richard Shusterman's Philosophy and Literary Theory*. Frankfurt. Peter Lang, 2010. Chinese translation: Wang Yaqin (Beijing: Chinese Academy of Social Sciences Press, 2019). 《"具身性" 的实用主义: 理查德·舒斯特曼的哲学与文学理论 》.

Alina Mitek-Dziemba, *Literatura i filozofia w poszukiwaniu sztuki życia: Nietzsche, Wilde, Shusterman.* Katowice: Wydawnictwo Uniwersytetu Śląskiego, 2011.

Dorota Koczanowicz and Wojciech Małecki, ed. *Shusterman's Pragmatism: Between Literature and Somaesthetics.* Amsterdam: Rodopi, 2012.

Jerold J. Abrams, ed. *Shusterman's Somaesthetics: From Hip Hop Philosophy to Politics and Performance Art.* Boston: Brill, 2022.

Liu Delin. *A Study on Shusterman's New Pragmatic Aesthetics.* Jinan: Shandong University Press, 2012. 《舒斯特曼新实用主义美学研究》.

Wei Shuanxi. *The Somatic Turn and The Transformation of Aesthetics: On Shustermann's Somaesthetics.* Beijing: Chinese Academy of Social Sciences Press, 2016. 《身体转向与美学的改造: 舒斯特曼身体美学思想论纲》.

Wang Yaqin. *Embodiment: Research on Richard Shusterman's Aesthetic Thought.* Beijing: Chinese Academy of Social Sciences Press, 2020. 《"具身化": 理查德·舒斯特曼美学思想研究》.

Valentina Antoniol and Stefano Marino, eds. *Foucault's Aesthetics of Existence and Shusterman's Somaesthetics: Ethics, Politics, and the Art of Living.* London: Bloomsbury, 2024.

Films about Richard Shusterman

Philosophical Encounters with Richard Shusterman. Directed by Paweł Kuczyński. Delos Films, 2013. A three-part educational documentary, each part approximately 30 minutes.

The Man in Gold. Directed by Paweł Kuczyński. Delos Films, 2021. 58 minutes.

Index